Cambridge Studies in Oral and Literate Culture   3

LITERACY AND SOCIAL DEVELOPMENT IN THE WEST: A READER

Cambridge Studies in Oral and Literate Culture
Edited by Peter Burke and Ruth Finnegan

This series is designed to address the question of the significance of literacy in human societies; it will assess its importance for political, economic, social and cultural development, and examine how what we take to be the common functions of writing are carried out in oral cultures.

The series will be inter-disciplinary, but with particular emphasis on social anthropology and social history, and will encourage cross-fertilization between these disciplines; it will also be of interest to readers in allied fields, such as sociology, folklore and literature. Although it will include some monographs, the focus of the series will be on theoretical and comparative aspects rather than detailed description, and the books will be presented in a form accessible to non-specialist readers interested in the general subject of literacy and orality.

Books in the series
1 Nigel Phillips: *'Sijobang': Sung Narrative Poetry of West Sumatra*
2 R.W. Scribner: *For the Sake of Simple Folk: Popular Propaganda for the German Reformation*

LITERACY AND SOCIAL DEVELOPMENT IN THE WEST: A READER

Edited by
HARVEY J. GRAFF

CAMBRIDGE UNIVERSITY PRESS

CAMBRIDGE
LONDON   NEW YORK   NEW ROCHELLE
MELBOURNE   SYDNEY

Published by the Press Syndicate of the University of Cambridge
The Pitt Building, Trumpington Street, Cambridge CB2 1RP
32 East 57th Street, New York, NY 10022, USA
296 Beaconsfield Parade, Middle Park, Melbourne 3206, Australia

First published 1981

Printed in the United States of America

Library of Congress catalogue card number: 81-10208

British Library Cataloguing in Publication Data
Literacy and social development in the West.
(Cambridge studies in oral and literate culture; 3)
1. Illiteracy – Social aspects
I. Graff, Harvey J.
306'.4   LC149
ISBN 0 521 23954 0 hard covers
ISBN 0 521 28372 8 paperback

For Nan and Gary

CONTENTS

ACKNOWLEDGEMENTS

During the time in which I prepared this collection, my research activities were supported by grants from the National Endowment for the Humanities, the Newberry Library, and the Spencer Foundation. This assistance I wish to acknowledge; for it, I express my gratitude. The Newberry Library ably supplied a base of operations. I thank my friends Kenneth Lockridge and Egil Johansson for permitting me to reprint their work, and my editor, Susan Allen-Mills, for her superb aid and advice. Vicki Graff, Carol Loverde, and Katy Smyser provided assistance in manuscript preparation. This book is for Nan and Gary.

INTRODUCTION

Harvey J. Graff

I

In almost any sphere of discourse or conversation today, it is difficult to avoid the subject of literacy. Literacy's currency is pervasive; the responses to the topic's introduction are often powerful, emotionally and intellectually. Throughout the Western world, perceived and sometimes documented 'crises' of literacy are proclaimed; elsewhere, in underdeveloping areas, 'crises' of *il*literacy garner attention. The amount of interest given to the presumed problems of literacy and illiteracy and the depth and breadth of response are revealing. On the one hand, they reflect the value accorded to literacy in modern societies and states, a value that is fundamentally an historical development. And, on the other hand, they reflect aspects of other contemporary crises – economic, political, cultural – all of which are related closely to literacy, whether in assumptions and theories or in actual practice. That concern and fears about the condition of literacy among youth and adult populations today are so grave and so tightly intermeshed with other serious current concerns across North America and Western Europe is an impressive testament. Identification of the centrality we attach to literacy and its presumed significance for advanced modern, democratic civilizations is made easier by these circumstances.

The value of literacy for achieving fulfilling, productive, expanding, and participating lives of freedom in modern societies is undoubted and unquestioned. At the same time, however, literacy does not seem to be well understood, popularly or academically. Despite its very real importance, it is quite likely that literacy's contributions are neither well appreciated nor are its limitations grasped. Whether seen as a concept; a skill, tool, or technique; or expected consequences from the possession of the tool, discussions of literacy suffer from serious confusion. An examination of attempts to define literacy or to explore its impacts in empirical terms all too readily affirms this point. We are heirs to a body of thinking, a set of legacies about literacy and its imputedly vast import. A source of anxiety and confusion in a changing world, this is also a historical outcome that can only be understood in historical terms. That is one reason, and one function, for this collection of writings on literacy and social development in the West. Contemporary understanding can be best advanced, in this case, as in many others, through a perspective grounded in history.

1

The roots of contemporary misgivings about the state of popular literacy are many and complex. Changing modes of communication have joined with changing political–economic and cultural conditions in an intellectual context of persisting assumptions and expectations about the necessary linkage of universal literacy with modernization. One commentator aptly notes, 'The assumption that literacy and progress were identical had become a dogma of progressive thought. Many thinkers believed that universal literacy was no less than the final milestone on the road to Utopia.' This, we must appreciate, was a product of post-Enlightenment social thought and a cause of institution-building throughout the West, although its origins in fact long predated that departure. Robert Disch continues, 'Subsequently the twentieth century inherited a mystique of literacy born out of two tendencies. One, essentially utilitarian, was committed to the functional uses of literacy as a medium for the spread of practical information that could lead to individual and social progress; the other, essentially aesthetic and spiritual, was committed to the uses of literacy for salvaging the drooping spirit of Western man from the death of religion and the ravages of progress.'[1]

The culmination of underlying historical developments is found in our belief in the necessity of mass literacy, its centrality to virtually all aspects of modern life and well-being, and its saving power. For example, one student of literacy and education admits ambivalence when he observes:

> In the popular imagination, literacy is the most significant distinguishing feature of a civilized man and a civilized society. Expressions of these attitudes are readily culled from the popular press . . . The assumption that nonliteracy is a problem with dreadful social and personal consequences is not only held by laymen, it is implicit in the writings of academics as well.

The problem, of course, is not that such views are erroneous, but that they are incomplete, and therefore misleading and distorting:

> But such an overwhelming concern with literacy can only increase one's suspicions that the significance of a universal high degree of literacy is grossly misrepresented. It is overvalued partly because literate people, such as educators, knowing the value of their own work, fail to recognize the value of anyone else's. More importantly, literacy is overvalued because of the very structure of formal schooling – schooling that, in Bruner's words, involves learning 'out of the context of action, by means that are primarily symbolic.' The currency of schools is words – words . . . that are shaped up for the requirements of literacy . . . We may have a distorted view of both the child and of social realities if we expect that the values and pleasures of literacy are so great that everyone, whether it is easy or difficult for him, or whether it leads to wealth or power . . . or not,

is willing to invest the energy and time required to reach a high level of literacy.[2]

That, however, is not all; the issues are broader. For virtually all approaches to literacy follow from conjunctures of historically-based assumptions: about the nature of social and economic development, of political participation and citizenship, of social order and morality, of personal advancement, and of societal progress. Our own normative theories are rooted in post-Enlightenment categories and concepts, typically refined and routinized during the nineteenth century. Origins of such approaches lie in the more distant past, as several of the selections here show.

Contemporary discussions about literacy, basic skills, and mass schooling are not unique or novel. They ring familiarly to those knowledgeable about the history of Western social thought, social change and development, and schooling. Rather than demeaning their significance, this fact should stimulate greater questioning of the uncritical acceptance of these legacies and greater awareness of literacy's historical course. It should contribute to new approaches to literacy, based in an awareness of the impact of the historical developments that underlie present means of transmission and concepts. For at least several centuries, the acceptance of the primacy of print and the abilities to read and reproduce it has become universal. The uses of literacy are still debated; its basic value is not. Throughout the West, the rise of literacy and its promulgation through different agencies of schooling is associated with a positive evaluation of mass access to reading and writing. Overwhelmingly, to be literate and to spread literacy were considered more and more important; opposition was branded reactionary and overcome (in theory, if not always in fact). Literacy, it was held, carried benefits to individuals as well as to societies, nations, and states. Ambiguities and contradictions were largely ignored, especially when seen in terms of the association of mass schooling with progress and enlightenment. Value to the community, self- and socioeconomic worth, mobility, access to information and knowledge, rationality, morality, and orderliness are among the many qualities linked to literacy for individuals.[3] Literacy, in other words, was one key component of the road to progress. Analogously, and perhaps even more significantly, these attributes were deeply important to the larger society in which the educated man or woman resided and to which he or she contributed. From productivity to participation, schooled and literate workers and citizens were required if the best path to the future and its fulfilment were to be followed.

The rise of literacy and its dissemination to the popular classes, therefore, was, and is, associated with the triumph of light over darkness, or liberalism, democracy, and universal unbridled progress; literacy takes its place among the other successes, and causes, of modernity and rationality. Cause and consequence, of course, are often confused; nevertheless, the value, the necessity of literacy for economic and social development, establishment and maintenance of democratic institutions, growth and advancement, and all the rest is seldom questioned.

The sanctity of this interpretation of modern history and society is no longer as secure as once thought.[4] Nor, with it, is the interpretation of the role of literacy within the larger complex that comprises social development, any more secure. Modern historical and social science scholarship is now in the midst of a challenging period of reevaluation and revision. This is particularly the case with respect to conceptualization and theory. The study of literacy is one important example of this transformation in approach and orientation. The importance of literacy, or at least its utility and potential, is not questioned; rather, its significance as a causal and independent factor is becoming qualified. A critical perspective has developed. Continuities as well as changes are discovered. The uses of literacy for conservative ends, for social and cultural control and hegemony, for example, are more often appreciated. The limits of literacy by itself as a critical contribution to individual and societal change are also attracting attention. Distinctions between quantities of literacy – simple social distributions – and qualities – levels of ability to use its skill – are gaining in research and interpretive interest. The setting in which literacy is transmitted, institutional arrangements, and motivations for dissemination are recognized as highly significant, too. Literacy training, it seems, often involves more than functional skill acquisition. Patterns of use of reading and writing abilities and their relationship to the demands that daily life and special exigencies place upon those abilities have received a new prominence, as has the key contemporary question of changes in the level of popular literacy skills over time. Contradictions between literacy's expected social, economic, cultural, and political relationships and the realities of its contribution are commonly noted. Indeed, some presumed causal connections may be reversed.

Both historical and contemporary studies, as illustrated by a number of the contributions to this volume, reflect this reorientation. They also, not surprisingly, illustrate the major new interest that has arisen around the entire subject. Not only are studies that focus upon literacy as the principal topic becoming more common, but literacy is also featured more regularly as an aspect or variable in a diverse range of research areas, from education and cultural studies to economic, demographic, developmental, linguistic, social structural, ethnographic, social relations and organizational subjects, for example. Among historians and others in the humanities and social sciences, traditional and normative perspectives about literacy's roles and meanings are reexamined, and literacy itself has become a significant, if somewhat new 'growth area'. New perspectives and concepts are now actively sought; literacy's contributions (and limitations) are studied rather than simply presumed. Literacy, in its many contexts, is seen as neither simple, direct, nor unambiguous. More than ever before, its contributions are the focus of research in terms of literacy's social, economic, cultural, and political relationships. That, too, is amply seen in the selections that follow.

II

The revision and reorientation of literacy studies, historical and contemporary, is a recent development. Systematic and critical research is not much more than a decade old. No new syntheses or consensuses have appeared. Indeed, the nature of the subject — the variety, and difficulty, and incompleteness of the sources; the problems and complications of definitions and concepts; and the power of legacies and expectations — strongly suggests that inclusiveness and definitiveness will not soon be forthcoming. Modes of analysis and avenues of interpretation are more pressing concerns. Nevertheless, the results of the last decade's research are important and impressive. The field of study and its centrality have been established, and this collection of historical studies should be seen as part of that larger, collective project. Changing patterns in the study of history, especially the rise of the 'new histories', closer relations between the humanistic and social scientific 'sciences of humanity', and the stimulation of contemporary issues all served to orient students in this direction.[5] Entirely new bodies of quantitative and qualitative data have been developed; new methods have been applied to their study. Theoretical perspectives, to orient research itself or to test ideas or theories, have become common practice. Continuing problems concern the interpretation of measures of literacy, such as signatures and marks, and the comparability of evidence across social and geographic space and through time. The issue of literacy's quality, as contrasted with its quantity, is among the major items on the current agenda.

No summary or evaluation of research can be presented here, although the studies that follow encourage some stock-taking. What has been achieved thus far is often descriptive, as a skeletal view of literacy's course over time and space is being delineated and fleshed out. Regional, sexual, religious, class, and occupational variations are identified; the effects of events, such as the French or American Revolutions, or processes, such as the Reformation or Commercial and Industrial Revolutions, are isolated. Research in this manner began with a small number of areas, principally in England, France, Sweden, the United States, and Canada; it has now expanded to include much more of Europe and more places in North America.[6] National surveys as well as local and regional case studies have been completed or are now under way. Much of this work seeks to illuminate the modern rise of literacy — 'the literacy transition' as it has been called — and thus has concentrated on the period from the seventeenth through the nineteenth centuries. Other students focus their attention on earlier and later time periods, expanding the history of literacy from a relatively truncated beginning (too often coinciding with the advent of printing), and adding immensely to our understanding. The beginnings of the course of literacy's dissemination among various social groups is being outlined. Present and future efforts aim to complete these time series and to expand their coverage, but even more to probe more deeply and attempt explanation and contextual interpretation.

As the examples collected in this book show well, important findings have resulted from this generation of modern researchers. In addition to the establishment of time series and group differentials, conclusions stress the nature of the early spread of literacy, the complexity of cultural communications, the interrelationships between the oral and literate media, the dynamic role of religion — especially but not exclusively Protestantism — in the spread of literacy, the significance of population concentration and access to means of schooling, the irregular pace of change, the roles of social stratification, inequality, and power, and the contributions of both personal motivation and institutional opportunities. Ambiguity and contradiction regularly mark findings and their interpretations. The limits of wholly functional analysis are clear. The French Revolution is sometimes seen as having contributed no direct stimulus to literacy, although its ideology had, it is suggested, a powerful role. The American Revolution was probably a similar force, although in a very different context. Industrialization's impact on literacy is hotly debated, and urbanization's role may be less than clearcut. The assumed links between literacy or schooling, on the one hand, and industrialization, urbanization, and modernization, on the other, are increasingly questioned, but it is agreed that literacy does make economic contributions to the individual and society. Literacy, nevertheless, has not always been sufficient to break the bonds of social ascription and to replace them with societies rooted in achievement. Rates of fertility and mortality influence literacy levels, and vice versa; these relationships, however, have not always proved to be simple or direct.[7] Overall, variation and contradiction mark the course of literacy's growth both within and among nations throughout the West.

Literacy studies are perhaps closer to a beginning than an end. Research is far from complete; the implications of findings are not always precise and certain; and controversy rises rather than abates. An important reevaluation has begun, yet we are far from new syntheses. With this research, moreover, has come the realization that the contexts of literacy, the needs for and uses of it, and the motivations that impel individuals to seek literacy and some to develop mass means for its transmission, are more interesting and important than raw series of data on changes in distributions of literacy skills. This is also reflected in the studies reprinted below. Literacy requirements, we now understand, vary among different social and economic groups, regions, and communities. Equally significantly, levels of literacy do not always relate directly to demands placed on them, and literacy in some cases can be nonfunctional. It is these differences in achieved literacy and the needs for and uses of its skills that students must now explain. For this, measures must be comparative; a focus on individuals, rather than solely on rates, better allows these questions to be confronted.

Peter Laslett stated well the challenge we face: 'The discovery of how great a proportion of the population could read and write at any one point in time is one of the most urgent of the tasks which face the historian of social structure, who is committed to the use of numerical methods.' Methods, he knew, were not enough. 'But the challenge is not simply to find the evidence and to devise ways of making it yield reliable answers. It is a challenge to the historical and literary imagination.'[8] That challenge is now being accepted by students of the past and others for the present. It is, we can agree, a challenge only heightened by the hard press of circumstances and serious concerns.

III

The importance of these results is clear; the studies that follow show them in some detail as they present the outlines of the history of literacy in the West. Their relevance to historical analysis *and* to social theory are both striking. Furthermore, the history of literacy speaks to yet another area of relevance, that of social policy. For among its findings are conclusions of more than historical or theoretical interest, although that is not required as a justification. The history of literacy, I believe, contributes to policy analysis and policy-making in the present day. Let us note several examples.

First is the concept of multiple paths to the making of literate societies and states. Historical findings confirm that there is *no one* route to universal literacy, that there is *no one* path destined to succeed in the achievement of mass literacy levels. This, of course, is contrary to the assumptions that led for several decades to the exportation of Western-based plans for mass schooling to underdeveloping areas in the world, contrary to a lesson that could have been drawn from the past. From the history of the West, one may distinguish specific contexts in which very different institutional and legal arrangements led to impressive increases in rates of popular literacy. The roles of private and public schooling, informal and formal, voluntary and compulsory education, were in some times and places sufficient for the broad expansion of the literate population. Very high levels of literacy were also possible before the development of modern, industrial, institutional, or urban societies. Mass literacy was achieved in Sweden, for example, without formal schooling, economic development, or instruction in writing. The impetus was religious; the forces of influence and compulsion were those of Church and State. Sweden, nevertheless, long remained a poor nation. The cases of Scotland and colonial New England are equally revealing.[9] In different contexts and cases, increasing rates of literacy followed from very different approaches and arrangements. The developmental and individual consequences were equally varied.

Just as the routes to literacy have varied, so have the impacts and concomitants. At the level of actual developments, there is little empirical support for the contemporary faith and policy assumption that poverty, disease, and general backwardness are inevitably and causally connected with illiteracy or that progress, health, and economic well-being are similarly linked with literacy. The belief in a modernization theory that social and economic progress follow from a change in persons from illiterate to literate is not only unconfirmed, but reflects a misplaced and exaggerated estimation of the power of literacy by itself. We do better to conceptualize literacy's correlates in more flexible, less unidirectional, and less causal ways. Historical patterns provide a set of experiences different from such expectations, and furnish a better guide to such crucial questions as how and to what degree basic literacy contributes to economic and cultural well-being in different circumstances. In the laboratory of the past, the costs and benefits of alternative paths and their effects can be discerned. For example, the connections and disconnections between literacy and commercial development, a favourable relationship, and literacy and industrialization, often an unfavourable linkage, at least in the short run, offer important case studies and analogues for analysis. If nothing else, the evidence of the past strongly indicates that a simple, linear, modernization model of literacy as a prerequisite for development, and development as a stimulant to increased levels of schooling, will not suffice.

A second example is implicit in the first. This is the relationship of literacy to paths of economic development – and, furthermore, with social development too. Relationships do not always prove to be direct; contradictory patterns are not unusual. Extensive development was possible before the modern era, in commercial, institutional, or social complexity, to take just three cases, without a base of extensive mass literacy. On the other hand, high levels of literacy do not always lead to modern, liberal, individualistic, democratic, participatory opportunities or arrangements, regardless of literacy's potential contributions. From the classical period onwards, leaders of polities and churches, reformers as well as conservers, have recognized the uses of literacy and schooling. Often, they perceived uncontrolled, untempered literacy as dangerous – a threat to social order, political integration, and authority. Yet, increasingly, they concluded that literacy, if transmitted through carefully controlled formal institutions created for that purpose and supervised closely, could be a powerful force in maintaining order, training up citizens, instilling morality and other valued attributes, and furthering progress. Such efforts have regularly marked the history of the Western world. Although they did not always have their sponsors' intended consequences, they did serve to channel and condition the uses and potentials of literacy. In grasping these integrating and hegemonic uses, we do not slight the important collective and individual uses of literacy that run counter to the efforts to restrain, control, and order. As the selections ably document, that consequence, if not the entire story, is no less important.[10]

A final example focuses on the question of the quality of literacy. The small amount of research that has considered qualitative abilities to use literacy's skills suggests conclusions of the greatest import. Investigations point to a great disparity between high levels of literacy's social distribution and the levels of usefulness of those skills. In Sweden, where the evidence is best, a great many persons who attained high levels of oral reading ability apparently did not have comparable skills in comprehending what they read. Less systematic evidence for other places in Europe and North America points toward similar conclusions. It is possible, therefore, that the measurement of the distribution of literacy in a given population may reveal relatively little about the uses to which those skills could be put and the demands they could meet. It is also possible that with increasing rates of popular literacy did not come ever-increasing capabilities (nor, for that matter, ever-declining, as has been suggested). Finally, and perhaps most significant today, such evidence places the often-asserted contemporary decline of literacy in a fresher and properly historical perspective. If, as seems possible, mass levels of ability to use literacy typically lagged behind the near universality of basic literacy rates, the frequently announced but ineffectively measured recent decline may be much less impressive a change than many have thought. Regardless, assessments of major shifts in communicative abilities require an evaluation over a longer period than they have received, regardless of the obstinacy or frailty of the available evidence. These, we note, are just a small number of the contributions that historical views of literacy can bring to contemporary understanding and policy formulation.

IV

In preparing this collection of materials on literacy and social development in the West, I have attempted to fulfil a number of purposes. Although the chronological and geographic coverage cannot be even, the selections collectively offer a substantive *history of literacy* from the Middle Ages through the very recent past. Together, these studies provide an introduction to *new, critical conceptual and empirical approaches* to literacy and its *social roles and meanings*. Diverse in interpretation and evaluation of the significance of reading and writing, they illustrate *innovative methods, sources, and modes of analysis*, typically of an *interdisciplinary* nature. They also show the uses of *case study* and more *general approaches* to research and analysis, of detailed *empirical* and broader *speculative efforts*. Literacy's relations to *social development* are a common concern. These studies reveal the *value of a historical approach* to literacy: for its own importance and for its *contribution to understanding the origins and the processes that led to circumstances with which we struggle today*. The need for *historical understanding* is made clearer; the links between the past and the present emerge from these analyses. The *contemporary implications*, by example and by analogy, implicitly and explicitly, of these studies are significant; they should be heeded.

Little more need be said by way of introduction. The organization of the collection is chronological; we begin in the eleventh century. *Clanchy* offers an interpretation of the increasing frequency of literacy in medieval England, discusses the meaning of literacy in premodern society, the forces that propelled its expansion, the obstacles, and the interrelations between literate and oral media and culture. This theme is also addressed in fascinating circumstances and details by *LeRoy Ladurie* for medieval France and *Davis* for early modern France. Cultural interactions and continuities, as well as changes, link these perspectives. *Eisenstein* makes a strong case for the impact of the innovation of movable typographic printing, and speculates about the changes that may have followed its advent and diffusion. *Davis* considers print in the lives of the *menu peuple*, or common people, during the following century. *Strauss* addresses the links between the Reformation and literacy and those between literacy and formal, institutional schooling in Luther's Germany. *Cressy* measures changing distributions of literacy in Tudor–Stuart England, and posits explanations for their uneven course. For the same years, *Spufford* focuses on individual readers and writers, and seeks to understand their motivations and life course consequences.

Johansson and *Lockridge* consider the 'transition' to near universal rates of literacy in the pre-industrial societies of, respectively, Sweden and colonial New England. In presenting pioneering case studies, they both offer original perspectives on the causes and consequences of changing levels of literacy. *Schofield* sketches the course of literacy levels in industrializing England, and, in so doing, he also raises serious questions about the causal and temporal connections between the two epochal transformations. *Furet and Ozouf*, in the conclusions to their major study of French literacy from the sixteenth through the nineteenth centuries, speculate about the social and cultural significance of the *alphabétisation* of the French population, with implications for other places in the West. *My own* piece offers a reinterpretation of the relationship between literacy and work and literacy and economic development in the nineteenth century, drawing upon North American and comparative evidence. In the final historical selection, excerpted from a study of rural political development, *Judt* discusses the role of literacy in the forces making for socialism in late-nineteenth century Provence.

The concluding contributions are neither primarily Western nor historical. In presentations originally to the 1975 Persepolis (Iran) International Symposium for Literacy, *Galtung* and *Verne* comment critically on usual assumptions and programmes for raising literacy levels in the underdeveloping parts of the world. Their positions force us to confront the present and the future in terms of the past. They provide a fitting conclusion – and, one hopes, point toward new beginnings – in the paths toward understanding literacy.

A note on further reading

I have chosen not to include a separate bibliography on literacy, past or present. For reasons of space and reasons that reflect the condition of a field of study very much in flux, this seemed less than imperative. The topic of literacy, as such, does not lend itself to definitive analysis and interpretation. As the foregoing introduction has argued, its study has been plagued by numerous complications: conceptual, empirical, evidential, interpretive, and the like. Nevertheless, I do not wish to leave the reader with no guide to the literature. Readers of this book should understand, first, that the notes that appear with each of the fifteen selections offer a good introduction to the most important secondary literature. In editing, I have as a rule removed citations to primary sources, but retained for bibliographic and pedagogical purposes those notes that identify historical and contemporary studies. A guide for further reading or for pursuing issues further may be compiled quickly by perusing the notes. Those seeking a more complete bibliography should consult my *Literacy in History: An Interdisciplinary Research Bibliography* (New York, 1981). This categorized compilation of over 4000 titles constitutes the fullest reference work now available (through 1979 publications) to literacy studies and closely related topics, as well as an introduction to the field and its sources.

A number of the selections chosen for this volume stem from larger works. Interested readers and students are encouraged to explore more deeply the works of Clanchy, LeRoy Ladurie, Strauss, Johansson, Lockridge, Furet and Ozouf, Graff, and the collection that included the articles by Galtung and Verne. In addition, since the time of the original appearance of articles included here, Eisenstein has completed a work of monumental proportions: *The Printing Press as an Agent of Change: Communications and Cultural Transformations in Early Modern Europe* (Cambridge, 1979); Cressy has published *Literacy and the Social Order: Reading and Writing in Tudor and Stuart England* (Cambridge, 1980). Cambridge University Press is also preparing an English translation of Furet and Ozouf's *Lire et écrire: L'alphabétisation des français de Calvin à Jules Ferry* (originally, Paris: Editions de Minuit, 1977). Under the editorship of Peter Burke and Ruth Finnegan, this press has initiated the first publication series devoted specifically to this topic: Cambridge Studies in Oral and Literate Culture, to which the present volume is a contribution.

For classical literacy, the several studies of Eric Havelock are the most exciting: *Preface to Plato* (Cambridge, Mass., 1961), *Prologue to Greek*

Literacy (Norman, Oklahoma, 1973), *Origins of Western Literacy* (Toronto, 1976), among others. Havelock's critics should also be noted. An introduction to Italian studies is *Alfabetismo e cultura scritta nella storia della società Italiana* (Perugia, 1978). Lucien Febvre and Henri-Jean Martin, *The Coming of the Book: The Impact of Printing, 1450–1800* (London, 1976, published in French, 1958) bears examination.

Older, but still useful introductory works should be consulted: Lawrence Stone, 'Literacy and Education in England, 1640–1900', *Past and Present*, 42 (1969), 61–139; Carlo Cipolla, *Literacy and Development in the West* (Harmondsworth, 1969); Jack Goody and Ian Watt, 'The Consequences of Literacy', in *Literacy in Traditional Societies*, ed. Goody (Cambridge, 1968), 27–68. The latter appeared first in *Comparative Studies in Society and History* in 1963, and should be read along with Goody's introduction to this important anthropological collection, in which some basic qualifications are introduced. Goody's more recent work, especially *The Domestication of the Savage Mind* (Cambridge, 1977) is also critical. In the same context, we note the seminal if highly problematic writings of Harold Innis and Marshall McLuhan, and the fascinating, continuing studies and reflections of Walter J. Ong, especially *The Presence of the Word* (New Haven, 1967), *Interfaces of the Word* (Ithaca, N.Y., 1977), and *Rhetoric, Romance, and Technology* (Ithaca, N.Y., 1971). Richard Hoggart's *The Uses of Literacy* (Boston, 1961) is a classic account. Daniel Calhoun's *The Intelligence of a People* (Princeton, 1973) is a brilliantly original approach to popular literacy levels.

Social science and other contemporary approaches to literacy reflect persisting paradigmatic confusion but also show increasing interest. There is no single good introduction. For normative perspectives, the many studies of sociologists Alex Inkeles and Daniel Lerner, social psychologist David McClelland, and economists—sociologists Mary Jean Bowman and C. Arnold Anderson provide an orientation. Related is Lucian Pye, ed., *Communications and Political Development* (Princeton, 1963). More recent and more innovative are: Mark Blaug, 'Literacy and Economic Development', *The School Review*, 74 (1966), 393–417; David R. Olson, 'Toward A Literate Society', *Proceedings*, National Academy of Education (1975–6), 109–78; Léon Bataille, ed., *A Turning Point for Literacy* (New York and Oxford, 1976); David Harmon, *Community Fundamental Education* (Lexington, Mass., 1974); Shirley Brice Heath, 'The Functions and Uses of Literacy', *Journal of Communication*, 30 (1980), 123–33; *Harvard Educational Review*, 47 (August 1977), 'Reading, Language, and Learning'; Egil Johansson, 'The Post-Literacy Problem – Illusion or Reality in Modern Society?', in *Time, Space, and Man: Essays in Micro-Demography*, ed. Jan Sundin and Erik Söderlund (Stockholm, 1979), 199–323; Michael Stubbs, *Language and Literacy: The Sociolinguistics of Reading and Writing* (London, 1980); Sylvia Scribner and Michael Cole, 'Literacy Without Schooling: Testing for Intellectual Effects', *Harvard Edu-*

cational Review, 48 (1978), 448–61, and 'Cognitive Consequences of Formal and Informal Education', *Science*, 182 (1973), 553–9; John Oxenham, *Literacy: Writing, Reading and Social Organization* (London, 1980). My *Literacy in History* provides a relatively full listing of relevant materials. The most promising new approaches are found in ethnographic studies of reading and writing in use, analysis of functional literacy requirements of jobs and social–cultural activities, and reconceptualizations of macro-relationships between literacy and social, economic, cultural, and political change.

1 LITERATE AND ILLITERATE; HEARING AND SEEING: ENGLAND 1066–1307*

Michael T. Clanchy

Literate and illiterate

In the summer of 1297 some jurors from Norfolk came to the court of King's Bench to attest that Robert de Tony was twenty-one years of age and was therefore entitled to have his wardship terminated. Proving the age of feudal heirs by sworn testimony was a routine procedure, in which each juror attempted to recollect some memorable event which coincided with the birth of the child in question. Jurors might recall, for example, specific gifts or public events or accidents to themselves or their neighbours.[1] Thus in a case in 1304 at Skipton in Yorkshire Robert Buck, aged forty-one, remembered being at school at Clitheroe where he had been so badly beaten that he ran away and that was twenty-one years ago. Such a cumbersome system was required because births were only rarely recorded in registers. This customary method of establishing the age of individuals by collective oral testimony is a good example of the medieval reliance on memory rather than written record.

The case from Norfolk in 1297 is exceptional in that the proof primarily depended not on the usual personal recollections, but on a record of the date of Robert de Tony's birth (4 April 1276), which had been written down in the chronicles of West Acre priory. This record had not been made at the time of Robert's birth, as he was born in Scotland, but a year or more later when he was brought down to West Acre priory, of which the de Tony family were the founders, by his mother. She seems to have been seeking the protection of the priory on her son's behalf and had his date of birth written down there to establish that he was the lawful de Tony heir. Because the circumstances of Robert's birth could not have been known to the Norfolk jurors from personal experience in the customary way, resort had to be made to the West Acre chronicle.

The first juror, William de la Sale of Swaffham, therefore gave evidence that he had seen the chronicle and read it and was thereby certain of Robert's age. Six other jurors agreed with William without exception or addition, that is, they too claimed to have read the chronicle and understood its significance. Three more likewise agreed and added ancillary recollections: Robert Corlu

*Reprinted from *From Memory to Written Record: England, 1066–1307* by Michael T. Clanchy, 175–91, 202–20, by permission of the publishers, Edward Arnold Ltd and Harvard University Press, © M.T. Clanchy 1979.

said his younger brother was born in the same year as Robert de Tony; John Townsend said he had a son born in the same year who was now twenty-one; John Kempe said his father had died five years after Robert had been brought down from Scotland. The eleventh juror, John Laurence, agreed with William 'with this exception, that he had not read the aforesaid chronicles because he is *laycus*'. The twelfth, Roger of Creston, attested the same. A thirteenth juror (why the evidence was taken from thirteen men instead of twelve is not explained), Thomas of Weasenham, said that he had neither seen nor read the chronicle, but he had learned of its contents from the prior. Thomas was not necessarily incapable of reading like John and Roger. He may have presented his evidence in this form simply because he had not been present on the day his fellow jurors saw the chronicle.

Thus, of the thirteen men examined, ten swore that they could read the entry in the chronicle, an eleventh may have been able to read, and two were unable to do so. The latter two were described as *layci* (laymen) presumably because they had no 'clergy' in the sense of a reading knowledge of Latin. Walter of Bibbesworth took it for granted in the 1250s or 1260s, the time when these Norfolk jurors were growing up, that the gentry usually had experience from childhood of the 'book which teaches us *clergie*'. Those without this knowledge were 'laymen' in the modern sense of being inexpert. The other jurors were 'clergy' only in the sense of knowing some Latin. William de la Sale and his fellows were no churchmen. They were knights and freemen of the neighbourhood, approximately the social equals of the heir in question, as required in jury trial procedure.

This case therefore shows that from a random sample of thirteen gentlemen of Norfolk at the end of the thirteenth century, ten could read an entry in a chronicle, two could not, and one's ability is unrecorded. Those who swore that they had read the chronicle were presumably telling the truth, as they risked being cross-examined in the King's Bench, and they had no apparent motive for perjuring themselves since they were not claiming benefit of clergy. The statement that two of the jurors were incapable of reading, together with the unspecific testimony about Thomas of Weasenham, adds credibility to the contrasting testimony of the rest. Although evidence of proof of age was sometimes falsified, there is no reason to reject the essential facts of this testimony. Obviously no generalizations about levels of literacy can be made from a unique case. On the other hand, the evidence of this case, that the great majority of the jurors examined were capable of reading one line of Latin in a chronicle, need cause no surprise. The procedure for giving juries' verdicts in royal courts, which depended on documents written in Latin and perhaps also in French and English, demanded a higher level of literacy among jurors than that. By 1297 the two who were unable to read at this elementary level are more surprising than the two who could do so.

Meanings of 'clericus' and 'litteratus'

The fact that most of these Norfolk gentlemen could read conflicts in appearance only with the medieval axiom that laymen are illiterate and its converse that clergy are literate. The terms cleric and lay, literate and illiterate, were used in ways which preserved intact the appearances of these fundamental axioms while acknowledging the realities of daily experience, where some clergy were ignorant and some knights knew more of books than brave deeds. Traditional roles had become confused, as Neal of Longchamp of Canterbury observed with regret in c. 1192: 'In the church today there are clergy without knowledge of letters, just as there are many knights without skill and practice in arms, who for that reason are called "Holy Mary's knights" by the others.' This discrepancy between theory and practice, between literature and life, did not of course mean that the ideals were immediately altered to fit the facts. On the contrary, the ideals of the learned cleric and the valorous knight became reinforced as fantasies, which had three or four centuries of vigorous life before them in literature and academic treatises.

The axiom that laymen are illiterate and its converse had originated by combining two distinct antitheses:

> *clericus: laicus*
> *litteratus: illiteratus*

The latter antithesis derived from classical Latin, where *litteratus* meant 'literate' in something like its modern sense and also (in the most classical usage of Cicero) described a person with *scientia litterarum*, meaning a 'knowledge of letters' in the sense of 'literature'.[2] The former antithesis derived from the Greek *kleros*, meaning a 'selection by lot' and hence subsequently the 'elect' of God in terms of Christian salvation, whereas *laos* meant the 'people' or crowd. Gradually in the process of Christian conversion those who were specially consecrated to the service of God, the *clerici* or 'clergy', became distinct from the mass of the people, the *laici* or 'laity'. The antithesis *clericus: laicus* was thus a medieval creation, while *litteratus: illiteratus* was of Roman origin. In the half millennium 500–1000 AD the reduction in the number of learned men in the west coincided with the expansion of Christianity by the conversion of the barbarians. As a consequence *clerici* began to be associated with *litterati*, although the two concepts had originally nothing in common. This association of ideas reflected the fact that outside the Mediterranean area nearly all Latinists were churchmen and most were monks. As academic standards declined, *litteratus*, which had meant 'lettered' or 'learned' for Cicero, more often came to mean 'literate' in the sense of having a minimal ability to read Latin. Such *litterati* were still learned compared with the great majority, who had no Latin or book learning at all.

These first clerical *litterati*, whose sparse knowledge had scarcely anything in common with the Latin scholars either of ancient Rome or of the Twelfth-Century Renaissance, established a privileged status for themselves in society by despising non-Latinists as an ignorant crowd of *laici*. In reality the *clerici* were unsure of their status, as Europe was dominated not by them but by warriors with a non-literate sense of values. Charlemagne and Alfred were exceptional in wanting the nobility to be better Latinists; their examples were lauded by the clergy to encourage the others. Dark-Age Europe was far from unique in creating an élite of priests who monopolized writing, yet who were constantly aware of their impotence vis-à-vis the dominant warlords. The supposed gulf between cleric and lay, between the elect and the damned, was some compensation to the clergy, although not even Pope Gregory VII could make it a reality for long in the terrestrial world.[3]

Thus by constant repetition the pairs of antitheses, *clericus: laicus* and *litteratus: illiteratus*, were coupled in the mind. The terms of each antithesis became interchangeable and ultimately synonymous. By the twelfth century *clericus* meant *litteratus*, *laicus* meant *illiteratus*, and vice-versa. The case from Norfolk has already illustrated *laicus* being used to mean *illiteratus*. The converse (*clericus* meaning *litteratus*) was discussed in detail in the 1170s by Philip of Harvengt, who observed that a person was not called a cleric unless he was 'imbued with letters', and hence:

> A usage of speech has taken hold whereby when we see someone *litteratus*, immediately we call him *clericus*. Because he acts the part that is a cleric's, we assign him the name *ex officio*. Thus if anyone is comparing a knight who is *litteratus* with a priest who is ignorant, he will exclaim with confidence and affirm with an oath that the knight is a better *clericus* than the priest . . . This improper usage has become so prevalent that whoever gives attention to letters, which is clerkly, is named *clericus*.[4]

Philip, like Neal de Longchamp and other writers on the state of the clergy, deplored the way real knights and clergy no longer fitted the traditional roles assigned to them. More important in the present context is his observation that a learned knight would be called a *clericus*, because that implies that a person described as *clericus* in a document was not necessarily a member of the clergy. Such a person is just as likely to have been an educated layman.

Philip of Harvengt's comments are best illustrated in England by Matthew Paris's obituary of Paulin Peyver or Piper, a steward of Henry III who died in 1251. He is described as *miles litteratus sive clericus militaris*, 'a literate knight or knightly clerk'. Matthew thus emphasized that these terms were interchangeable in Paulin's case. Paulin was a cleric only in the learned sense, as he had numerous knights' fees and a wife and legitimate children. Similarly the Northamptonshire knight, Henry de Bray, who was born in 1269 and wrote his own cartulary, noted that his maternal grandfather, Richard lord of

Harlestone, 'was called Ricardus Clericus because he was *litteratus*'. The most familiar example of this usage is the nickname 'Clerk' or 'Beauclerk' given to Henry I. How learned Henry really was is a separate and controversial question; certainly he was described by Orderic Vitalis as *litteratus* and 'nurtured in natural and doctrinal science'.[5] A *clericus* in common parlance was therefore a person of some scholarly attainments, regardless of whether he was a churchman. As early as the third decade of the twelfth century a polemic of English origin, commenting on the large number of schoolmasters, asked rhetorically: 'Are there not everywhere on earth masters of the liberal arts, who are also called *clerici*?'[6] Peter the Chanter summarized the situation in around 1200: 'There are two kinds of *clerici* and in both there are good and bad, namely those who are ecclesiastics and those who are scholastics.'[7]

The use of *clericus* and *litteratus* as interchangeable terms, both meaning 'learned' or 'scholarly', is clearest in Jocelin of Brakelond's descriptions of the debates within Bury St Edmunds abbey over the election of Abbot Samson in 1182 and Prior Herbert in 1200. On each occasion the more scholarly monks argued that they must be governed by *litterati* and not by the ignorant. Their opponents teased them with a new litany. 'A bonis clericis, libera nos, Domine!' (From all good clerics, good Lord, deliver us), and with puns about learning Latin grammar, 'Our good *clerici* have declined so often in the cloister that now they themselves have declined.' *Clericus* was a relative term. Thus Jocelin has one monk say: 'That brother is something of a cleric [*aliquantulum clericus*], although much learning [*littere*] doth not make him mad.' On another occasion Jocelin told of how Hubert Walter, the archbishop of Canterbury, had to admit that Abbot Samson was a better *clericus* than he was, meaning that Samson was the better scholar. The way Jocelin uses *clericus* is explained by Philip of Harvengt, who notes that when we meet a monk of humanity and charity,

> We ask him whether he is a *clericus*. We don't want to know whether he has been ordained to perform the office of the altar, but only whether he is *litteratus*. The monk will therefore reply to the question by saying that he is a *clericus* if he is *litteratus*, or conversely a *laicus* if he is *illiteratus*.

It might be added that a monk who aspired to Christian humility would not call himself *litteratus*, even if he were of scholarly inclinations. Thus Adam of Eynsham, in his life of St Hugh of Lincoln, claims not to know how to satisfy the *litterati*, who will cavil at his style and simple narrative. Adam is using here the hagiographer's common device of making his story appear more truthful by being naive.

As *clericus* and *litteratus* both meant learned, it followed that a person of no great book learning was a *laicus*, a 'layman', even if he were a monk or a priest. Thus Archbishop Hubert Walter was described by the chronicler of St Augustine's abbey at Canterbury as *laicus et illiteratus*. Hubert was not of

course a layman in the ecclesiastical sense, nor was he illiterate in any modern sense, as he was the chief justiciar and chancellor who did more than any
other individual to create the royal archives. The St Augustine's abbey
chronicler was using *laicus* and *illiteratus* as terms of abuse – he also called
Hubert a legal *ignoramus* – but he was not using these terms inaccurately.
Hubert was a *laicus* in Philip of Harvengt's sense and *illiteratus* in Jocelin's, as
he lacked the academic learning of Bologna or Paris. That academic snob,
Gerald of Wales, alleged that Hubert's Latin was shaky and that his only
school had been the Exchequer.

Like *clericus*, *litteratus* was a relative term. Whether a particular individual
was appropriately described as *litteratus* was a matter of opinion, since essentially it meant 'learned'. The same man might be *litteratus* in one assessment
and *illiteratus* in another. Thus Ralf Nevill, Henry III's chancellor and bishop
of Chichester, was certified by a papal legate as *litteratus* when elected dean
of Lichfield in 1214, but *illiteratus* by another papal adviser in 1231 when his
candidature for the archbishopric of Canterbury was rejected. Conscientious
churchmen considered Ralf to be a worldly administrator. Like Hubert Walter,
he was no *clericus* or *litteratus* in the ideal sense of being either the elect of
God or a scholar. On this occasion in 1231 the successful candidate for
Canterbury, St Edmund of Abingdon, was both. Hubert and Ralf were not
the only distinguished churchmen and administrators to be described as
illiteratus. To their company should be added Roger bishop of Salisbury,
Henry I's chief justiciar, and the controversial Abbot Ording of Bury St
Edmunds. In the exalted view of John of Salisbury, who aspired to Ciceronian
standards, all those who are ignorant of the Latin poets, historians, orators
and mathematicians should be called *illiterati* 'even if they know letters'.[8]

John's contention is taken for granted by Walter Map when he describes a
boy he had known, who was a paragon and was 'educated among us and by
us'; yet 'he was not *litteratus*, which I regret, although he knew how to transcribe any series of letters whatever.' Walter would have liked to have described
this boy as *litteratus*, since he was one of his kinsmen, but he had to admit
that nice penmanship was no substitute for scholarship. He adds that the boy
left England and became a knight of Philip of Flanders (1168–91). At his
learned court, where many of 'the order of laymen' knew 'letters' (according
to Philip of Harvengt), this boy would presumably not have been numbered
among the *milites litterati*. The ability to write well comprised the technical
skill of an artist and was not an integral part of the science of letters. Writing
is not included among the skills which cause Philip of Harvengt's knight who
is *litteratus* to be described as a *clericus*. In Philip's opinion the essential
abilities are to read, understand, compose by dictation, make verse and express
oneself in the Latin language. The medieval *miles litteratus* was thus a gentleman educated in the classics, he embodied a recurrent ideal in European
culture.

The way the words *clericus* and *litteratus* were used has been discussed in detail here because such examples demonstrate that neither word, when applied to an individual, can be accurately translated by its modern equivalent. A *clericus* was not necessarily either a 'cleric' or a 'clerk', although he was someone with a reputation for erudition. Likewise a person described as *litteratus* was much more than 'literate' in the modern sense. Counting the number of persons called *clericus*, or making lists of knights described as *litteratus*, provides examples of persistent and characteristic medieval ways of thinking, but it throws no light on whether such persons, whether designated cleric or lay by ecclesiastical law, were 'literate' in a twentieth-century sense of that word.

The question of the literacy of the laity

Discussions of medieval literacy have been bedevilled by the difficulty of distinguishing between the modern 'literate' and the medieval *litteratus*. When a knight is described as *litteratus* in a medieval source, his exceptional erudition is usually being referred to, not his capacity to read and write. Such knights were rare because good Latin scholars have always been rare among country gentry and government officials in England. A few existed even in this period. Thus shortly after the Conquest a Norman called Robert, *miles ille litteratus*, endowed St Albans abbey with an income to provide books for the church. He probably had a greater interest in books than most of the monks. About a century later Gerald of Wales tells how a *miles litteratus* appeared as a ghost, demanding to play a game of capping Latin verses with a learned master, for that had been his 'social recreation' when he was alive. Similarly Matthew Paris is recording his admiration for the learning and not the elementary schooling of John of Lexington, when he describes him as *miles elegans* (refined) *et facundus* (eloquent) *et litteratus*, or of Roger de Thurkelby, *miles et litteratus*. John was the keeper of the royal seal, whose obituary Matthew was writing in 1257, while Roger was one of the few royal judges who possessed legal wisdom in Matthew's opinion.

The historian's initial difficulty, when discussing the literacy of the laity, is to avoid anachronisms. Medieval ideas of literacy were so different from those of today that some modern questions are meaningless. To ask, 'Were laymen illiterate?', is a tautology: of course *laici* were *illiterati* because these terms were synonyms. Faced with the question another way round, 'Were laymen literate?', a medieval schoolman might have thought that he was being invited to take part in an exercise in elementary dialectic. Asking whether laymen were literates was like asking whether evil was good or black was white. Every bachelor of arts knew that the validity of axioms such as these was not affected by individual cases of moral imperfection or greyness in this imperfect world. The axiom that *clerici* were *litterati* and its converse belonged to the same order of thinking. Contemporaries, like Philip of Harvengt or

Jocelin of Brakelond, knew of numerous exceptions in their daily experience, but they saved the appearances of the rules by calling learned knights *clerici* and ignorant monks *laici*. Such axioms cannot be equated with twentieth-century historians' generalizations, which derive from an assessment of a multitude of individual cases. Scholastic axioms derived their validity not from individual experience but from universal rules, which were superior and prior to particular cases because they were part of a divine order of things. When explaining medieval ways of thought it is correct to say that all laymen were considered illiterate, yet it would be mistaken to conclude from that proposition that in any particular time or place all non-churchmen were unable to read or write. Scholastic axioms differ from real cases.

Another anachronism is the assumption that the capacity to read and write is a simple and constant measure which readily applies to medieval cases. The automatic coupling of reading with writing and the close association of literacy with the language one speaks are not universal norms, but products of modern European culture. Literacy in this modern sense is so deeply implanted from childhood in every twentieth-century scholar that it is difficult to liberate oneself from its preconceptions, or to avoid thinking of it as an automatic measure of progress. Over the last two centuries medievalists have painfully learned to overcome anachronisms when discussing feudal society or scholastic philosophy. Yet, when they reach elementary education and literate skills, they tend to assume that these problems can be readily understood by applying modern criteria and experience to the medieval past. Past ideas must be analysed in their own terms before they are assessed in modern ones.

As the citations from Walter Map and Philip of Harvengt have already illustrated, reading and writing were not automatically coupled at the end of the twelfth century, nor was a minimal ability to perform these actions described as literacy. Writing was a skill distinct from reading because the use of parchment and quills made it difficult. Likewise the traditional emphasis on the spoken word caused reading to be coupled more often with speaking aloud than with eyeing script. Although the average medieval reader had been taught to form the letters of the alphabet with a stylus on a writing tablet, he would not necessarily have felt confident about penning a letter or a charter on parchment. Scholars and officials employed scribes, particularly for drafting formal legal documents, just as typists are employed today. To this rule there are exceptions, of which the most spectacular is the beautifully written will of Simon de Montfort, as it states in its text that it is written in the hand of his eldest son, Henry.[9] Wills were unusually personal documents, intimately associated with the family circle, because their main purpose was to ensure the testator's state of grace at death rather than the worldly disposition of his property; hence Henry was performing a special act of filial devotion in writing his father's will.

Another fundamental difference between medieval and modern approaches to literacy is that medieval assessments concentrate on cases of maximum ability, the skills of the most learned scholars (*litterati*) and the most elegant scribes, whereas modern assessors measure the diffusion of minimal skills among the masses. Consequently modern assessments of literacy have been primarily concerned with the minimal ability of persons to sign their own names and the development of elementary schools in which this ability is taught as the basic educational skill. In twelfth- and thirteenth-century England the ability to sign one's name was likewise considered important, but it was not directly associated either with writing or with schools. The personal signature or sign manual was not accepted by itself as a lawful symbol of authentication on a document unless the signatory were a Jew. A Christian was required either to sign with a cross, indicating that he was making a promise in the sight of Christ crucified, or more commonly he affixed to the document his *signum* or seal.

In medieval England possession of a seal bearing the owner's name comes closest to the modern criterion of making the ability to sign one's own name the touchstone of literacy. Although the possessor of a seal might not be able to write, he or she was a person familiar with documents and entitled to participate in their use. Neither the medieval seal nor the modern sign manual on a document indicates that the signatory has anything more than a minimal competence in the skills of literacy. Such a person need not be *litteratus* in a medieval sense nor 'educated' in a modern one. If possession of a seal is taken as the medieval equivalent of the modern sign manual as a measure of minimal literacy, the growth of literacy (in this modern sense) can be approximately assessed. Scarcely anyone apart from rulers and bishops possessed seals in 1100, whereas by 1300 all freemen and even some serfs probably had them. Thus the statute of Exeter of 1285 expected 'bondsmen' to use them when they authenticated written evidence. How far the expectations of this statute reflected actual practice is a matter for conjecture, although instances can be readily cited as early as the 1230s of smallholders and tenants owing labour services affixing their personal seals to charters. The extent of minimal literacy in this sense among the peasantry by 1300 has been underestimated because historians have been reluctant to allow such competence even to the gentry.

The discrepancies between modern and medieval conceptions of what constituted literacy go deeper than differences in minimal requirements. The variety of languages in which spoken and written thoughts were formulated in medieval England made any capacity to read or write an intellectual achievement. This variety also obstructed the rapid spread of literacy, in the modern sense of the majority of people acquiring a minimal ability to read and write the language they spoke. Elementary instruction in reading and writing started from Latin because that was the traditional language of literacy and sacred Scripture. Those who wrote in vernaculars, whether in Middle English or French, were building novel and complex structures on a foundation of Latin.

Neither Middle English nor French was sufficiently standardized, or well enough established as a literary language, to become the basis of elementary instruction in reading and writing until well after 1300. If a person in Edward I's reign or earlier had learned to read in English or French but not in Latin, he could never have become *litteratus*, nor could he have understood the majority of writings circulating in his own lifetime because these were in Latin. English and French had to have become common business and literary languages before it was practical or desirable to initiate literate skills with them.

Nevertheless by 1300 the supremacy of Latin, and the privileges of the *clerici* and *litterati* who upheld it, was increasingly being challenged, both by writings in vernaculars and by anti-clericalism. Boniface VIII introduced his bull *Clericis Laicos* in 1296, directed primarily at Edward I and Philip IV of France, with the provocative words: 'That laymen are notoriously hostile to clerics antiquity relates and recent experience manifestly demonstrates.'[10] Yet English non-churchmen were slower than their French counterparts to abandon Latin as the basis of literate skills, probably because of the competition between English and French as alternative literary languages. In general from *c.* 1300, lawyers and government officials preferred French, while creative writers favoured English. Moreover, in the later Middle Ages an elementary reading knowledge of Latin became a matter of life and death for Englishmen. Any person charged with felony, who could read a prescribed verse from the Bible, was theoretically entitled to benefit of clergy and hence escaped the death penalty.[11] Now that middle-class laymen were beginning to assert themselves, they took over the old association of *clericus* with *litteratus* and turned it to their own advantage in order to save themselves from hanging. *Litteratus* was thus reduced from meaning a person of erudition to meaning a person with a minimal ability to read, albeit in Latin. A *clericus* was still a *litteratus*, but he was now neither a churchman nor a scholar: he was anyone who was literate in this minimal sense. By the middle of the fifteenth century London tradesmen are being described as *litterati.*[12] Consequently after 1300 it became relatively common to be literate. What had changed, however, was not necessarily the proportion of persons in the population who had mastered reading and writing, but the meanings of words. A *clericus* was now a common clerk and a *litteratus* was a minimal literate. The literacy of the laity had been achieved, perhaps not so much by the efforts of schoolmasters and the mysterious forces of progress, as is sometimes alleged, as by the method which Humpty Dumpty explained to Alice in *Through the Looking-Glass*: 'When *I* use a word, it means just what I choose it to mean, neither more nor less . . . The question is which is to be master — that's all.' Verbally at least, the *laici* had mastered the *clerici* and *litterati*; and from that mastery the modern concept of literacy, meaning a minimal ability to read, was born.

Knowledge of Latin among non-churchmen

To avoid ambiguities the question, 'Were laymen literate?', needs recasting. A more productive question to ask is, 'Did non-churchmen know any Latin?', since Latin was the foundation of literacy in England in this period. The latter question has been progressively answered in the affirmative by scholars over the past fifty years. Starting at the top of the social hierarchy, historians have demonstrated that at least an acquaintance with Latin became increasingly widespread over the two centuries 1100–1300.

Independently of each other in the 1930s, V.H. Galbraith in Britain and J.W. Thompson in California demonstrated that the kings of England from Henry I onwards were instructed in Latin and that Henry I and Henry II were even considered *litterati* by some contemporaries.[13] More importantly, Henry II showed his mastery of written instruments in a series of judgments concerning the charters of the abbeys of St Albans in 1155, Battle in 1157 and 1175, and Bury St Edmunds in 1187.[14] He evidently enjoyed presiding over legal wrangles between abbots and bishops in his court, as it gave him an opportunity to scrutinize their charters and demonstrate that he was their master in intellect and legal wisdom as well as in material power. Peter of Blois was probably not exaggerating when he states that among Henry's commonest forms of relaxation were private reading and working with a group of *clerici* to unravel some knotty question: at his court there was 'school every day'. By 'school' Peter did not mean an elementary school, but a circle of learned schoolmen discussing *questiones* as they did at Paris or Oxford. From King John's reign onwards elementary instruction in Latin was taken for granted: 'Henceforth all our kings were taught letters in their youth, and their literacy, as distinct from their culture, has no particular importance.'[15]

The example set by the kings inevitably gave the baronage and gentry a motivation to learn some Latin, both to avoid looking foolish at court (where there was school every day), and to have sufficient understanding of the written demands, expressed in Latin, which began to pour from the royal Chancery and Exchequer. For these reasons H.G. Richardson and G.O. Sayles in 1963 widened the range of those who had 'a limited knowledge of Latin, a knowledge to be easily and rapidly acquired by any intelligent youth' from kings to the baronage and gentry of twelfth-century England.[16] Their conclusion concerning the baronage is cautious and unexceptionable: 'Without rashly generalizing from what may perhaps be called a handful of cases, it may fairly be said that they create a presumption that a man of noble birth will in his youth have had the opportunity of learning something of Latin letters.'[17] Richardson and Sayles also suggested that even some of the lesser knights read and wrote Latin. This suggestion is based on the written replies to Henry II's inquest into knights' fees in 1166 and his Inquest of Sheriffs in 1170. The argument is that 'the more informal documents, those that have no marks of clerkly skill' were written by the knights themselves.[18] Although the assumption that such men would or could write on parchment is contentious, the lesser conjecture that many knights read the royal writs themselves and drafted their own replies is possible.

The strongest argument of Richardson and Sayles for a relatively wide acquaintance with Latin is that royal officials like sheriffs and judges, most of whom were non-churchmen, had to have a working knowledge of Latin because they performed offices 'demanding the use of written instruments'.[19] Although such officials usually employed clerks to do their writing, and to read letters aloud to them, they had to understand enough Latin to master the business in hand and not be misled by their clerks or by the litigants' lawyers. At least one of Henry II's lay sheriffs, Richard sheriff of Hampshire, wrote as well as read in Latin, as his holograph acknowledgement of a debt to William Cade is extant.[20]

The presumption that officials knew some Latin, which applies to officers of the central government by 1200, extends to manorial and village stewards, bailiffs, beadles and reeves by 1300. On the basis of this evidence M.B. Parkes, in a recent contribution to the literacy of the laity question, argues that historians should allow for an 'extent of pragmatic literacy among the peasantry'.[21] His arguments are strengthened by the instances of peasants using seals and charters which have already been discussed. Parkes cites Walter Map, who took it for granted that 'serfs [*servi*], whom we call peasants [*rustici*], are eager to educate their ignominious and degenerate children in the [liberal] arts.' Walter deplored this because a liberal education was appropriate only for freedom. The question had arisen one day when he and the chief justiciar, Ranulf de Glanvill, were discussing why it was that the clerical judges of Henry II were harsher than the lay ones. Walter's explanation was that the clerics did not behave like gentlemen because they were serfs in origin. Although Walter was only expressing a personal opinion, and his opinions were often perverse and ironical (Walter was a clerical justice himself), his remarks had some basis in fact.

Starting at the top of the hierarchy with kings and descending through barons and knights, historians of medieval literacy have reached the peasants at the bottom and are suggesting that even some of them were acquainted with Latin. N. Orme has recently surveyed literacy (mainly in the later Middle Ages) from the top of society to the bottom as an introduction to his study of medieval schools.[22] He divides people into seven classes – clergy; kings and princes; nobility and gentry; administrators and lawyers; merchants, craftsmen, artisans; villeins; women. For the twelfth and thirteenth centuries a fourfold classification into kings and princes, nobility or baronage, gentry or knights, and peasantry (both free and unfree) is more appropriate. Neither the clergy nor women were separate social classes, as they derived their place in society from their families. Nor were administrators and lawyers yet a distinct class, as the legal profession (in a literate sense) only emerged in the late thirteenth century.

It might be thought that merchants are worth distinguishing as a group, as their families were at the forefront of education in the city states of Flanders and Northern Italy. In England, however, merchant dynasties like those of London took on the social colouring of the landed gentry and were not, in the thirteenth century anyway, a distinct 'bourgeoisie'. Knightly merchants were as educated as other knights. With lesser merchants, it is doubtful whether literacy in Latin was yet an essential skill, as they worked from memory and tally sticks. Book learning and book keeping became crucial to lesser merchants only when they ceased to travel with their wares and sat in offices instead. On the whole, that is a development of the fourteenth century rather than the twelfth, as far as England is concerned. St Godric, who mastered the *mercatoris studium* without any formal education, is probably typical of eleventh- or twelfth-century experience. Financiers, on the other hand, like William Cade or Osbert Huitdeniers (Eightpence) of London, who employed the young Thomas Becket as a clerk and accountant, needed as much Latin as the judicial side of their business (writing and enforcing bonds for loans) required. But financiers are not a sufficiently homogeneous group to constitute a social class, as many of them were Jews; they were literate in Hebrew and often in Latin as well.

The knowledge of the peasantry (both free and unfree), at the bottom of the social pyramid, remains to be discussed. The suggestion that some peasants were acquainted with Latin is not implausible when the role of the church in village life is considered. Theoretically at least every adult in England should have known some Latin because of its use in the liturgy. The attitude of the western church towards Latin was ambivalent. The identification of *clerici* with *litterati*, which implied that only Latinists were the elect of God, was counterbalanced by the perennial message of the Gospels insisting that Christian teaching should be conveyed to everybody, and therefore to the crowd of *laici*. Various attempts had consequently been made to translate prayers, Scripture and the church's teaching into vernacular languages. The works of Alfred and Aelfric are obvious examples of such attempts in pre-Conquest England.

By the eleventh century an uneasy compromise seems to have been reached whereby, for the people at large, the irreducible minimum of Christian teaching — namely the Lord's Prayer and the Creed — was to be recited in Latin, while sermons, homilies and the like were expressed in the vernacular. Thus a law of Cnut enjoined every Christian to apply himself until he could at least 'understand aright and learn the *Pater Noster* and the *Credo*'. Although this law does not mean that everybody is to read Latin, they are to recite these two Latin texts by heart. Hence one of the glosses accompanying this law adds that Christ himself first recited the *Pater Noster*. That Latin texts are meant and not English translations is suggested by the use of the Latin names for the texts and also by the glosses which describe the penalties for failing to learn them. If the texts had been in the vernacular, there would presumably have been no problem about learning them.

As it was, most people probably did not find this minimal amount of Latin overwhelmingly difficult because they were accustomed to using their ears to learn and furthermore they heard these texts recited whenever they went to church. Assuming that most of the population were minimally conscientious about their religious duties, we are led to the conclusion that most people could recite a little Latin. They had thus taken the first step towards literacy, as paradoxically they could speak *litteraliter*. Those who reached slightly greater competence, in other words, those who understood what they recited and could perhaps also distinguish the letters of the alphabet, would not have been altogether at a loss if they were required to sign their names with seals on Latin charters.

A conjecture of this sort, concerning the level of education of the mass of medieval people, is impossible to prove because evidence of any sort about elementary instruction, and particularly about that of ordinary people, is rare. The biographies of saints sometimes provide glimpses of childhood, but the only detailed description of an English saint of this period of undoubted peasant origins is the life of St Godric, which was written (in various versions) from his own recollections. Although he features in numerous social histories, because he is the first English example of the Dick Whittington type who made his fortune as a merchant, Godric's story is worth examining again from the point of view of what sort of education he acquired.

Godric was born in Norfolk in *c.* 1065 of parents who were good, though poor and ignorant. Since he had no wish to remain a peasant, but to exercise his mind, he exerted himself to study. So he strove to learn to be a merchant (*mercatoris studium*), first by selling things locally, then by joining travelling chapmen and ultimately by becoming an international shipman. As merchants travelled with their wares, he mastered navigation and practical maritime astronomy. Business combined well with religion, as he journeyed to the shrines at Lindisfarne and St Andrews, and beyond Britain to Rome, Santiago and Jerusalem. For a while he returned to Norfolk and became steward and general manager to a certain rich man. Godric was a pious but not yet a bookish man, although he had known the Lord's Prayer and the Creed 'from the cradle' and he often pondered them on his journeys. At about the age of forty a kinsman in Carlisle gave him a Psalter, from which he learned the Psalms most diligently, retaining them in his memory. This was an abbreviated version of the Psalter, commonly called 'St Jerome's Psalter'. The book must have been quite large, as Godric permanently distorted his little finger by carrying it around, even to bed. After further travels he came to Durham, where he learned more Psalms 'and afterwards he learned the whole Psalter.' By staying around St Mary's church at Durham, where 'boys were learning the first elements of letters', he tenaciously applied his memory to 'hearing, reading and chanting' and thus became 'firm and certain' in the liturgy. Finally he settled at Finchale, near Durham, as a hermit.

Because Godric was self-educated, both the devil and the monks of Durham adopted a patronizing attitude towards him. The twelfth-century devil shared Walter Map's opinion of serfs who had advanced in the world and called Godric a 'stinking old peasant', while his chief biographer, Reginald of Durham, quite often describes him without malice as *laicus*, *illiteratus* and *idiota*. Technically Reginald was correct, as Godric was not a *clericus* and *litteratus*. Nevertheless Reginald revealed his own ignorance of the effects of travel on an intelligent man, when he considered it miraculous that Godric understood 'French or Romance', even though his mother tongue was English. Reginald likewise considered that it was the Holy Spirit, rather than his native wit, which enabled Godric to understand the Latin conversation of four monks from Durham, who had been sent to cross-examine him. By these means Godric was able to give an impressive exposition of the Scriptures to them (in English), 'as if he were an outstanding *litteratus*'. The information provided by Godric's biographers about his knowledge was not recorded for its own sake, as it was intended as evidence of his religious devotion and of those miraculous powers which were the indispensable sign of a saint. Nevertheless the various versions of the life are sufficiently circumstantial and consistent to provide a historical record of one man's self-education and rise from the mass.

Godric's life story provides numerous correctives to the modern tendency to assume that schools are the beginning and end of education. He received his instruction in the Lord's Prayer and the Creed 'from the cradle', presumably meaning from his parents. He is therefore an example of Christian law being applied in practice, as it was the duty of every parent to teach his child the *Pater Noster* and the *Credo*. Thereafter Godric was self-taught. He learned numeracy and navigation, the *mercatoris studium*, by experience. Literacy obviously presented greater problems. Godric may never have learned to write and his knowledge of Latin depended primarily on hearing and memorizing. Although he could never become *litteratus* by this method, he could evidently cope with the normal uses of Latin in ecclesiastical circles. Gerald of Wales gives an example of another hermit and traveller, Wecheleu, who had likewise miraculously learned Latin by ear. The fact that such knowledge was considered miraculous suggests, however, that Latin was thought difficult to learn without formal instruction in grammar. Nevertheless even Latin was in its rudimentary stages primarily a spoken language, to which children were introduced by the church's liturgy and prayers in the home.

Although a man like Godric, who had memorized whole portions of the liturgy, could not pass as a Latinist among the *litterati*, he could probably make as good a show of Latin as some clergy. His self-taught Latin only became a problem when he wanted to be accepted as a conscientious church-man and monk. In lay society Godric's lack of a formal education had not prevented him from mastering the *mercatoris studium*, or from becoming a rich man's steward. In the latter capacity tally sticks and a trained memory were more useful than parchments, although if Godric had lived a century later, he might have found it more difficult to conduct business without writing. Yet before deciding that Godric could not have succeeded a century later, it is worth recalling that the greatest of all medieval stewards and business managers, Hubert Walter, was likewise described as *laicus et illiteratus*. Like Godric, he had little or no formal schooling and was ignorant of elemen-tary Latin grammar, if Gerald of Wales is to be believed. A little Latin, like a little literacy in more recent times, could get a man a long way in ordinary business, deplorable as that was in the eyes of scholars.

Hearing and seeing

'Fundamentally letters are shapes indicating voices. Hence they present things which they bring to mind through the windows of the eyes. Frequently they speak voicelessly the utterances of the absent.' In these antitheses John of Salisbury's *Metalogicon* grapples with the basic problems of the relation-ship between the spoken and the written word. The difference between sounds or voices (*voces*) and things or realities (*res*) was complicated for him, writing in the mid-twelfth century, by the controversy between Nominalists and Realists, between those who argued that universals were mere names and those who claimed they were real things. This philosophical controversy is not our concern here. John's remarks are relevant because, like much of *Metalogicon*, they seem to reflect his own experience as a secretary and drafter of letters as well as exemplifying current scholastic thought.

Numerous charters of the twelfth century are addressed to 'all those see-ing and hearing these letters, in the future as in the present' or to 'all who shall hear and see this charter'; these two examples come from the charters of Roger de Mowbray who died in 1188. The grantor of another charter, Richard de Rollos, actually harangues his audience, 'Oh! all ye who shall have heard this and have seen!' Early charters likewise quite often conclude with 'Goodbye' (*Valete*), as if the donor had just finished speaking with his audi-ence. Documents made it possible for the grantor to address posterity ('all who shall hear and see') as well as his contemporaries. In the opening words of the Winchcombe abbey cartulary, 'when the voice has perished with the man, writing still enlightens posterity.' Writing shifted the spotlight away from the transitory actors witnessing a conveyance and on to the perpetual parchment recording it. By the thirteenth century, when charters had become more familiar to landowners, donors cease addressing their readers, as Richard de Rollos did, and likewise they no longer conclude with *Valete*. Once it was understood that charters were directed to posterity, it must have seemed foolish to say 'Goodbye' to people who had not yet been born. In place of such conversational expressions, thirteenth-century charters are more stereo-typed; they are often impersonally addressed in some such form as 'Let all persons, present and future, know that I, A of B, have given X with its appurtenances to C of D.'

A comparable change occurs in wills. Until the thirteenth century the will was an essentially oral act, even when it was recorded in writing. The persons present witnessed the testator making his bequests 'with his own mouth'; they 'saw, were present, and heard' the transaction.[23] By the end of the thirteenth century a man's final will no longer usually means his wishes spoken on his deathbed, but a closed and sealed document. The witnesses no longer heard him; instead they saw his seal being placed on the document. When wills were first enrolled, as they were in London from 1258, the formula of probate still put emphasis on the witnesses who had seen and heard. But a generation later, by the 1290s, the London roll often omits the names of the witnesses, presumably because the written will was the preferred evidence.[24] The validity of the will now depended primarily upon its being in a correct documentary form and not on the verbal assurances of the witnesses. This is another illustration of the shift from memory to written record between 1100 and 1300. Wills had been made in writing by the Anglo-Saxons; the novelty lay in their being closed and sealed documents.

Symbolic objects and documents

Before conveyances were made with documents, the witnesses 'heard' the donor utter the words of the grant and 'saw' him make the transfer by a symbolic object, such as a knife or a turf from the land. William the Conqueror went one better and jokingly threatened to make one donee 'feel' the conveyance by dashing the symbolic knife through the recipient abbot's hand saying, 'That's the way land ought to be given.'[25] Such a gesture was intended to impress the event on the memory of all those present. If there were dispute subsequently, resort was had to the recollection of the witnesses. Similar rules applied to the oral 'records' of courts, which were retained (in theory at least) in the memory of those present. For example, if the record of the county court were disputed, the aggrieved litigant brought forward two witnesses who each gave evidence of what they had heard and seen. In such a case in 1212 the prior to Ware (in Hertfordshire) defended himself by 'one hearing and one understanding', namely Jordan of Warew and Robert of Clopton; Robert also offered to prove the prior's allegation by battle, 'as he was present and heard this'. In this case some distinction is evi-dently being attempted between the knowledge of the two witnesses: Jordan had heard, or at least understood, less of the proceedings than Robert. Likewise at Cheshunt (in Hertfordshire) in a seignorial court in 1220 a litigant challenged the record by 'one person hearing and another seeing'. Which testimony was thought preferable in this instance, that of the person who heard or of the other who saw, is unclear. These two exceptional cases suggest that the legal commonplace of making a record by 'hearing and seeing' was not a mere formula made meaningless by repetition.

Documents changed the significance of bearing witness by hearing and seeing legal procedures, because written evidence could be heard by reading aloud or seen by inspecting the document. In John of Salisbury's definition, letters 'indicate voices' and bring things to mind 'through the windows of the eyes'. Once charters were used for conveyances, 'hearing' applied to anyone hearing the charter read out loud at any time, instead of referring only to the witnesses of the original conveyance. From there it was a short step to substitute 'reading' for 'seeing', as one of Roger de Mowbray's charters does, which is addressed to 'all his own men and to the rest, *reading* or hearing these letters'. This phrase plays also with the ambiguity of the word 'letters', which in Latin (as in English) means both alphabetic symbols and missives.

A curiously worded grant for St Mary's priory at Monmouth is addressed to the donors, Richard de Cormeilles and Beatrice his wife, instead of to the recipients. The charter rewards Richard and Beatrice with divine bliss because they have given the tithes of Norton-Giffard to Mary the mother of God. She is the ostensible grantor of the charter, though the document itself was presumably written by a monk of St Mary's priory which was the terrestial beneficiary. The writer's Latin is eccentric — for example he spells *uxor* (wife) as *hucxor* — but revealing in its phraseology. He includes the phrase *sicut presens breve loquitur* (as the present writing speaks), whereas ordinary usage would have *dicitur* (says) or *testatur* (attests) in place of *loquitur*. The writer also makes it clear that the named witnesses, who 'saw and heard the gift solemnly exhibited by a book upon the altar', are 'subsequent' and therefore secondary to the evidence of the writing itself. In making the writing 'speak' and in putting the pre-literate witnessing ceremony of seeing and hearing into a subsidiary role, the naïve writer of this charter has exemplified John of Salisbury's scholastic definition (which is contemporary with the charter) that letters 'speak voicelessly the utterances of the absent', the absent in this instance being the grantor, Mary the mother of God.

Once property was conveyed in writing, it would have seemed logical for the charter to supersede the symbolic object, such as the knife or turf, which had formerly been used in the witnessing ceremony. As the grant to Monmouth priory shows, that object had sometimes itself been a writing — a book solemnly exhibited upon an altar. Traditionally the book used for this purpose was the text of the Gospels. For example a gift of a saltpan was made to St Peter's priory at Sele in Sussex in 1153 'by the text of the Holy Gospel upon the altar of St Peter, many persons hearing and seeing'. The Gospel book was used because it was customary to reinforce oaths with it (as is still the practice in law courts); thus in Edward I's wardrobe there was kept 'a book, which is called *textus*, upon which the magnates were accustomed to swear'. To replace a Gospel book by a charter in a conveyancing ceremony was a relatively small change in appearance (it was simply substituting one document for another), but a large one in substance. The charter in its text actually 'represented' (in John of Salisbury's definition) in a durable record the terms of the conveyance, whereas the Gospel book merely symbolized the solemnity of the occasion for the witnesses. The Monmouth priory charter therefore distinguishes the written grant (*breve*), which 'speaks' to the hearers, from the symbolic book (*liber*) which is 'exhibited' to the viewers.

Nevertheless, although it seemed logical to dispense with symbols and make full use of the potentialities of writing, contemporaries continued with their pre-literate habits long after charters had become common. In the rare instances where the conveyance appears to be made by the written document itself (as in the Monmouth priory charter), we should probably assume that the document is serving the ancient function of a symbolic object, rather than being considered primarily for its contents in a modern literate way. There are examples of the conveyancing document being presented on the altar like a Gospel book. In a charter of 1193 the abbot of Glastonbury states that 'the present charter was placed on the altar of St Mary by me as an offering, the clergy and people of the same vill [of Street in Somerset] standing round.' In the Guthlac roll (probably dating from the late twelfth century) King Ethelbald and twelve other benefactors of Crowland abbey in Lincolnshire are depicted pressing forward with opened scrolls to lay at the altar and shrine of St Guthlac. The writing on the scrolls is specific, giving in Latin the name of each donor and the property donated, such as, 'I, Alan de Croun give you, Father Guthlac, the priory of Freiston with appurtenances.' One or two of the benefactors have their mouths open, as if voicing their gifts. As some of these charters cannot be traced and may well have been forged, the Guthlac roll could have been intended to provide a kind of documentary proof of the gifts in this peculiar form.

An explicit instance of a conveyance by the charter itself is a gift made by William of Astle in *c.* 1200 to the Knights Hospitaller. The last witness is Ivo clerk of Stafford, representing the Hospitallers, 'in whose hand I, William, have made seisin with this charter in the church of Alderly'. The usual rule was that a conveyance could not be made by a document alone, but depended on the recipient having 'seisin' (meaning actual possession of the property). Nevertheless the exception to this rule in William of Astle's charter may merely prove it, as the charter, conveyed from hand to hand, is a substitute for the usual object symbolizing the transaction.

The unfamiliar idea of a writing being interpreted primarily as a symbolic object, rather than as a documentary proof, is most clearly evident when the object written upon is not a parchment, but something else. Thus an ivory whip-handle found at St Albans abbey had an inscription on it stating that 'this is the gift of Gilbert de Novo Castello for four mares.' The object, a whip, appropriately symbolized the gift of horses; the writing was ancillary. Similarly a knife is still preserved at Durham, which symbolized Stephen of Bulmer's agreement (perhaps made in the 1150s) with the monks of Holy Island at Lindisfarne about the chapelry of Lowick.

This knife is particularly interesting because its haft bears an inscription, which is comparable with the St Albans whip-handle and other inscribed knife hafts no longer extant. Whereas the hafts of these other knives were made of ivory, Stephen's is of hard horn (perhaps a deer's) and the inscriber has had difficulty making much impression on it. He was not perhaps an experienced carver but a scribe, possibly a monk of Lindisfarne, who only had a pen knife readily available. Although the lettering of the inscription is shaky and uneven, it is conceived in a bold monastic hand. Along one side of the knife's haft is written *Signum de capella de lowic* (the sign for the chapel of Lowick) and on the other side *de capella de lowic & de decimis de lowic totius curie & totius ville* (for the chapel of Lowick and for the tithes of Lowick from the whole court and the whole vill). As well as this inscription on the haft, a parchment label is attached (written in a comparable bold monastic hand), which gives fuller details of the agreement. This label cannot be described as a charter, as it is irregular in shape and is written on both sides. A statement on its dorse helps explain the purpose of the knife. It records that Stephen of Bulmer had not come in person to make the agreement at Holy Island, but sent Lady Cecily and Aschetin, the *dapifer* or steward, in his place. Probably Aschetin brought the knife with him as a symbol of Stephen's consent. It may well have been Stephen's own carving knife; the haft is heavy and shows signs of use and, although the blade is broken near the top, what remains of the knife still measures 13½ cm. It would thus have been an appropriate object for a steward, who probably carved at his lord's table, to bring as durable and substantial evidence that he truly represented his master.

Why go to the trouble of trying to write on a knife, when pen and parchment did the same job more efficiently? Ordinary writing materials were evidently available, as Stephen's knife has the parchment label on it as well as the inscription. The explanation may be that the parties to this agreement had more confidence in the evidence of the knife than in writing. Knives were traditional symbols for conveyances, whereas charters authenticated by seals were a relative novelty, though they should have been familiar to the monks of Lindisfarne if not to a northern knight like Stephen of Bulmer. Some contemporaries may also have thought that a knife was more durable than, and therefore preferable to, parchment and sealing wax. It was true that only the sparsest details of a conveyance could be engraved on the handle of a knife or a whip, but the tradition had been that the true facts of a transaction were engraved on the hearts and minds of the witnesses and could not be fully recorded in any form of writing however detailed. The symbolic knife would have been retained regardless of whether it had anything written on it, because it preserved the memory of the conveyance.

Only literates, who could interpret the 'shapes indicating voices' (in John of Salisbury's definition of letters), were going to be convinced that the writing was superior to the symbolic object. Such objects, the records of the non-literate, were therefore preserved along with documents. Another example is the knife by which Thomas of Moulton gave the church of Weston in Lincolnshire to Spalding priory, which was deposited in its archive (*in secretario*) according to the charter confirming the gift. This latter knife is no longer preserved. To later archivists, knives and other archaic relics meant nothing unless they had inscriptions connected with them; such things were thrown away as medieval rubbish, because the language of memory which they expressed had no significance for literates.

It is possible that the seals, *signa* in Latin, attached to charters were seen by many contemporaries in a similar way as inscribed 'signs'. To students of diplomatics today seals are a method of authenticating documents which preceded the sign manual or written signature. To medieval people they may have appeared rather as visible and tangible objects symbolizing the wishes of the donor. The seal was significant even without the document. Early seals (that is, twelfth-century ones) tend to be disproportionately large – often 6 or 7 cm in diameter – compared with the writings to which they are attached. John of Salisbury, writing on behalf of Archbishop Theobald of Canterbury about the safekeeping of seals, says that 'by the marks of a single impress the mouths of all the pontiffs may be opened or closed.' Just as letters 'speak voicelessly the utterances of the absent', seals regulate that speech. Emphasis on the spoken word remained.

The 'signs' attached to documents, whether they took the form of inscribed knives or impressed wax or even ink crosses made by the witnesses, all helped to bridge the gulf between the traditional and the literate way of recording transactions. Pre-literate customs and ceremonies persisted despite the use of documents. The doctrine of livery of seisin – the rule that a recipient must have the property duly delivered to him and enter into possession (that is, seisin) of it, whether there was a document of conveyance or not – became a fundamental principle of the common law; but there are exceptions to it, like the charter of William of Astle to the Knights Hospitaller which has already been discussed. The treatise ascribed to Bracton insists (in the first half of the thirteenth century) that 'a gift is not valid unless livery follows; for the thing given is transferred neither by homage, nor by the drawing up of charters and instruments, even though they be recited in public.' Written words were thus entirely inadequate, and even spoken ones were insufficient, without physical symbols: 'If livery is to be made of a house by itself, or of a messuage for an estate, it ought to be made by the door and its hasp or ring, by which is understood that the donee possess the whole to its boundaries.' It followed also that a gift 'may be valid though no charter has been made . . . and conversely the charter may be genuine and valid and the gift incomplete.' The physical symbol, the door hasp or ring in Bracton's example, continued to epitomize the whole gift better than any document.

Likewise the drafting rule became general that the past tense should be used in charters for the act of giving: 'Know that I, A of B, *have* given', not simply 'I give'. This emphasized that the ceremonial conveyance was the crucial transaction, whereas the charter was merely a subsequent confirmation of it. This rule only became firmly established in the thirteenth century. Numerous charters of the twelfth century depart from it, presumably because their more amateur draftsmen did not appreciate the relationship between written record and the passage of time. Similarly a generation or two after Bracton the need for the livery of seisin rule was not apparent to ordinary people. Some Derbyshire jurors, who had supposed in 1304 that a charter might suffice without it, were described by a second group of jurors as 'simple persons who were not cognizant with English laws and customs'. The doctrine of seisin, which had once been a self-evident and commonsense rule, had become with the spread of literacy one of those technical mysteries in which the common law abounded.

The spoken versus the written word

The increasing use of documents created tension between the old methods and the new. Which was the better evidence, for example, seeing a parchment or hearing a man's word? How was the one to be evaluated if it conflicted with the other? A good illustration of this particular dilemma is Eadmer's account of the investiture controversy between St Anselm, archbishop of Canterbury, and Henry I. Both Anselm and the king had sent envoys to Pope Paschal II; Anselm sent two monks of Canterbury, while the king sent the archbishop of York and two other bishops. The envoys returned to England in September 1101 with papal letters addressed to the king and to Anselm, prohibiting royal investiture of churches and exhorting resistance to them. When the pope's letter to Anselm had been publicly read out, Henry's envoys objected. They claimed that Paschal had given them a purely verbal message that he would treat the king leniently on the investiture question and would not excommunicate him; the pope had added that he did not wish this concession to be put in written form (*per carta inscriptionem*) because other rulers would use it as a precedent. Anselm's envoys replied that the pope had given no verbal message which conflicted in any way with his letters. To this Henry's bishops answered that Paschal had acted in one way in secret and another in public. Baldwin of Bec, Anselm's chief envoy, was outraged at this allegation and said that it was calumny on the Holy See.

Dissension then arose in the audience. Those favouring Anselm maintained that credence should be given to 'documents signed with the pope's seal' (*scriptis sigillo pape signatis*) and not to 'the uncertainty of mere words'. The king's side replied that they preferred to rely on the word of three bishops than on 'the skins of wethers blackened with ink and weighted with a little lump of lead'. They added further venom to the argument by alleging that monks were unreliable anyway, as they should not be engaged in worldly business. Eadmer puts the controversy into dialogue form:

> Anselm's monks: 'But what about the evidence of the letters?'
> Henry's bishops: 'As we don't accept the evidence of monks against bishops, why should we accept that of a sheep-skin?'
> Anselm's monks: 'Shame on you! Are not the Gospels written down on sheepskins?'

Obviously the conflict could not be quickly resolved. In Lent 1102 Anselm set out for Rome and opened on his way another letter from the pope, in which Paschal denied that he had ever given contradictory verbal instructions to the bishops or said that he was reluctant to set a precedent in writing.[26] Who was telling the truth is of course impossible to resolve. Paschal was attempting to make peace and settle the investiture controversy by diplomacy. He may well therefore have said something off the record to the bishops which they had possibly exaggerated. Like all statesmen, the pope obviously had to make a formal denial of such secret negotiations once they became public.

The substance of the story is not our concern here, but the attitudes it reveals towards documentary evidence. Papal letters, sealed with the leaden bull and bearing the symbols and monograms of curial officials, were the most impressive documents produced in medieval Europe, their only rival being Byzantine imperial letters. Yet in Eadmer's story the papal bull is disparagingly described as a sheepskin blackened with ink with a bit of lead attached to it, an extreme example of a document being treated simply as a physical object rather than for its contents. Anselm's supporters were entitled to riposte that the Gospels too were written on parchment – in other words, that Christianity was essentially the religion of a book. At Orléans in 1022 a group of heretics had been burned for disparaging the book learning of the clergy cross-examining them, which they had called human fabrications 'written on the skins of animals', whereas the heretics claimed to believe 'in the law written in the inner man by the Holy Spirit'.[27] The heretics had therefore been arguing that the true written law (*lex scripta*) was not canon law nor Justinian's code, but inspiration retained in the mind alone; real writing was not man-made script on animal parchment. Such an idea may well have derived from the Scripture itself, most probably from St Paul's Second Epistle to the Corinthians, 'written not with ink, but with the spirit of the living God . . . for the letter killeth, but the spirit giveth life.'[28] Early in the thirteenth century St Francis was to take up this theme as part of his revolt against the spiritually empty book learning of some monks: 'Those religious have been killed by the letter who are not willing to follow the spirit of the divine letter, but only desire to know words and interpret them for other men.'[29] As so often in his work, Francis blended orthodox and heretical viewpoints in an insight of his own. Literacy was not a virtue in itself. Emphasis on the word inscribed spiritually on the minds of men, as contrasted with letters written on parchment, retained its strength in the Christian message as it did in secular conveyancing ceremonies.

The argument of Henry I's envoys, that their word was better evidence than a papal bull, would not in fact have appeared as outrageous or surprising to contemporaries as Eadmer suggests in his account of the controversy with Anselm. The principle that 'oral witness deserves more credence than written evidence' was a legal commonplace. It was cited for example by Hubert Walter, archbishop of Canterbury, in a letter to Innocent III in 1200 controverting Gerald of Wales's well documented claim to be bishop-elect of St David's.[30] Gerald conceded the point in his reply to the pope, but added that he had brought both documents and witnesses. Behind this principle lay the correct assumption that numerous documents used in legal claims, from the Donation of Constantine downwards, were forgeries. Not all those who relied on the traditional use of the spoken word, rather than parchments, were necessarily therefore obscurantist conservatives. The technology of written record was insufficiently advanced to be efficient or reliable. As a consequence, documents and the spoken word are frequently both used in a way which appears otiose to a modern literate. To make a record often meant to bear oral witness, not to produce a document. For example, in the civil war of Stephen's reign Robert earl of Gloucester and Miles earl of Hereford made a treaty of friendship in writing, in the form of a sealed letter; yet both parties in this document also name witnesses, who are 'to make legal record of this agreement in court if necessary'.

The rule that oral witness is preferable to documents, like the rule that seisin is superior to a charter, shows how cautiously – and perhaps reluctantly – written evidence was accepted. Much important business continued to be done by word of mouth. Bearers of letters were often given instructions which were to be conveyed *viva voce*, either because that was convenient and traditional or because the information was too secret to write down. Twice, for instance, in March 1229 Henry III sent messengers to the count of Toulouse. In their mouths, the king wrote, he had put matters which they would disclose more fully to the count, since the business (presumably concerning a truce with Louis IX) could not be committed to writing because of the dangers of the roads. Similarly in the period of the baronial rebellion, when Henry was in France in 1260, he wrote to the earl of Gloucester instructing him to report on the state of the kingdom by Gilbert Fitz Hugh, the king's serjeant, who would tell the earl more fully *viva voce* about the king's situation. In such negotiations the letter itself did not convey essential information but, like a modern ambassador's letter of credence, was a symbolic object replacing the messenger's ring or other *signum* which had formerly identified him as a confidential agent of his master.

Oral messages were also used to give instructions which later generations would have put in writing. For example, in 1234 John le Franceis and John Mansel were authorized by royal letters of credence to conduct inquiries concerning Jews in certain counties and give instructions to sheriffs *viva voce*. An interesting but non-English case of oral delivery is the poem which the troubadour, Jaufre Rudel, lord of Blaye in the Gironde, sent to the Comte de Marche in *c.* 1150 'without a parchment document' (*senes breu de parguamina*) by the mouth of the jongleur, Filhol.[31] The jongleur is thus being used as a kind of living letter. There is, however, a paradox in all such evidence, since historians can only know of the survival of oral ways of conveying information by extant written evidence. Jaufre Rudel's poem, once sent without a script, is written down nonetheless.

Much business was still done by word of mouth for the obvious reason that documents were bound to be relatively rare until printing made their automatic reproduction possible. The usual way of publishing new laws and regulations was by proclamation. The following instances from the Chancery records of Henry III for 1234 are typical. On 28 August the sheriff of Northumberland and some others were ordered to have it proclaimed (*clamari facias*) that pleas were to be adjourned until the coming of the eyre justices. On 29 August all sheriffs were to proclaim the regulations for supervising hundred courts in accordance with the revision of Magna Carta in 1234. On 1 September the sheriff of Norfolk and Suffolk was to proclaim throughout the two counties that no Jew was to lend money to any Christian in the king's demesne.[32] Matthew Paris suggests that Henry III pursued a policy of legislating by proclamation: in 1248 the people were harassed by diverse precepts promulgated 'by the voice of a crier' (*voce preconia*) throughout the cities of England; the king established a new fair at Westminster, for example, in this way. The proclamation to which Matthew gives most attention likewise occurred in 1248, when the king 'ordered it to be proclaimed as law by the voice of a crier' that henceforward no man might castrate another for fornication except a husband in the case of his wife's adulterer. The reason for this was that John le Bretun had castrated the Norfolk knight, Godfrey de Millers, for lying with his daughter.

How extensively or frequently proclamations of this sort were made is not clear. Proclamations were a quick and effective way of conveying information in crowded cities like London, but were obviously less practical in the countryside. Most references to proclamations concern cities. For example, in 1252 Henry III had it proclaimed throughout London that no one should lend money to the abbot of Westminster; or in the preceding year a proclamation had been made against the royal judge, Henry of Bath, in London and in the king's court. One consequence for the history of Henry III's government's use of the spoken word for legislation is that all trace of it is lost, unless a chronicler happened to record it or the Chancery rolls refer to it incidentally. Edward I is considered a great lawgiver partly because the legislation of his time is preserved in the statute rolls. In Henry III's reign less was written down, though a comparable amount of legislative activity probably took place.

Magna Carta became the great precedent for putting legislation into writing. Yet even it was not officially enrolled in the royal archives, although it was proclaimed extensively and repeatedly. Within a few days of King John's assent to it letters were sent to all his sheriffs, foresters, gamekeepers, watermen and other bailiffs informing them of the agreement between the king and the barons, 'as you can hear and see by our charter which we have had made thereon', which they were ordered to have read publicly throughout their bailiwicks. As a result, in theory at least, everyone in England should have heard Magna Carta read out, although it is unlikely that a sufficient number of copies were available.[33] Similarly when the barons again had the upper hand in 1265, they ordered the terms of Henry III's oath to keep peace with them to be published in the full county court at least twice every year, at Easter and Michaelmas. In 1300 transcripts of Magna Carta and the Charter of the Forest were delivered to every sheriff to read out 'before the people' four times a year, at Christmas and Midsummer as well as at Easter and Michaelmas. Nevertheless by 1300 there had been a significant change, as considerable emphasis was now being put on seeing the document as well as hearing it. Sealed transcripts of Magna Carta were sent to all judges, sheriffs and civic officials and also to all cathedral churches. A precedent for the latter had been made in 1279 when Archbishop Pecham's council at Reading had ordered a copy of Magna Carta to be posted up in every cathedral and collegiate church in a public place 'so that it can be clearly seen by the eyes of everyone entering'; in the spring of each year the old copy was to be taken down and a new fair copy substituted for it.[34]

The clergy therefore assumed that the general public could read, or would at least be impressed by seeing the Latin text of Magna Carta. The royal government likewise was sufficiently alarmed to make Pecham have all these copies removed from church doors shortly afterwards. An even earlier precedent, though a fantastic one, occurs in Andrew the Chaplain's *Ars Amandi* of the later twelfth century. The king of love had written out the rules of love on a parchment for a British knight. His lady then called together a court of numerous knights and their ladies, each of whom was given a written copy of the rules to take home and issue to all lovers in all parts of the world. Like Archbishop Pecham, Andrew the Chaplain probably had higher expectations of the reading ability of the public than were justified.

Public readings of documents were done in the vernacular as well as in Latin and might reach a wider audience in that way. Thus in 1300, according to the chronicler Rishanger, Magna Carta was read out at Westminster 'first in Latin [*litteraliter*] and then in the native tongue [*patria lingua*]'. Similarly a year earlier letters of Pope Boniface VIII about the peace between England and France had been read out in Parliament 'in Latin for the literate and in the native tongue for the illiterate'. Also in 1299, according to the Worcester annals, royal letters concerning a new perambulation of the forests were 'proclaimed in the city of Worcester in the mother tongue [*materna lingua*]'.[35] The 'paternal' or 'maternal' language might mean either English or French. Thus in 1254 the papal excommunication of infringers of Magna Carta was ordered to be published 'in the English [*Anglicana*] and French [*Gallicana*] tongues' whenever and wherever appropriate. The use of English and French in this instance was probably a reiteration of existing practice, rather than an innovation, as it is likely that Magna Carta itself had been proclaimed throughout the land in both English and French in 1215.

The distinction the chroniclers wished to emphasize in the citations above was between the language of literacy (Latin) and spoken language; they were less concerned with which vernacular was used. To pedantic Latinists vernacular simply meant the spoken language. Gerald of Wales hoped that someone would translate his work into French and claimed that Walter Map used to tell him that he (Gerald) had written much, whereas Walter had said much. Although Gerald's writings (*scripta*) were more praiseworthy and durable than Walter's speeches (*dicta*), Walter had the greater profit because his *dicta* were accessible, since they were expressed in the common idiom, while Gerald's *scripta* were appreciated only by the declining few who knew Latin. In fact the distinction Gerald drew here between himself and Walter Map was misleading, as Walter also was a precocious Latinist.[36] Possibly Gerald felt that Walter had been a more successful preacher and *raconteur* in the vernacular than he was. The point of the story from our angle, regardless of whether it is true or not, is that Gerald felt that the spoken vernacular brought greater prestige than written Latin.

Listening to the word

Whatever the language, and whether the record was held solely in the bearer's memory or was committed to parchment, the medieval recipient prepared himself to listen to an utterance rather than to scrutinize a document visually as a modern literate would. This was due to a different habit of mind; it was not because the recipient was illiterate in any sense of that word. In his account of his claim to be bishop-elect of St David's Gerald of Wales describes a private audience in the pope's chamber with Innocent III in 1200, when the pope looked up a register listing all the metropolitan churches of Christendom and went through the rubrics until he found Wales. But when at a subsequent private audience Gerald showed the pope a transcript of a letter of Eugenius III which Gerald had found in another papal register, Innocent handed the transcript to Cardinal Ugolino and told him to read it; 'and when it had been read and diligently heard, the pope replied that he was well pleased with it.' Gerald's account of the earlier audience depicts the pope browsing through a reference book as a modern literate would do; but when at the subsequent audience the pope needs to absorb carefully the details of a letter, he has it read to him instead of scrutinizing it. Reading aloud in this case is not being done to enable everyone present to learn the contents of the letter, as the only persons at this private audience are Innocent, Gerald and Ugolino who is supporting him. Nor obviously was Innocent incapable of reading the script of papal registers. Yet he evidently found it easier to concentrate when he was listening than when he was looking; reading was still primarily oral rather than visual.

Indications of the same habit of mind appear in the 'auditing' of monetary accounts. Abbot Samson of Bury St Edmunds 'heard' the weekly account of his expenditure, yet he obviously could have consulted such a document (if the account were in documentary form at all), as his biographer Jocelin says that he inspected his *kalendarium* (his register of rents and so on) almost every day 'as though he could see therein the image of his own efficiency as in a mirror'. The modern word 'audit' derives from a time when it was the habit to listen to, rather than to see, an account. Thomas of Eccleston in his description of the arrival of the Franciscan friars in England in 1224 records that when the superior heard the first annual account of the London friars and realized how little they had to show for such lavish expenditure, he threw down all the tallies and rolls and shouted 'I'm caught' and 'he never afterwards wanted to hear an account'. In this instance accounts in writing existed, in the form of both wooden tallies and parchment rolls, yet the superior 'heard' them nonetheless. H.J. Chaytor points out, however, that one must be careful of colloquial speech in such an instance as this. For example modern English uses the phrase 'I have not heard from him for some time' to mean 'I have had no letter'.[37]

Similarly in law courts, 'inspecting' a document might mean hearing it read aloud. Thus in 1219 in an action of warranty of charter in Lincolnshire William of Well, the defendant, is reported in the plea roll to 'have come and claimed a hearing [*auditum*] of his father's charter' and it was duly heard. A generation later, in a similar action in Berkshire in 1248, the abbot of Beaulieu who was the defendant claimed that the plaintiff should 'show' him the charter by which he should warrant her. The contrasting emphasis on hearing and seeing in these similar claims only thirty years apart may indicate a general change of attitude developing within this period, if only in the minds of the enrolling clerks; or more likely the two cases show the differing approach to documents of a knight, William of Well, and a monk, the abbot of Beaulieu.

Literary works, especially vernacular ones, were frequently explicitly addressed by the author to an audience, rather than to readers as such. Thus the nun of Barking in her French version of Ailred's life of Edward the Confessor in *c.* 1163 requests 'all who hear, or will ever hear, this romance of hers' not to despise it because the translation is done by a woman.[38] In the *Romance of Horn* by Master Thomas the author begins by addressing his audience: 'Gentlemen, you have heard the lines of parchment' (*Seigneurs, oi avez le vers del parchemin*). The parchment is evidently thought of here as a direct substitute for a jongleur; it speaks and is heard, like the charter of Richard de Cormeilles for St Mary's priory at Monmouth. Likewise in the *Estoire de Waldef* (dating from *c.* 1190) the author refers to the *Brut* story:

> If anyone wants to know this history
> Let him read the *Brut*, he will hear it there
> [*Qui l'estoire savoir voldra*
> *Lise le Brut, illoc l'orra*].[39]

A modern literate would not say 'he will *hear* it there', but 'he will *find* it' or '*see* it there.' The emphasis in such works on hearing does not necessarily mean that their contents stem directly from oral tradition, but that reading continued to be conceived in terms of hearing rather than seeing. Until cheap printing supplied every 'reader' with his own book, the emphasis on hearing was understandable.

Latin works too were generally intended to be read aloud – hence the speeches and frequent use of dramatic dialogue in monastic chronicles. Eadmer concludes the first book of his *Life of St Anselm* with an interval, as in a play: 'But here, lest our unpolished speech [*oratio*] weary your readers or hearers by being too long drawn-out, we shall make our first halt in the work.' Traditional monastic reading in particular bore little relation to a modern literate's approach to a book. *Lectio* was 'more a process of rumination than reading, directed towards savouring the divine wisdom within a book rather than finding new ideas or novel information'.[40] The process is well illustrated by St Anselm's *Meditation on Human Redemption*: 'Taste the goodness of your redeemer . . . chew the honeycomb of his words, suck their flavour which is sweeter than honey, swallow their wholesome sweetness. Chew by thinking, suck by understanding, swallow by loving and rejoicing.' Reading was a physical exertion, demanding the use not only of the eyes, but of tongue, mouth and throat. Writing was a similar act of endurance, requiring three fingers to hold the pen, two eyes to see the words, one tongue to speak them, and the whole body to labour.[41] For these reasons some monks argued that work in the *scriptorium* was an adequate substitute for manual labour.

The system of punctuating and abbreviating words in Latin works was likewise intended primarily to assist someone reading aloud, rather than a person silently scrutinizing the page. N.R. Ker cites the case of a manuscript where the Latin word *neque* (neither), which is written out in full, has been amended throughout to *neq*; he suggests that writing *neque* out in full was likely to mislead an oral reader into stressing the second syllable; writing out the word in full was an error on the scribe's part which has been duly corrected. Some abbreviations were therefore intended to help pronunciation, rather than save the scribe's time when copying a book. Ideally a 'reader' was expected to look at the text as well as listen to it, but that was the exception and not the rule. In the *Life of St Margaret* of Scotland the author considered it a point worth remarking that Margaret's daughter, Matilda (Henry I's queen), 'desired not only to hear, but also to inspect continually the impress of the letters' of her mother's life.[42] A school manual, not English unfortunately and later than our period, sums up in a dialogue the medieval meaning of 'reading' (*lectio*):

'Are you a scholar, what do you read?'

'I do not read, I listen.'

'What do you hear?'

'Donatus or Alexander, or logic or music.'[43]

Donatus's *Ars Minor* and Alexander's *Doctrinale* were Latin textbooks. The term 'reading' a subject has been preserved at Oxford and Cambridge, whereas some undergraduates think that 'reading' implies studying books instead of hearing lectures, medieval students understood *lectio* primarily to mean that the master read while they listened.

Whole books were published by being read aloud. Gerald of Wales says that he published his *Topography of Ireland* in this way in *c.* 1188 by reading it at Oxford to different audiences on three successive days. But Gerald's action was not typical, as he boasts that 'neither has the present age seen, nor does any past age bear record of, the like in England.' The normal way of disseminating scholarly works, as distinct from popular romances, was by the modern method of circulating copies. For instance Herbert of Bosham assumed in his life of Becket that his readers will be able to study Becket's correspondence, which he omits for the sake of brevity, 'because that book of letters is already in the possession of many persons and churches'. If Becket is thought too exceptional an example because of his extraordinary popularity, Eadmer mentions in his appendix to St Anselm's *Life* that he intends to make a new start, because the *Life* has already 'been transcribed by many and distributed to various churches'. Distributing copies did not of course rule out public readings; on the contrary, as more books became available, the practice may have grown even more widespread.

Just as reading was linked in the medieval mind with hearing rather than seeing, writing (in its modern sense of composition) was associated with dictating rather than manipulating a pen. Reading and writing (in the sense of composition) were therefore both extensions of speaking and were not inseparably coupled with each other, as they are today. A person might be able to write, yet not be considered literate. As we have seen, Walter Map mentions a boy 'who was not *litteratus*, although he knew how to transcribe any series of letters whatever'. Literacy involved being learned in Latin, whereas writing was the process of making a fair copy on parchment, which was the art of the scribe. Some authors (notably the great monastic historians Orderic Vitalis, William of Malmesbury and Matthew Paris)[44] did their own writing, but they are the exceptions and they distinguished that activity from composition.

Medieval distinctions are well illustrated by Eadmer. He explains that he had to conceal from St Anselm that he was 'writing' his biography. When he had begun the work 'and had had already transcribed on to parchment a great part of what I had composed [*dictaveram*] in wax', Anselm asked 'what it was I was composing and copying' (*quid dictitarem, quid scriptitarem*). The process of composing on wax tablets is thus described in Latin by the word *dictitare* (literally, 'to dictate'), even though in Eadmer's case he was dictating to himself. The use of 'writing' (*scriptitare*) is confined to making the fair copy on parchment. Similarly when Orderic Vitalis wishes to say that before the time of William the Conqueror the Normans had concentrated on war rather than reading and writing, the phrase he uses is *legere vel dictare*, not *legere vel scribere*. Numerous other examples of using 'dictate' where a modern literate would use 'write' could be given.[45] Dictating was the usual form of literary composition and the *ars dictaminis*, taught in the schools as part of rhetoric, was the skill governing it. Letter writing was thus an intellectual skill using the mouth rather than the hand. Peter of Blois, a busy secretary of state like John of Salisbury, boasted that the archbishop of Canterbury had seen him dictating to three different scribes on diverse subjects, while he dictated and wrote a fourth letter all at the one time.[46]

Reading aloud and dictating permit the non-literate to participate in the use of documents, whereas reading and writing silently exclude the illiterate. When the voice is used, the clerk or scribe becomes no more than a medium between the speaker or hearer and the document. Neither the hearer of a book nor the *dictator* of a letter needs to be a master of every detail of the scribal technique himself, just as modern managers are not required to type or to programme computers. Obviously it is helpful if the manager understands how these things are done and has some experience of them, but this expertise is not indispensable. For these reasons medieval kings and their officials, such as sheriffs in the counties, did not need to be literate in the modern sense. Lack of literacy did not mean that they were ignorant or incapable of coping with business; they were as literate as the tasks required. As the number of documents increased and habits of silent visual reading became more common, levels of literacy (in the modern sense) presumably increased also; but there is no evidence of a crisis suddenly demanding numerous literates. Because the pre-literate emphasis on the spoken word persisted, the change from oral to literate modes could occur slowly and almost imperceptibly over many generations.

The text usually quoted to show that medieval attitudes towards literacy were similar to modern ones is John of Salisbury's quotation in *Policraticus* that 'Rex illiteratus est quasi asinus coronatus' (an illiterate king is like a crowned ass).[47] In this passage John is primarily concerned that the prince should have wisdom, which is gained by reading the law of God daily. For that reason, and not for administrative requirements, the prince needs skill in letters. John concedes moreover that it is not absolutely necessary for the prince to be *litteratus*, provided he takes advice from *litterati*, that is, from priests who like Old Testament prophets will remind the prince of the law of God. 'Thus the mind of the prince may read in the tongue of the priest. For the life and tongue of priests are like the book of life before the face of the peoples.' John is obviously thinking here of the spiritual, and not the worldly, value of reading. His discussion emphasizes that an illiterate prince can participate in wisdom through the medium of the priest's voice. The prince is not excluded by being illiterate: 'nor is he altogether destitute of reading [*lectionis*] who, even though he does not read himself, hears faithfully what is read to him by others.' John thus shows that in his day non-literates could participate in literate culture; he is not arguing for the absolute necessity of rulers being literate in either the medieval sense of being learned in Latin or the modern sense of having a minimal ability to read and write. Ironically the king of England at the time, Henry II, was literate in every sense of the word; yet he was not a good king by John's definition, as he refused to listen to the lectures of priests and was responsible for the murder of Becket.

2   CULTURAL EXCHANGES: EARLY FOURTEENTH-CENTURY MONTAILLOU*

Emmanuel LeRoy Ladurie

How far was cultural transmission in Montaillou and other villages of the same type due to books and writing? The preaching of the Authiés, decisive for Montaillou, was essentially based on the influence of books.

> Pierre and Guillaume Authié [says the peasant Sybille Pierre] were clerks; they knew the law [as notaries] ; they had wives and children; they were rich. One day, Pierre, in his house, was reading a certain passage in a book. He told his brother Guillaume, who happened to be present, to read the passage.
>
> After a moment, Pierre asked Guillaume: 'How does it strike you, brother?'
>
> And Guillaume answered: 'It seems to me that we have lost our souls.'
>
> And Pierre concluded: 'Let us go, brother; let us go in search of our souls' salvation.'
>
> So they got rid of all their possessions and went to Lombardy, where they became good Christians; there they received the power of saving the souls of others; and then they returned to Ax-les-Thermes.

We can only guess what the book was that lay behind the Authiés' Cathar vocation. But one thing is certain: in the legal circles which gave rise to the economic and juridical renaissance of the thirteenth and fourteenth centuries, books were not entirely absent. There were even small libraries, some of them incubating heresy. The spread of the use of paper and the wide written use of the Occitan language could only favour these dangerous tendencies, also stimulated by the professional activity of the notaries, among them the Authié clan which exercised so much influence on Montaillou.

'Fourteen years ago', related in 1320 Pierre de Gaillac of Tarascon-sur-Ariège, once employed as a clerk by Arnaud Teisseire, doctor at Lordat and son-in-law of Pierre Authié,

> I lived for half a year in the house of Arnaud Teisseire, writing out the contracts deposited in his office; one day when I was looking through his papers to find his books of notes, I found a certain book

*Reprinted from *Montaillou: The Promised Land of Error* by Emmanuel LeRoy Ladurie, 233–41, by permission of the publishers, Scolar Press and George Braziller, Inc. Copyright English translation, 1978, by Scolar Press. First published in French by Editions Gallimard © 1975, translated by Barbara Bray.

written on paper in the vulgar tongue and bound in old parchment. I spent some time reading it. In it I found arguments and discussions in the vulgar tongue concerning the theories of the Manichean heretics and of the Catholics. Sometimes the book agreed with the views of the Manicheans and disagreed with those of the Catholics; and sometimes the opposite. While I was reading the book, my employer, Master Arnaud Teisseire, came in; suddenly, and in a fury, he snatched the book out of my hands; he hid it; and during the following night I heard him beating his wife and Guillaume, his bastard son, because I had managed to find the book. Whereupon, blushing and ashamed, I went back home to Tarascon-sur-Ariège. The third day Master Arnaud came to fetch me; and took me back with him.

This passage reveals the danger inherent in books themselves. Some peasants ended up thinking that everything which was written down must be heresy. 'One night', said the stock-farmer Michel Cerdan, 'during the night before full moon, I got up before dawn, in summer, to lead my cattle to pasture; I saw some men in a meadow behind the house of Arnaud Teisseire reading something written, by the light of the moon; I am sure they were heretics.'

In the region of Aude and Ariège there was a small 'socio-economic base' for the making of books. Leaving aside Pamiers, which was an intellectual centre, quite unimportant villages like Belpech (in present-day Aude) and Merviel (Ariège) might contain a parchment-maker or a 'scriptor' of books. Small as their production was, it sufficed, through the agency of the good-men to 'infect' Sabarthès and the Pays d'Aillon. The process was speeded up when paper arrived to supplement parchment. So there were some links between learning and popular culture, and these were helped by the circulation of a few books, though of course such interaction was much slower and more fortuitous than nowadays.

Nevertheless, books remained rare and precious. The respect felt for them by the illiterate people of the village paralleled their touching reverence for learning and for people who were educated. Guillemette Maury of Montaillou, exiled in Catalonia, was overcome with admiration for the *parfait* Raymond Issaura of Larcat. 'He can preach very well, he knows many things about our faith.' Urged on by Guillaume Bélibaste, she actually adored the Cathar Bible itself, composed by God in Heaven.[1] And so a goodman without his books was a soldier without his gun. The *parfait* Raymond de Castelnau — he was about forty, tall, of a ruddy complexion, white-haired and with a Toulouse accent — told the shepherds of Montaillou how sorry he was because 'I have left my books at Castelsarrasin.'

One of the reasons why books were so highly regarded was that almost no one had access to them. Apart from the goodmen themselves, only the priests owned or borrowed books or were able to read them. The priest Barthélemy Amilhac owned a book of hours which, when he was in prison, earned him the mockery of the Albigensian Bernard Clergue. It was this book that Barthélemy thought of pawning or selling to finance his flight to Limous with his mistress. Pierre Maury met a Gascon priest, of whom all we know is that he came from a rich family, was thirty years old, had grey-green eyes and brown hair and owned the *Book of the faith of the heretics* bound in red leather. In Junac, a village of peasant farmers and mountain blacksmiths, the perpetual *vicaire*, Amiel de Rives, possessed a *Book of homilies*, or at least read such a book, though it might have belonged to his parish church. He extracted from it heretical views which he subsequently used in his sermons, in the presence of his parish priest, the local lord, and a large number of his parishioners. In Montaillou itself part of the prestige and charismatic power of the priest Pierre Clergue derived from the fact that for some time he had in his possession a 'calendar' called, again, the *Book of the heretics*, or *Book of the holy faith of the heretics*, lent to him by Guillaume Authié. The various names by which this one book was referred to suggests that it was some kind of calendar 'followed or preceded, within the same binding, by a short edifying text'. The popular literature of the early eighteenth century was to include many 'little blue books' which similarly mingled calendar, almanac and religious text. At all events, this one book, part of the circulating library of the Authié brothers which contained three volumes, did not remain long with the priest. After giving various public lectures from it around the fire in people's homes, Pierre Clergue returned the book through Guillaume Belot to its rightful owners. But its temporary presence in the Clergue *ostal* was an event in the village of Montaillou, and attracted the attention of four witnesses, among them Raymonde Arsen, an illiterate servant maid. The shepherd Jean Maury, for his part, suggests that it was this 'calendar' which brought about the complete conversion to Catharism of the four Clergue brothers, the priest chief among them. Indeed, the impact of such a book could not have been negligible in the house of Bernard Clergue, generally regarded in Montaillou as a learned man. For his brother the priest, who by definition had a certain amount of intellectual equipment, the influence of the written word was something which went without saying.

Sometimes other books circulated among the people of Montaillou, thanks to goodmen such as the ex-weaver Prades Tavernier.

> One day [says Guillemette Clergue], I intended to take my mule to the fields to collect turnips; but first I had to give it some hay. So I went into the barn where my mother kept hay and straw, to get some. But I hid from my brother, for he might stop me. And right at the top of the said barn I saw Prades Tavernier sitting: by the rays of the sun, he was reading in a black book the length of someone's

hand. Prades, taken by surprise, got up as if he meant to hide, and said: 'Is that you, Guillemette?'

And I answered: 'Yes, Monsieur, it's me.'

But the reading of suspicious books was not only practised in solitude in Montaillou. Now and then the goodmen would share the benefits with the illiterate peasants around the fire of their *domus*.

> One evening [said Alazaïs Azéma, widow and peddler of cheese], at the time when I used to frequent the heretics, I went into the house of Raymond Belot not knowing that there were heretics there that day. In the house, sitting by the fire, I found the heretics Guillaume Authié and Pons Sicre; also present were Raymond, Bernard and Guillaume Belot, the three brothers, together with their mother, Guillemette 'Belote'. Guillaume Authié the heretic was reading a book and also speaking to those present . . . He referred to Saint Peter, Saint Paul and Saint John, the Apostles; so I sat down on a bench beside Guillemette; the Belot brothers were sitting on another bench; and the heretics on a third. Until the end of the sermon.

In slightly larger, more urban and distinguished villages than Montaillou there were sometimes, beside the priest and the *parfait*, some ordinary laymen who were literate and could read Occitan or even Latin.

> Nineteen or twenty years ago [said Raymond Vayssière of Ax-les Thermes], I was sunning myself beside the house I then owned in Ax (I later sold it to Allemande, the mistress of the present priest at Junac); and four or five spans away, Guillaume Andorran was reading aloud from a book to his mother Gaillarde. I asked: 'What are you reading?'
>
> 'Do you want to see?' said Guillaume.
>
> 'All right,' I said.
>
> Guillaume brought me the book, and I read: 'In the beginning was the Word . . .'
>
> It was a 'Gospel' in a mixture of Latin and Romance, which contained many things I had heard the heretic Pierre Authié say. Guillaume Andorran told me that he had bought it from a certain merchant.

The number of books in circulation in the fourteenth century was of course infinitely smaller than in the eighteenth. But the contrast between town and country later noted by Nicolas Rétif was already marked. In the local town of Pamiers the homosexual Arnaud de Verniolles read Ovid; there were Jewish refugees, Waldensian residents and schoolmasters, each with his own small but daring library. But only a few works of edification, Catholic in the lowlands, Cathar in the mountains, ever penetrated as far as the villages. And indeed it was the new presence of the occasional Albigensian volume that encouraged the modest triumphs of heresy in Ariège.

In Montaillou there were several strata of literacy. At the top there was a literate and 'charismatic' élite, whose only representatives were the Authiés and a few other *parfaits* like Issaura or Castelnau who circulated among the Catalan diaspora. These men had access to what Jacques Authié called the double scripture: the bad scripture which emanated from the Roman Church, and the good scripture, the scripture which saved, known to the goodmen and proceeding from the Son of God.

A literate élite, constituting the second stratum, knew something of Latin but possessed no specific charisma. The Register contains quite good descriptions of this élite in villages other than Montaillou but similar to it: in Goulier (Ariège) one Bernard Franc, a farmer who planted his millet just the same as everyone else, was also a clerk in minor orders and knew some Latin.

> One Sunday four years ago [said Raymond Miégeville of Goulier], Mass had just been said in the church of Saint Michael in Goulier. I had remained behind in the sanctuary by the altar, together with Arnaud Augier, Guillaume Seguela, Raymond Subra, Bernard Maria and Bernard Franc, all of Goulier. Then Bernard Franc and Arnaud Augier, who were clerks, began to argue in Latin; and the rest of us, the laymen, whose names I have just given, could not understand what they were saying to one another. Suddenly, after the discussion in Latin, Bernard Franc started to speak in the vulgar tongue; and he said: 'There are two Gods! One good, the other bad.'
> We protested.

Thus for a peasant like Raymond Miégeville the distinction between Latin and the vulgar tongue corresponded quite simply to the contrast between cleric and layman. Similarly, in Ax-les-Thermes, the local people assumed that the priest was able to write (in Latin) to his bishop. The same was true in Montaillou for Pierre Clergue the priest, and his successor or substitute, Raymond Trilh.

Below the latinist clerics, who might well be only ordinary farmers, there was another cultural level — that of the more cultivated laymen, able to read a text so long as it was written in the vulgar tongue, Occitan. These people were described as *sine litteris*, without letters (i.e. Latin letters). Ordinary people regarded them as distinctly inferior to the Latinists. Witness the condescending tone in which the sheep-farmer Raymond Pierre speaks of the ex-weaver Prades Tavernier, elevated to the rank of *parfait* though no one was very sure that he had the requisite knowledge.

> Pierre, Guillaume and Jacques Authié [said Raymond Pierre], are wise men; many people are very fond of them. Anyone who makes them presents does himself good. So the Authiés are overwhelmed

with presents, and lack for nothing. On the other hand, André Prades Tavernier is not so highly regarded; he is ignorant of letters. He has much less knowledge and fewer friends than the Authiés. That is why he is poor; so people have to give him presents in order that he may have clothes, books and all the rest.

A final barrier separated the few individuals who were literate in the vulgar tongue from the common herd of illiterates. This barrier, too, was a cultural reality, but it appears not to have caused friction or to have wounded anyone's pride: the people on both sides of the frontier all really belonged to the same world.

But the number of actual illiterates raises problems about the transmission of ideas derived from books. Out of some 250 inhabitants in Montaillou, no more than four were definitely literate;[2] even an ex-*châtelaine* like Béatrice was illiterate, unlike her daughters. She was unable to write love-letters to her sweetheart, who knew how to read and write, and was reduced to sending him messages by word of mouth through a little boy.

All this being so, the purely oral transmission of books was of supreme importance. Out of some dozens of heretical meetings that we know of in Montaillou and elsewhere, only two are clearly seen to have been held by *parfaits* actually using books. The other meetings were entirely 'verbal', the *parfait* speaking to the believers and sympathizers without any reference to written matter. Most of the time, books only appeared at Montaillou in order to be placed for a few minutes on the head of someone dying, in the last stages of the *consolamentum*. Outside Montaillou there is evidence of books being used as objects upon which witnesses, friends or fellow-conspirators pledged their truthfulness.[3] In the absence of written records the memory, both visual and auditory, was highly developed among the people of Montaillou. Hence also the importance of preaching and of eloquence in general. 'When you have heard the goodmen speak,' said Raymond Roussel, steward of the château of Montaillou, 'you can no longer do without them, you are theirs for ever.' Pierre Authié, like his son Jacques, was said to have 'the mouth of an angel', though their pupil, Guillaume Bélibaste, was thought to be completely undistinguished in this respect.

There were other connections between what was written and what was oral. For example, an idea in circulation in peasant and artisan circles of upper Ariège asserted that the world was eternal. There was of course a basis for this notion in folklore, but it also owed something to written culture, both literary and philosophical, retransmitted to the people by such instructors as the quarrier Arnaud de Savignan of Tarascon-sur-Ariège, who flouted Christianity by claiming that the world had no beginning and would have no end. He quoted two sources: the local proverb about men always sleeping with other men's wives, and the teaching of his master, Arnaud Tolus, overseer of the schools at Tarascon. Tolus's teaching was probably based on books.

Another example is the way the influence of the troubadours was passed on. According to the Fournier Register, though this evidence is only negative, Montaillou and similar villages were not directly affected and, apart from noblemen's castles, troubadour influence is seen only in Pamiers. But even in this urban context poems were transmitted chiefly by word of mouth: people whispered Pierre Cardenal's *cobla* to one another in the choir of the church at Pamiers.

Attitudes and ideas were also transmitted directly: from father to son, mother to daughter, aunt to nephew, or older brother or cousin to younger brother or cousin and so on. Pierre Maury remarks: 'My father's house in Montaillou was destroyed three times for heresy; and there is no question of my making up for it; I must remain faithful to the beliefs of my father.' Similarly Jean Maury, Pierre's brother, says:

> I was then twelve years old, and looked after my father's sheep. One evening, going back to my father's house, I found sitting by the fire my father, my mother, my four brothers and my two sisters. In the presence of my mother and brothers and sisters my father said to me: 'Philippe d'Alayrac and Raymond Faur are good Christians and goodmen. They are men of good faith. They do not lie.'

Another instance of a parent passing on religious attitudes to his child is offered by the case of Pierre Maury and his proposed marriage, later, to a little girl at that time aged six.

'And how do you know,' asked Pierre, 'that Bernadette, when she is grown up, will have the understanding of good?'

'The little girl's father,' answered Bernard Bélibaste, 'will bring her up so well that, with the help of God, she will have the understanding of good.'

Guillaume Austatz was won over to heretical ideas partly through the influence of his mother, who had been subject to direct propaganda on the part of Pierre Authié. Mother and son used to discuss the Cathar missionary's ideas during long evenings round the fire, or on the way to and from Carcassonne. And many others, like Jean Pellissier and Vuissane Testanière, had been exposed to hererodox influences on the part of an aunt, a mother, a husband and so on.

Generally speaking, cultural transmission rarely operated through a peer group. As we have seen, it is doubtful whether there was an effective group of young people as such in Montaillou. Basically, the right to transmit or retransmit culture was something acquired either through age or through social superiority (the priest vis-à-vis his parishioners; an employer vis-à-vis his employee; the owner of a pasture vis-à-vis the lessee). The older generation in general taught the younger generation.

It could be a father, mother or aunt who in this respect enjoyed the privilege of age; but it could also be a husband, an older person or merely an employer.

3   SOME CONJECTURES ABOUT THE IMPACT OF PRINTING ON WESTERN SOCIETY AND THOUGHT: A PRELIMINARY REPORT*

Elizabeth L. Eisenstein

I have found it useful, in any case, to start taking stock by following up clues contained in special studies on printing. After singling out certain features that seemed peculiar to typography, I held them in mind while passing in review various historical developments. Relationships emerged that had not occurred to me before, and some possible solutions to old puzzles were suggested. Conjectures based on this approach may be sampled below under headings that indicate my main lines of inquiry.

A. A closer look at wide dissemination: various effects produced by increased output

Most references to wide dissemination are too fleeting to make clear the specific effects of an increased supply of texts directed at different markets. In particular they fail to make clear how patterns of consumption were affected by increased production. Here the term 'dissemination' is sufficiently inappropriate to be distracting. Some mention of cross-fertilization or cross-cultural interchange should be included in surveys or summaries. More copies of one given text, for instance, *were* 'spread, dispersed, or scattered' by the issue of a printed edition.[1] For the individual book-reader, however, different texts, which were previously dispersed and scattered, were also brought closer together. In some regions, printers produced more scholarly texts than they could sell and flooded local markets.[2] In all regions, a given purchaser could buy more books at lower cost and bring them into his study or library. In this way, the printer provided the clerk with a richer, more varied literary diet than had been provided by the scribe. To consult different books it was no longer essential to be a wandering scholar. Successive generations of sedentary scholars were less apt to be engrossed by a single text and to expend their energies in elaborating on it. The era of the glossator and commentator came to an end, and a new 'era of intense cross referencing between one book and another'[3] began. More abundantly stocked bookshelves increased opportunities to consult and compare different texts and, thus, also made more probable the formation of new intellectual combinations and permutations.

*Reprinted from Elizabeth L. Eisenstein, 'Some Conjectures about the Impact of Printing on Western Society and Thought: A Preliminary Report', *Journal of Modern History*, 40 (1968), 7–29, by permission of the University of Chicago Press, © 1968, by the University of Chicago Press.

Viewed in this light, cross-cultural interchanges fostered by printing seem relevant to Sarton's observation: 'The Renaissance was a transmutation of values, a "new deal," a reshuffling of cards, but most of the cards were old; the scientific Renaissance was a "new deal," but many of the cards were new.'[4] Combinatory intellectual activity, as Koestler has recently suggested, inspires many creative acts. Once old texts came together within the same study, diverse systems of ideas and special disciplines could be combined. Increased output directed at relatively stable markets, in short, created conditions that favored, first, new combinations of old ideas and, then, the creation of entirely new systems of thought.

Merely by making more scrambled data available, by increasing the output of second-century Ptolemaic maps and twelfth-century *mappae mundi*, for instance, printers encouraged efforts to unscramble these data. Hand-drafted portolans had long been more accurate, but few eyes had seen them.[5] Much as maps from different regions and epochs were brought into contact, so too were diverse textual traditions previously preserved by specially trained groups of schoolmen and scribes. It should be noted that cross-cultural interchange was not solely a consequence of augmented output. For example, texts were provided with new illustrations drawn from artisan workshops instead of scriptoria. Here again, different traditions were brought into contact. In this case, words drawn from one milieu and pictures from another were placed beside each other within the same books.[6] When considering new views of the 'book of nature' or the linking of bookish theories with observations and craft skills, it may be useful to look at the ateliers of Renaissance artists. But one must also go on to visit early printers' workshops, for it is there above all that we 'can observe the formation of groups . . . conducive to cross-fertilization'[7] of all kinds.

Cross-cultural interchange stimulated mental activities in contradictory ways. The first century of printing was marked above all by intellectual ferment and by a 'somewhat wide-angled, unfocused scholarship'.[8] Certain confusing cross-currents may be explained by noting that new links between disciplines were being forged before old ones had been severed. In the age of scribes, for instance, magical arts were closely associated with mechanical crafts. Trade skills were passed down by closed circles of initiates. Unwritten recipes used by the alchemist were not clearly distinguished from those used by the apothecary or surgeon, the goldsmith or engraver. When 'technology went to press', so too did a vast backlog of occult lore, and few readers could discriminate between the two.

The divine art or 'mystery' of printing unleashed a 'churning turbid flood of Hermetic, cabbalistic, Gnostic, theurgic, Sabaean, Pythagorean, and generally mystic notions'.[9] Historians are still puzzled by certain strange deposits left by this flood. They might find it helpful to consider how records derived from ancient Near Eastern cultures had been transmitted in the age of scribes.

Some of these records had dwindled into tantalizing fragments pertaining to systems of reckoning, medicine, agriculture, mythic cults, and so forth. Others had evaporated into unfathomable glyphs. All were thought to come from one body of pure knowledge originally set down by an Egyptian scribal god and carefully preserved by ancient sages and seers before becoming corrupted and confused. A collection of writings containing ancient lore was received from Macedonia by Cosimo de' Medici, translated by Ficino in 1463, and printed in fifteen editions before 1500. It seemed to come from this body of knowledge — and was accordingly attributed to 'Hermes Trismegistus'. The hermetic corpus ran through many more editions during the next century before it was shown to have been compiled in the third century A.D. On this basis we are told that Renaissance scholars had made a radical error in dating.[10] But to assign definite dates to scribal compilations, which were probably derived from earlier sources, may be an error as well.

The transformation of occult and esoteric scribal lore after the advent of printing also needs more study. Some arcane writings, in Greek, Hebrew or Syriac, for example, became less mysterious. Others became more so. Thus hieroglyphs were set in type more than three centuries before their decipherment. These sacred carved letters were loaded with significant meaning by readers who could not read them.[11] They were also used simply as ornamental motifs by architects and engravers. Given baroque decoration on one hand and complicated interpretations by scholars, Rosicrucians, and Freemasons on the other, the duplication of Egyptian picture writing throughout the Age of Reason presents modern scholars with puzzles that can never be solved. In brief, when considering the effects produced by printing on scholarship, it is a mistake to think only about new forms of enlightenment. New forms of mystification were entailed as well.

It is also a mistake to think only about scholarly markets when considering the effects of increased output. Dissemination as defined in the dictionary does seem appropriate to the duplication of primers and *ABC* books, almanacs, and picture Bibles. An increased output of devotional literature was not necessarily conducive to cross-cultural interchange. Catechisms, religious tracts, and Bibles would fill some bookshelves to the exclusion of all other reading matter. A new wide-angled, unfocused scholarship had to compete with a new single-minded, narrowly focused piety. At the same time, guide-books and manuals also became more abundant, making it easier to lay plans for getting ahead in this world — possibly diverting attention from uncertain futures in the next one. It is doubtful whether 'the effect of the new invention on scholarship' was more important than these other effects 'at the beginning of the sixteenth century'.[12] What does need emphasis is that many dissimilar effects, all of great consequence, came relatively simultaneously. If this could be spelled out more clearly, seemingly contradictory developments might be confronted with more equanimity. The intensification of both religiosity and secularism could be better understood. Some debates about periodization also could be bypassed. Medieval world pictures, for example, were duplicated more rapidly during the first century of printing than they had been during the so-called Middle Ages. They did not merely *survive* among the Elizabethans. They became *more available* to poets and playwrights of the sixteenth century than they had been to minstrels and mummers of the thirteenth century.

In view of such considerations, I cannot agree with Sarton's comment: 'It is hardly necessary to indicate what the art of printing meant for the diffusion of culture but one should not lay too much stress on diffusion and should speak more of standardization.'[13] How printing changed patterns of cultural diffusion deserves much more study than it has yet received. Moreover, individual access to diverse texts is a different matter than bringing many minds to bear on a single text. The former issue is apt to be neglected by too exclusive an emphasis on 'standardization'.

B. Considering some effects produced by standardization

Although it has to be considered in conjunction with many other issues, standardization certainly does deserve closer study. One specialist has argued that it is currently overplayed.[14] Yet it may well be still understressed. Perhaps early printing methods made it impossible to issue the kind of 'standard' editions with which modern scholars are familiar. Certainly press variants did multiply, and countless errata were issued. The fact remains that Erasmus or Bellarmine could issue errata; Jerome or Alcuin could not. The very act of publishing errata demonstrated a new capacity to locate textual errors with precision and to transmit this information simultaneously to scattered readers. It thus illustrates, rather neatly, some of the effects of standardization. However fourteenth-century copyists were supervised, scribes were incapable of committing the sort of 'standardized' error that led printers to be fined for the 'wicked Bible' of 1631.[15] If a single compositor's error could be circulated in a great many copies, so too could a single scholar's emendation.[16] However, when I suggest that we may still underestimate the implications of standardization, I am not thinking primarily about textual emendations or errors. I am thinking instead about the new output of exactly repeatable pictorial statements, such as maps, charts, diagrams, and other visual aids;[17] of more uniform reference guides, such as calendars, thesauruses, dictionaries; of increasingly regular systems of notation, whether musical, mathematical, or grammatical. How different fields of study and aesthetic styles were affected by such developments remains to be explored. It does seem worth suggesting that both our so-called two cultures were affected. Humanist scholarship, belles lettres, and fine arts must be considered along with celestial mechanics, anatomy, and cartography.[18]

Too many important variations were, indeed, played on the theme of standardization for all of them to be listed here. This theme entered into every operation associated with typography, from the replica casting of precisely measured pieces of type[19] to the subliminal impact upon scattered readers of repeated encounters with identical type styles, printers' devices and title-page ornamentation.[20] Calligraphy itself was affected. Sixteenth-century specimen books stripped diverse scribal 'hands' of personal idiosyncracies. They did for handwriting what style books did for typography itself; what pattern books did for dressmaking, furniture, architectural motifs, and ground plans. In short the setting of standards — used for innumerable purposes, from cutting cloth to city-planning — accompanied the output of more standardized products.

Here, as elsewhere, we need to recall that early printers were responsible not only for issuing new standard reference guides but also for compiling many of them.[21] A subsequent division of labor tends to divert attention from the large repertoire of roles performed by those who presided over the new presses. A scholar—printer himself might serve as indexer—abridger—lexicographer—chronicler. Whatever roles he performed, decisions about standards to be adopted when processing texts for publication could not be avoided. A suitable type style had to be selected or designed and house conventions determined. Textual variants and the desirability of illustration and translation also had to be confronted. Accordingly, the printer's workshop became the most advanced laboratory of erudition of the sixteenth century.

Many early capitalist industries required efficient planning, methodical attention to detail, and rational calculation. The decisions made by early printers, however, directly affected both toolmaking and symbol-making. Their products reshaped powers to manipulate objects, to perceive and think about varied phenomena. Scholars concerned with 'modernization' or 'rationalization' might profitably think more about the new kind of brainwork fostered by the silent scanning of maps, tables, charts, diagrams, dictionaries, and grammars. They also need to look more closely at the daily routines pursued by those who compiled and produced such reference guides. These routines were conducive to a new *esprit de système*. 'It's much easier to find things when they are each disposed in place and not scattered haphazardly', remarked a sixteenth-century publisher.[22] He was justifying the way he had reorganized a text he had edited. He might equally well have been complaining to a clerk who had mislaid some account papers pertaining to the large commercial enterprise he ran.

C. Some effects produced by editing and reorganizing texts: codifying, clarifying, and cataloguing data

Editorial decisions made by early printers with regard to layout and presentation probably helped to reorganize the thinking of readers. McLuhan's suggestion that scanning lines of print affected thought processes is at first glance somewhat mystifying. But further reflection suggests that the thoughts of readers are guided by the way the contents of books are arranged and presented. Basic changes in book format might well lead to changes in thought patterns. Such changes began to appear in the era of incunabula. They made texts more lucid and intelligible. They involved the use 'of graduated types, running heads . . . footnotes . . . tables of contents . . . superior figures, cross references . . . and other devices available to the compositor' – all registering 'the victory of the punch cutter over the scribe'.[23] Concern with surface appearance necessarily governed the handwork of the scribe. He was fully preoccupied trying to shape evenly spaced uniform letters in a pleasing symmetrical design. An altogether different procedure was required to give directions to compositors. To do this, one had to mark up a manuscript while scrutinizing its contents. Every scribal text that came into the printer's hands, thus, had to be reviewed in a new way. Within a generation the results of this review were being aimed in a new direction – away from fidelity to scribal conventions and toward serving the convenience of the reader. The competitive and commercial character of the new mode of book production encouraged the relatively rapid adoption of any innovation that commended a given edition to purchasers. In short, providing built-in aids to the reader became for the first time both feasible and desirable.

The introduction and adoption of such built-in aids, from the 1480s on, has been traced and discussed in special works on printing but has been insufficiently noted in other accounts. We are repeatedly told about 'dissemination', occasionally about standardization, almost never at all about the codification and clarification that were entailed in editing copy.[24] Yet changes affecting book format probably contributed much to the so-called rationalization of diverse institutions. After all, they affected texts used for the study and practice of law – and consequently had an impact on most organs of the body politic as well.[25] This has been demonstrated by a pioneering study of the 'englishing and printing' of the 'Great Boke of Statutes 1530–1533'.[26] I cannot pause here over the many repercussions, ranging from statecraft to literature, that came in the wake of Tudor law-printing according to this study. To suggest why we need to look at new built-in aids, I will simply point to the introductory 'Tabula' to the 'Great Boke'; 'a chronological register by chapters of the statutes 1327–1523'. Here was a table of contents that also served as a 'conspectus of parliamentary history'[27] – the first many readers had seen.

This sort of spectacular innovation, while deserving close study, should not divert attention from much less conspicuous but more ubiquitous changes. Increasing familiarity with regularly numbered pages, punctuation marks, section breaks, running heads, indexes, and so forth helped to reorder the thought of *all* readers, whatever their profession or craft. Hence countless

activities were subjected to a new *esprit de système*. The use of arabic numbers for pagination suggests how the most inconspicuous innovation could
have weighty consequences – in this case, more accurate indexing, annotation,
and cross-referencing resulted.[28] Most studies of printing have quite rightly
singled out the provision of title pages as the most important of all ubiquitous
print-made innovations.[29] How the title page contributed to the cataloguing
of books and the bibliographer's craft scarcely needs to be spelled out. How it
contributed to a new habit of placing and dating in general does, I think, call
for further thought.

On the whole, as I have tried to suggest throughout this discussion, topics
now allocated to bibliophiles and specialists on printing are of general concern
to historians at large – or, at least, to specialists in many different fields. The
way these fields are laid out could be better understood, indeed, if we opened
up the one assigned to printing. 'Until half a century after Copernicus' death,
no potentially revolutionary changes occurred in the data available to astron-
omers.'[30] But Copernicus' life (1473–1543) spanned the very decades when a
great many changes, now barely visible to modern eyes, were transforming
'the data available' to all book-readers. A closer study of these changes could
help to explain why systems of charting the planets, mapping the earth, syn-
chronizing chronologies, and compiling bibliographies were all revolutionized
before the end of the sixteenth century.[31] In each instance, one notes, ancient
Alexandrian achievements were first reduplicated and then, in a remarkably
short time, surpassed. In each instance also, the new schemes once published
remained available for correction, development, and refinement. Successive
generations of scholars could build on the work of their sixteenth-century
predecessors instead of trying to retrieve scattered fragments of it.

The varied intellectual revolutions of early modern times owed much to
the features that have already been outlined.[32] But the great tomes, charts,
and maps that are now seen as 'milestones' might have proved insubstantial
had not the preservative powers of print also been called into play. Typographical fixity is a basic prerequisite for the rapid advancement of learning.
It helps to explain much else that seems to distinguish the history of the past
five centuries from that of all prior eras – as I hope the following remarks
will suggest.

D. Considering the preservative powers of print: how fixity and accumulations altered patterns of cultural and institutional change[33]

Of all the new features introduced by the duplicative powers of print, preservation is possibly the most important. To appreciate its importance, we need
to recall the conditions that prevailed before texts could be set in type. No
manuscript, however useful as a reference guide, could be preserved for long
without undergoing corruption by copyists, and even this sort of 'preservation'

rested precariously on the shifting demands of local elites and a fluctuating incidence of trained scribal labor. Insofar as records were seen and used, they were vulnerable to wear and tear. Stored documents were vulnerable to moisture and vermin, theft and fire. However they might be collected or guarded within some great message center, their ultimate dispersal and loss was inevitable. To be transmitted by writing from one generation to the next, information had to be conveyed by drifting texts and vanishing manuscripts.

When considering developments in astronomy (or geography or chronology) during the age of scribes, it is not the slow rate of cognitive advance that calls for explanation. Rather, one might wonder about how the customary process of erosion, corruption, and loss was temporarily arrested. When viewed in this light, the '1,800 years' that elapsed between Hipparchus and Copernicus[34] seems less remarkable than the advances that were made in planetary astronomy during the 600 years that elapsed between Aristotle and Ptolemy. With regard to all computations based on large-scale data collection, whatever had once been clearly seen and carefully articulated grew dimmed and blurred with the passage of time. More than a millennium also elapsed between Eratosthenes and Scaliger, Ptolemy and Mercator. The progress made over the course of centuries within the confines of the Alexandrian Museum seems, in short, to have been most exceptional.[35] To be sure, there were intermittent localized 'revivals of learning' thereafter, as well as a prolonged accumulation of records within certain message centers. Ground lost by corruption could never be regained, but migrating manuscripts could lead to abrupt recovery as well as to sudden loss. Yet a marked increase in the output of certain kinds of texts resulted generally in a decreased output of other kinds. Similarly, a 'revival' in one region often signified a dearth of texts in another.

The incapacity of scribal culture to sustain a simultaneous advance on many fronts in different regions may be relevant to the 'problem of the Renaissance'. Italian humanist book-hunters, patrons, and dealers tried to replenish a diminished supply of those ancient texts that were being neglected by scribes serving medieval university faculties. Their efforts have been heralded as bringing about a 'permanent recovery' of ancient learning and letters.[36] If one accepts the criteria of 'totality and permanence' to distinguish prior 'revivals' from the Renaissance,[37] then probably the advent of the scholar—printer should be heralded instead. He arrived to cast his Greek types and turn out grammars, translations, and standard editions in the nick of time – almost on the eve of the Valois invasions.[38]

Once Greek type fonts had been cut, neither the disruption of civil order in Italy, the conquest of Greek lands by Islam, nor even the translation into Latin of all major Greek texts saw knowledge of Greek wither again in the West. Instead it was the familiar scribal phrase *Graeca sunt ergo non legenda* that disappeared from Western texts. Constantinople fell, Rome was sacked. Yet a cumulative process of textual purification and continuous recovery had been launched. The implications of typographical fixity are scarcely exhausted by thinking about early landmarks in classical scholarship and its auxiliary sciences: paleography, philology, archeology, numismatics, etc. Nor are they exhausted by reckoning the number of languages that have been retrieved after being lost to all men for thousands of years. They involve the whole modern 'knowledge industry' itself, with its mushrooming bibliographies and overflowing card files.

They also involve issues that are less academic and more geopolitical. The linguistic map of Europe was 'fixed' by the same process and at the same time as Greek letters were. The importance of the fixing of literary vernaculars is often stressed. The strategic role played by printing is, however, often over-looked.[39] How strategic it was is suggested by the following paraphrased summary of Steinberg's account:

> Printing 'preserved and codified, sometimes even created' certain vernaculars. Its absence during the sixteenth century among small linguistic groups 'demonstrably led' to the disappearance or exclusion of their vernaculars from the realm of literature. Its presence among similar groups in the same century ensured the possibility of inter-mittent revivals or continued expansion. Having fortified language walls between one group and another, printers homogenized what was within them, breaking down minor differences, standardizing idioms for millions of writers and readers, assigning a new peripheral role to provincial dialects. The preservation of a given literary language often depended on whether or not a few vernacular primers, catechisms or Bibles happened to get printed (under foreign as well as domestic auspices) in the sixteenth century. When this was the case, the subsequent expansion of a separate 'national' literary culture ensued. When this did not happen, a prerequisite for budding 'national' consciousness disappeared; a spoken provincial dialect was left instead.[40]

Studies of dynastic consolidation and/or of nationalism might well devote more space to the advent of printing. Typography arrested linguistic drift, enriched as well as standardized vernaculars, and paved the way for the more deliberate purification and codification of all major European languages. Randomly patterned sixteenth-century typecasting largely determined the subsequent elaboration of national mythologies on the part of certain separate groups within multilingual dynastic states. The duplication of vernacular primers and translations contributed in other ways to nationalism. A 'mother's tongue' learned 'naturally' at home would be reinforced by inculcation of a homogenized print-made language mastered while still young, when learning to read. During the most impressionable years of childhood, the eye would first see a more standardized version of what the ear had first heard. Particu-larly after grammar schools gave primary instruction in reading by using vernacular instead of Latin readers, linguistic 'roots' and rootedness in one's homeland would be entangled.

Printing helped in other ways to permanently atomize Western Christendom. Erastian policies long pursued by diverse rulers could, for example, be more fully implemented. Thus, the duplication of documents pertaining to ritual, liturgy, or canon law, handled under clerical auspices in the age of the scribe, was undertaken by enterprising laymen, subject to dynastic authority, in the age of the printer. Local firms, lying outside the control of the papal curia, were granted lucrative privileges by Habsburg, Valois, or Tudor kings to service the needs of national clergies.[41] The varied ways in which printers contributed to loosening or severing links with Rome, or to nationalist senti-ment, or to dynastic consolidation cannot be explored here. But they surely do call for further study.[42]

Other consequences of typographical fixity also need to be explored. Religious divisions and legal precedents were affected. In fact, all the lines that were drawn in the sixteenth century (or thereafter), the condemnation of a heresy, the excommunication of a schismatic king, the settling of disputes between warring dynasts, schisms within the body politic — lines that prior generations had repeatedly traced, erased, retraced — would now leave a more indelible imprint. It was no longer possible to take for granted that one was following 'immemorial custom' when granting an immunity or signing a decree. Edicts became more visible and irrevocable. The Magna Carta, for example, was ostensibly 'published' (i.e., proclaimed) twice a year in every shire. By 1237 there was already confusion as to which 'charter' was involved.[43] In 1533, however, Englishmen glancing over the 'Tabula' of the 'Great Boke' could see how often it had been repeatedly confirmed in successive royal statutes.[44] In France also the 'mechanism by which the will of the sovereign' was incorporated into the 'published' body of law by 'regis-tration' was probably altered by typographical fixity.[45] Much as M. Jourdain learned that he was speaking prose, monarchs learned from political theorists that they were 'making' laws. But members of parliaments and assemblies also learned from jurists and printers about ancient rights wrongfully usurped. Struggles over the right to establish precedents probably became more intense as each precedent became more permanent and hence more difficult to break.

On the other hand, in many fields of activity, fixity led to new departures from precedent marked by more explicit recognition of individual innovation and by the staking of claims to inventions, discoveries, and creations. By 1500, legal fictions were already being devised to accommodate the patenting of inventions and the assignment of literary properties.[46] Upon these foun-dations, a burgeoning bureaucracy would build a vast and complex legal struc-ture. Laws pertaining to licensing and privileges have been extensively studied. But they have yet to be examined as by-products of typographical fixity. Both the dissolution of guild controls and conflicts over mercantilist policies might be clarified if this were done. Once the rights of an inventor could be legally fixed and the problem of preserving unwritten recipes intact was no longer posed, profits could be achieved by open publicity, provided new restraints were not imposed. Individual initiative was released from reliance on guild protection, but at the same time new powers were lodged in the hands of a bureaucratic officialdom. Competition over the right to publish a given text also introduced controversy over new issues involving monopoly and piracy. Printing forced legal definition of what belonged in the public domain and clear articulation of how one sort of literary product differed from another.[47] When discussing the emergence of a new kind of individualism, it might be useful to recall that the eponymous inventor and personal authorship appeared at the same time and as a consequence of the same process.

The emergence of uniquely distinguished, personally famous artists and authors out of the ranks of more anonymous artisans and minstrels was also related to typographical fixity. Cheaper writing materials encouraged the separate recording of private lives and correspondence. Not paper mills but printing presses, however, made it possible to preserve personal ephemera intact. As an expanding manuscript culture found its way into print, formal compositions were accompanied by intimate anecdotes about the lives and loves of their flesh-and-blood authors. Was it the 'inclination' to 'publish gossip' that was new in the Renaissance,[48] or was it, rather, the possibility of doing so? The characteristic individuality of Renaissance masterpieces surely owes much to the new possibility of preserving the life-histories of those who produced them. As art historians have shown, the hands of medieval illuminators or stone-carvers were, in fact, no less distinctive. Their personalities remain unknown. Vestiges of their local celebrity have vanished. They must therefore be portrayed as faceless master guildsmen in terms of the garb they wore or the life-style they shared with colleagues. What applies to personality may also apply to versatility. Alberti probably was not the first architect who was also an athlete, orator, scholar, and artist. But he *was* the first whose after-dinner speeches, boasts about boyhood feats, and 'serious and witty sayings' were collected and transmitted to posterity along with the buildings he designed and formal treatises he composed. He may be displayed at home and in public, as an athletic youth and elderly sage, moving through all the ages of man, personifying earlier archetypes and collective roles. Possibly this is why he appears to Burckhardt in the guise of a new ideal type, *homo universalis.*[49]

Similar considerations are also worth applying to authors. The personal hand and signature of the scribe was replaced by the more impersonal type style and colophon of the printer. Yet, by the same token, the personal, private, idiosyncratic views of the author could be extended through time and space. Articulating new concepts of selfhood, wrestling with the problem of speaking privately for publication, new authors (beginning, perhaps, with Montaigne) would redefine individualism in terms of deviation from the norm and divergence from the type. The 'drive for fame' itself may have been affected by print-made immortality. The urge to scribble was manifested in Juvenal's day as it was in Petrarch's. But the *insanabile scribendi cacoethes* may have been reoriented once it became an 'itch to publish'.[50] The wish to see one's work in print (fixed forever with one's name, in card files and anthologies) is different from the urge to pen lines that could never get fixed in a permanent form, might be lost forever, altered by copying, or – if truly memorable – carried by oral transmission and assigned ultimately to 'anon'. When dealing with priority disputes among scientists or debates about plagiarism among scholars, the advent of print-made immortality has to be taken into account. Until it became possible to distinguish between composing a poem and reciting one or between writing a book and copying one, until books could be classified by something other than incipits, how could modern games of books and authors be played?

Many problems about assigning proper credit to scribal 'authors' may result from misguided efforts to apply print-made concepts where they do not pertain. The so-called forged book of Hermes is a good case in point. But countless other scribal works are too. Who *wrote* Socrates' lines, Aristotle's works, Sappho's poems, any portion of the Scriptures? Troublesome questions about biblical composition, in particular, suggest how new forms of personal authorship helped to subvert old concepts of collective authority.[51] Veneration for the wisdom of the ages was probably modified as ancient sages were retrospectively cast in the role of individual authors – prone to human error and possibly plagiarists as well.[52] Treatment of battles of books between 'ancients and moderns' might profit from more discussion of such issues. Since early printers were primarily responsible for forcing definition of literary property rights, for shaping new concepts of authorship, for exploiting best sellers and trying to tap new markets, their role in this celebrated quarrel should not be overlooked. By the early sixteenth century, for example, staffs of translators were employed to turn out vernacular versions of the more popular works by ancient Romans and contemporary Latin-writing humanists.[53] This might be taken into account when discussing debates between Latinists and advocates of new vulgar tongues.[54]

It is also worth considering that different meanings may have been assigned terms such as 'ancient' and 'modern', 'discovery' and 'rediscovery', 'invention' and 'imitation' before important departures from precedent could be permanently recorded. 'Throughout the patristic and medieval periods, the quest for truth is thought of as the *re*covery of what is embedded in tradition ... rather than the *dis*covery of what is new.'[55] Most scholars concur with this view. It must have been difficult to distinguish discovering something new from recovering it in the age of scribes. To 'find a new art' was easily confused with retrieving a lost one, for superior techniques and systems of knowledge *were* frequently discovered by being recovered.[56] Probably Moses, Zoroaster, or Thoth had not 'invented' all the arts that were to be found.[57] But many were retrieved from ancient giants whose works reentered the West by circuitous routes. The origins of such works were shrouded in mystery. Their contents revealed a remarkable technical expertise. Some pagan seers were believed to have been granted foreknowledge of the Incarnation. Possibly they had also been granted a special secret key to all knowledge by the same divine dispensation. Veneration for the wisdom of the ancients was not incompatible with the advancement of learning, nor was imitation incompatible with inspiration. Efforts to think and do as the ancients did might well reflect the hope of experiencing a sudden illumination or of coming closer to the original source of a pure, clear, and certain knowledge that a long Gothic night had obscured.

When unprecedented innovations did occur, moreover, there was no sure way of recognizing them before the advent of printing. Who could ascertain precisely what was known — either to prior generations within a given region or to contemporary inhabitants of far-off lands? 'Steady advance,' as Sarton says, 'implies exact determination of every previous step.' In his view, printing made this determination 'incomparably easier'.[58] He may have understated the case. *Exact* determination must have been impossible before printing. Given drifting texts, migrating manuscripts, localized chronologies, multiform maps, there could be no systematic forward movement, no accumulation of stepping stones enabling a new generation to begin where the prior one had left off. Progressive refinement of certain arts and skills could and did occur. But no sophisticated technique could be securely established, permanently recorded, and stored for subsequent retrieval. Before trying to account for an 'idea' of progress, we might look more closely at the duplicating process that made possible a continuous accumulation of fixed records. For it seems to have been permanence that introduced progressive change. The preservation of the old, in brief, launched a tradition of the new.

The advancement of learning had taken the form of a search for lost wisdom in the age of scribes. This search was rapidly propelled after printing. Ancient maps, charts, and texts once arranged and dated, however, turned out to be dated in more ways than one. Ordinary craftsmen and mariners appeared to know more things about the heavens and earth than were dreamt of by ancient sages. More schools of ancient philosophy than had previously been known were also uncovered. Scattered attacks on one authority by those who favored another provided ammunition for a wholesale assault on all received opinion. Incompatible portions of inherited traditions were sloughed off, partly because the task of preservation had become less urgent. Copying, memorizing, and transmitting absorbed fewer energies. Some were released to explore what still might be learned. Studying variant versions of

God's words gave way to contemplating the uniformity of His works. Investigation of the 'book of nature' was no longer undertaken by studying old glyphs and ciphers. Magic and science were divorced. So too were poetry and history. Useful reference books were no longer blotted out or blurred with the passage of time. Cadence and rhyme, images and symbols ceased to fulfil their traditional function of preserving the collective memory. The aesthetic experience became increasingly autonomous, and the function of works of art had to be redefined. Technical information could be conveyed more directly by plain expository prose and accurate illustration. Although books on the memory arts multiplied after printing, practical reliance on these arts decreased. Scribal schemes eventually petrified, to be ultimately reassembled, like fossil remains, by modern research. The special formulas that had preserved recipes and techniques among closed circles of initiates also disappeared. Residues of mnemonic devices were transmuted into mysterious images, rites and incantations.[59]

Nevertheless, scribal veneration for ancient learning lingered on, long after the conditions that had fostered it had gone. Among Rosicrucians and Freemasons, for example, the belief persisted that the 'new philosophy' was in fact very old. Descartes and Newton had merely retrieved the same magical key to nature's secrets that had once been known to ancient pyramid-builders but was later withheld from the laity or deliberately obscured by a deceitful priesthood. In fact, the Index came only after printing and the preservation of pagan learning owed much to monks and friars. Enlightened freethinkers, however, assigned Counter-Reformation institutions to the Gothic Dark Ages and turned Zoroaster into a Copernican. Similarly, once imitation was detached from inspiration and copying from composing, the classical revival became increasingly arid and academic. The search for primary sources was assigned to dry-as-dust pedants. But the reputation of ancient seers, bards, and prophets was not, by the same token, diminished. Claims to have inherited their magic mantle were put forth by new romanticists who reoriented the meaning of the term 'original' and tried to resurrect scribal arts in the age of print. Even the 'decay of nature' theme, once intimately associated with the erosion and corruption of scribal writings, would be reworked and reoriented by gloomy modern prophets who felt that regress, not progress, characterized their age.

E. Amplification and reinforcement: accounting for persistent stereotypes and increasing cultural differentiation

Many other themes imbedded in scribal writings, detached from the living cultures that had shaped them, were propelled as 'typologies' on printed pages. Over the course of time, archetypes were converted into stereotypes, the language of giants, as Merton puts it, into the clichés of dwarfs. Both 'stereotype' and 'cliché' are terms deriving from a typographical process developed three and a half centuries after Gutenberg. They point, however, to certain other features of typographical culture in general that deserve closer consideration. During the past five centuries, broadcasting new messages has also entailed amplifying and reinforcing old ones. I hope my use of the terms 'amplify' and 'reinforce' will not distract attention from the effects they are meant to designate. I am using them simply because I have found no others that serve as well. Some such terms are needed to cover the effects produced by an ever-more-frequent repetition of identical chapters and verses, anecdotes and aphorisms drawn from very limited scribal sources. This repetition is not produced by the constant republication of classical, biblical, or early vernacular works, although it undoubtedly sustains markets for such works. It is produced by an unwitting collaboration between countless authors of new books or articles. For five hundred years, authors have jointly transmitted certain old messages with augmented frequency even while separately reporting on new events or spinning out new ideas. Thus, if they happen to contain only one passing reference to the heroic stand at Thermopylae, a hundred reports on different military campaigns will impress with a hundredfold-impact Herodotus' description on the mind of the reader who scans such reports. Every dissimilar report of other campaigns will be received only once. As printed materials proliferate, this effect becomes more pronounced. (I have encountered several references to Thermopylae in the daily newspaper during the past year.) The same is true of numerous other messages previously inscribed on scarce and scattered manuscripts. The more wide ranging the reader at present, the more frequent will be the encounter with the identical version and the deeper the impression it will leave. Since book-writing authors are particularly prone to wide-ranging reading, a multiplying 'feedback' effect results. When it comes to coining familiar quotations, describing familiar episodes, originating symbols or stereotypes, the ancients will generally outstrip the moderns. How many times has Tacitus' description of freedom-loving Teutons been repeated since a single manuscript of *Germania* was discovered in a fifteenth-century monastery? And in how many varying contexts – Anglo-Saxon, Frankish, as well as German – has this particular description appeared?

The frequency with which all messages were transmitted was primarily channeled by the fixing of literary linguistic frontiers. A particular kind of reinforcement was involved in relearning mother tongues when learning to read. It went together with the progressive amplification of diversely oriented national 'memories'. Not all the same portions of an inherited Latin culture were translated into different vernaculars at the same time.[60] More important, entirely dissimilar dynastic, municipal, and ecclesiastical chronicles, along with other local lore, both oral and scribal, were also set in type and more permanently fixed. The meshing of provincial medieval *res gestæ* with diverse

classical and scriptural sources had, by the early seventeenth century, imbedded distinctively different stereotypes within each separate vernacular
literature.[61] At the same time, to be sure, a more cosmopolitan *Respublica
litterarum* was also expanding, and messages were broadcast across linguistic
frontiers, first via Latin, then French, to an international audience. But
messages received from abroad were not amplified over the course of several
centuries in the same way. They only occasionally reinforced what was
learned in familiar tongues at home.[62]

On the other hand, the fixing of religious frontiers that cut across linguistic
ones in the sixteenth century had a powerful effect on the frequency with
which certain messages were transmitted. Passages drawn from vernacular
translations of the Bible, for example, would be much more thinly and
weakly distributed throughout the literary cultures of Catholic regions than
of Protestant ones.[63] The abandonment of church Latin in Protestant regions
made it possible to mesh ecclesiastical and dynastic traditions more closely
within Protestant realms than in Catholic ones – a point worth noting when
considering how church–state conflicts were resolved in different lands.
Finally, the unevenly phased social penetration of literacy, the somewhat
more random patterning of book-reading habits, and the uneven distribution
of costly new books and cheap reprints of old ones among different social
sectors also affected the frequency with which diverse messages were received
within each linguistic group.

4   PRINTING AND THE PEOPLE:
EARLY MODERN FRANCE*

Natalie Zemon Davis

Here are some voices from the sixteenth century. 'The time has come . . . for women to apply themselves to the sciences and disciplines.' Thus the rope-maker's daughter Louise Labé addresses her sex when her collected poems are printed in Lyon in 1556. 'And if one of us gets to the point where she can put her ideas in writing, then take pains with it and don't be reluctant to accept the glory.' Ten years later in Cambrai, a Protestant linen-weaver explains to his judges about the book in his life: 'I was led to knowledge of the Gospel by . . . my neighbor, who had a Bible printed at Lyon and who taught me the Psalms by heart . . . The two of us used to go walking in the fields Sundays and feast days, conversing about the Scriptures and the abuses of priests.' And listen to the printers' journeymen of Paris and Lyon in 1572, in a brief they printed to convince Parlement and public that they needed better treatment from their employers: 'Printing [is] an invention so admir-able . . . so honorable in its dignity, and profitable above all others to the French. Paris and Lyon furnish the whole of Christendom with books in every language.' And yet 'the Publishers and master Printers . . . use every stratagem to oppress . . . the Journeymen, who do the biggest and best part of the work of Printing'. And finally, Pierre Tolet, doctor of medicine, justify-ing in 1540 his translation of some Greek texts into French, printed for the use of surgeons' journeymen: 'If you want a servant to follow your orders, you can't give them in an unknown tongue.'

These quotations suggest the several and complex ways in which printing entered into popular life in the sixteenth century, setting up new networks of communication, facilitating new options for the people, and also providing new means of controlling the people. Can this be true? Could printing have mattered that much to *the people* in a period when literacy was still so low? How can one detect its influence? And what do I mean anyway by 'popular' and 'the people'?

Indeed, these words were ambiguous in sixteenth-century literate usage, as in our own. On the one hand, 'the people' could refer to all the natives in the kingdom (*le peuple françoys*) or the body of citizenry and inhabitants to which a law was promulgated. On the other hand, the word could refer to a more limited but still large population: those who were commoners, not

*Reprinted from *Society and Culture in Early Modern France* by Natalie Zemon Davis, 189–226, by permission of the publisher, Stanford University Press, © 1973, 1975, Natalie Zemon David.

noble; of modest means or poor, not wealthy; unschooled, not learned. For Claude de Seyssel in his *Grand' Monarchie* of 1519, the 'little people' lived in both the town and the countryside, and were those who worked the land and those who carried on the crafts and lesser mysteries. Recent studies of popular culture in the seventeenth and eighteenth centuries have used 'people' in de Seyssel's sense, but have stressed peasants more than city-dwellers. Geneviève Bollème has talked of the *'petites gens'*; Robert Mandrou has been concerned with 'popular milieus', especially in the countryside.[1]

The connection between these milieus and the printed book has been considered in several ways. First, there are those studies that take 'popular literature' as their source material and make a thematic analysis of its contents. Lewis B. Wright's *Middle-Class Culture in Elizabethan England* (1935) is the classic example of such an undertaking for a literate urban grouping comprising merchants, tradesmen, and skilled artisans. Robert Mandrou's subject has been the blue-covered books that were peddled out of Troyes in the seventeenth and eighteenth centuries to villages over a wide geographical area, whereas Geneviève Bollème has examined a large sample of French almanacs. Their goal has been to discover not so much new or continuing patterns of communication, but rather 'the outlook of the average citizen' (Wright), or a popular 'vision of the world' (Mandrou). Why this confidence in inferring from the book its readers' outlook? Because, so it is argued, the Elizabethan literature was written 'for or by the plain citizen'; because the publishers of the *Bibliothèque bleue* stayed in close touch through their peddlers with village needs and tastes.[2]

In establishing the characteristics of a body of printed literature, these studies have been invaluable and even surprising. For disclosing the outlook of a given social group, though, they have some methodological drawbacks. Popular books are not necessarily written by *petites gens*. Master André Le Fournier, author of a 1530 compilation of household recipes and cosmetics for women, was a regent of the Faculty of Medicine at Paris, and he was by no means the only university graduate to engage in such an enterprise. Nor are popular books bought and read only by *petites gens*. The *Grand Calendrier et compost des bergers*, for instance, the archetype of the French almanac, was read perhaps by countryman but surely by king. François Ier had a copy in the royal collection, and a mid-sixteenth-century edition, now at the Houghton Library, belonged to the king's advocate at Sens.[3] The *Tresor des povres*, a traditional collection of medical remedies, was owned in sixteenth-century Paris by a councillor's wife and a bookbinder.[4]

Finally, it is especially important to realize that people do not necessarily agree with the values and ideas in the books they read. For instance, M. Mandrou concludes from the fairy stories and saints lives in the *Bibliothèque bleue* that it functioned as escape literature for the peasants, an obstacle to the understanding of social and political realities. Perhaps. But without independent evidence, can we be sure of how a rural audience took its tales of marvels, especially at a period when people might dress up as ghosts to teach children a lesson or might protect peasant rebels by saying they were 'fairies' who came from time to time.[5] When a peasant read or was read to, it was not the stamping of a literal message on a blank sheet; it was the varied motion of 'a strange top' (to use Jean-Paul Sartre's metaphor for the literary object), set to turning only by the combined effort of author and reader.[6]

Thus we can best understand the connections between printing and the people if we do two things: first, if we supplement thematic analysis of texts with evidence about audiences that can provide context for the meaning and uses of books; second, if we consider a printed book not merely as a source for ideas and images, but as a carrier of relationships. The data to support such an approach are scattered in the pages of the original editions themselves; in studies of literacy and dialects, book ownership and book prices, author-ship and publication policy; and in sources on the customs and associational life of peasants and artisans. The theory to assist such an approach can be found in part in the work of Jack Goody and his collaborators on the impli-cations of literacy for traditional societies – especially in their discussion of the relations between those who live on the margins of literacy and those who live at its center. Additional theoretical support exists in the fertile essays of Elizabeth L. Eisenstein on the impact of printing on literate elites and on urban populations in early modern Europe – especially when she talks of 'cross-cultural interchange' between previously 'compartmentalized systems'. Both Goody and Eisenstein have insisted to critics that they do not intend technological determinism, and I am even more ready than they to emphasize the way that social structure and values channel the uses of literacy and printing.[7]

This essay, then, will consider the context for using printed books in defined popular milieus in sixteenth-century France and the new relations that printing helped to establish among people and among hitherto isolated cultural traditions. Were there new groups who joined the ranks of known authors? What was the composition of 'audiences' – those who actually read the books – and of 'publics' – those to whom authors and publishers addressed their works?*

These relations are especially interesting to trace in the sixteenth century. In the cities, at any rate, the basic innovations occurred quite rapidly. By mid-century all the major centers of publication had been established in France: Paris, Lyon, Rouen, Toulouse, Poitiers, Bordeaux, Troyes. Some forty towns had presses by 1550; about sixty had them by 1600. Moreover, economic control in the industry was not yet firmly in the hands of merchant—

---

*This distinction is a necessary one, but is not made in everyday speech. I follow the terminology of T.J. Clark, *Image of the People. Gustave Courbet and the Second French Republic, 1848–1851* (New York, 1973), p. 12.

publishers and commercial booksellers, as it would be after the Religious Wars. Decisions about what was profitable and/or beneficial to print were made also by 'industrial capitalists' and artisans, that is, by publisher—printers, like Jean I de Tournes in Lyon and the Marnef brothers in Poitiers; such decisions were even sometimes made by simple master printers publishing their own editions. This diversity may help explain the wide range in the *types* of books that appeared before mid-century. In these decades there proliferated most of the forms to be published in France up to 1700. The same is true of patterns in book ownership. For example, virtually no Parisian artisans other than printers in the generation that died around 1500 owned printed books; by 1560, the percentage of Parisian artisans and tradesmen possessing books in inventories after death had reached the level (not very high, to be sure) that Henri-Jean Martin has documented for mid-seventeenth-century Paris.[8]

This brings me to a last point about method. Rather than thinking diffusely about 'the people', I am trying wherever possible to ask how printing affected more carefully defined milieus — namely, cohesive, social groups some of whose members were literate. In the countryside this means the entire settled population of a village where anyone was literate. In the cities this means the small merchants and the craftsmen (masters and journeymen), and even semi-skilled workers (such as urban gardeners and fishermen) having some connection with urban organizations such as confraternities or guilds. It means their wives, themselves ordinarily at work in the trades, and even women in the families of the wealthier merchants. It means domestic servants, male or female, who might be living in their households. It does not include the un-skilled dayworkers, the *gagnedenier* and *manouvriers*, the *portefaix* and *crocheteurs*, the vagabonds and permanent beggars. This floating mass was just illiterate; and however resourceful their subculture, the only reader to whom they listened with any regularity was the town crier ordering them to show up for work cleaning sewage or else leave town under penalty of the whip.

Nor am I including the lower clergy or the backwoods noblemen and their wives, even though they might in the sixteenth century sometimes cluster on the borderline between literacy and illiteracy and as individuals play a role in village life. They are distinguished from the peasants and the urban *menu peuple* not by the criterion of literacy but by their estate and their relations to spiritual and emotional power, to jurisdiction and to property.

I

Let us look first to the peasants. The penetration of printing into their lives was a function not just of their literacy but of several things: the cost and availability of books in a language that they knew; the existence of social occasions when books could be read aloud; the need or desire for information that they thought could be found in printed books more easily than elsewhere; and in some cases the desire to use the press to say something to some-one else.

In the countryside we meet a world that sees letters infrequently, whether written or printed. Suggestive of their relevance in the days before printing is a rural festival in Torcy around 1450, where a mock herald – a miller's son – with a mock seal pretends to read to the harvest queen from a blank parchment, whereas in fact he is improvising farcical jokes. Parchment or paper might come into the peasants' life when transactions were being recorded by courts, seigneurs, or rent-collectors, but peasants might equally expect to see these materials used, say, in a humiliating headdress for local offenders. (In the Ile-de-France in the fifteenth century a dishonest chicken-grower is led to punishment wearing a miter with chicks and other fowl painted on it and 'an abundance of writing', and in 1511 a lax forest ranger is paraded around in a paper miter decorated with standing and fallen trees.)[9]

Rural literacy remained low throughout the sixteenth century. Of the women, virtually none knew their ABC's, not even the midwives. As for the men, a systematic study by Emmanuel LeRoy Ladurie of certain parts of the Languedoc from the 1570s through the 1590s found that three percent of the agricultural workers and only ten percent of the better-off peasants – the *laboureurs* and *fermiers* – could sign their full names.* In the regions north and southwest of Paris, where the speech was French, the rates may have been slightly higher, and rural schools have been noted in several places. But the pupils who spent a couple of years at such places learning to read and write and sing were drawn from special families (such as that of a barber-surgeon in the Forez, who sent his boys to a school and rewarded its rector with a chapel in 1557) or were intended for nonagricultural occupations (such as the serf's son in the Sologne who went to school 'to learn science' because he was 'weak of body and could not work the soil').[10]

Surely a lad ambitious to be a *fermier* in the mid sixteenth century would need to keep accounts, yet not all economic pressures pushed the prosperous peasant to literacy. Charles Estienne's agricultural manual advised the landed proprietor that his tenant farmer need not have reading and writing (one can lie on paper, too) so long as he was experienced and wise in agricultural ways. A peasant in the Haut-Poitou in 1601, designated tax assessor of his village,

*Estimates of ability to read based on studies of ability to sign one's name are, of course, approximate. One can learn to read without learning to write and vice versa. Nevertheless, the two skills were most often taught together in the sixteenth century. Statistics on ability to sign, then, give us the order of magnitude of the number of readers. For a discussion of techniques of measuring literacy in the early modern period, see R.S. Schofield, 'The Measurement of Literacy in Pre-Industrial England', in J.R. Goody, ed., *Literacy in Traditional Societies* (Cambridge, Eng., 1968), pp. 311–25, and F. Furet and W. Sachs, 'La Croissance de l'alphabétisation en France, XVIIIe–XIXe siècle', *Annales. Economies, Sociétés, Civilisations* 29 (1974): 714–37.

tried to get out of it by pleading illiteracy. As for sales of land, marriage contracts, and wills, there were itinerant scribes and notaries aplenty who were
happy to add to their income by performing these services for the peasants.

The country boys who really learned their letters, then, were most likely
those who left for the city to apprentice to crafts or to become priests, or the
few lucky sons of *laboureurs* who, at a time when fellowships for the poor
were being taken over by the rich, still made it to the University of Paris. One
such, the son of a village smith from Brie, became a proofreader in Lyon after
his university years, and at his death in 1560 was in possession of a precious
manuscript of the Theodosian Code.

But when they came back to visit, such men did not leave books in their
villages. 'Our little Thomas talks so profoundly, almost no one can understand
him' was the observation of Thomas Platter's relatives when he passed through
his Swiss mountain home during his student years in the early sixteenth century. One can imagine similar remarks exchanged by peasants in France about
a son who had studied books in a strange language or learned his craft in a
different dialect. As the peasants' inventories after death* were virtually without manuscripts in the fifteenth century, so they were almost without printed
books in the sixteenth.[11] Why should this be so? Surely a *laboureur* who
could afford many livres worth of linens and coffers in the 1520s could
afford three sous for a *Calendrier des bergers*, two sous for the medical manual
Le Tresor des povres, or even two and a half livres for a bound and illustrated
Book of Hours, which might be a credit to his family for generations.[12]

Yet just because one can afford books does not mean that one can have
ready access to them or need them or want them. A literate *laboureur* in
some parts of France during the sixteenth century might never meet a bookseller: his nearest market town might have no presses if it were a small place,
and peddlers' itineraries still reached relatively few parts of the countryside.[13]

*No study has yet been made of the book holdings of rural *curés* in sixteenth-
century France. Albert Labarre examined inventories after death of 23 *curés*
of rural parishes in the Amiénois from 1522 to 1561 (fifteen had books, eight
had none), but, as he points out, these men were all living in Amiens. Except
when the resident *curé* kept a school, we would expect that he would possess
little more than a breviary and a missal, and perhaps a book of saints' lives. In
his *Propos rustiques* of 1547, Noel du Fail pictured a rural *curé* of earlier
decades at a feast-day banquet, not reading aloud, but chatting with parishioners about the text for the day and with the old midwife about medicinal
herbs. The education of the rural clergy was, of course, very uneven well into
the seventeenth century. Only then do we find French bishops requiring *curés*
to own specified books. A. Labarre, *Le livre dans la vie amiénoise du seizième
siècle* (Paris, 1971), pp. 107–11. Noel du Fail, *Les propos rustiques*, ed. A. de
la Borderie (Paris, 1878), p. 21. T.-J. Schmitt, *L'organisation ecclésiastique et
la pratique religieuse dans l'archidiaconé d'Autun de 1650 à 1750* (Autun,
1957), pp. 132–3. J. Ferté, *La vie religieuse dans les campagnes parisiennes,
1622–1695* (Paris, 1962), pp. 186–94.

If he did come upon a bookseller, his wares might be in a language the peasant had difficulty reading, since so little printing was done in vernaculars other than French. Only five books printed in Breton during the sixteenth century could be found by an eighteenth-century student of that language, and the first work in Basque came out in 1545 and had very few imitators.[14] Provençal was favored by several editions, mostly of poetry, but the various regional dialects, from Picard to Poitevin, rarely appeared in print at all.

In any case, how much were printed books really needed in the sixteenth-century village? A *Shepherds' Calendar* was a useful, though not always essential, supplement to oral tradition. (Indeed, sometimes as I read the different sixteenth-century editions of the *Calendrier des bergers*, I wonder to what extent contemporary compilers and publishers envisaged a peasant public for them. They appear a cross between a folklorist's recording and a pastoral, a shaped vision of the peasant world for country gentlemen and city people and a way for such readers to identify themselves with the simple wisdom of 'the great shepherd of the mountain'. The appearance in Paris in 1499 of a *Shepherdesses' Calendar*, a literary contrivance modeled after the earliest *Calendrier* and printed by the same atelier, tends to support this view.)[15] The *Shepherds' Calendar* told which sign the moon was in and its phases, the dates of fixed and movable feast days, and the timing of solar and lunar eclipses. For the most important findings about the year in which the calendar was printed, pictorial devices were given to aid the barely literate. For full use of the various tables, genuine ability to read was required.*

Now except for the eclipses, peasants had their own equivalent devices to calculate these results, which they then recorded 'in figures on little tablets of wood'. These 'hieroglyphic Almanacs' were still being made by peasants in the Languedoc in 1655: 'On a morsel of wood no bigger than a playing card,' said an observer in the Albigeois region, 'they mark by a singular artifice all the months and days of the year, with the feast days and other notable things.' Why should they then feel the lack of a *Shepherds' Calendar*?

Other parts of the *Calendrier* might have been enjoyable for peasants, such as the recommendations on regimen or the physiognomic signs that warned one who was crafty and who was kind. Yet here, too, rural communities were well supplied with proverbs and old sayings that covered many of these contingencies, sometimes even more aptly than the uniform teaching of the *Calendar*. (Can both Provençaux and Picards have agreed that black

---

*The *Shepherds' Calendar* was not published annually. The dates for the new moon could be read off for 38 years; the eclipses were predicted for a century or more. For any year after the year of its printing, the dates of the days of the week, the exact time of the new moon, and the position of the moon in the zodiac had to be worked out from the tables.

In Noel du Fail's *Propos rustiques*, the village copy of *Calendrier des bergers* is owned by old Maistre Huguet, former village schoolteacher, who reads aloud from it from time to time (p. 15).

curly hair meant a melancholy, lewd, evil-thinking person? Can both Bretons and Gascons have agreed that redheads were foolish, senseless, and disloyal?) The gynecological sections of some *Calendars* (such as Troyes, 1541, and Lyon, 1551) were trifling compared to the wide lore of the village midwife. And let us hope that traveling barbers did not base their bleeding only on the crude illustration of the veins that recurred in these editions.

Similarly, the agricultural advice in the *Shepherds' Calendar* was only of occasional usefulness. Peasants did not really need its woodcuts – a delight though they were to the eyes – to teach them, for instance, that in March it was time to prune the vines. As the old saying went:

> Le vigneron me taille
> Le vigneron me lie
> Le vigneron me baille
> En Mars toute ma vie.

Finally, though I have come upon no example before 1630 of a rural *curé* in possession of a *Shepherds' Calendar*, we can imagine such a priest in the earlier period reading aloud from the extensive religious passages of the book, or even better, showing the villagers the articulated trees of virtue and vice and the pictures of punishments in Hell. This might happen, but could these woodcuts compete with the Last Judgments, the dance of death, the saints' lives, and the Biblical scenes already coloring the walls and filling the windows of so many rural churches at the end of the Middle Ages? And would the seven ways of knowing God and self and the six ways of fulfilling baptism, wise though they might be, do much to lessen the peasants' dependence on ritual, to move peasant religion toward reading? In short, *Le Grand Calendrier des bergers*, if any of its editions found their way to the village in the sixteenth century, may have jogged the peasants' memory and enriched and perhaps helped standardize its visual store. But it can hardly have brought them much new information or changed significantly their reliance on oral transmission and their relationships with nonpeasant groups.

The festive and musical life of the peasants was also nourished primarily by local tradition and experience and by what the peasants learned from traveling players and saw and heard themselves at fairtime in a nearby center. For example, the unmarried youth of the village, organized into Abbayes de Jeunesse, composed chants and playlets to mock the domestic and sexual foibles of older villagers. Thus a mid-sixteenth-century charivari song might be made up on the spur of the moment because a newly wed husband had failed three nights running to consummate his marriage. In the version that has come down to us:

> Quand ils ont sceu au village
> Que ce mary
> N'avoit non plus de courage
> Q'une soury

Ils ont faict charyvary
Pour la riser . . .
En tres grande diligence
Un bon garcon
Du village par plaisance
Fit la chanson.

In parts of the Auvergne, *reinages* were organized annually in which the right to costume oneself as king, queen, dauphin, constable, and the like was auctioned off to the villager who gave the most wax to the parish church or a local convent.[16] Religious drama also emerged from this nonliterate milieu: in the late fifteenth century, four inhabitants of Triel (Ile-de-France) put on the Life of Saint Victor and got into trouble for taking a statue from the church and using it irreverently as a prop; in 1547, three *laboureurs*, unable to sign their names, contracted with a village painter to make 'portraits' for the Life of the child martyr Saint Cyr that they were playing on Sundays in their hamlet of Villejuive.[17]

Farces, moralities, and mysteries were pouring from the presses of Paris and Lyon in the first part of the sixteenth century, but these rural performances used no printed book and probably did not even have a text behind them. So too, it became the fashion in the mid-century to publish so-called '*chansons rustiques*' as part of general collections of songs without music, but there is no evidence that these were aimed at or bought in the villages.[18]

And yet there were a few ways that printing did enter rural life in the sixteenth century to offer some new options to the peasants. The important social institution for this was the *veillée*, an evening gathering within the village community held especially during the winter months from All Saints' Day to Ash Wednesday.[19] Here tools were mended by candlelight, thread was spun, the unmarried flirted, people sang, and some man or woman told stories – of Mélusine, that wondrous woman-serpent with her violent husband and sons; of the girl who escaped from incest to the king's palace in a she-donkey's hide; of Renard and other adventuresome animals.[20] Then, if one of the men were literate and owned books, he might read aloud.

In principle, printing increased significantly the range of books available for the *veillée*. In fact, given the limited channels of distribution in the sixteenth century and the virtuosity of the traditional storyteller, even a rural schoolteacher might have very few books. According to Noel du Fail, a young lawyer from a seigneurial family in upper Brittany who wrote in 1547 a story of a peasant village, the village books were 'old': *Aesop's Fables* and *Le Roman de la Rose*. Now both of these had printed editions and urban readers in the late fifteenth and early sixteenth centuries. By the 1540s, however, the learned were enjoying Aesop in fresh Latin and Greek editions or in new French rhyme; and, though still appreciative of the thirteenth-century *Roman*, they were feeling ever more distant from its sense and style, even in the updated version given them by Clément Marot. In contrast, peasants would have had no reason to supplant the early editions that Marot and his publisher disdained as full of printing errors and *'trop ancien langaige'*.[21]

Did such reading aloud change things much in the village? *Reading* aloud? We might better say 'translating', since the reader was inevitably turning the French of his printed text into a dialect his listeners could understand. And we might well add 'editing' – if not for *Aesop's Fables*, whose form and plots were already familiar to peasants, then for the 22,000 lines and philosophical discourses of the *Roman*. In a community hearing parts of the *Roman* for the first time, new relationships were perhaps set up with old chivalric and scholastic ways of ordering experience; some new metaphors were acquired and varied images of women and love added to the listeners' existing stock. Who do you yearn to be, or to love? Mélusine or the Rose? A good question, but it hardly constitutes a connection with the distinctive features of 'print culture'.*

As early as the 1530s, however, some *veillées* were being treated to a book that was in the vanguard and more disruptive of traditional rural patterns than Aesop, the *Roman de la Rose*, or the *Calendrier*: the vernacular Bible. In Picardy a cobbler reads it to the villagers at the *veillées* until he is discovered by a nearby abbey. Here the literalness of the text was important. The Bible could not be 'edited' or reduced to some formulaic magic. It had to be understood, and there were probably no pictures to help. In the Saintonge and elsewhere during the 1550s, Philibert Hamelin, his pack filled with Bibles and prayer books that he had printed at Geneva, comes to sit with peasants in the fields during their noonday break and talks of the Gospel and a new kind of prayer. Some are delighted and learn; others are outraged and curse and beat him. He is sure that one day they will know better.[22]

*Noel du Fail was quite particular about the books that he placed in the village. When a pirated edition of his *Propos* came out in Paris in 1548 with other books added to his list, he suppressed them in his new edition at Lyon in 1549. In 1573, however, the Parisian publisher Jean II Ruelle added five titles that may have had some hearing in the countryside: a late-fifteenth-century poetic history of the reign of Charles VII; two medieval romances (including *Valentin et Orson*, which has thematic material relating to the old rural custom of the chase of the wildman or of the bear); an account by Symphorien Champier of the chivalric deeds of the good knight Bayard; and the Miracles of Our Lady. Some of these were part of the *Bibliothèque bleue* of the seventeenth century (du Fail, *Propos*, pp. iv–xii, 138, 187).

On a rainy evening in February 1554, the Norman gentleman Gilles de Gouberville read to his household, including the male and female servants, from *Amadis de Gaule* (A. Tollemer, *Un Sire de Gouberville, gentilhomme campagnard au cotentin de 1553 à 1562*, with an introduction by E. Le Roy Ladurie [reprint of the 1873 ed., Paris, 1972], p. 285). This chivalric tale had only recently been translated from the Spanish and printed in France.

I think these books would have been received by peasants in the same way as the *Roman de la Rose* and *Aesop's Fables*.*

In the Orléanais a forest ranger buys a vernacular New Testament, a French Psalter, and the Geneva catechism from a bookseller at a fair and goes alone into the forest of Marchenoir to read them. Over in the mountains of the Dauphiné a peasant somehow teaches himself to read and write French and divides his time between plowing and the New Testament. The story goes that when reproached by the priests because he did not know the Scripture in Latin, he laboriously spelled it out until he could contradict them with Latin citations.

Finally, evangelical peddlers begin to work the countryside systematically. A carter, a native of Poitiers, loads up in Geneva with Bibles, Psalters, and Calvinist literature published by Laurent de Normandie and looks for buyers in the Piedmont and the rural Dauphiné. Five craftsmen from scattered parts of France are arrested in 1559 in a village in the Lyonnais with literature from Geneva in their baskets. Even the Inquisitor wonders why they should want to sell such books to '*gens rustiques*'.[23]

As it turned out, of course, the Calvinist message never won the massive support of the French peasants. Rural Protestantism was to be chiefly the affair either of seigneurs and great noble houses, whose tenants or subjects would then attend Reformed services perforce, or of special regions like the Cévenol, where (as LeRoy Ladurie has shown) initial commitment came from the relatively high concentration of rural artisans, especially in the leather trades.[24] For most peasants, the religion of the Book, the Psalm, and the Consistory gave too little leeway to the traditional oral and ritual culture of the countryside, to its existing forms of social life and social control.

This Calvinist inflexibility is illustrated by the character of a new *Calendrier* that originated in Geneva in the late 1550s and was published in great numbers in the 1560s there, in Lyon, and elsewhere. The engravings for each month still depicted rural scenes, sometimes with great charm. But information on the moon's location in the zodiac either was given not in tables but in *words*, or more often was suppressed altogether (perhaps because it was feared that it would be put to astrological use); and the many saints whose names and pictures marked the traditional *Calendrier* were banished as 'superstitious and idolatrous'. Instead, the Reformed *Calendrier* listed 'historical' dates that would show God's ways to man. Thus Noah's progress in the ark and events in the life of Christ were recorded in their place. On January 26 or 27, 815, Charlemagne died. On February 18, 'the feast of fools was celebrated at Rome, to which corresponds Mardi Gras of the Papists . . . successors of the Pagans'. March was the month of Martin Bucer's death, July that of Edward IV. Constantinople was taken by Mahomet II May 29, 1453. On August 27, the 'reformation according to the truth' took place in Geneva. Under October was remembered Martin Luther's attack on indulgences.[25]

It was an interesting innovation, this slender *Calendrier historial*, which was often slipped in with the Reformed Psalter or New Testament (and even

appeared, as they did, in Basque).[26] But how would peasants have responded
to it? First, it was harder for the semiliterate to decipher than the Catholic
calendar, and it had less astronomical fact. But most of all, no matter how
curious the new historical items were, the peasants' year was here stripped
beyond recognition, empty even of the saints by which they named their days.
Protestant publishers wanted *gens rustiques* to buy these books, but they had
not tailored them to a peasant public.*

Still, even if the Bible did not become a permanent fixture in most rural
households, merely to think of selling to them on a large scale was something
new. Who first opened up the rural markets for the peddlers' books of the
seventeenth century? Not a simple printer of rural background; he would
remember the illiteracy of his village. Not an ordinary publisher of popular
literature; he would worry about meager profits. But zealous Protestants
could overlook all that, could face the possibilities of destroyed merchandise
and even death for the sake of 'consoling poor Christians and instructing
them in the law of God'.[27]

If printing and Protestantism opened new routes for selling books in the
countryside, the press also facilitated the *writing* of a few new books for a
peasant public. What happened, I think, was that the printing of 'peasant lore',
as in the *Shepherds' Calendar* and in books of common proverbs, brought it
to the attention of learned men in a new way. These men were discovering
the thoughts not of their local tenants or of the men and women from whom
they bought grain at market but of The Peasants. And, dedicated to the
'illustration' of the national tongue and to the humanist ideal of practical
service, they decided that they must correct rural lore and instruct The
Peasants. Thus, Antoine Mizaud, doctor of medicine, mathematician, and professor at Paris, writes an *Astrologie des Rustiques* to tell countryfolk without
the time to acquire perfect knowledge of the heavens how to predict the
weather by sure terrestrial signs. (Mariners, military commanders, and
physicians should find it useful, too.) Thus, somewhat later, the royal surgeon
Jacques Guillemeau writes a book on pregnancy and childbirth 'not for the
learned . . . but for young Surgeons, little versed in the art, dispersed here and
there, far away from the cities'.

---

*The *Calendriers historials* were all anonymous and were given their form and
content by those that published them. The *Calendrier*'s first creator was
Conrad Badius, son of a printer in Paris. Of sixteen other *libraires* and *impri-
meurs* associated with the editions in Geneva and Lyon in the 1560s, nine of
them − and these the most important − were of urban origin. The pictures
show some attention to agricultural detail: the ox-drawn light plows (*araires*)
of the Languedoc figure in some, whereas the horse-drawn heavier plows
(*charrues*) of the north appear in others. But some calendars put animal and
instrument together in less likely combinations; and a 1566 Lyon edition has
placed mowing in the month before reaping − and none provides advice on
crops.

Some new kinds of almanacs appear on an annual basis now, authored by doctors of medicine and 'mathematicians', containing bits of possibly novel *agricultural* information, such as when to plant fruits and market vegetables. ('Tested by M. Peron and Jean Lirondes, old gardeners at Nîmes', says one edition, which then tells about the *choux cabus*, artichokes, melons, and other plants that distinguished the seventeenth-century Languedoc garden from its modest fifteenth-century forebear.) Though these almanacs were conceived for a diverse public, they probably were expected to reach some peasant readers – certainly more than were the justly celebrated agricultural manuals of Charles Estienne, Jean Liebault, and others. These latter treatises were intended for landowners, gentlemen farmers, and seigneurs, who would then teach their lessees, tenants, and hired servants what to do.*

The most interesting of these new almanacs, however, was written by Jean Vostet in 1588 and occasioned by the Gregorian calendar reform of six years before. As his patron, the prior of Flammerécourt in Champagne, had said, the ten cut days 'had rendered useless the ancient observations of the peasants . . . had ruined their verses and local memory [*leurs vers et mémoire locale*] '. So Vostet went through the year's poems and proverbs – culled from sayings and from old manuscript and printed *Calendars* and *Prognostications* – occasionally correcting them when he thought the advice bad or 'superstitious' and rewriting them to make up for the lost days. For example, the Bear decides about winter's length no more at Candlemas but on February 12; the hog's acorns are put in doubt not by a rainy St James' day but by a rainy

---

*As Corinne Beutler points out in an excellent review of sixteenth-century agricultural literature, these manuals were addressed to the nobility and landed proprietors, who were then expected to teach their unlettered peasants ('Un chapitre de la sensibilité collective: la littérature agricole en Europe continentale au XVIe siècle', *Annales. Economies, Sociétés, Civilisations* 28 [1973]: 1282, 1292–4). This is clear not only from the introductions to the manuals, but from the assumed public for some of their chapters. Charles Estienne devotes a long section to the kind of *fermier* and *fermière* that the proprietor should hire after he has constructed his farmhouse. Literacy is not a requirement for the tenant, as we have seen, and thus Estienne is not thinking of him as the *reader* of his text (*L'agriculture et la maison rustique de M. Charles Estienne Docteur en Medecine* [Paris: Jacques Du Pays, 1564], chaps. 7–8).

Olivier de Serres, after a preface discussing the limitations of the agricultural understanding of unlettered peasants (an understanding based on experience alone), goes on to a chapter on the different kinds of arrangements by which the Father of the Family may rent out or administer his land. We are long past the time, he writes with ironic wistfulness, when the Father of the Family dirtied his hands working the soil himself. He thinks some of his readers may have to be absent from their property because of service to the king, judicial or financial office, or commercial enterprise. (*Theatre d'Agriculture et Mesnage des Champs d'Olivier de Serres, Seigneur de Pradel* [Paris: Jamet Mettayer, 1600], Preface and Book I, chap. 8. Signature at the end of Table in copy at the Bancroft Library: 'de Menisson'. Marginalia in French, German, and Latin, by different hands, in the chapter on medicinal plants.)

Saint Gengoul's. Instead of it being a good idea to bleed your right arm on March 17, Saint Gertrude's Day, you now should do it two days after the Annunciation. This will keep your eyes clear for the whole year. All this is rather different from the Calvinist *Calendrier historiale*, and not merely because the Protestants refused to accept the pope's reformed calendar until the eighteenth century. (Did Vostet's new sayings catch on? At least in the printed literature they did. We find them in the seventeenth- and eighteenth-century almanacs, but coupled, alas, with the verses they were supposed to supersede.)

Jean Vostet was a man of minor learning, but another book imagined for a peasant public (though actually printed only in Latin during the sixteenth century) was by the eminent jurist René Choppin. It was called *On the Privileges of Rustic Persons*, and Choppin wrote it in 1574 at his estate at Cachan, where he, 'half-peasant', was on vacation from the Parlement of Paris. Surveying his fields and flocks, he thought how little jurists had done to recompense the men by whose labor they lived. Why had no one told the peasants of their legal privileges and rights, so they need not be diverted from the plow to wasteful cases in the courts? He would relieve their ignorance in a treatise which, drawing on Roman law, customary law, royal ordinances, and decisions of the Parlements, would answer a host of questions concerning peasants – from the status of persons to disputes over pasture.

Was Choppin really trying to make the law accessible to the peasants? Despite the claims of this 'semi-paganus' that he wished the 'Diligent Husbandman' to read his own law, the promised French translation did not appear till several years after his death. He spoke of the countryfolk with a pastoral nostalgia for their sincerity and an employer's suspicion of their laziness. But especially he visualized peasants as clients or opposing parties, and the book was directed to lawyers who would plead for or against them in various courts. It was a genuine contribution to the slow process of unification of French law – though one about which Choppin felt defensive. Writing about rustic things after writing about the royal domain might be thought, as the proverb said, to be going from horses to asses. As for the 'asses', it seems unlikely that they read about their privileges. Indeed, we have no *sure* evidence that any of these books addressed to a rural public ever actually reached a peasant audience. Probably some of the almanacs did circulate in the countryside, for they appear in the peddlers' packs in the seventeenth century.

What can we conclude, then, about the consequences of printing for the sixteenth-century peasant community? Certainly they were limited. A few lines of communication were opened between professor and peasant – or rather between bodies of cultural materials, as in the case of some traditional lore that was standardized and disseminated by the press, perhaps with a little correction from above. Expectations were higher by 1600 that a printed book might come into the village and be read aloud at the *veillée*, even where the little spark of Protestantism had burned out in the countryside. But oral culture was still so dominant that it transformed everything it touched; and it still changed according to the rules of forgetting and remembering, watching and discussing. Some printed medieval romances may have come to the peasants from the cities, but they cannot have played the escapist role that Mandrou has claimed for them in the seventeenth century. Peasants in the Lyonnais, in the Ile-de-France, and in the Languedoc put on tithe strikes just the same; villages in Burgundy forced their lords to enfranchise about half of their service population; peasants in Brittany, the Guyenne, Burgundy, and the Dauphiné organized themselves into emergency communes, communicated with each other, and rebelled under traditional slogans, ensigns, and captains with festive titles – all neither deflected nor aided by what was being said in print.[28] Indeed, those who wished to control the countryside and bring it to order by means other than sheer force – whether bishop, seigneur, or king – would have to send not books but messengers, whose seals would not be mock and who would disclose verbally the power behind the papers that they read.

II

In the cities, the changes wrought or facilitated by printing in the life of the *menu peuple* had greater moment. The literacy rate had long been higher among urban artisans and tradesmen than among peasants, but the gap widened – at least for males – in the early sixteenth century. The old choir-boy schools still performed their service for the sons of some artisans and petty traders, and more important, the numbers of vernacular schoolteachers and reckonmasters multiplied. For instance, in Lyon in the 1550s and 1560s, some 38 male teachers of reading, writing, and arithmetic can be identified (very roughly one for every 400 males under the age of twenty in the city), quite apart from the masters at the Latin Collège de la Trinité. They marry the daughters of taverners and the widows of millers; they live in houses with pouchmakers and dressmakers; they have goldsmiths, printers, barber-surgeons, coopers, and gold-thread-drawers among their friends. In addition to these teachers, newly established municipal orphanages in some cities provided simple instruction for poor boys, and at times even orphan girls were taught their ABC's.[29]

This press for literacy was associated with technological, economic, and social developments. Printing itself created a populous cluster of crafts (including bookbinding and typecasting) where literacy rates were high. Of 115 printers' journeymen assembled in Lyon in 1580 to give power of attorney, two-thirds could sign their names fully; and the journeymen were already demanding that all apprentices know how to read and write, even those who would be but simple pressmen. In other crafts, such as painting and surgery, literacy was spurred by the desire for a higher, more 'professional' status and the availability of vernacular books for training. Even the royal sergeants, a group among the *menu peuple* previously noted only for their skill with the rod, began to live up to a 1499 decree requiring them to read and write.

Literacy was not, of course, distributed evenly among the *menu peuple*. An examination of the ability to sign of 885 males involved in notarial acts in Lyon in the 1560s and 1570s spreads the trades out as follows (masters and journeymen combined):

Very high: apothecaries, surgeons, printers.

High: painters, musicians, taverners, metalworkers (including gold trades).

Medium (about 50 percent): furriers and leatherworkers, artisans in textile and clothing trades.

Low to very low: artisans in construction trades, in provisioning, transport; urban gardeners; unskilled dayworkers.

In Narbonne, for about the same time, LeRoy Ladurie found that one-third of the artisans could sign their names; another third could write initials; and only one-third were totally foreign to letters. At Montpellier the percentage of craftsmen who could make only marks was down to 25 percent. This range among the artisans contrasts both with the almost complete literacy of well-off merchants of all kinds and with the low rate of literacy among urban women outside the families of lawyers, merchant-bankers and publishers.[30]

City-dwellers were also more likely than countryfolk to be able to understand French. Towns were, of course, constantly replenished by people from rural areas with their local patois and even by people from foreign lands, and the urban speech itself was not independent of the big patterns of regional dialect. Nevertheless, French was increasingly the language of royal government (after 1539 all judicial acts were to be in French) and of other kinds of exchange; in an important southern center like Montpellier it could be heard in the streets already by 1490.[31] Thus the urban artisan had potentially a more direct access to the contents of the printed book – whose vernacular was French, as we have seen – than a peasant who could read handwritten accounts in Provençal but would have had to struggle over a printed *Calendrier*.

From simple literacy to actual reading is something of a step. Studies based only on inventories after death in sixteenth-century Paris and Amiens suggest that the step was not always taken. In the early years of the century, if an artisan or small shopkeeper in Paris owns a book at all, it is likely to be a manuscript Book of Hours. By 1520 printed books appear, displacing the manuscripts but existing along with the religious paintings, sculpture, and wall hangings that even quite modest families possess. Most artisans, however, had no books at their death. They represent only about ten percent of book owners in Paris and twelve percent of book owners in Amiens (or seventeen percent, if we include barbers and surgeons), that is, well below the proportion of the *gens mécaniques* in the urban population at large. And when they do have books, outside of printers' stock, there are not very many of them. Out of all the editions in the Amiens inventories, only 3.7 percent were in artisanal hands (six percent, if we include barbers and surgeons); and apart from the latter group, the median size of the library was one book![32]

In Amiens that one book was most likely to be a Book of Hours, or perhaps a French *Golden Legend* (the medieval book of saints' lives popular throughout the sixteenth century), or a vernacular Bible. Or else it might be a technical work, such as a pattern book for cabinetmaking or painting. In Paris in 1549, a tanner dies owning a *Golden Legend* and the *Mer des Histoires*, a thirteenth-century historical work still being printed in the 1530s and 1540s; a barber-surgeon leaves behind six French volumes on the art of surgery.[33] Clearly the literate were often without private libraries and, at least on their deathbed, do not appear to have taken much advantage of the varied fruits of the 'admirable invention'.

There were some economic reasons for this, even though printed books were cheaper by far than manuscripts had been. A twenty-four page sermon on poor relief cost as much as a loaf of coarse bread in the 1530s; an easy little arithmetic, half a loaf. A few years later, a full news account of the seizure of Rhodes could be almost as expensive as a pair of children's shoes; a book of Christmas carols, as much as a pound of candlewax. In the 1540s a French history could cost more than half a day's wages for a painter's journeyman or a printer's journeyman, and almost a whole day's wages for a journeyman in the building trades.[34] In the 1560s the cheapest 'hand-size' New Testament in French was not much less. Understandably, some artisans complained that they could not afford to buy it, thus prompting a Protestant polemicist to ask them whether 'they didn't have all the Instruments of their craft, however much poverty made it difficult to buy them' and how could they pass up a Book of such utility as the Bible?[35]

In fact, artisans found ways to have access to printed materials without collecting them privately. They bought a book, read it until they were finished, or until they were broke or needed cash, and then pawned it with an innkeeper or more likely sold it to a friend or to a *libraire*. Thus one Jean de Cazes, a native of Libourne, purchased a Lyon Bible in Bordeaux for two écus (an expensive edition), read it, and sold it to someone from the Saintonge before he was arrested for heresy in 1566 at the age of 27.[36] Books were relatively liquid assets and were less subject to depreciation than many other personal items. One kept to the end, if one could afford it, only those editions that were needed for constant reference or were wanted as permanent family property − thus the Hours, the Bibles, and the workbooks that show up in the inventories after death. Possibly, too, in the absence of public libraries, literate artisans and shopkeepers lent each other books from their small stores as did more substantial collectors (the poet François Béroald had three leaves of his account book devoted to loaned books); and they may even have passed on books as gifts more often than we know. Theirs was a world in which 'secrets' — the secrets of the craft, the secrets of women — had never been private possessions but corporate ones, shared, told, passed on so they would not be forgotten. What happens when scarce printed books enter such a world? They flow through the literate segments of the *menu peuple* rather than remain hoarded on an artisan's shelf.

Books were also shared in reading groups which, as in the countryside, brought the literate and illiterate together. The traditional winter *veillée* was not the regular setting, however; for outside the building trades many crafts-men worked winter and summer, by candlelight if necessary, till eight or even ten o'clock at night.[37] Gatherings of family and friends for singing, games, cards, storytelling, and perhaps reading were more likely special occasions, like feast days. Certain books were designed to be read aloud or consulted in the shop, such as pattern books for textile design and the French translation of Birunguccio's *Pirotechnia*, an excellent manual on metallurgical processes. So, too, the oft-printed little arithmetics that taught petty business operations 'by the pen' in Arabic numerals and by counting stones (*jetons*) 'for those who don't know how to read and write' were resources for apprentices and adults in an atelier even more than for an instructor in a little school. One *Brief Arithmetic* promised to teach a tradesman all he needed to know in fifteen days' time and added mnemonic verses to help him catch on.

Reading aloud in one connection or another must have been especially common in the printing shop. I am thinking not merely of the discussion of copy among scholar—printers, authors, and editors, but of reading in snatches that could reach out to the journeymen and to the spouses and daughters helping to hang up the freshly printed sheets. Thus one Michel Blanc, a simple pressman in Lyon in the late 1530s, knew enough of Marot's poems, which were printed in his shop, for his son to remember later how he had been 'brought up in his youth on Marot'. Possibly men may sometimes have taken books into the tavern for reading. As for the women, they surely did some of their reading aloud among their own sex; an example might be the Life of Saint Margaret, with prayers for the pregnant and the parturient.

But the most innovative reading groups were the secret Protestant assemblies on feast days or late at night in private homes — innovative among other reasons because they brought together men and women who were not necess-arily in the same family or craft or even neighborhood. Thus a 1559 assembly in Paris included a goldsmith's journeyman from the Gâtinais, a university student from Lyon, a shoemaker's journeyman, and several others, all from different parts of the city. An early conventicle in the town of Saintes, organ-ized by two poor artisans in 1557, had access to one printed Bible, from which passages were written down for discussion. Encouraged by Deuter-onomy 6: 7 to speak of God's law however small their learning, the artisans scheduled written exhortations every Sunday by the six members who could read and write. Like the heretical linen-weavers of Cambrai, with their printed Bible in the fields, these Protestants read, talked, sang, and prayed.

In short, reading from printed books does not silence oral culture. It can give people something fresh to talk about. Learning from printed books does not suddenly replace learning by doing. It can provide people with new ways to relate their doings to authority, new and old.

Nor should printing be viewed merely as purveying to the *menu peuple* the science of university graduates, the doctrine of the religious, the literary pro- duction of the educated, and the orders of the powerful. Artisans, tradesmen, and women composed themselves a few of the books they read.* To be sure, some such persons had in the fourteenth and fifteenth centuries quietly authored manuscripts – of craft secrets, of mechanical inventions, of poems. But the authors had failed to become widely known and, with the exception of outstanding figures like the literary Christine de Pisan, their works were not reproduced later by the presses.

But now many individuals without the ordinary attributes expected of an author in the later Middle Ages get their books printed – and they have an audience. Their tone might range from the confident ('I've tested sundials for a long time') to the apologetic ('Excuse my unadorned language . . . I am not Latin'), but they are sure that their skills, observations, or sentiments give them something distinctive to say. Like the learned writer, they imagine varied publics for their work: their own kind and those on a higher level. Like the learned writer, they present themselves to the unknown buyers of their books in proud author portraits quite different from the humble donor pic- ture characteristic of the medieval manuscript. Thus Milles de Norry, previously a modest reckonmaster in Lyon, gazes from his 1574 commercial arithmetic, fitted out with a ruff and a Greek device.[38]

This widening of the circle of authors had diverse causes besides printing, but it was given some permanence by the new form of publication. Now practicing apothecaries get into print, like Pierre Braillier of Lyon, who dared to attack *The Abuses of Ignorance of Physicians*, and Nicolas Houel of Paris, who encroached on the physicians' field by writing on the plague and who published a treatise on poor relief as well. Now surgeons write on their art and even on medicine (and we must remember that they are still considered *gens mécaniques* in the sixteenth century, despite the gains of some of them in learning, status, and wealth). Ambrose Paré's first book appears in 1545, when he is a mere army surgeon and master at the Hôtel-Dieu in Paris; and at

*Anonymous city lore and song, like peasant sayings, found their way into print, as did innumerable stories and poems in which artisans and servants were the actors (such as *Le caquet de bonnes Chambrieres, declarant aucunes finesses dont elles usent vers leurs maistres et maistresses*, printed at Lyon about 1549). The authorship of such material and its relation to actual popular life and sources are such complex problems that we cannot consider them here.

least nineteen other surgeons have vernacular texts printed from the 1540s through the 1580s. Sailors publish accounts of their travels to the New World. Poems come out from a cartwright in the Guyenne, a wine merchant in Toulouse, and a trader in Béthune, the last including a 'Hymn to Commerce'.

The most self-conscious artisan–author, however, was the potter Bernard Palissy. To the readers of his important dialogues on chemistry and agriculture he says that some will think it impossible that 'a poor artisan . . . destitute of Latin' could be right and ancient learned theorists wrong. But experience is worth more than theory. If you don't believe what my books say, get my address from the printer and I will give you a demonstration in my own study. What we see here is not merely fresh communication between craftsman and scholar (much discussed by historians of science), and between practice and theory (the participants in Palissy's dialogues); we see also a new kind of relation between an author and his anonymous public.*

Another entrant into the ranks of authors was, of course, the self-educated scholar-printer. Elizabeth Eisenstein has rightly stressed the novelty of this figure, who combined intellectual, physical, and administrative forms of labor.[39] Indeed, it was not only men like Badius, the Estiennes, Gryphius, and the de Tournes who had such a creative role; lesser masters and even journeymen could shape the content of the books they printed. Sometimes their names are appended to prefaces; sometimes, as with the proof-reader Nicolas Dumont, it is only by luck that we catch a glimpse of their work as authors. A native of Saumur, Dumont was so busy preparing and correcting copy in Paris in the years 1569 to 1584 'that he scarcely had time to breathe'. Yet he sometimes got hold of a press and printed pamphlets, he translated

*This formal invitation from the author for direct response from readers is found in other printed books as well. It is the product of a situation in which the author expects that a large number of unknown readers will be seeing his work in the near future and will be able to locate him easily. (It goes well beyond the practice of the medieval author who, as John Benton has informed me, either urged his readers to write improvements on the manuscript or – more likely – anathemized readers and scribes who tampered with his text, but who did not invite correspondence.) Robert I Estienne asked readers of his *Dictionnaire Francoislatin* to send him any works he might have omitted that they found in Latin authors and 'good French authors', as well as to correct any faults they found in his definitions of hunting terms (Paris: Robert I Estienne, 1549, '*Au lecteur*' and p. 664). Both the physician Laurent Joubert and the bibliophile François de La Croix du Maine asked for information from their readers, as we will see below. Authors may also have received unsolicited letters: Ambrose Paré asked young surgeons using his *Oeuvres* (1575) to let him know graciously of any faults they might find rather than slander him. The reckonmaster Valentin Mennher did not especially want to hear from readers about the mistakes in his arithmetic texts: 'Please just make corrections on the page rather than by useless words.' The errors in a 1555 Lyon edition of his work were the printer's fault, not his (*Arithmetique Seconde par M. Valentin Mennher de Kempten* [Antwerp, Jean Loc, 1556], f. Z viii^r).

various works from Latin to French; and, in particular, he composed little news stories about Henri III's doings in France and Poland, the seizure of Tunis from the Turks, and other current happenings. Whether he presented his stories as 'letters' from unnamed gentlemen observers or as anonymous eyewitness accounts, Dumont in many ways anticipated the reporter of the periodical press.

Female writers also appeared in print in noticeable numbers – more than twenty had some reputation. Mostly they came from families of gentlemen or lawyers, were involved in humanist circles, and published poems or translations. Their works still show signs of womanly modesty: they are dedicated to other women ('because women must not willingly appear in public alone, I choose you for my guide'); they address themselves to 'female readers'; they defend themselves against the reproach that silence is the ornament of women. A few of them transformed the image of the author even more: Louise Labé, the ropemaker's daughter, whose appeal to women to publish we heard at the opening of this essay (and contemporary evidence indicates that many well-born women did shyly keep their poems in manuscript); Nicole Estienne, printer's daughter and physician's wife, whose verses on 'The Miseries of the Married Woman' had two editions; and the midwife Louise Bourgeois. Once midwife to the poor of her Paris neighborhood, later midwife to the family of Henri IV, Bourgeois wrote on her art, believing herself the first woman to do so. Her wide practice, she claimed, would show up the mistakes of Physicians and Surgeons, even of Master Galen himself. She looks out with poise from her engraving at the reader, this skilled woman who corrected men, publicly and in print.

Finally, groups among the *menu peuple* sometimes spoke to the public collectively through the press. The *compagnonnages* of the journeymen of Lyon and Paris, as we have seen, printed the brief that they presented to the Parlement of Paris in 1572. This document raised a dozen objections to a royal edict on printing and attacked the journeymen's employers as tyrannical and avaricious oppressors, who worked them to poverty and illness. Their employers answered, also in print, that the journeymen were debauched conspiratorial 'monopolists', trying to reduce their masters to servitude and destroy the industry. A printed protest was used again in Lyon in 1588, when master printers and journeymen were on the same side against the merchant-publishers, who were ignoring them in favor of the cheaper labor of Geneva. Here are precocious examples of artisans trying to influence literate public opinion in a labor dispute.

Groups also tried on occasion to influence public opinion in regard to political matters. Here I am thinking of the urban Abbeys of Misrule, festive societies of neighborhood or craft, which directed their charivaris and mockery not only against domestic scandals but against misgovernment by their betters. For a long time, the Abbeys had left their recreations unrecorded; but in the sixteenth century they began to print them. Thus readers outside Rouen could learn about the 1540 Mardi Gras parade at that city — with its float bearing a king, the pope, the emperor, and a fool playing catch with the globe — and could ponder its mocking verses about hypocrisy in the church, about how faith was turning to contempt (*foy* to *fy*) and nobility to injury (*noblesse* to *on blesse*). In the Lyon festivals of the 1570s through the 1590s, the Lord of Misprint tossed printed verses to the spectators and subsequently published the scenarios, with their complaints about the high cost of bread and paper, about the fluctuations in the value of currency, and especially about the folly of war in France.

This body of pamphlet literature, small and ephemeral though it is, suggests two interesting things about the relation of printing to the development of political consciousness. First, though most early polemical literature disseminated outward and downward the political and religious views of persons at the center (whether at the center of royal government or at the center of strong resistance movements like the Huguenots and the Holy Catholic League), it occurred to some city people on the margins of power to use the press to respond. Second, the addition of printed pamphlets to traditional methods for spreading news (rumor, street song, private letters, town criers, fireworks displays, bell-ringing, and penitential processions) increased the *menu peuple*'s stock of detailed information about national events. In the 1540s, the Rouen festive society could count on spectators and readers knowing the facts of local political life, but references to national or European events were usually general and even allegorical. By the end of the century in Lyon, however, the Lord of Misprint could expect that his audience would also recognize joking references to recent sumptuary legislation and to controversial decisions of the Parlement of Paris.

Readers may be thinking that these varied works authored by the *menu peuple* were such a tiny fraction of the total printed corpus of sixteenth-century France that no educated contemporary would have paid attention to them. In fact they were noticed, favorably and unfavorably. The visionary bibliographer François de La Croix du Maine, who built up a library of thousands of volumes and who sent out printed requests all over Europe for information about authors, was happy to include most of the people and books we have been considering here in his *Bibliotheque* of 1584.* He made

---

*Thus among sixteenth-century authors either writing in French or translating into French, La Croix listed 110 physicians, but also 25 surgeons (22 of whom had works in print) and nine apothecaries (eight with works in print). He included 40 female writers from the end of the fifteenth century to 1584 (at least sixteen had works in print, as far as he knew); Christine de Pisan, composing her *City of Ladies* around 1405, seems to have been aware of no other contemporary female authors.

In 1579 at Le Mans, La Croix had 350 copies printed of the initial statement of his project, including his request for information about or from

no critical exclusions: Nicole Estienne and Nicolas Dumont are set in their alphabetical places just as are Pierre de Ronsard and Joachim du Bellay in his 'general catalogue' of all authors, 'women as well as men, who had written in our maternal French'.

We also have a reaction from a humanist and poet deeply concerned about the character of French culture. As a member of the Pléiade, Jacques Peletier had devoted himself to the vernacular tongue and had also celebrated the printing press:

> Ah . . . one can print in one day
> What it would take thirty days to say
> And a hundred times longer to write by hand.

High quality in vernacular publication would be guaranteed, so he had argued hopefully, by right and clear Method — right method for ordering poetry, mathematics, medicine, music, even spelling. But what would happen now that all kinds of people were publishing books? In an ironic anonymous essay, he urged every village, every curate, every trader, every captain to write his piece; every parish, every vineyard must have its historian. *'Ecrivons tous, sçavans et non sçavans!'* And if we do badly? Well, never mind. Our books can be used by the ladies who sell toilet paper at the Paris bridges.

How indeed could the learned control not only aesthetic quality but also true doctrine and science if just anyone could get books printed, and if these books were being made available by the press in the vernacular to large numbers of ill-educated city people? The central book in the religious debate was, of course, the vernacular Bible, and for several decades the doctors of theology (strongly backed by secular law) tried to defend their monopoly on its interpretation by denying the right of the uneducated to read it. The debate was sometimes face to face, between doctor of theology and craftsman: 'Do you think it's up to you to read the Bible,' asked the Inquisitor in a Lyon prison in 1552, 'since you're just an artisan and without knowledge?' 'God taught me by His Holy Spirit', said the craftsman. 'It belongs to all Christians to know it in order to learn the way to salvation.'[40]

The debate also took place in print. 'God does not want to declare his secrets to a bunch of *menu peuple*', said the great Jesuit Emond Auger. 'Intoxicated by I know not what phrases from the Apostles, badly quoted and even worse understood, they start to abuse the Mass and make up questions.' Understanding comes not from 'a bare and vulgar knowledge of the words', but from the special vocation of those who have studied.[41] A young Protestant pastor answered: the pope and his doctors of theology forbid the

authors. He received six answers. He repeated the request in the 1584 edition of the *Bibliotheque*, this time remembering to suggest ways in which mail might reach him at Paris (*Premier volume de la Bibliotheque du sieur de la Croix-du-Maine* [Paris: Abel l'Angelier, 1584], *'Preface aux lecteurs'* and pp. 523, 529, 538–9).

Bible to everyone but themselves, because they know that once their lives and doctrine are examined by the Word of God, they will have to give their goods to the poor and start working with their hands. They permit a poor craftsman to read a book on love or folly, to dance or play cards, but they see him with a New Testament in his hands and he is a heretic. But our Lord has commanded us 'Search the Scriptures.' And the early Fathers exhorted the people – craftsmen, women, and everybody in general – to read it in their houses and often, and especially before going to sermons so they could understand them. The pastor ends up reminding his readers that reading *alone* was not the path to true doctrine. The Protestant method for guaranteeing orthodoxy was in the last instance censorship and punishment; but in the first instance it was *the combination of reading with listening to a trained teacher.*

Ultimately, despite the triumphs of the Counter-Reformation in France, the doctors of theology had to abandon their position, in fact if not always in public. Force simply would not work. What had guaranteed the clerical monopoly two hundred years before had really been a limited technology and the Latin language. Already at the end of the fourteenth century, vernacular Bibles, Biblical digests, and picture books were being used by lay families here and there. Once the first presses were installed in France, the stream of French Bibles and Bible versions began without waiting for the Reformation. No legislation, no inquisition, no procedures of censorship could stop the new relations between reading, listening, and talking that had grown up among city people – relations which Catholic humanists as well as Protestants had been ready to encourage. After the 1570s, it became legal for a French Bible – a Catholic revision of the Genevan Scripture approved by the Theology Faculty of Louvain – to circulate in France. In cheap, small format, the New Testament had some success among Catholic laymen in the cities.[42]

What was needed to maintain Catholic orthodoxy was a mode of control more suited to printing than an archaic form of sacerdotal monopoly and more effective than censorship. In 1524, a Franciscan religious who was translating and commenting a Book of Hours for a circle of noblewomen pointed the way. Everyone is admitted to preaching, no matter how unlearned, said Brother Gilles; need seeing words be more dangerous than hearing them? The answer was to make the bare text safe by clothing it with orthodox exposition. The Jesuits were to go on and fix the meaning of a devotional text by an accompanying standardized religious picture or emblem. By 1561 in Lyon, the Jesuit Possevino paid for the printing of orthodox little booklets and distributed them free in the streets. By the late sixteenth century, the Catholic laity had a growing body of spiritual literature *in which the eye was guided by exposition and illustration.*

A similar though less intense debate occurred over the dissemination of medical information to laymen. Vernacular *Regimens against the Plague* and collections of remedies for ill health and women's disorders were old genres;

printing did no more than increase their numbers. In the 1530s, however, doctors of medicine began to publish translations of Greek medical texts and of Doctor Guy de Chauliac's fourteenth-century Latin treatise on surgery, as well as systematic examinations of medicine and surgery in French for the specific use of surgeons' journeymen, 'who have begged us to do it', 'whose ignorance must be dispelled', and 'who are today more studious than many physicians'. These books were used by the young surgeons who attended occasional lectures and dissections given by physicians at the Hôtel-Dieu at Lyon, special courses at the Faculty of Medicine at Montpellier, and the classes supported by the surgeons' confraternity of Saint-Côme at Paris; they were used also by older surgeons in the cities who wanted to improve their skill.[43] The next step was the publication by doctors of medicine of new regimens of health and medical advice on child-rearing in the vernacular, very often dedicated to women.

The arguments used in defense of these editions, offered by Catholic humanists and Protestants alike, resemble those used in defense of vernacular Bibles and doctrinal literature. As printers pointed out that Saint Jerome had translated the Bible into a vernacular, so the physician Vallembert pointed out in his 1565 pediatric manual that Galen and Avicenna had written in their vernacular. An English medical popularizer spoke against his critics in the very terms that the early Protestant Antoine de Marcourt had used against the engrossing 'merchants' of the Faculty of Theology: 'Why grutch [grudge] they phisike to come forth in Englysche? Wolde they have no man to know but onley they? Or what make they themselves? Marchauntes of our lyves and deathes, that we shulde bye our healthe onely of them, and at theyr pryces?' A French work by the Protestant Laurent Joubert makes the comparison explicit: those doctors of medicine who say that it is wrong to teach people how to maintain their health are no better than doctors of theology who deprive them of spiritual food. To those who objected to instructing surgeons in French, Joubert's son answered that good operations could be performed in any language and that misunderstanding of a Latin text was as possible as misunderstanding of a French one ('should we burn all Latin books because of the danger that some clerk will misinterpret the law therein?'). And anyway, if we are willing to read books aloud to surgeons' journeymen, why not put them in French? 'Must we put a lower value on the living voice than on the written paper?'

Laurent Joubert's volumes are especially useful for a study of the new relations between groups of people and between cultural traditions facilitated by printing. For twenty-five years he had been trying to stamp out false opinions in medicine, and in 1578 he decided to compile a new kind of book — *Erreurs Populaires* about health and medicine from conception to grave that he would collect and correct. 'Popular errors' came from several sources, he explained: from weaknesses in the soul and human reasoning; from ignorant oral traditions, especially those of midwives; and from people's having heard too much from physicians and having a crude understanding of it. It seems to me, however, that as the sense of the errors in peasant lore was sharpened for the learned by the printing of that lore (as we have seen above), so the printing of all kinds of vulgar regimens, traditional books of secrets, and remedies created for Joubert the concept of general errors and made them accessible to correction.

In any case, in Volume One he got through conception and infancy, demonstrating, for instance, that it was *not* true that male children were born at full moon and female children at new moon and that it *was* true that at certain times of night or monthly period one could be sure of conceiving a male. He then told his readers that he would wait to publish Volume Two until they had had a chance to send him more popular errors. They could just address him at the University of Montpellier, where he was Chancellor of the Faculty of Medicine. Dr Joubert received 456 sayings and queries from readers within a year, which he duly published and, where possible, corrected or explained in Volume Two.

Joubert's *Popular Errors* illustrates the central paradox in the impact of printing on the people. On the one hand, it can destroy traditional monopolies on knowledge and authorship and can sell and disseminate widely both information and works of imagination. It can even set up a new two-way relationship between author and anonymous audience. But printing can also make possible the establishment of new kinds of control on popular thought. To quote once more the physician and translator Pierre Tolet, 'If you want a servant to follow your orders, you can't give them in an unknown tongue.' Joubert's goal and that of the other popularizers was not to eliminate the distinction between expert and inexpert or to weaken the profession of medicine. It was to raise the surgeons from their 'routine illiterate practice' while defining their field to keep even the most skillful of them under the authority of the physicians. It was to raise the people to a better understanding of how to take care of themselves while convincing them more effectively to obey the doctor's orders.

On the whole, it seems to me that the first 125 years of printing in France, which brought little change in the countryside, strengthened rather than sapped the vitality of the culture of the *menu peuple* in the cities — that is, added both to their realism and to the richness of their dreams, both to their self-respect and to their ability to criticize themselves and others. This is because they were not passive recipients (neither passive beneficiaries nor passive victims) or a new type of communication. Rather they were active users and interpreters of the printed books they heard and read, and even helped give these books form. Richard Hoggart, in his remarkable study of working-class culture in present-day England (*The Uses of Literacy*) has found a salty, particularistic, resourceful layer of culture existing along with a 'candy-floss', slack, uniform one. If this is possible in the twentieth century, with its powerful and highly competitive mass media and centralized political institutions, all the more readily could the sixteenth-century populace impose its uses on the books that came to it. Oral culture and popular social organization were strong enough to resist mere correction and standardization from above. Protestantism and certain features of humanism converged with printing to challenge traditional hierarchical values and to delay the establishment of rigid new ones. Economic control of publishing was not concentrated in the houses of great merchant—publishers, but was shared by a variety of producers. Monopolies in knowledge had broken down but had not been replaced by effective political and religious censorship and by the theory and laws of private property in ideas.

If in a different context printing may lead the people to flaccidity, escape, and the ephemeral, in the sixteenth century the printers' journeymen could claim with some reason that printing was 'the eternal brush which gave a living portrait to the spirit'.

5 TECHNIQUES OF INDOCTRINATION:
THE GERMAN REFORMATION*

Gerald Strauss

To speak of a 'widened gap between literate and oral cultures', as recent students of the social impact of printing have done,[1] is to exaggerate. If there were two cultures, they interpenetrated so deeply and at so many points that neither could have flourished independently. This is not to deny that graduates of institutions of learning differentiated themselves from their 'non-learned' countrymen. Indeed, I will argue later that this separation, insofar as it sets clerics and churchmen apart from their flocks, is a factor in the Reformation's failure to make good its pedagogical promise. But the distinction between the learned and the laity was a function more of the offices to which formal education gave admittance than of education itself. It was certainly not a product of literacy, which in any case was by all appearances much more widespread among the broad population than has usually been recognized.

Literacy touches the subject of Reformation pedagogy at many critical points and raises questions of great interest to historians of early modern Europe. The relationship between the Protestant Reformation and the extension of reading has intrigued scholars for a long time. It was also of concern to the reformers themselves, who saw it as a difficult and problematic issue. Clearly, they encouraged reading among their followers, favoring – in principle at least – the spread of literacy to the whole population.[2] But in the aftermath of the events of the 1520s and 1530s reformers experienced some misgivings about the wisdom of a massive application of this principle. Expansion of vernacular education appeared to be starving serious learning of its recruits, while independent Bible reading was coming under suspicion for nourishing the seeds of an uncontrollable sectarianism. These doubts were never completely laid to rest. Throughout the century they surfaced at moments of stress and anxiety. With the adoption of the catechism as a corrective to religious instability, however, and with revitalized gymnasiums and seminaries promising a reliable supply of trained pastors, literacy became a safe policy to pursue. Magistrates and rulers had their own reasons for encouraging this trend,[3] and in response to the shift in their attitude elementary

*Reprinted from *Luther's House of Learning: Indoctrination of the Young in the German Reformation* by Gerald Strauss, 193–202, by permission of the publisher, The Johns Hopkins University Press, © 1978, by The Johns Hopkins University Press.

schools proliferated in the second half of the sixteenth century, as has been seen.

The educational laws of the Lutheran Reformation gave concrete expression to official intentions of propagating literacy. In Saxony, for example, the school ordinance of 1580 stipulated that even in the smallest and poorest villages, where the people were too hard-pressed to instruct their own children, too poor to hire a teacher, and too thin on the ground to support a Latin school, a sexton ought to be available to teach reading and writing 'because children of working people [*arbeitender leute Kinder*] should, for the sake of their own and our common welfare, receive in their early youth instruction in prayers, catechism, and writing and reading'. In the duchy of Lauenburg, also in 1580, visitors admonished country people to 'keep their children in school so that they will learn to read and write'. Householders — as has been shown in an earlier chapter — were expected to preside over Bible readings, and although it was acknowledged that not every *Hausvater* and *Hausmutter* could perform this duty, the assumption was always that they ought to be able to do it. Indeed, literacy seems to have been regarded as a normative, certainly as a desirable, skill. Those who lacked it could turn to teach-yourself books, whose titles explain both their purpose and the nature of their appeal: Jakob Griessbeutel's *A Most Useful Book of Sounds, Illustrated with Figures Giving the True Sound of Each Letter and Syllable, from Which Young Men, Husbands and Wives and Other Adults, Also Children, Women as Well as Men, Can Easily Learn to Read in as Little as 24 Hours*; Valentin Ickelsamer's *A Correct and Quick Way to Learn Reading* and *A German Grammar from Which Every Man Can Teach Himself to Read* . . . ; or Peter Jordan's *The Layman's School: An Easy and Quick Method for Learning to Write and Read. With a Technique for Instructing the Hard-of-Learning and Dull-Witted without the Use of Letters, but through Figures and Characters Attractive to Look at and Easy to Remember*. 'Such books,' writes Jordan, 'are used everywhere. Each year a new title appears on the market.' With some initial help from a practiced reader (even a child would do) an interested layman could now achieve functional literacy by himself. Ickelsamer, the favorite among these popular 'grammarians', advocated the phonetic method as the best approach to teaching adults. Teach the alphabet from the sound of the word, he said, not vice versa. 'Take the name Hans,' he explained; 'You have four sound changes in this word, which are represented by four letters. First, you hear a strong exhaling noise, as when someone heaves a deep sigh. This is the H, which you breathe into the vowel A. Following this there is a sound through the nose and finally you hear a sibilant like the hissing of a snake.' For the next step, Ickelsamer continues, imagine a picture to associate each of these sounds with a written letter. Let us say that you want to read the word *Mertz* (*März*, March). First note the four sound changes, then think of an animal or object vividly representing each of these sounds. Draw a cow over the moo-sound M, over the goat sound E put a goat, a dog over the growl R, and finally a bird over the sparrow cry Tz. Nothing could be easier or more entertaining.

There is much evidence that a strong interest at the grass roots supported the attempt to raise literacy. Whenever a government moved to curtail or abolish a vernacular school, either for the sake of economy or in order to protect the Latin curriculum, it met stubborn opposition from the affected community. The municipality of Heidenheim in the duchy of Württemberg is a case in point. Its town fathers engaged their prince in a heated correspondence in the mid-1560s over the closing of the German school in their borough. 'Our young people,' they wrote to Duke Christoph, 'most of whom have no aptitude for Latin and are growing up to be artisans, are better served by a German teacher than a Latin master, for they need to learn writing and reading, which is of great help to them in their work and livelihood.' They did not like the alternative of a new Latin school, where all boys would learn to read, and a few would stay on to become scholars. Their interests were practical, and reading and writing was their foremost concern, 'for these skills,' they maintained, 'do honor to God and promote trade and an honorable walk of life'. When the Bavarian government proposed the closing of German schools in the duchy's villages, the territorial estates objected, saying that 'not all peasant children want to be like their parents . . . and whoever can't read or write his mother tongue is little more than a dead person'.

Literacy was coming to be recognized as an indispensable skill for every occupation tied to commerce and exchange. 'Our burghers here,' reported the pastor of a town in Württemberg, where the German school had closed down, 'deem it their greatest complaint that their sons have been deprived of the opportunity to learn writing, reading, and reckoning before they are apprenticed to the trades.' When asked how a smallish city like Coburg could support three vernacular schools in the 1560s, a local official explained, 'because we have so many artisans, journeymen, and vine dressers here'. Apart from the utility of literacy, there was, of course, the pleasure to be derived from reading. Printed books made quick converts. 'My father,' wrote Hermann von Weinsberg, the advocate and politician of Cologne, 'although a layman, went to school to the age of twelve and, having learned to write, read, and reckon, he developed such a taste for . . . books that he spent all his time studying them, telling the rest of us at table every day of the things he had learned. And he never ceased to marvel at the riches contained in books . . . Indeed, he often praised book reading as a source of useful and helpful knowledge to men.' This is not an isolated story. If most men made slower progress than the elder Weinsberg, who advanced from ABC and primer to Livy and Herodotus (in German translation, of course), few lacked the opportunity to acquire a serviceable command of the written language.

A religious motive was rarely given for the wish to become literate, but

Protestant churchmen declared reading to be a normative obligation on all Christians. 'Attend to reading, preaching, and teaching', the authors of the school of Mecklenburg quoted from 1 Tim. 4:13 (somewhat out of context), adding, lest the point be missed, 'in saying this, Paul has intentionally put reading in first place'. Authors of books of self-instruction also believed that by teaching people to read they were helping to prepare them for the word of God. 'Now that the Bible has been printed in German,' wrote Johann Kolross in introducing his *Manual of German Orthography* in 1530, 'all the artisans and housemaids, though working all day in the sweat of their brows, want to spend their evenings pondering the word of God.' The observation may not be entirely accurate, but its motive was genuine. 'Only a few rare spirits achieve enlightenment without reading', said Ortholph Fuchssperger in his *Art of Reading* in 1542. 'Most of us depend on books for what we need to learn about our duties toward God and our fellowmen.' 'I was moved [to write this book]' Valentin Ickelsamer explained in the preface to his *German Grammar* of 1534, 'not only because I know that reading brings much pleasure to those who have mastered it, but also because this skill is a splendid divine gift, which we should use to honor God by reading, singing and writing. Never before has the art of reading been so beneficial,' he added, 'as in our day, when each man by himself can know and judge the word of God.' (Ickelsamer, it is pertinent to interject, had been a partisan of Karlstadt's in the early 1520s.) He suspected that a corrupt world would ultimately prove unworthy of this divine gift. But to the few true Christians among the host of sinners it would, he thought, bring great spiritual profit. Ickelsamer did not fail to list some mundane advantages as well. 'Everybody nowadays wants to be adept at a skill with which one discovers, understands, and remembers everything in the world and can communicate it to others, no matter how far away they are.' His book, he contends, can prepare anyone to be ready within a few days to read and write. He himself had taught people to read in as little as a week; in fact, he says, it can even be done overnight. A promotional interest is certainly not absent from these claims. On the other hand, it is true that, given the incentive to learn, some leisure time, and a bit of help at the start, no one needed to remain illiterate.

But adults were not the main concern of the Reformation pedagogues who had attached their hopes to future generations. Turning the young into qualified readers was clearly a problem of schooling. As has been shown, vernacular schools sprang up nearly everywhere in the course of the sixteenth century. Strassburg had nine elementary schools for boys and six for girls in 1535. In Hamburg each parish had not only a school for boys, but also one where girls learned 'reading, writing, sewing, and the fear of God, good manners and honorable conduct'. In other German cities — Catholic as well as Protestant — the situation was similar. A visitation in Munich in 1560 showed that every parish had an elementary school.

For small towns, villages, and hamlets, the evidence is spottier, but the conclusion seems warranted that most rural people had access to elementary schooling (though they did not necessarily avail themselves of it). The school situation in Württemberg was described in an earlier chapter; abundant visitation documents in the Stuttgart archives suggest that every town and every large village (*Flecken*), as well as a preponderance of the smaller villages, had, from the 1550s onward, a vernacular school where, no matter how unsatisfactory its physical condition, reading, writing, and catechism were taught to as many children as parents saw fit to send. The same can be said of the principality of Coburg, as shown by notations in the Coburg visitation documents in the 1570s: 'small school here, children learning to read and pray, hard-working schoolmaster'; 'pious sexton, does his best in reading and writing with the children'; 'tiny school, reading only, difficult to get a teacher to stay here'; 'teacher not very competent, only catechism and German hymns'; 'schoolmaster here is an artisan, hard-working, has 4—5 pupils in wintertime, teaches reading and praying'. When the Upper Palatinate was visited in 1579 and 1580, the inspectors found that more than three-quarters of the territory's *Flecken* and villages had some kind of school (many of them poorly attended, however). In the Electorate of Saxony, village schools were common by the 1570s, as the protocols in the archives of Dresden and Weimar demonstrate. But the same sources show also that numerous communities were still without teachers in 1590, and that many schools survived precariously, attended only occasionally by half a dozen peasant children and taught by an overworked and underpaid sexton ('a poor old man', 'a hard-working but unlearned man') or a rural artisan ('a poor day laborer', 'a poor bookbinder' or linen weaver, cooper, printer, or carpenter).

On close inspection of the documents it appears that the fate of a village school, and the number of pupils it attracted, were functions less of the support of territorial rulers or magistrates than of the concern with education, or lack of it, of the local elite: village elders, jurors, church deacons. Where these worthies valued book learning, where they could persuade or browbeat their neighbors to pay for it, and where their own children acted as examples to the rest, a school usually survived. Governments played their part, of course: prodding, dangling the promise of financial help before an eager or a reluctant commune, occasionally granting a subsidy. But local interest was of the essence, and the visitation protocols tell us where it existed and where not.

Needless to say, economic and social conditions had much to do with the response villagers made to schools. 'People here are unwilling to send their barefoot children to the school in Grossenbuch during the winter months', states a Saxon protocol; 'the cold, snow, and storms are so severe that no one would chase a dog over the raging brooks and narrow planks'. If a little money could be squeezed from the public treasury, such an isolated community might set up its own subsidiary school (*Nebenschule*) to spare children the long trip to the parish village, where the *Hauptschule* was situated. Many of these tiny ABC and catechism schools had a mere handful of pupils: 'Sachsenburg: few inhabitants, school has only three or four boys, but they are all learning their prayers and the ABC.' Sextons did the teaching where no schoolmaster could be hired.

Governments set the procedures used in teaching reading and writing in German-speaking schools. These rules had not changed since antiquity and were not much influenced by the theories of advocates of 'method' in education. Moving from the simple to the complex, from parts to the whole, ABC learning started the pupil on letters (learned by name and sound), advanced him to syllables, then to words, eventually to sentences, from there straight to the German catechism. Compared with this 'synthetic' system, the phonetic, or analytic, method advocated by Ickelsamer seemed natural and fast-moving, but it did not make its way into the schools, where tradition reigned with its reliance on slow, repetitious, cumulative, habit-forming drill. Under this system it took a six-year-old child one to two years to learn to read, provided, said Neander, he was not rushed but was allowed to progress slowly and methodically at his own pace.

Although unattractive on psychological grounds, the synthetic system probably worked as well as any. Its proponents, at any rate, were enthusiastic about it, and even its detractors could criticize only its demands on the child's memory and attention span. The following example shows how one teacher, Hans Fabritius, author of a manual on his craft, conducted his elementary reading lesson:

> *Master:* My dear pupil, say after me: a.e.i.o.u.
> *Pupil:* I can do this already. *M.* Tell me, then, which is the a among these vowels? *P.* Is that what they are called, vowels? *M.* Yes, they are called vowels. You cannot write a word without the use of one. That's why we must learn them especially well. *P.* Write them out for me, please. *M.* Here they are: i.u.a.e.o. Now say them. *P.* I.u.a.e.o. *M.* And now in reverse order. *P.* O.e.a.u.i. *M.* Do you think you will remember and recognize them from now on? *P.* Yes, surely I shall.

And so on to consonants. In Augsburg (according to a *ratio docendi* submitted by one schoolmaster to the magistrates) the scene looked as follows: 'Prayers finished, the youngest boys stand before a board on which the letters of the alphabet are written. One letter after another is read out to them and its shape explained. For example: O is like a ring, a short stroke with a little dot on top is an i, and so forth. This is kept up until all the children have learned the letters', after which they attempted simple words, written out in spaced syllables, before going on to Luther's Shorter Catechism. Critics occasionally scoffed at so mechanical a routine and pointed to the distorted sense children were apt to gain from intoning 'Him—Him—el—el: Himmel, Christ—Christ—

us—us: Christus.' But the old procedure remained inviolate. 'If the word is a long one, let the boys say the first syllable twice; otherwise they will forget it before reaching the end of the word.' In Saxony, in 1580, according to the school ordinance,

> When young boys first come to school, give them a copy of the ABC booklet specially printed with Dr. Luther's catechism. Don't press them too hard at first, but be sure that they repeat all the letters from the beginning every time they learn a new one. To discover how well they remember them, have them occasionally name a letter outside the regular order, from the middle or near the end of the alphabet. When you are certain they have mastered the alphabet, teach them the syllables, using the Lord's prayer as your text. All this time pay close attention to their pronunciation, and do not allow the boys to slur or drawl their vowels and consonants in the manner of their natural speech, but make them separate and distinguish the sounds clearly from one another, as is done in Latin diction.

The rest was drill: 'What is the first letter in *pater*? It's a p. Show me the p in the alphabet. What comes after the p? An a. Show me the a.' And so on.

What do these facts suggest about the literacy of the general population? And what is the evidence for my contention that reading and writing were more widespread among the common folk of early modern Germany than has been thought? Let it be admitted at once that the evidence is circumstantial. Students of the incidence of literacy in traditional societies have usually resorted to counting signatures given in circumstances that allow them to relate signers to their social origins, and then quantify the results.[4] Such data exist for Germany too. The so-called Fraternal Book (*Bruderschaftsbuch*) of the city of Frankfurt am Main, for example, holds for the years 1417 to 1524 hundreds of signatures of artisans from all parts of Germany. Another quantifiable, albeit secondhand, indicator is the large number of entries in Frankfurt's citizen registers (*Bürgerbücher*), where the names of applicants for lower municipal offices in the fifteenth and sixteenth centuries bear in nearly every instance the note 'can read and write'. Most of my exhibits, however, are of the kind usually disparaged as 'impressionistic' or 'literary' — in other words they are indirect. None will by itself, nor will they all together, constitute a demonstration. I offer them here for what they are worth.[5]

The strongest argument is the distinct sense one gains from the sources that by the middle of the sixteenth century literacy was taken for granted in the elevated ranks of society, regarded as normal among artisans, and noted without astonishment in the peasantry. One can take the heroes and heroines of Jörg Wickram's courtly novels (written in the 1530s, 1540s and 1550s) as an initial example. They are prolific letter writers, all of them, and Wickram evidently thought it unnecessary to explain or justify their writing skill. This is no less true of the burgher novels, where nearly everyone reads and writes. Wickram's popularity, and that of the half-dozen or so writers who equaled his contemporary fame as a storyteller, is itself a comment on reading ability in urban circles.[6] But books and pamphlets were found in the homes of the lowly as well. The learned peasant encountered by Wickram's pilgrim errant[7] could not, despite obvious exaggeration, have struck his readers as an absurdly implausible character without stripping the poem of its chief didactic point. That there was reading in rural cottages is known also from more immediate sources. Investigations in Bavaria during the reigns of Albrecht V and Wilhelm V brought to light a large number of materials lumped together as 'wicked sectarian and seditious Bibles, postils, prayer books, scurrilous pamphlets, and tracts, translated into German and put into print', along with the discovery that a considerable portion of the population 'in towns and larger villages [*Städte und Märkte*]' could read these books. The Bavarian authorities say explicitly that this group included 'common burghers' (*gemeine bürger*), artisans, 'ordinary men' (*der gemein man*), as well as peasants. When the government instructed officials in the Munich district to 'visit [i.e., inspect and report on] the homes of all those peasants who can write and read and possess written or printed books', it must have known that the search would not be for a needle in a haystack.

While evidence of this kind has no statistical force, it does help provide a context in which to interpret more ambiguous pieces of information. For instance, pastors in Albertine Saxony were instructed in 1555 to make an annual house inspection in the sparsely populated outlying villages of their respective parishes 'and subject those inhabitants who cannot read [*so nit lesen können*] and who are unknown to him to a catechism examination'. I take this as an indication that literacy was, to say the least, not uncommon among the Saxon peasantry. There is, of course, evidence on the other side as well. The preface to Ambrosius Moibanus's catechism of 1534 refers to the continued need for preachers 'in this age of printing, when books can be read at home, but not by those who do not know how to read at all, and these are always the greater part. Books benefit the minority', Moibanus continues, 'and we need preachers and teachers to serve the majority who cannot read'. Another example of counterevidence comes from a prosperous region in Württemberg, where visitors reported at the end of the sixteenth century that although the district had 'many substantial villages and farms, few people in them can write and read'. At about the same time the *Geistliche Rat*, the highest ecclesiastical authority in Bavaria, reported to the duke that catechism instruction in the diocese of Friesing was proceeding very slowly because 'our subjects there can neither read nor write'. If these statements are true as they stand, they seem to represent atypical situations. Of course the larger the town and the better off its citizens, the greater the inducements to literacy. *Winkelschulen* – unlicensed private schools where only utilitarian skills were taught and the time-consuming burdens of catechism drill and hymn-singing were held to a minimum — flourished in many of the larger towns despite determined attempts to suppress them. The stubborn support burghers gave to these schools is strong evidence for the interest of townspeople in gaining and preserving the skill of letters.

The direct connection between literacy and elementary schooling is, at any rate, no longer a matter for debate.[8] Sixteenth-century governments were convinced of this link. Since the proliferation of vernacular elementary schools is a documented fact, it can, I think, be taken that literacy increased commensurately. Of course there are reasons to hedge this assertion with caveats. School attendance was a serious problem, particularly in the countryside. Nonetheless, one who has spent much time with the sources cannot suppress the conclusion that reading was a common rather than an uncommon pursuit for a large number of people in nearly all walks of German society in the sixteenth century. The pedagogical endeavor of the Reformation presupposed a society whose members were, or were being trained to be, readers. The evidence suggests that they were not wrong in this supposition.

6 LEVELS OF ILLITERACY IN ENGLAND 1530–1730*

David Cressy

While remaining appropriately humble about the crudity of his data and the limitations of his sources, the social historian who is willing to employ numerical methods and statistical procedures can make reasonably confident estimates of the extent of illiteracy in early modern England. A careful examination of the ability of witnesses before the ecclesiastical courts to sign their depositions, of testators to sign their wills, of applicants for marriage licences to sign the allegations and bonds, and of subscribers to protestations and declarations actually to write their names on the document, reveals a pattern of widespread but unevenly distributed illiteracy.[1] The best of these sources provides evidence not only on the social structure of illiteracy, but also on its changing level between the sixteenth and the eighteenth centuries. Progress towards the reduction of illiteracy was decidedly erratic.

In this article I shall discuss some of the difficulties in defining and measuring illiteracy. The depositions of the Consistory Court of the diocese of Norwich will be used to delineate the social dimensions of illiteracy under Elizabeth and the Stuarts. Finally, attention will be drawn to certain shifts in the level of illiteracy which might be associated with changes in the provision of education. The evidence of the Norwich depositions will be used to reconstruct the movement of illiteracy from the Reformation to the early eighteenth century.

Some of the most tantalizing and important questions about Tudor and Stuart illiteracy are at present unanswerable. Although we would like to know what sectors of the population could read the tracts of the Reformation or newspapers and pamphlets of the Civil War, or what proportion could pen a letter or draw up a bill of sale, there is no direct way to obtain this information. We can guess at the size and character of the reading public but we cannot measure it.[2] Nor can we discover how many people could both read and write, or could write with any more fluency than was required to sign their names. Theoretically it may be useful to distinguish passive literacy, an ability to read without knowledge of writing, from active literacy, where writing as well as reading had been mastered, but the documents at our disposal do not permit such sophistication. Many of the gradations of illiteracy,

*Reprinted from David Cressy, 'Levels of Illiteracy in England, 1530–1730', *Historical Journal*, 20 (1977), 1–23, by permission of the publisher, Cambridge University Press, © Cambridge University Press, 1977.

from total ignorance of the written word through partial illiteracy to full and fluent skill, are lost to history.

Only one type of literacy is directly measurable, the ability or inability to write a signature, and that may be the least interesting and least significant. People who formed signatures are counted as literate; those who made marks in default are counted as illiterate. All percentages of illiteracy cited in this paper are based on this simple distinction. It is, of course, an unsatisfactory criterion, but as a measure that is 'universal, standard and direct' it provides a fruitful starting place.[3]

Illiteracy measured this way may be taken, with some misgivings, to signify a cut-off point in the middle range, somewhere between a rude ability to read and actual fluency in writing. The imprecision though alarming, does not seriously jeopardize the inquiry since we are more interested in the progress and relative performance of different social groups than in absolute levels.

Pre-industrial England was a partially literate society encompassing a broad range of literate skills. Some people, we have no way to discover how many, could have been able to read without knowing how to write or even to sign their names. The existence of this semi-literate segment of the population, whose literacy was passive rather than active, is suggested by the conventional ordering of the curriculum in Tudor and Stuart elementary education. The sequence of instruction was such that a child would learn to read the alphabet, syllables, words and then sentences before he ever held a pen or attempted to write. As a basic literate skill, reading was taught first. Writing, if it was taught at all, was a separate, secondary activity, not to be started until the primary skill of reading had been mastered.[4] Because of this the percentages cited here refer to the upper limits of illiteracy.

People who could sign their names could probably read as well. The sequence of instruction argues against the suggestion that an otherwise illiterate person might somehow have mastered the trick of writing his name. The penmanship involved in such a seemingly simple task implies a wider familiarity with the world of letters. The occasions which required a signature were so few before the eighteenth century and the opprobrium attached to making a mark so slight or non-existent that learning a signature for its own sake must have been uncommon. There were no advantages in pretending to be literate when one was not; a signature had none of the power of a neck verse.[5]

Of all the sources which can be made to yield evidence of distribution of illiteracy the depositions are the most rewarding. Valuable information can be obtained from wills, marriage licences, Protestations and Hearth Tax records, but no other series of documents so clearly exposes the sexual, social and occupational dimensions of illiteracy over an extended period of time. Unlike wills the depositions are not unduly biased towards the prosperous and decrepit. They were not restricted, as marriage licences were, to 'such persons as be of good state and quality', nor were deponents exclusively male. The depositions contain much more information than Protestation or Hearth Tax returns and are available for many more years in the sixteenth and seventeenth centuries. Their advantages greatly outweigh the problems.

The preface to each deposition made before an ecclesiastical court was supposed to record the name, age, sex and marital status, occupation or social status, place of residence and length of time there, previous residences and place of birth of each witness, together with his relationship to the principal parties of the case. Having testified, all witnesses were required to 'write their Names or usual Mark to these their Depositions with their own hand, lest the Register, or any other should afterwards vitiate this Deposition in any particular'. Unfortunately the care taken by diocesan and archidiaconal registers to record every item varied from place to place and time to time. Occasionally such important details as the occupation of the deponent were omitted, and rarely the testimony was even left unsigned. In most cases, however, we know at least the name, approximate age, occupation and place of residence of each deponent, and whether or not he could sign his name.

Witnesses were summoned to testify in a great variety of causes, from tithe and probate disputes to defamations and sexual offences. They were drawn from every age group and from all social strata, but greater weight may have been attached to the testimony of an older man or someone of higher social standing. Even if witnesses called to testify before the courts were not proportionately representative of the population at large there is sufficient evidence among the depositions to control for bias and arrange them into appropriate social categories.

Depositions survive in great numbers from many of the old ecclesiastical jurisdictions. In the diocese of Norwich, which included Norfolk, Suffolk and a strip of Cambridgeshire, the Consistory Court maintained one of the most complete records. Full biographical details are preserved of nearly all the witnesses testifying before the court. Deposition books or bundles signed or marked by the deponents, survive for most years in the late sixteenth, seventeenth and early eighteenth centuries. From October 1618 to February 1629 the record is missing, and there are no depositions from July 1647 to April 1661 when the court was suppressed by the revolution, but otherwise the documentation is abundant. Of some 20,000 depositions preserved from 1580 to 1700 a total of 6,786 has been sampled and subjected to analysis. Almost a thousand more were sampled from the early eighteenth century. The results are summarized in Tables 6.1, 6.2 and 6.3.

Deponents did not appear in an order associated with their social position, nor did the same number of witnesses testify in each case, so their order in the documents can be regarded as effectively random. This permits the use of certain statistical tests which were designed to operate with randomly drawn samples. To ensure that every deposition had an equal chance of

Table 6.1. *Illiteracy of social groups in the diocese of Norwich, 1580–1700*

Group	Number sampled	% illiterate	95% confidence interval
Clergy and professions	332	0	–
Gentry	450	2	±1
Yeomen	944	35	±3
Tradesmen and craftsmen	1,838	44	±2
Husbandmen	1,198	79	±3
Labourers	88	85	±7
Women	1,024	89	±2

being selected a systematic sampling procedure was devised with a random start in every volume.[6]

Before progressing to the results of this sampling it should be pointed out that illiteracy figures from the diocese of Norwich do not necessarily apply to the rest of England. East Anglia under Elizabeth and the Stuarts was a prosperous and densely settled area, in close economic and cultural contact with London and the continent. The religion and politics of the region, at least of its leading families, was generally regarded as progressive. If literacy was associated with wealth, puritan sympathies and proximity to London the diocese of Norwich may have been one of the more literate parts of the country. On the other hand East Anglia had, like other grain growing areas, a large population of poor labourers who were mostly illiterate.[7] Labourers appeared infrequently before the Consistory Court but 85 per cent of those who made depositions could not sign them. The massive illiteracy of the labouring poor may have depressed the literacy level of the region as a whole.

The one opportunity to compare the regional distribution of illiteracy in seventeenth-century England, which is provided by the Protestation and similar declarations of the 1640s, has frustratingly little evidence from Norfolk and Suffolk. Over the country as a whole some 70 per cent of the male subscribers were unable to write their own names. The home counties performed somewhat better, with 65 per cent male illiteracy in Essex. No reliable estimate can be made of the overall male illiteracy of the diocese of Norwich, but it is unlikely to have been better than in Essex or worse than the country at large.[8]

The whole structure of illiteracy in the diocese of Norwich is clearly established by the study of depositions. Table 6.1 shows the percentage in various social categories who could not sign their names, and Table 6.2 shows the illiteracy of men in some of the most frequently encountered trades and crafts. Only the more common ranks and occupations have been included. Where samples are particularly small, of course, the figures should be treated with caution. We may be 95 per cent confident that the true illiteracy of yeo-

Table 6.2. *Illiteracy of tradesmen and craftsmen in the diocese of Norwich, 1580–1700*

Occupation	Number sampled	% illiterate	95% confidence interval
Grocers	49	6	±7
Haberdashers	11	9	±17
Merchants	25	12	±13
Bakers	33	27	±16
Tanners	36	31	±15
Wheelwrights	16	31	±23
Innkeepers	25	36	±19
Maltsters	22	36	±20
Brewers	32	41	±17
Weavers	225	42	±6
Glovers	25	44	±19
Tailors	139	44	±8
Blacksmiths	49	45	±14
Butchers	60	48	±13
Shoemakers	79	58	±11
Sailors	27	59	±19
Carpenters	91	64	±10
Millers	20	70	±20
Gardeners	11	73	±26
Masons	21	76	±18
Bricklayers	24	88	±13
Shepherds	10	90	±16
Thatchers	33	97	±6

men in East Anglia lay in the range of 35±3 per cent but the illiteracy of, say, shoemakers should be more properly estimated as 58±11 per cent and brick-layers 88±13 per cent. Despite some large margins of possible error associated with sampling a clear ranking of illiteracy does emerge. Illiteracy was rare among shopkeepers, men of commerce and the ruling elite; between a third and a half of skilled craftsmen could not sign their names; while threequarters or more of the labouring people were illiterate. Illiteracy expanded from clean, prestigious and profitable trades to rough, dirty, outdoor activities. The major stratification of gentry, yeomen, husbandmen and labourers accords exactly with contemporary and traditional accounts of the social order.[9]

In general, the possession of literate skills varied with social and economic circumstances. Clergymen, lawyers and schoolmasters possessed a versatile range of reading and writing skills because that was a prerequisite of their vocation. Gentlemen too were expected to be fully and actively literate. Their education normally prepared them for the business of local administration, estate management, political gossip and civilized intercourse which went with their rank. Their literacy was appropriate to their needs. However, illiteracy was not unknown even among the elite. Of the gentlemen testifying before the Norwich Consistory Court in the seventeenth century 2 per cent were unable to sign their depositions. When gentlemen's wills are examined the proportion making marks rises to five per cent. Medical problems, such as blindness, palsy or dyslexia, could have prevented their writing, and the infirmities of age no doubt frustrated the attempts of some gentlemen to sign their wills. Others just could not write. Gentility was not impugned by illiteracy, although it may have been inconvenient. Apparently illiterate members of a generally literate class could retain their status and exercise their power despite this handicap.

The literacy of yeomen was substantially inferior to that of the gentry, but way ahead of the husbandmen and poorer countryfolk. Some 35 per cent of the yeomen giving evidence before the Consistory Court at Norwich between 1580 and 1700 could not sign their depositions. By all accounts the yeomen of Elizabethan and early Stuart England were a thrusting, dynamic group, working hard, amassing land and profits, apeing their betters and setting their sons up as gentlemen. Thomas Fuller describes yeomen as 'gentlemen in ore . . . in the temperate Zone, betwixt greatness and want', and their moderate literacy confirms this comfortable assessment.

A group pursuing upward mobility needs all the advantages it can muster, and literacy was surely useful to the yeomen in their economic affairs as well as their social aspirations. It was not, however, absolutely essential. Favourable leases and carefully framed wills might be achieved by a yeoman who could write, but scriveners were available for those who could not. The yeomen were the natural audience for certain types of printed material. Almanacs, guides to good husbandry, even books of etiquette, appear to have a yeoman readership in mind and such books are occasionally mentioned in a yeoman's probate inventory.[10] Yeomen who were forty shilling free-holders were enfranchised and could vote for the county member in parliamentary elections. They belonged to the political nation, at least to its outer fringes. Being literate for the most part they were aware of the gentry's politics and religion and may even have emulated them. The extent to which these yeomen partook of such elite concerns as puritanism or constitutional theory may be a measure of their desire to be associated with the gentry. Being literate the yeomen had the opportunity to interpret the bible and dally with sedition, opportunities from which they normally refrained.

Tradesmen and craftsmen were not much less literate than yeomen, although a broad range of ability is obscured in this composite category. As reference to Table 6.2 will show, illiteracy levels varied with the particular trade or craft being followed, but were roughly commensurate with occupational requirements. Artisans and outside workmen were often illiterate, while shopkeepers and merchants could commonly sign their names. Crafts-

men who were unable to write sometimes demonstrated a degree of penmanship by sketching representational marks, a tailor drawing some scissors or a
mason depicting his hammer.[11] Many of these trades people could no doubt
read, even if they had trouble writing, and the class as a whole might be
characterized as being on the brink of literacy.

Farm labourers and building workers, at the base of the social structure,
were not expected to be literate. Nor, when they appear in the records, do
they show many signs of being able to write. Among seventeenth-century
deponents 79 per cent of the husbandmen, 85 per cent of the labourers, 88
per cent of the bricklayers and 97 per cent of the thatchers could not sign
their names. Their marks were often crude scrawls, a stab at the paper instead
of an accomplished cross. Many of them may never have held a pen before.
Very few would have been able to read.

The massive illiteracy of these people, who comprised more than half of
the population, was not simply a product of restricted educational opportunities. The husbandmen and labourers were not encouraged to acquire
literacy, had few means by which they could acquire it, and, in the routine of
their lives and within their horizons, had little use for literate skills. A
seventeenth-century sermon reassures the husbandman, 'Though you cannot
read a letter in the book, yet if you can, by true Assurance, read your name
in the *Book of Life*, your scholarship will serve . . . If you cannot write a
word, yet see you transcribe the fair copy of a godly, righteous, and sober
life, and you have done well.' Even under protestantism, with its emphasis on
the gospel, salvation did not require literacy. If you could not read the prayer
book or bible it was enough to recite the catechism and listen to the sermon.

No doubt the farm workers could communicate admirably with their
fellows with tales, jokes and conversation. They could probably predict the
weather, mend a fence or cure a sick horse with less trouble than their literate
social superiors, and may even have despised the gentlefolk and tradesmen
who lacked these elementary skills. Literacy was not considered appropriate
for the rural poor; they did not need it, nor did they have it. They were not,
of course, entirely cut off from written or printed matters. If one in five or
six could sign their names then presumably a greater proportion could read.
The presence of even one reader among a group of rural labourers could act as
a significant bridge to the literate world.[12] But normally these ordinary
people were indifferent to the political and religious controversies which
exercised their betters. They might, at times, become aroused, but without
full literacy they could not easily be politicized.

Most women too were unable to sign their names. Women in Tudor and
Stuart England were not normally taught to write, although there may have
been some intermittent provision for some of them to learn to read. The fully
literate woman was a rarity. The domestic routine to which most women
were confined required many skills, from beer brewing to child rearing, but it

did not require literacy. In Norfolk and Suffolk 95 per cent of the female deponents sampled between 1580 and 1640 could not sign their names, a proportion which slowly diminished to 82 per cent in the period 1660 to 1700. East Anglian women as a whole were no more literate, and had no more need of literacy, than building workers and rural labourers.[13]

The social structure of illiteracy is relatively simple to chart and not hard to understand. Limited educational opportunity in a hierarchically organized society, together with the scant need of literacy in many occupations, may adequately explain the social distribution of illiteracy. More troublesome, however, are variations in illiteracy over time. There appears to have been no steady, cumulative progress in the reduction of illiteracy in the early modern period. Nor did the different social groups maintain the same level of illiteracy in relation to each other at all times from the sixteenth to the eighteenth century. Rather, the record reveals an irregular fluctuation, a series of spurts and setbacks, plateaux, arrests and accelerations in the progress of literacy, which sometimes involved large sectors of society but at other times were confined to particular sets or specific social groups.

The movement of illiteracy observed in the depositions is simply shown by grouping the evidence in ten-year periods. The abilities of gentlemen and clerics at one end of the scale and of labourers and women at the other did not change significantly between 1580 and 1700 but there was considerable volatility in the performance of yeomen, husbandmen and tradesmen. Table 6.3 shows the illiteracy of men in these groups in the diocese of Norwich decade by decade from 1580 to 1700, with figures added from the 1720s for comparison. Rapid progress in the reduction of illiteracy at the beginning of the period was slowed down and in some cases reversed by the end.

The late sixteenth century saw general and substantial progress in reducing illiteracy. Yeomen improved from 55 per cent unable to sign the depositions in the 1580s to 38 per cent in the 1590s; husbandmen improved from 93 to 87 per cent and tradesmen from 61 to 55 per cent in the same brief period. No other period experienced such solid and widespread progress. Tradesmen and husbandmen continued to improve during James' reign, but yeomen held steady at the level they reached in the 1590s. Yeomen began to improve again by the 1630s, but by this time the other two groups had suffered setbacks. On the eve of the Civil War tradesmen and husbandmen in East Anglia were as illiterate as they had been at the death of Elizabeth. Further improvements were found in the decade of the Restoration but they could not be sustained. The measured illiteracy of yeomen fluctuated over a broad range in the later seventeenth century but this may owe more to the small size of the sample than to actual shifts in illiteracy. In aggregate the evidence from 1660 to 1700 shows 27 per cent of the yeomen unable to sign their names. Illiteracy among tradesmen and craftsmen was reduced in the post-war period, but their subsequent progress was erratic. Under Charles II and James II the tradesmen

Table 6.3. *Illiteracy in the diocese of Norwich by decade, 1580–1730*

Decade	Yeomen		Husbandmen		Tradesmen	
	No.	%	No.	%	No.	%
1580s	78	55	94	93	98	61
1590s	112	38	121	87	161	55
1600s	89	39	108	79	151	48
1610s	84	38	91	77	126	44
1620s	–	–	–	–	–	–
1630s	90	32	84	86	140	49
1640s	36	28	23	78	90	52
1650s	–	–	–	–	–	–
1660s	37	24	82	71	176	33
1670s	24	12	56	82	149	35
1680s	42	45	38	89	174	44
1690s	33	18	40	82	125	30
1720s	46	26	39	87	104	34

showed more signs of drifting back into illiteracy than of its further conquest. Husbandmen also performed well in the 1660s but the rest of the Stuart
period saw them sink to appallingly high levels of illiteracy. Husbandmen at
the end of the seventeenth century were as deep in illiteracy as their predecessors a century before.

The evidence from the depositions of the 1720s finds no improvement
among husbandmen and little change in the other main groups. With few
exceptions the movement of illiteracy, so promising during Elizabeth's reign,
became sluggish and quagmired in the seventeenth century. The figures for
the 1660s reflect a second period of improvement, which soon ended. Each
group slid back to a performance in the 1680s which was among their worst
ever. The evidence for much of the Stuart period shows slow progress, stagnation or actual reversals in the literacy of yeomen, tradesmen and husbandmen. The overall pattern shows none of the gradual elimination of illiteracy
which might have been expected.

The movement of illiteracy in the sixteenth and seventeenth centuries can
be plotted with greater precision by attending to the time when people
acquired their literacy, as children, rather than when they displayed it, as
adult deponents. Although there may have been opportunities to learn to
write in later life it is reasonable to assume that most people learned, or failed
to learn, literate skills while they were young. The exact relationship between
education and literacy is still unclear, but again it seems reasonable to believe
that most people who learned to write did so as a result of some instruction,
whether formal or informal, and that this took place during childhood or

adolescence. Tudor and Stuart educational writers considered the school years to range from about five to fifteen and assumed that schoolboys would be able to read and write by the age of nine, ten or eleven. If we wish to examine the changing levels of illiteracy in terms of school generations, it is a simple matter to subtract the age of each deponent from the date of his deposition to find his year of birth, and to add ten to bring him to the age of a schoolboy.

One problem with this procedure is that literacy might have deteriorated with advancing age, thereby distorting the statistics. Some of the elderly deponents who made marks may once have been taught to write and might be found signing their names when they were younger. There was in fact an association between illiteracy and senility, which is apparent when wills are compared to depositions. Illiteracy levels calculated from the marks and signatures on wills are consistently higher than those derived from depositions.[14] Deponents could be senile too. Witnesses aged above sixty were more likely to have made marks than signatures, but there was no clear association between illiteracy and advancing years for any other age group. So long as the more elderly deponents were evenly distributed through the various school generations and the lapse from literacy remained fairly constant, the analysis is not seriously jeopardized.[15]

Additional advantages accrue from re-sorting the deponents into their school generations. The threshold of knowledge about illiteracy can be pushed back at least to the 1530s. Although we have no direct evidence of illiteracy patterns in the mid-Tudor period they can be reconstructed from data accumulated at a later time. Witnesses before the Consistory Court in the last half of Elizabeth's reign belonged to every school generation of the sixteenth century. A sixty year old yeoman making his deposition in 1583 would have been of school age at the time of the Reformation. One who was forty in 1583 could have learned to read under Edward or Mary. Survivors from school generations before 1530 who appeared in the deposition books have been eliminated from this discussion lest their great age distort the illiteracy statistics, but otherwise no attempt has been made to control for age. The resorting procedure also overcomes the problem of missing evidence for the 1620s and 1650s. Members of the school generations who might have made depositions at those times are found distributed through the records from other decades.

The depositions of yeomen, husbandmen and tradesmen sampled from the diocese of Norwich from 1580 to 1730 have been processed to show the movement of illiteracy by school generations from 1530 to 1710. The results, shown in Figure 6.1, have been subjected to an eleven year moving average in order to overcome some of the problems of small numbers of deponents in individual years and to smooth year to year fluctuations. Not all the fluctuation has been eliminated, but the general movement is clear.

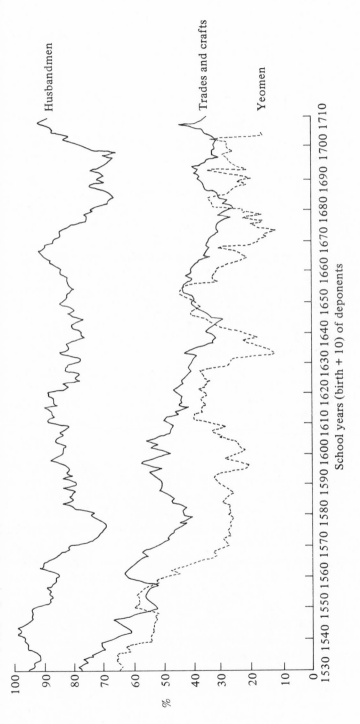

Figure 6.1 Illiteracy of social groups, diocese of Norwich 1530–1710

The figure reveals the existence of eight distinct phases in the movement of illiteracy which can be summarized as follows:

(1) 1530—1550 improvement.
(2) 1550—1560 setbacks.
(3) 1560—1580 rapid improvement.
(4) 1580—1610 setbacks.
(5) 1610—1640 improvement.
(6) 1640—1660 serious setbacks.
(7) 1660—1680 improvement.
(8) 1680—1710 setbacks.

Each phase lasted roughly a generation, some twenty or thirty years. There appears to have been a cyclical pattern, with progress in the reduction of illiteracy followed by stagnation or reversal, followed in turn by a new phase of improvement.

The extent to which these changes in levels of illiteracy reflect the changing educational climate of the Tudor and Stuart period is not immediately clear. Articulate opinion was constantly shifting, with arguments for the greater availability of schooling vying with demands for its stricter control. Enthusiasm for educational expansion contested with fears that widespread learning would endanger religion, the State and the entire social order. If there was any cyclical pattern to these intellectual and political currents it is difficult to discern. The main streams of educational thought at any one time were intertwined with older outmoded views and prophetic fringe propaganda. Intellectual currents are in any case a poor guide to the actualities of educational provision. Ideas in the minds of educational commentators did not necessarily have any impact on schools.

Certain aspects of the changing educational climate are susceptible to numerical analysis. Figures showing the number of endowed school foundations each decade, the amount of charitable giving to schools in particular and to education in general, and the flow of students into the university of Cambridge, have been assembled in Table 6.4. These figures are themselves beset with imperfections, and do not in any case purport to represent the entire educational situation, but they may be taken as a rough index of educational vitality. They allow us to interpret the eight phases in the movement of illiteracy in terms of developments in the history of education. It could be objected that changes in the level of illiteracy among East Anglian yeomen, husbandmen and tradesmen owed little or nothing to changes in the provision of education, mostly of an elite nature, charted for the country as a whole. But even if no direct connexion is established we can examine whether conditions favourable to the advance of education were synchronized with periods of diminishing illiteracy. The analysis would be more satisfactory if we possessed regional indices of educational change or national figures for the distribution of illiteracy.

Table 6.4. *Educational progress 1500–1700*

	School foundations	Gifts to schools, £	Gifts to all education, £	Cambridge matriculations
1500s	6	4,230	30,174	–
1510s	9	10,062	27,896	–
1520s	13	9,527	46,288	–
1530s	8	7,380	12,235	–
1540s	39	8,227	17,727	1,584*
1550s	47	21,173	30,593	1,624
1560s	42	10,377	27,296	2,748
1570s	30	22,647	36,344	3,438
1580s	20	19,172	44,863	3,443
1590s	24	20,540	31,444	2,416*
1600s	41	30,315	60,791	2,699*
1610s	41	97,774	133,093	3,879
1620s	26	63,119	116,239	4,208
1630s	32	29,392	73,471	3,726
1640s	15	33,345	53,549	2,623
1650s	42	55,388	75,750	2,543
1660s	34	–	–	3,035
1670s	36	–	–	2,902
1680s	28	–	–	2,260
1690s	26	–	–	1,905

*Adjusted estimate.

The totals of school foundations are derived from the work of the Schools Inquiry Commission of 1867–8 which, pursuing historical research in the service of modernization, carefully tabulated the founding of endowed schools from the twelfth to the nineteenth century. No other source so conveniently and accurately documents the creation of schools. Although shortlived private schools are omitted from the list and a few endowments may have been overlooked, a check against other sources proves the commission's work to be reliable. Nevertheless, caution is enjoined. Some of the foundations listed were in fact re-foundations or re-organizations of schools that already existed. Others, though formally established and endowed at a given date, did not immediately come into operation as places of education. The legal creation of an institution did not necessarily lead to an immediate augmentation of learning.

Amounts of educational charity, expressed to the nearest pound, are taken from *Philanthropy in England, 1480–1660* by W.K. Jordan.[16] The problems with these figures are well known, especially their disregard of inflation which undercut the real value of later endowments, and the avoidance of probate records from the lesser courts where many wills of yeomen and modest gentlemen were proved. Nevertheless, Jordan's totals, based on a study of twelve English counties including Norfolk, can be taken to indicate the level of investment in education. Comparable figures after 1660 are not available.

Cambridge matriculation figures are taken from the manuscript matriculation registers, adjusted where necessary by reference to college admission books and university graduations to show decennial totals.[17] The actual size of the undergraduate population at Cambridge is not directly represented by these figures since a varying proportion of students declined to matriculate. They may be taken as a guide to the changing intake.

The graph shows that illiteracy scores were falling among yeomen and tradesmen who were of school age in the years immediately following the Henrician Reformation. Husbandmen were slow to join in this movement and did not begin to make progress until the early 1540s. The evidence of literacy suggests that elementary education was flourishing in the decade after the break with Rome. The revolution of the 1530s, the royal coup over the Church and the dissolution of the monasteries, had no adverse effect on children learning to write. It was not until the reign of Edward VI, famed for its grammar school foundations, that the growth of literacy was arrested. Tradesmen and husbandmen in the school generation of the 1550s ceased improving and held steady at a literacy plateau. The illiteracy of one cohort of yeomen, educated *c.* 1548—58, was even higher than in the previous generation.

Given our limited knowledge of pre-Elizabethan educational conditions the explanation of these movements must be tentative. Commonweal reformers were agitating on behalf of educational expansion but they are not known to have been particularly successful in creating more schools.[18] The rhetoric of educational reform was not necessarily matched by its performance. Indeed, the record of endowing and founding of schools in the 1530s is not at all distinguished compared to subsequent achievements.

The decade before the Reformation saw a peak in the cash value of educational charity, but much of this was composed of gifts to the universities. The 1530s saw a slump both in gifts to schools and in overall educational philanthropy. A reduced rate of giving continued into the 1540s, but educational charity was again bountiful in the 1550s. Almost three times the amount of money was given to schools in the 1550s as in the 1530s. Yet literacy was improving in the 1530s and deteriorating in the 1550s. Inflation eliminates some of the difference in the worth of the bequests but an apparent paradox remains. The record of school foundations matches the record of philanthropy. Nine schools were founded in the 1510s, thirteen in the 1520s, only eight in the 1530s, and then there was a rush of foundations, 39 in the 1540s and 47 in the 1550s. The charitable and institutional evidence points to an educational expansion in the late Henrician, Edwardian and Marian periods, when the evidence of illiteracy points to a slump. How is this disparity to be reconciled?

A partial explanation may lie in the elite nature of the schools whose existence is best documented. Most of the foundations recorded by the Schools Inquiry Commission were grammar schools dedicated to the parsing and translating of Latin, while little of the charity that Jordan has documented was intended for elementary instruction. The lack of a clear correlation between endowments and the ability to write is therefore no surprise. The geographic mismatch between East Anglian illiteracy and national figures for schools and charity may further disturb any correlation. Even if educational bequests did contribute to the reduction of illiteracy a time lag would be expected between the date of an endowment and the time of its impact. It might then be argued that the bountiful educational charity of the 1520s was associated with improving literacy in the 1530s, while the Henrician and Edwardian school foundations of the 1540s and 1550s influenced the growth of literacy under Elizabeth in the 1560s and 1570s.

Unsettling political events rather than reduced support for education may explain the abrupt halt in the reduction of illiteracy at the beginning of Edward's reign. If the chantries really were reponsible for a large measure of elementary instruction, as A.F. Leach believed, their dissolution in 1547 would have been temporarily disruptive of teaching to write.[19] Some chantries were made into grammar schools but the legal and organizational problems involved could take a decade or more to resolve. The same problems beset the re-organization of cathedral schools under Henry VIII. The Reformation brought confusion. Whatever educational impulse was associated with it in the 1540s and early 1550s was not likely to bear fruit until the next generation. Social and political turmoils frustrated the acquisition of literacy. The troubles of 1549, especially Ket's rebellion in the heart of East Anglia, may have further dislocated an educational system already weakened by the dissolutions and uncertainties. Some of the illiterate deponents of the 1548–58 school generation may not have learned to read and write because educational facilities went untended during their childhood. The setback to literacy, discovered through the depositions, exactly coincides with a decade of peasant rebellion and revolutions in religious policy, in which schoolmasters were as likely to be distracted as anyone else.

A period of energetic educational advance, lasting almost to 1580, began with the accession of Elizabeth. All social groups were affected. The husbandmen who were of school age at this time improved from almost 90 per cent to less than 70 per cent unable to sign the depositions. Not for another hundred years were husbandmen to be so swept up by an educational movement. Tradesmen improved from more than 60 per cent unable to sign to less than 40 per cent, while yeomen improved from 56 to 26 per cent. The literacy figures give further substance to the characterization of the period after 1560 as one of 'educational revolution'.[20] Political, religious and humanist propaganda was running in favour of education. Marian exiles were concerned to create a learned protestant clergy, while Ascham and his contemporaries were perfecting the education of the lay aristocracy. Such a cultural climate could not but be helpful to the advance of basic literacy.

Undergraduate admissions at the universities reached unprecedented numbers in the early part of Elizabeth's reign. Matriculations at Cambridge rose from 160 a year in the 1550s to more than 340 a year in the 1570s and 1580s. University graduates (and drop-outs, often met in the records as *literati*), unable to find immediate employment in the church, became schoolmasters. Thirty-five per cent of the schoolmasters licensed in the diocese of London in the 1590s were graduates and 31 per cent were *literati*. In the diocese of Norwich in the 1580s 30 per cent of newly licensed teachers were graduates and 47 per cent were *literati*. The expansion of higher education helped to raise the quality and size of the school teaching force.[21]

There was a proliferation of grammar schools in this period of rising literacy. Edwardian foundations were overcoming their early organizational problems and receiving charters and other forms of endorsement from the Elizabethan regime. New schools were created, but not so many as in the 1550s. The Schools Inquiry Commission found 42 foundations in the 1560s and 30 in the 1570s, whereas 47 schools dated their origins from the 1550s. Charitable giving to education was at a reduced level in the 1560s, although it reached new peaks in the 1570s. Jordan found bequests of £21,173 to schools in the 1550s, only £10,173 in the 1560s, and £22,647 in the 1570s. If we take inflation into consideration, as Jordan did not, the value of the early Elizabethan endowment is further reduced.

Although the figures for philanthropy and school foundations are out of phase with other indices of educational vitality, the bulk of the evidence, strengthened by the literacy figures, points to the first two decades of Elizabeth's reign as a period of unusual educational excitement and achievement. It may be no coincidence that Shakespeare and his talented literary contemporaries were of school age at this time.

Most accounts of Tudor and Stuart education assume a more or less steady expansion from the accession of Elizabeth to the Civil War. The evidence of illiteracy suggests that progress was far from steady. There is substantial evidence to characterize the period 1580–1610 as one of 'educational recession'. Every index of educational progress bears marks of this recession.

Literacy was stagnating or deteriorating in the second half of Elizabeth's reign. Husbandmen quickly relinquished the advanced position staked out by the school generation of the 1570s, retiring to the illiteracy doldrums for the next one hundred years. The literacy of tradespeople also went into decline in the 1580s and 1590s, after substantial improvements earlier in the reign. Yeomen managed to sustain their mid-Elizabethan level until the end of the sixteenth century, but could make no further progress. The fluctuations of the 1590s announce no clear direction for the literacy of yeomen, but they too slid into decline at the beginning of James' reign.

The evidence of illiteracy in East Anglia suggests that the educational boom of the 1560s came to a standstill around 1580 and had developed into a serious recession by the end of the century. Evidence from educational records also points to a late Elizabethan setback which few historians have noted. Even the observation that admissions to Oxford and Cambridge slumped in the 1580s has not been allowed to overshadow the celebration of the 'educational revolution' of 1560 to 1640.[22] University admissions were falling in the last part of Elizabeth's reign. Although new colleges were founded and building works were undertaken the undergraduate population was drastically reduced. One third fewer students matriculated at Cambridge in the 1590s than in the 1580s and matriculations in the 1600s were still below the level of the 1570s.[23] Fewer boys were prepared for university entrance, while the pool of potential schoolmasters with university experience was also diminished. The extent to which religious restrictions or financial problems kept students away is a subject which demands further attention. By the end of the sixteenth century a university education was less desirable, or less possible, than in the previous generation.

Charitable giving to education was also depressed at the end of Elizabeth's reign, while soaring inflation undercut the real value of endowments. The 1590s, a decade of economic crisis, saw the smallest sum philanthropically bestowed on education in thirty years. Fewer new schools came into existence. Only 20 schools were founded in the 1580s and 24 in the 1590s, the smallest decadal totals since the Reformation.

All indicators of educational progress point to a serious recession. In as far as it can be glimpsed, the personnel of education also suffered. Country schoolmasters had been highly visible in the ecclesiastical visitation and licensing records of the diocese of Norwich before 1590, but they had virtually disappeared by 1610. As many as 200 active schoolmasters can be identified in Norfolk and Suffolk in the 1580s, 170 in the 1590s, 92 in the 1600s and even fewer in the 1610s.[24] Although the correspondences are imperfectly synchronized there is substantial evidence to associate the decline in literacy with a national and regional collapse of educational provision.

The recovery began during James' reign. Tradesmen and craftsmen were the first to show progress, improving their literacy throughout the early Stuart period and surpassing their mid-Elizabethan peak by the eve of the Civil War. Yeomen had been stagnating at an uncharacteristically high level of illiteracy during the Jacobean period but they too improved during Charles' reign. The exceptionally advanced position of the school generation of 1633 may be a fluke of the sample, but the overall movement is indicative of renewed progress. Yeomen who were of school age in the 1630s were more literate than ever before. Even the husbandmen of this school generation show tentative signs of escaping their high illiteracy.

The early Stuart recovery of literacy reflects a second stage in the inter-

rupted 'educational revolution'. All indices confirm this revival. The crisis
that had removed country schoolmasters from the diocesan records, whatever
its cause, was over by the 1620s. Most of the East Anglian communities
which had schoolmasters at the turn of the century were again being served in
the 1620s and 1630s, but freelance teachers were still less widespread than in
the 1580s.[25] Students were again populating the universities in large numbers,
peaking at Cambridge in the 1620s and Oxford in the 1630s. Between 1610
and 1640 some 400 students a year were matriculating at Cambridge, more
than at any other time in the Tudor or Stuart period. Educational philanthropy also reached a peak during James' reign. Record sums were given to
schools, £97,774 in the 1610s, £63,119 in the 1620s, tailing off to £29,392
in the 1630s. Much of this money was directed to the endowment of new
schools. The Schools Inquiry Commission traced 41 foundations of the 1600s
and another 41 of the 1610s. Totals for the 1620s and 1630s, when 26 and
34 schools were founded, reflect the reduced giving of those decades. The
greatest investment in education was made in the early part of the seventeenth
century, as if to compensate for the weakened educational provision of the
1580s and 1590s. This lavish endowment of educational facilities may be
associated with the pronounced improvement in illiteracy levels in the 1630s.

The revival was abruptly terminated by the onset of civil war. The illiterate
deponents who were of school age in the 1640s, even more than their ancestors
under Edward and Mary may be regarded as victims of political events which
seriously disrupted educational provision. The illiteracy of tradesmen and
craftsmen rose from 30 to 42 per cent and that of yeomen from around 20
per cent to as high as 43 per cent before the slide was arrested in the 1650s.
The slight progress seen among husbandmen of the 1630s school generation
was wiped out in the 1640s. All the evidence from the depositions points to a
catastrophic collapse of elementary education in the period of the Civil War
and its aftermath. Other indices of educational provision support this assessment.

Some schoolmasters left their posts while others were ejected, leaving
many of the elementary schools unmanned. At Grimstone in Norfolk, for
example, the inhabitants complained that 'through these distracted times . . .
the school house is fallen into decay, the master gone, and error and malig-
nancy like to flow in'. University admissions plummetted as Oxford became
the Royalist headquarters and Cambridge a Parliamentary garrison and
prison. Only 45 students matriculated at Cambridge in 1643 compared to 315
in 1640 and 450 in 1639. Jordan found more money given to schools in the
1640s than in the previous decade, but educational charity as a whole was
depressed. Only 15 schools were founded in the 1640s, compared to 32 in the
1630s. The provision of education was necessarily subordinated to the more
pressing military and political concerns, and illiteracy expanded as a result.

However well-intentioned the revolutionaries may have been about extending popular education they were not able to attend to it until the relative stability of the 1650s. There is no dearth of evidence in the writings of men like Samuel Hartlib and Comenius that great plans were afoot for transforming educational provision, but there is equally no evidence that any of them came to fruition.[26]

The restoration of literacy was in hand before the Restoration of the king. 1656 brought some relief to the education-starved inhabitants of Grimstone when the Council voted £30 to support a schoolmaster there. Forty-two new schools came into existence in the 1650s, as many as at the height of the 'educational revolution', and there was a moderate expansion of educational charity. The graph shows a renewed attack on illiteracy from a little before 1660 to around 1680. Tradesmen and yeomen made solid progress in the Restoration era and even husbandmen began to emerge from illiteracy in the late 1660s.

University admissions were again buoyant in the 1660s, although matriculations did not reach their pre-war level. Cambridge matriculations in the 1660s were the highest since the 1630s, and higher than in any subsequent decade before the nineteenth century. If there was an educational boom under Charles II it was of modest proportions. Information about the quantity and direction of charity after 1660 is not readily available and there are no figures to compare with those assembled by Jordan. Schools were founded at a substantial if unspectacular rate, 34 in the 1660s and 36 in the 1670s. Country schoolmasters appear infrequently in the ecclesiastical records of the later seventeenth century, but that may reflect evasion of control as much as a shortage of teachers. We may conclude that the business of education went on in a routine fashion in the 1660s and 1670s, sufficient to sustain the growth of literacy but without the energy of earlier decades. Leaders of opinion in the second half of the seventeenth century were no longer enthusiastic about education and some, such as Edward Chamberlayne, blamed the schools and universities for 'our late unhappy troubles'.[27]

The end of the seventeenth century saw literacy faltering once again. Tradesmen experienced a setback in the 1690s while the yeomen of school age in the 1680s and 1690s were somewhat more illiterate than their predecessors of the 1670s. Husbandmen performed quite well in the late seventeenth century but slid back into higher illiteracy at the beginning of the eighteenth. This halt to the growth of literacy was associated with a malaise affecting educational provision.

Progressively fewer endowed schools were founded in the late seventeenth and early eighteenth centuries, 36 in the 1670s, 28 in the 1680s, 26 in the 1690s and 24 in the 1700s. University enrolments continued to shrink; fewer students matriculated at Cambridge in the 1690s than at any time since the mid sixteenth century. The rural teaching force in East Anglia, which relied on the universities for much of its manpower, was in steady decline; 195 men had subscribed as schoolmasters in the diocese of Norwich in the 1660s, 94 in the 1670s, 81 in the 1680s and only 37 in the 1690s. Nonconformist reluctance to subscribe may explain part of this shrinkage, but many village schools ceased to function. The educational climate at the end of the seventeenth century was less conducive to the spread of literacy than it had been in some earlier phases.

Faced with a situation of darkening illiteracy, which some commentators associated with idleness and vice, an attempt was made at the turn of the century to reinvigorate popular education. Charity schools were primarily intended to socialize the poor, to produce 'honest and industrious servants', but they also spread literacy.[28] The slight improvement in the literacy of tradesmen of the 1695—1704 school generation might be attributable to the efforts of the charity schoolers, but the improvement was not sustained.

Despite the difficulties of defining and measuring illiteracy its outlines can be clearly established. Illiteracy was much more widespread among women than among men, and a man's illiteracy level was strongly associated with his occupation or his position in the social order. The social structure of illiteracy hardly changed, even though actual illiteracy levels varied within the social group. Yeomen never approached the competence of gentlemen while husbandmen were always inferior to yeomen. Among the composite category of tradesmen and craftsmen bricklayers never approached the literacy of weavers and they in turn were consistently more illiterate than grocers. Evidence from marriage records of the eighteenth century shows a stratification by the inability to sign very similar to that found in depositions of the sixteenth and seventeenth centuries.[29]

The study of illiteracy illuminates shifts in educational provision which have so far received little attention. The evidence of the depositions, whether examined by decade of observation or processed to show school generations, shows the movement of illiteracy to have been more volatile than was formerly suspected. Phases of improvement, stagnation and decline cannot always be explained by reference to indices of educational activity, but their discovery provokes many questions. We particularly need to know how widespread was elementary instruction, how the availability of schooling varied from time to time as well as place to place, and the degree to which education was sensitive to changes in politics or the economy. The history of education alone will not account for the varying levels of illiteracy but an important task will be to compile better indices of educational change.

7 FIRST STEPS IN LITERACY: THE READING AND WRITING EXPERIENCES OF THE HUMBLEST SEVENTEENTH-CENTURY SPIRITUAL AUTOBIOGRAPHERS*

Margaret Spufford

The spiritual autobiographies of the seventeenth century include the first subjective accounts, written by men from the countryside from yeoman parentage or below, of childhood, education, the importance of literacy and the importance that their religious convictions had for them. They therefore contain first-hand accounts, or rather fragments of accounts, of the amount of education available, and its effects, by the relatively humble. They thus provide insight into the effects of literacy which is not provided by any other source.

There are very, very few of these accounts, and those which do exist suffer from the disadvantage of the *genre*. The spiritual autobiographers were Puritans and dissenters,[1] and therefore were socially slanted in whatever way Puritans and dissenters were socially slanted. They must also be considered even more a-typical than Puritans and dissenters in general, because the urge to write autobiography in itself defines an exceptional man.[2] Lastly, even within the whole group of autobiographers, those who bothered to set the stage for their spiritual experiences within any framework of place, parentage and education were exceptional again. Most of them simply launched into the account of the work of God in their souls which was the purpose of their writing, without even the slightest account of their age, the region of England or the social group from which they came. There is no means of knowing whether those who do give some detail of parentage or education were drawn to do so by temperament, and were equally representative of the whole group of autobiographers whatever its social composition.

However, it is interesting, despite all these *caveats*, that those among the autobiographers who do bother to describe their social backgrounds were drawn mainly from just those groups in rural society which were most literate, had more educational opportunity and also provided most converts to Quakerism than any other in some areas.[3] They were largely yeomen's sons, together with some wholesalers. They did not come exclusively from this sort of background, however. I have concentrated more here on the few who were either born in less prosperous circumstances, or who lost their fathers before their education was completed, and so abruptly descended the social scale, and, as

*Reprinted from Margaret Spufford, 'First steps in literacy: The reading and writing experiences of the humblest seventeenth-century spiritual autobiographers', *Social History*, 4 (1979), 407–35, by permission of the publisher, Methuen and Co. Ltd, © Margaret Spufford, 1979.

they describe their surroundings, give us some account of the less literate world below the level of the yeoman. It is, therefore, the least typical of the autobiographers who are discussed most fully here.

Despite the problem of typicality the autobiographers present, it seems entirely fair to assume that this group gives the reader some insight into the range of opportunities and experience in seventeenth-century England which was open to other, non-Puritan boys from similar social backgrounds. This account is therefore based on their experiences. Some of this group of auto-biographers were only able to attend school for a very short time, and their accounts of the stage of proficiency in reading or writing they had reached by six, seven or eight years old give a very useful guide to the time it took to learn to read and write in the seventeenth century, and the ages at which it was customary to acquire the different skills. The incidental description of these autobiographers of their different social worlds and range of contacts also gives an impression of the diffusion of literate skills at different levels of seventeenth-century society.

The ability to sign one's name[4] has been conclusively shown to be tied to one's social status in Tudor and Stuart East Anglia,[5] for the simple reason that some degree of prosperity was necessary to spare a child from the labour force for education as soon as it was capable of work. So literacy was economically determined. Between 1580 and 1700, 11 per cent of women, 15 per cent of labourers and 21 per cent of husbandmen could sign their names, against 56 per cent of tradesmen and craftsmen and 65 per cent of yeomen. Grammar school and even more university education was heavily socially restricted and only sons of yeomen from amongst the peasantry had much chance of appearing in grammar school or college registers.[6] This somewhat gloomy picture fails to stress the small but significant groups of signatories in even the most illiterate social groups who were able to write their names. It dwells on grammar and university education to the exclusion of the patchy, sporadic, but very real elementary education available in Tudor and Stuart England.[7] At the same time, Cressy admits, 'we do not know whether the acquisition of literacy was exclusively the product of formal elementary schooling, or at what stage in a person's life he learned, or failed to learn, to write the letters of his name'. The experiences of the spiritual autobiographers throw a great deal of light on just these problems.

Because the acquisition of reading and writing skills was socially stratified, I have organized this account in ascending order, starting with the poorest. Viewed from this angle, those yeomen's sons whose fathers could support them through a university education appear highly privileged, and I have in fact ignored them in favour of those autobiographers whose experiences represent those of that part of society which is outside the cognizance of historians working from college admission registers. The evidence is of course impressionistic. It is the qualitative evidence which puts at least some flesh on the quantitative skeleton of literacy provided by the signatures. It illuminates a murky and ill-defined world in which grammar schooling was practically irrelevant and yet reading and writing skills were sought after.

Useful though it is, such a discussion of basic 'literacy' which attempts particularly to gain an impression of the diffusion of the ability to read, and the period of schooling necessary to acquire the ability, necessarily comprehends very different degrees of the skill under one heading. Is one inquiring, Schofield asks, about the ability to read a simple handbill, a local newspaper or the works of John Locke?[8] Here, inevitably, I find myself discussing under the heading 'reading ability' a Wiltshire labourer who could read *Paradise Lost* with the aid of a dictionary, the Gloucestershire shepherds who could sound out words to teach an eager boy to read, and a blind thresher in Yorkshire who made a name for himself as a 'famous schoolteacher' whose pupils probably learnt to 'read' by rote learning only. It is obvious that completely different levels of fluency and skills are involved, but there is no way of distinguishing them. The problem can only be stated. I have deliberately let the autobiographers speak for themselves wherever possible. Since the point is to demonstrate that very limited educational opportunity did not debar at least a few people, who may of course have been highly exceptional, from the development of interests involving literary skills, the way in which men who left school at six, seven or nine later expressed themselves on paper is in itself meaningful.

Before working through the experiences of the autobiographers from the poorest upwards, it is useful to consider the specific information the autobiographies give us about the length of time it took some of them to acquire the skills of reading and of writing. This provides a background which makes it easier to assess the probable effects of the limited educational experiences of the poorer children. The seventeenth-century educationalists suggested that in the country schools, children normally began at seven or eight. Six was early. This fits well, on the whole, with the experience of the autobiographers, who learnt to read with a variety of people, mostly women, before starting writing with the 'formal' part of their education at seven, if they got that far.[9]

A bright child was able to learn to read in a few months in the seventeenth century, although so much must have depended on intelligence, the sort of teacher available, and the size of group he was in, that it is difficult to generalize. Oliver Sansom, born in 1636 in Beedon in Berkshire, wrote: 'When I was about six years of age, I was put to school to a woman, to learn to read, who finding me not unapt to learn, forwarded me so well, that in about four months' time, I could read a chapter in the Bible pretty readily.' Latin and writing began at seven. John Evelyn, the diarist, began his schooling earlier, at four, when he joined the village group to begin the 'rudiments' in the local church porch. But he was not 'put to learn my Latin rudiments, and to write' until he was eight. James Fretwell, eldest son of a Yorkshire timber-merchant, born in 1699, began lessons earlier still.

> As soon as I was capable of learning [my mother] sent me to an old school-dame, who lived at the very next door . . . But I suppose I did but continue here but a few days, for growing weary of my book, and my dame not correcting me as my mother desired, she took me under her pedagogy untill I could read in my Bible, and thus she did afterwards by all my brothers and sisters . . . And as my capacity was able, she caused me to observe what I read, so I soon began to take some notice of several historical passages in the Old Testament.

He was admitted to the small grammar school of Kirk Sandall,

> my dear mother being desirous that I should have a little more learning than she was capable of giving me . . . where [the master] placed me amongst some little ones, such as myself . . . when he called me up to hear what I could say for myself, he finding me better than he expected, removed me higher, asking my mother if she had brought me an Accidence, which I think she had; so she had the pleasure of seeing me removed out of the horn-book class, which my master at first sight thought most suitable for me.

The master's assumption was not surprising. James was then aged four years and seven months. He was obviously precocious. Other precocious children's achievements were also recorded because they were unusual. Oliver Heyward married the daughter of a Puritan minister who had learnt both to read and to write fluently before the normal age in the 1640s. 'She could read the hardest chapter in the Bible when she was but four years of age' and was taught to write by the local schoolmaster 'in learning whereof she was more than ordinarily capable, being able at six yeares of age to write down passages of the sermon in the chappel'. Anne Gwin of Falmouth, daughter of a fisherman and fishmerchant, born in 1692, likewise 'took to learning very Young, and soon became a good Reader, viz. when she was but about Three yeares and a Half old, she wrote tolerably well before five'. The biographers of these girls recognized their unusual forwardness; it seems safer to use Oliver Sansom as a specific example of the time it took normal children to learn to read.

The autobiographers give the impression that, unless their schooling had already been broken off, they were reading fluently by seven at the latest, even if, like young Thomas Boston, who 'had delight in reading' the Bible by that age, and took it to bed at night with him, 'nothing inclined me to it but . . . curiosity, as about the history of Balaam's ass'.

Writing began with Latin, if a grammar school education was in prospect, whether the boy began this stage of his education at seven like Oliver Sansom, at eight like John Evelyn, or at four like the forward little James Fretwell. It is even more difficult to find evidence on the time it took to master the second skill than the first. Yet one piece of very precise evidence does survive.

Alderman Samuel Newton of Cambridge kept a diary from 1664 to 1717. It contains very little personal information, amongst the accounts of corporation junketings and funerals of prominent persons. But on 12 February 1667, Alderman Newton wrote: 'On Tuesday was the first time John Newton my sonne went to the Grammar Free Schoole in Cambridge'. In October the same year, between a note on the assembly of parliament and a family baptism, appears an entry in a child's hand:

> I John Newton being in Coates this nineteenth day of October Anno Domini 1667 and not then full eight yeares old, wrote this by me
> John Newton.

There is no paternal comment on this entry, but Alderman Newton must have shared his son's satisfaction in the new achievement to allow the entry to be made. Obviously, to the seven-year-old John, the new skill of writing, which had taken six months to acquire, was a matter of as much pride as his emergence into manhood in his newly acquired breeches.

It seems likely, as a rule-of-thumb guide, that children who had the opportunity to go to school until they were seven were likely to be able to read. Those who remained at school until eight were likely to be able to write.

If it took the autobiographers, who may have been exceptionally gifted, four to six months to learn to read, and they began to acquire the skill at various ages from four to six, it seems reasonable to double this learning period to allow a margin of safety for less intelligent or forward children.[10] A working hypothesis would then be that children who had the opportunity of going to school would have learnt to read by seven. Similarly, since the autobiographers normally began the writing part of their curriculum at seven, and it took John Newton six months to write a good hand, it seems reasonable to double this period also, and suggest that the ability to write was normally acquired by eight.

If these hypotheses are accepted, it follows from the evidence collected by Cressy on occupational differences in ability to sign, showing that only 15 per cent of labourers and 21 per cent of husbandmen, as against 65 per cent of yeomen could sign, that these percentages roughly represent the proportion of those social groups which had the opportunity for schooling between seven and eight. Nothing could show more clearly that the economic status of the parents was the determinant of schooling,[11] along, of course, with the existence of some local teaching. The children of labourers and, to a lesser extent, of husbandmen, were needed to join the labour force as soon as they were strong enough to contribute meaningfully to the family economy.

It is difficult to conceive that they could have made a real contribution before six. The case of Thomas Tryon, whose father urgently needed his son's earnings, but still sent him to school from five until he was nearly six, bears this out. So does the literary evidence of Thomas Deloney, who was himself a weaver, who wrote in one of his extravagant novels glorifying the clothing trade in 1599 of a golden age in the past when:

> poor people whom God lightly blessed with most children did by meanes of this occupation so order them that by the time they were come to be six or seven years of age, they were able to get their own bread.

John Locke, who was by no means unacquainted with the realities of childhood, recommended as a commissioner of trade concerned with encouraging linen-manufacture in Ireland in 1696 that families without estate of 40/— a year should be compelled to send their children of both sexes aged between six and fourteen, to spinning schools. There they should work a ten-hour day. Parents should be free to send four to six-year olds also, if they so chose. The element of choice disappeared at six; obviously, to Locke, this was the viable age to start work.[12]

Further evidence for a starting age of six or seven comes from workhouse regulations of the sixteenth and seventeenth centuries governing the ages at which children could be set to work. These seem particularly likely to be reliable, since a municipal workhouse was very unlikely not to try to profit from children's labour if it were possible to do so. Westminster workhouse, in 1560, sent its children over six, but not yet twelve, 'to wind Quills for weavers'.[13]

The Aldersgate workhouse, in 1677, admitted children of from three to ten, and its founder wrote 'as to young children, there is nothing they can more easily learn than to spin linen, their fingers, though never so little, being big enough to pull the flax and make a fine thread'. At the time, in 1678 and 1681 when he wrote, he had 'some children not above seven or eight years old, who are able to earn two pence a day'.[14] In 1699, the Bishopgate workhouse was established for all poor parish children over the age of seven. They were to be employed from seven in the morning until six at night, with an hour off for dinner and play, and two hours' instruction in reading and writing.[15] This workhouse, which was, incidentally, a humane one by contemporary standards, was obviously run on the assumption that its children could all work these hours. It is highly significant, therefore, that it did not admit children under seven. It looks very much as if seven was thought to be the age at which a child could cope with a full working day and start to earn a wage which began to be significant.[16] It was also the age at which Tudor parents had a statutory duty to see that their sons practised regularly at the butts, that is, were strong enough to begin to be thought significant in the adult world of the militia. Obviously, rural children could only be regularly employed in areas where textile industries provided the kind of outwork performed by these city orphans. In many areas, their opportunities for work were likely to be more seasonal, and more along the lines described by Henry Best. His 'spreaders of muck and molehills' were for the most part women, boys and girls, and they were paid 3*d*. a day for the 'bigger and abler sort' and

2*d*. a day for the 'lesser sort'. Obviously a child was started at work before seven if there was a great need, as the cases of Thomas Tryon and the Westminster workhouse children show.

If seven were indeed the age at which a child could earn significant wages, and was regarded as an embryonic member of the militia as well as the workforce, it also seems to have been the age at which reading had probably been mastered, but writing not yet embarked on. If this conclusion is true, it is an important one. It indicates that reading skills, which unfortunately by their nature are not capable of measurement, were likely to have been very much more socially widespread in sixteenth- and seventeenth-century England than writing skills, simply because the age at which children learnt to read was one at which children of the relatively poor were not yet capable of much paying labour, and were therefore available for some schooling. The restriction of writing ability to a small percentage of labourers' and husbandmen's sons, and its much wider spread amongst the sons of the yeomanry is at once explained. Reading skills are likely to have been very much more diffused. It was, of course, the ability to read (and not the ability to write) that laid the way open to cultural change.

The argument can, of course, be started the other way round. We know that 15 per cent of labourers' sons could sign their names and presumably could read; we know that a much higher proportion of yeomen's sons could do so. We therefore know that economic necessity is likely to have been the factor that limited the opportunity to learn. It seems that a boy was physically strong and co-ordinated enough to contribute to the family budget in a significant way at some age between six and eight. The crucial question is whether this point was nearer six, or nearer seven. On the answer to this, as well as the local availability of schooling, depended the number of boys, from different occupational backgrounds, who could read.

No identifiable autobiographer was fathered by an agricultural labourer, although at least one autobiographer became an agricultural labourer. Thomas Tryon, of the autobiographers who identified their backgrounds, came from the poorest home, and he certainly had the most prolonged struggle to get himself an education. He was born in 1634 at Bibury in Oxfordshire, and was the son of a village tiler and plasterer 'an honest sober Man of good Reputation; but having many Children, was forced to bring them all to work betimes'. Tilers and plasterers were building craftsmen, and as such were more prosperous than agricultural labourers, but the purchasing power of their wages was very low in the early seventeenth century.[17]

The size of the family did much to dictate educational opportunity, for obvious reasons. Again and again, only children or those from small families amongst the autobiographers appear at an advantage. Despite his numerous siblings, young Thomas was briefly sent to school. 'About Five Year old, I was put to School, but being addicted to play, after the Example of my young

School-fellows, I scarcely learnt to distinguish my Letters, before I was taken away to Work for my Living.' This seems to have been before he was six, although his account is ambiguous. At six young Thomas Tryon was either not strongly motivated, as he obviously thought himself from his mention of the importance of play, or he was not well taught. Yet it is worth remembering that he was removed from school to work at about the age Oliver Sansom began to learn. His failure to learn to read was going to take great determination to repair.

His contribution to the family economy began immediately and he obviously took tremendous pride in his ability to contribute: 'The first Work my Father put me to, was Spinning and Carding, wherein I was so Industrious and grew so expert that at Eight Years of Age I could Spin Four Pound a day which came to Two Shillings a Week.' He continued to spin until he was twelve or thirteen but by the time he was ten 'began to be weary of the Wheel' and started to help the local shepherds with their flocks on Sundays, to earn a penny or twopence on his own account. When his father wished to apprentice him to his own trade he obeyed very reluctantly, for by this time he was determined to become a shepherd. 'My Father was unwilling to gratifie me herein . . . but by continually importuning him, at last I prevailed, and he bought a small number of Sheep; to the keeping and management whereof, I betook myself with much satisfaction and delight, as well as care.' But now, at last, at the age when his most fortunate contemporaries were about to go to University,[18] the desire for literacy gripped Thomas. It is worth quoting his account of the way he managed to satisfy it in full.

> All this while, tho' now about Thirteen Years Old, I could not Read; then thinking of the vast usefulness of Reading, I bought me a Primer, and got now one, then another, to teach me to Spell, and so learn'd to Read imperfectly, my Teachers themselves not being ready Readers: But in a little time having learn't to Read competently well, I was desirous to learn to Write, but was at a great loss for a Master, none of my Fellow-Shepherds being able to teach me. At last, I bethought myself of a lame young Man who taught some poor People's Children to Read and Write; and having by this time got two Sheep of my own, I applied myself to him, and agreed with him to give him one of my Sheep to teach me to make the Letters, and Joyn them together.

The difficulty Thomas found in learning to write, as opposed to learning to read, seems very important. Although his fellow shepherds, as a group, were not 'ready' readers, they did, again as a group, possess the capacity to help him to learn to spell out words. He was not dependent on only one of them to help him. But although these Gloucestershire shepherds could read, they could not write at all. A semi-qualified teacher was called for, and it took some effort to find him.

Thomas Tryon eventually went to London as an apprentice. His addiction to print continued. He made time to read by sitting up at night for two or three hours after his day's work was finished. His wages went on education. 'Therewith I furnished myself with Books, paid my Tutors and served all my occasions.' He was particularly interested in the art of medicine which he defined as the 'whole study of Nature' and within that, astrology, which he defined as the 'Method of God's government in Nature . . . [which] ought no more to be condemned because of the common abuse of it, than Religion ought, because its so commonly perverted to Superstition, or made a Cloak to Hypocrisie and Knavery'. Even after his marriage at thirty-five, he remained an incurable self-improver and then took music lessons.

> About Five and Thirty Years, I attempted to learn Musick and having a natural propensity thereto, made a pretty good progress on the Base-viol, tho' during the time of my learning, I . . . stuck as close to my working Trade, as ever before; so that I could only apply an Hour or Two to Musick, taking my opportunities at Night, or in a morning as best I could; and the time others spent in a Coffee-house or Tavern, I spent in Reading, Writing, Musick or some useful Imployment; by which means I supplyed what I could the defect of Education.

His written works which reflected his own range of interests included *The Country Man's Companion*, *The Good Housewife made a Doctor*, *Dreams and Visions*, *Book of Trade*, *Friendly Advice to the People of the West Indies*, *A New Method of Education* and, most surprisingly of all, *Averroes Letter to Pythagoras*. It is a remarkable publication list for a boy who left school at six before he could read.

When Thomas Tryon came to write down his 'Principles' for the religious group he founded, his own experiences, including his battle for literacy, were directly reflected in them. In his 'Laws and Orders proper for Women to observe', he wrote, amongst various rules for the upbringing of children which were, on the whole, remarkably sane and tolerant:

> At a Year and a Half or Two Years Old, shew them their Letters, not troubling them in the vulgar way with asking them what is this Letter, or that Word; but instead thereof, make frequent Repetitions in their hearing, putting the Letters in their Sight. And thus in a little time, they will easily and familiarly learn to distinguish the Twenty Four Letters, all one as they do the Utensils, Goods, and Furniture of the House, by hearing the Family name them. *At the same time*, teach your Children to hold the Pen, and guide their Hand; and by this method, your Children, un-accountably to themselves, will attain to Read and Write at Three, Four, or Five years old . . . When your Children are of dull Capacities and hard to Learn, Reproach them not nor expose them, but taking them alone . . . shew them

the Advantages of Learning, and how much it will tend to their advancement.

His advocacy of flash-cards has a strangely modern ring about it, as does his suggestion of teaching writing at the same time as reading. His assumption that the teaching of reading is the natural function of the mother, is an interesting one, particularly since several of the autobiographers were in fact taught to read by their mothers. The few literate women in seventeenth-century society may well have had a disproportionately large influence.

A boy from a husbandman's background, rather than a skilled labourer's, was more likely to be lucky enough to be spared from work for long enough to gain a rudimentary education, although his education was likely to be constantly interrupted by more pressing agricultural business. Thomas Carleton described the situation of such a boy very well.

> I sprang of mean (though honest) Parents according to the flesh, my Father being a Husbandman, in the County of Cumberland, I (according to his pleasure) was educated sometimes at School, sometimes with Herding, and tending of Sheep, or Cattel, sometime with the Plow, Cart, or threshing-Instrument, or other lawfull labour.

This background of sporadic schooling enabled him, when the spiritual need took him, to 'give myself to reading and Searching of the Scriptures'. Intermittent educational experience like this was probably typical of the fifth of the husbandmen[19] who were lucky enough to get as far as learning to write their names.

John Bunyan, the best known of all the seventeenth-century dissenters, came of poor parentage, although his parents were more prosperous or their family less numerous than Thomas Tryon's. He never had to struggle for a basic education as Tryon did. His father held a cottage and nine acres in Bedfordshire. This was barely adequate for subsistence. He eked out a living by tinkering rather than by wage-labour, and so is classifiable either as a husbandman on his acreage, or as a poor craftsman on his trade. Despite their relative poverty, Bunyan wrote 'notwithstanding the meanness of . . . my Parents, it pleased God to put it into their Hearts to put me to School, to learn both to read and write'. He was fully conscious of having had educational advantages which exceeded his parents' social position.

Amongst the autobiographers who described their parentage only Baxter and Bunyan also confessed to the reading of cheap print as a childhood sin. The yeoman's son, Richard Baxter, listed amongst his early sins committed about the age of ten, 'I was extremely bewitched with a love of romances, fables and old tales, which corrupted my affections and lost my time'. He also gives a very rare glimpse of a chapman at work in the 1630s: 'About that time it pleased God that a poor pedlar came to the door that had ballads and some good books: and my father bought of him Dr Sibb's *Bruised Reed*.'

Bunyan is also likely to have got his reading matter from the chapmen, either at the door or at market. Elstow, where he was brought up, is two miles from the county-town of Bedford, which was not a large enough provincial town to have a bookshop in the seventeenth century. Moreover, the reading matter he describes is chapmen's ware. He was much more specific than Baxter about his tastes in his youth. He wrote:

> give me a Ballard, a News-book, *George* on Horseback or *Bevis of Southampton*, give me some book that teaches curious Arts, that tells of old Fables; but for the Holy Scriptures, I cared not. And as it was with me then, so it is with my brethren now.

The implication is plain that either Bunyan's relations or his peer group were, at the time Bunyan was writing in the 1660s, commonly readers of the ballads and chapbooks which Bunyan himself avoided after his conversion.

Bunyan's reading seems to have left some mark on him.[20] *Bevis of Southampton* was a typical, breathless, sub-chivalric romance in which adventure follows adventure in quick succession. The hero's mother betrays his father to death and marries his murderer. Her son first escapes and keeps his uncle's sheep on a hill near his father's castle, then is sold into slavery to the 'paynims'. There he refuses to serve 'Apoline' their god, kills a gigantic wild boar, is made a general over twenty thousand men, and wins the love of the princess. Alas, he is betrayed, and thrown into a dungeon with two dragons who quickly get the worst of it. He is still able to kill his jailer, after seven years on bread and water, and runs off with the princess and a great store of money and jewels. He is next attacked by two lions in a cave, meets 'an ugly Gyant thirty foot in length and a foot between his eyebrows', defeats him and makes him his page, and kills a dragon forty foot long. He then has the heathen princess baptised, and after numerous further adventures invades England, avenges his father's death, marries his paynim lady, and is made Lord Marshall. There is no attempt at characterization and the whole piece of blood-and-thunder writing seems aimed at pre-adolescent or adolescent males; very successfully, if Bunyan's testimony is to be believed. Although his own writing was very far removed from this, some of his imagery does seem to have come from his early reading. The lions Christian met by the way, the description of the monster Apollyon and the cave where the giants Pope and Pagan dwelt all owe something to it, as perhaps, does Giant Despair himself. It is worth remembering also that Bunyan's own voluminous output was surely aimed at the rural readership he knew in the villages around Bedford amongst which he had his ministry. He knew his readership was familiar with the giants, lions, dragons and battles of the chapbooks, just as it was with the cadences of the Authorized Version.

Arise Evans, who came from the Welsh border, was born in 1606 or 1607. His father was a good deal better off than either Bunyan's or Tryon's, and sounds indeed like a prosperous yeoman, or even a minor gentleman, from his son's description:

> My father being a sufficient man of the Parish did entertain the
> Curate always at his Table, and gave him a little Tenement of Land
> to live upon; and by reason of this kindness to the Minister, which
> had but small allowance from the Parson of the Parish, that had all
> the Tithes. The Minister was diligent to do my father's family what
> good he was able: and as soon as I began to speak plain, I was put to
> school to him.

But when Arise was only six, his father died.

A surprisingly large number of autobiographers who give any factual details
of themselves at all dwell on the deaths of one, or both of their parents. It
seems that as many as one eighth of children may have lost their fathers by
the time they were seven, the age at which I suggest they might have learnt to
read, but not to write.[21] The death of the father leaving a young family always
meant that the family economy collapsed. A son still at school usually left,
either to earn his living, or to help his mother. Frequently he seems to have
slithered down the social scale permanently; it is for this reason that some
account of the life of a farm labourer survives. It was written by a boy who
was at grammar school until his father's death, but who became an in-servant
in husbandry after his mother's remarriage. The death of the mother involved
less economic hardship, but often considerable psychological distress for the
child. Historical demographers have so far emphasized infant mortality rates a
good deal more than parental mortality rates. It seems that the social and personal consequences of as many as one child in eight losing its father when it
was seven or less, were considerable, and deserve more attention.

The death of Arise Evans's father involved both economic and psychological
hardship for him; indeed, it seems from his autobiography that the trauma
involved could well have been one of the causes of his later emotional un-
balance and rather dubious visions. He had thought that he was his father's
favourite child. Certainly his father had shown great pride in his ability to
read aloud and had shown him off to visitors.

> It was not long before I attained to reade English perfectly, to the
> admiration of all that heard me: and because I was so young and so
> active in learning, all concluded that God had designed me for some
> great work . . . But . . . death takes away my father before I was
> seven years old, and now he forgets me at his death, that was his
> delight a little before; and making his last Will, he leaves a Portion to
> all his children by name, and to many of his kindred . . . But I was
> not so much as mentioned in his Will, nor any thing left for me, so
> that I came soon to know the folly of vain confidence in man . . .
> After this I was taken from school, when I had learned the *Accidence*
> out of Book, but never came to *Grammar*, or to write.

Arise never tells us how or when he did learn to write. Certainly, he had no
opportunity at the normal age. At eight when he should have learnt to write,

he was apprenticed to a tailor, far younger than usual. He retained from his brief period of education until some time in his seventh year a passion for the written word which he was hardly ever able to satisfy. One of the stories he tells dramatically illuminates this thirst for information and for books which he would satisfy at the cost of enormous personal discomfort, if only it were possible. At twenty-two he set off, like so many others, to work his way to London.

> And at Coventre I wrought and stayed a quarter of a year, by reason of an old Chronicle that was in my Master's house that showed all the passage in Brittain and Ireland from Noahs Floud to William the Conquerour, it was of great volume, and by day I bestowed what time I could spare to read, and bought Candles for the night, *so that I got by heart the most material part* of it.

This desire for information, together with the problems of even finding time to absorb it during the working day, or a source of light to read it by at night, seems to have been common to all largely self-educated working men at all periods. The physical difficulties the autobiographers encountered in the seventeenth century were fundamentally the same as those of their nineteenth-century heirs.[22]

Thomas Chubb, like Arise Evans and Thomas Tryon, was a boy from a rural background who moved to town, although in his case the town was Salisbury, not London. Also, like Arise Evans, the death of his father affected his prospects, though not so seriously. He was the son of a maltster of East Harnham, born in 1679. His father died when he was nine, leaving a widow and five children, of which he was the youngest. He wrote of himself in the introduction to a lengthy work on the Scriptures.

> The Author was taught to read English, to write an ordinary hand, and was further instructed in the common rules of arithmetick; this education being suitable to the circumstances of his family and to the time he had to be instructed in. For as the Author's mother laboured hard, in order to get a maintenance for herself and family, so she obliged her children to perform their parts towards it. Accordingly, the Author was very early required to perform such work and service as was suitable for his age and capacity; so that he had neither time nor means for further instruction than the above mentioned.

When he was fifteen, in 1694, he was apprenticed to a glover in Salisbury. It is not certain from his account that he left school at nine, on his father's death, but it seems probable, since he would then have had two years in which to learn writing and elementary arithmetic. He had obviously attended one of the schoolmasters who was so frequently licensed in visitation records to teach 'to read, write and caste an accompte'.[23] He was never intended, or never had the chance, to embark on a grammar school curriculum. After he had served his apprenticeship he became a journeyman, but was handicapped as a glover by his weak sight. So, after 1705 he lived with, and worked for, a tallow-chandler. He served in the chandler's shop, and made gloves part-time only. He never married and it sounds as if his experience of poverty after his father's death had influenced him heavily in this:

> The Author . . . [judged] it greatly improper to introduce a family into the world, without a prospect of maintaining them, which was his case; such adventures being usually attended with great poverty . . . And tho', according to the proverb, God does not send mouths without sending meat to fill them; yet our Author saw, by daily experience, that meat to some was not to be obtained but with great difficulty. And as to trusting to providence, in such cases, the Author . . . did [not] find, that providence interposed to extricate it's . . . dependents out of their difficulties.

Thomas Chubb gives an account of the way his first tract came to be published. The fascination of this lies not in the account of the tract itself, but the way it reveals his own habits of written composition since his boyhood, and the literary activities of a whole group of young men like himself in Salisbury.

> When the reverend Mr. Whiston published his historical preface to those books he entitled *Primitive – christianity revived* . . . about 1711, that preface happened to fall into the hands of the Author and some of his acquaintance, who were *persons of reading* in Salisbury; and as some of his friends took part with Mr. Whiston in the main point controverted, viz. the single supremacy of the one God and the father of all; so some were against him, *which introduced a paper – controversy betwixt them*. And as the Author's friends were shy of expressing themselves plainly and fully upon the question, but chose rather to oppose each other by interrogations; so this appeared to the Author a way altogether unlikely to clear up the case, and bring the point debated to an issue . . . he was naturally led to draw up his thoughts upon the subject in the way that he did, as it appeared to him a more probable means of bringing the controversy to a conclusion. And this the Author did without . . . even a thought of it's being offered to publick consideration, but only for his own satisfaction, and for the information and satisfaction of his friends in Salisbury, to whom then his acquaintance was confined; *he having accustomed himself from his youth to put his thoughts into writing*, upon such subjects to which his attention had been called in; . . . thereby to arouse and satisfy himself, and then commit them to the flames, *which had been the case in many instances*. The Author . . . arranged his sentiments on the aforementioned subject . . . it was exposed to the view and perusal of his acquaintance . . . some of whom approved the performance, . . . but others thought

the contrary, and this induced a controversy in writing betwixt the Author and some of those who thought differently . . . and several letters and papers passed betwixt them.

Eventually one of Chubb's friends took the manuscript he had composed on this latest occasion to Whiston himself to ask for his opinion. Whiston had the manuscript published, and so the work of the Salisbury journeyman first reached the printed page.

He had a cool, rational, exploratory cast of mind. He was a theist, who denied the divinity of Christ, and looked with a critical eye on the Scriptures.

> This collection of writings has been the parent of doctrines most dis-
> honourable to God, and most injurous to men; such as the doctrine
> of absolute unconditional election and reprobation, of religious per-
> secution and the like . . .
>
> Besides, this book, called the holy Bible, contains many things that
> are greatly below, and unworthy of, the Supreme Deity . . . That
> [God] should . . . approve of, or countenance, such malevolent
> desires as these, 'Let his children be fatherless and his wife a widow;
> let his children be continually vagabonds, and beg . . . let his posterity
> be cut off, and in the generation following let their name be blotted
> out'. I say that such trifling observations, and such malevolent
> desires as these, should be considered as the offspring of God, is
> playing at hazard indeed.

His collected works, which included a treatise on 'Divine Revelation in General, and of the Divine Original of the Jewish, Mohometon and Christian Revelation in Particular' ended with a typical statement 'in what I have offered to the world, I have appealed to the understandings, and not to the passions of men'. His achievement is not as startling as Thomas Tryon's, but the vivid image of this urban artisan, too poor to marry and support a family, a part-time journeyman-glover with bad sight, a part-time assistant to a chandler, weighing out candles in the shop and at the same time ordering his thoughts to commit them to paper for his own pleasure, or that of his friends, in their next 'paper-controversy' is a fascinating one. This lively literate atmosphere of serious debate on theological subjects amongst the journeymen who were 'persons of reading' in early eighteenth-century Salisbury was, of course, urban, but Thomas Chubb participated in it, and apparently led it, from an education in a rural hamlet which taught him to read, write and count, prob-ably all before his tenth year, in the 1680s.

Shortly before Chubb began to write for publication in the second decade of the eighteenth century, Stephen Duck, the first of the eighteenth-century poets of the countryside to come from a humble rural background himself, was born at Chorlton St Peter, at the northern edge of the Salisbury Plain. His education was exactly similar to that of Thomas Chubb; he learnt to read and to write English and the 'arithmetic [which] is generally join'd with this

Degree of Learning'. His first biographer, Joseph Spence, wrote that he was not taken from school until he was fourteen, which sounds improbably late. His father was able to set him up on a small-holding after he left school, but after its failure he made his living as a day-labourer. His great opportunity for self-improvement came when he made friends with a man who had acquired two or three dozen books while in service in London. Amongst these were seven of Shakespeare's plays, Dryden, Virgil, Seneca, Ovid, the *Spectator* and Milton's *Paradise Lost*, which Duck read twice with the aid of a dictionary before he could understand it. He relied extensively on his memory, just as Arise Evans had done. When he first read Pope's *Essay on Criticism*, he memorized almost the whole of it overnight. The verses in the *Spectator* first triggered him into composing his own poetry. His own personal experience of day-labour and his absorption with these literary models and their vocabulary lay behind his most original poem, *The Thresher's Labour*.

Even though we are now considering a period in the 1720s, Stephen Duck's ability to read Milton, Dryden and Shakespeare and his ability to compose his own verses is invaluable evidence of the degree of literacy a basic seventeenth-century education could bestow. Of course, this day-labourer, like his older contemporary in Salisbury, the chandler's assistant, was a highly exceptional man. Nevertheless, he demonstrates the literate skills a boy from a poor rural background could develop, given an education until eight or nine in the seventeenth-century basic subjects, reading, writing and simple arithmetic.

Josiah Langdale was the first of the autobiographers considered here whose background was prosperous enough for long enough to bring him within reach of a grammar school education. He was born in 1673 in the village of Nafferton in the East Riding, and went to school 'after I grew up', as he wrote. His labour was not required until the death of his father, before he was nine. Then his mother found his labour essential to the family economy. Like Tryon, he took great pride and pleasure in his skills, which in his case were specifically rural, not industrial.

> I then was taken from School, and being a strong Boy, of my Years, was put to lead Harrows and learn to Plow, Also, in the Summer Time, I kept Cattel (we having in our Country both Horses and Oxen in Tethers) and moved them when there was Occasion with much Care, for I loved to see them in good Liking. In those Days, both when I followed the Plow and kept Cattel in the Field, I was religiously inclined . . . I had not time for much Schooling, being closely kept to what I could do in our way of Husbandry, yet I made a little Progress in Latin, but soon forgot it; I endeavoured how-ever, to keep my English, and could read the Bible, and delighted therein . . .
>
> I now being about Thirteen Years of Age, and growing strong, did my Mother good service; having attain'd to the knowledge of ordering

my Plow, and being expert in this Employment could go with Four horses, and plow alone, which we always did except in Seed time; I very much delighted in holding the Plow, It being an Employment suitable to my Mind, and no Company to disturb my Contemplation, therefore I loved it the more, and found by experience that to have my mind inward and to contemplate the Ways and Works of God was a great Benefit and Comfort to me.

Josiah's inclinations were not all devotional, however, and he was much drawn towards dancing, which was an important adolescent pastime in Nafferton. He gives the only account I have seen of the way this important leisure activity was learnt in the countryside. At this point his account becomes confused, for he seems to have learnt dancing after school at night, before he was fourteen, even though he had left regular school, and lost his Latin before he was nine. It sounds as if he attended sporadically when agricultural routine allowed it, after his ninth year. Just possibly the schooling that included Latin, before this, had been outside Nafferton, unless country masters able to teach grammar also frequently taught dancing at night.

> Dancing took much with the young People of our Town . . . Much Evil was committed at this School . . . The Dancing Master was a Fidler and Jugler, and after we broke up School every Night he went to play his Tricks. I did not learn many Dances before it became an exceeding Trouble to my Soul and Spirit . . . After some time my Playfellows would entice me to Feasts, where young men and women meet to be merry . . . and such Like was I invited to, under a Pretence to improve our Dancing.

Josiah's fortunes changed again when his mother remarried after seven years of widowhood, and no longer needed him. At that point the fifteen-year-old became an in-servant in husbandry. His spiritual search continued, and was fed by an influential close friend in his second year as a servant. His account of his friend shows just how limited seventeenth-century literacy could be.

> After I was come to my new Master, he had a young strong Man that was his Thresher, but he was blind, and had been so for about Twenty Years, who had lost his Sight when about Ten Years of Age; He was never Taught further than the Psalter as I have heard him often say; yet this Man taught our Master's Children, and afterwards became a famous Schoolmaster . . . He was a Man of great Memory, and of good Understanding.

If reading could be taught by the blind, the role of memorization and rote-learning must have been very great indeed.

Josiah's description of his conversations and recreations with this friend gives some insight into the world of this literate pair of labourers in the 1680s, and the astonishingly cool and appraising round of sectarian sermon-tasting they indulged in, and their worries about the necessity of the sacraments, which held them back from Quakerism for some time. Their opinions were based on Bible reading.

> We would walk out together on First-Day mornings in the Summer-time several Miles a-foot, to hear such Priests as were the most famed for Preaching; and as we walked together we should have such Talk as was profitable. One Time as we were coming home from hearing one of the most famous and learned of these Priests in our Country, Well, said he, Josiah, I am weary with hearing these Priests, they are an idle Generation, they cannot be Ministers of Jesus Christ; This Sermon that we heard to Day I heard this man preach some years ago; as soon as he took his Text I thought how he would manage it, and accordingly as I thought he would go on so he did — I do not know, said he, what People to join in Society with — I have looked in my Mind over the Church of England, Presbyterians, Baptists and the Quakers, and do say the Quakers excel all people in Conversation . . . but, said he they do not use Baptism and the Lords Supper . . . So, as I followed my Business, which was mostly Plowing, serious thoughts began again to flow afresh in upon me . . . We Two would often go on First Day Mornings into the Field, taking a Bible with us, and there we would sit down together, and after I have read a while, we have sat silent, waiting with Desires in our Hearts after the Lord.

The blind thresher and the literate ploughman had possibly become in-servants for the same reasons that their education had been disrupted, in one case the accident or disease that had caused blindness, in the other the demographic accident of parental loss. But there must have been a constant trickle of semi-literate people into agricultural labour for just these reasons, and although this literate pair in Yorkshire were probably unusual, they were certainly not unique. Richard Baxter's first 'stirrings of conscience' in about 1630 in rural Shropshire were prompted by 'a poor day-labourer' in the town who normally did 'the reading of the psalms and chapters' in church, and who lent Baxter's father 'an old, torn book . . . called *Bunny's Resolution*' which influenced young Richard. These examples of literate labourers may be taken to represent the 15 per cent of labourers between 1580 and 1700 who could sign their names.[24] We may firmly deduce from the evidence of the order in which reading and writing was taught, and the experience of the autobiographers given above, that those who could sign their names could all read. The existence of this literate group amongst agricultural labourers is one of the reasons which leads me to stress the magnitude of the change in English society between 1500 and 1700. It proves my contention that illiteracy was everywhere face to face with literacy, and the oral with the printed word. Schofield suggested some time ago that 'there were probably groups in the population, such as agricultural labourers in certain parts of the country, which were entirely cut off from any contact with the literate culture'.[25] Cressy recently concurred. Although he conceded that the presence of even one reader amongst a group of rural labourers could act as a significant bridge to the literate world, he feels that 'normally these ordinary people were indifferent to the political and religious controversies which exercised their betters'.[26] Langdale's account of lively debate scarcely bears him out. I think the combination of the existence of a measurable proportion of labourers able to sign over a period of time, combined with the amount of cheap print in circulation, combined again with the brief impressions I am able to gather from Langdale, Baxter, and Thomas Tryon's group of reading shepherds, justifies the disagreement. It seems, from the life expectancy for adult males in the seventeenth century, and the proportion of children who lost their fathers early, that there was a constant slithering down the social ladder. The steady trickle of semi-educated orphaned boys into apprenticeship and into service was one of the ways largely illiterate groups came to contain 'literate' members in the sixteenth and seventeenth centuries.

All the autobiographers quoted so far either come from too poor a background, or suffered too much from their father's early death to go to grammar school. The next group of men come from yeomen or trading backgrounds, and their education was interrupted by their fathers at an appropriate point in time when they had absorbed as much as would be of use. They were never intended for the universities. A third of the autobiographers who identified their social backgrounds and their educational experiences fully became apprentices at fourteen.[27] Here is a very important correction to a view of seventeenth-century education based on university entrants alone. Such a view necessarily completely neglects the flow of boys from the schools into the various trades. The evidence of the autobiographers suggests this flow was very considerable. The boys involved came from a tremendous social and economic range.

George Trosse of Exeter was the son of a prominent lawyer who had married the daughter of a merchant who had twice been Mayor. George shone at grammar school and his master objected when he was removed at fifteen 'having a mind to be a Merchant'. Alderman Newton of Cambridge certainly took great pride in his son's intellectual achievement, or he would not have allowed him to celebrate his new skill of writing at seven by making an entry in his own diary; but proud as he was of this grammar school product, he apprenticed him to a dry-salter at fourteen. The boys concerned were not merely sons of townsmen, however. The autobiographies contain ample evidence of the degree of magnetism exerted by the towns. London was, of course, pre-eminent. The autobiographies provide a mass of evidence on the formative effects of their apprenticeships then, and the Puritan meetings and occasions they then attended. Their backgrounds were as diverse as the distances they travelled to get there. Arise Evans had walked across country from Wales, Thomas Tryon from Gloucestershire. William Crouch was the son of a substantial yeoman of Hampshire, and his father's early death and the Civil War combined deprived him of both his inheritance on the land which he expected from his father's will, and also the grammar school education he regarded, with some justification, as his right as a yeoman's son. He also ended up, after much wandering, as a London apprentice. Benjamin Bangs, son of a prosperous Norfolk yeoman who died when he was a small child, has a similar history, except that he was more humbly apprenticed to a local shoemaker, and ended in London more by accident than design.

The provincial towns also drew in boys from rural backgrounds. Thomas Chubb was only one of the boys who went to Salisbury. The fanatic William Dewsbury was apprenticed to a clock-maker in Leeds at thirteen, specifically because he wanted to explore Quakerism and knew he could do so there. William Edmundson, yet another orphan, the youngest of six children, of a Westmorland family whose mother died when he was four, his father when he was eight, also lost his portion under his father's will. He was apprenticed to a carpenter and joiner in York. George Bewley was a second generation Quaker, born in Cumberland in 1684. He attended a school about a mile from home until he was twelve, when he was sent to board with an uncle to attend a school twenty miles away. This sounds like a grammar education. At fourteen, he was sent as apprentice to a Quaker linen-draper in Dublin. His parents kept in touch with him by letter, and more interesting, his sister, the eldest child, frequently wrote him long letters also. Apart from these boys from the country apprenticed to masters in provincial towns, many others were simply apprenticed to local craftsmen in their own area. The outstanding example is, of course, George Fox, the Leicestershire weaver's son apprenticed to a shoe-maker. The main utility of a seventeenth-century education, judging from the autobiographies, was to prepare boys for an apprenticeship. A university education beginning for some of the autobiographers at about fourteen was a highly specialized and rare type of apprenticeship preparing boys for the Church.

Boys who came from slightly more prosperous backgrounds than those just described or who had not been precipitated down the social ladder by their father's death, sons of wholesale traders and yeomen, were given a grammar education to an appropriate level of usefulness, before being claimed from school by their fathers. Some of them were simply sons of yeomen, being prepared for the activities and lives of the more prosperous farmers who acted as local officials in their areas, with no thought of a university training. Grammar education often seems to have been assumed by such people, university education was not. The next group of autobiographers gives some insight into the social world of the yeomen, and its expectations.

James Fretwell, who was born right at the end of the seventeenth century, came from a family of yeomen and traders, timber merchants, horse-breeders and dealers, carpenters and brasiers. James's father, who was born in the 1670s, went to grammar school, but his father removed him to 'put him to his own business' after 'he had learn'd so far as my grandfather thought was needful'. He was a substantial timber-merchant. The family pattern was repeated. James went to grammar school before he was five. Because this school was five miles away it was too far for such a small child to walk, although he began by trying it, so he was boarded out during the week with a widow who lived near the school. The autobiographers were commonly boarded out like this, to get over the problems of accessibility caused by scattered schools. Between five and fourteen, James and his younger brother went to three separate schools and were boarded with three different families. It is just possible from his account that the availability of relatives or ex-servants with whom to board the children dictated the change of school. By the time he left the second, at thirteen, he 'had made an entrance into Greek'. When he was fourteen, his father 'thinking I had got as much of the learned languages as would be of service to a tradesman . . . thought it time to learn something which was more immediately related to the qualifying of me for business: therefore he sent me to Pontefract, to learn to write and to accompt'. He was taught by a Quaker linen-draper, who kept a school which was partly run by his apprentice who 'was a good penman'. James who was fluent in Latin and had had two years Greek seems to have been astonishingly uncertain of his writing. Again, the separation between the two skills is emphasized: 'I had learn't some little to write before, but nothing of accounts that I remember. Here it was that I got what learning I have of that kind. I went through most of the rules of vulgar arithmetick and decimal fractions, with some little of practical geometry.' Then James, like his father before him, left school. There was never any thought of university for him.

Oliver Sansom had been born over sixty years earlier, at Beedon in Berkshire, and was also the son of a timber-merchant, who had married a yeoman's daughter. His educational experiences closely paralleled James Fretwell's. He began later. At seven, he was sent to board with an aunt to learn 'latin, and writing'. He had another change of schools at ten, but 'stayed not long there, my father having occasion to take me home to keep his book, and look after what I was capable of in his business, which was dealing in timber and wood'. Oliver Sansom's autobiography, together with that of the Quaker John Whiting of Somerset gives most insight into the literate yeoman world of the seventeenth century. It was a world in which the ability to read was assumed, without question. The very unself-consciousness of the incidental remarks that give away the manner in which literate skills were used in everyday living, amongst wives and daughters as well as friends, are revealing of the way in which literacy was an accepted skill. Oliver Sansom 'took great delight, even in my tenders years, in reading the Holy Scriptures, and other godly books

which I met with'. When he married, his wife was 'of a good yeomanry family
and had been brought up in a sober and suitable way of education . . . I
walked as before, in great seriousness of mind, and spent much time in reading good books, the holy Scriptures more especially; with which my wife and
her relations, as well as my own, were greatly affected.' Oliver's autobiography
includes a whole series of letters written to his wife during his lengthy series
of imprisonments. More important, when he had smallpox he adjured his
wife, 'I desire thee not to venture to come to me, until thou hear further
from me, but let me hear from thee as often as thou canst'. His wife's sister
also wrote to him in prison. In 1670 he wrote, 'I would have thee remember
me dearly to thy sister, and let her know that I received her letter and was
sweetly refreshed in the sense of the love of God which is manifested in and
through her'.

Oliver Sansom's father had bought him a 'copyhold estate' at Boxford,
near Newbury, after his marriage, and he settled down to lead the life of a
yeoman farmer. He had one serving man to help him, so his acreage cannot
have been very large. But he was a person of consequence in the neighbourhood, well liked by his neighbours despite his Quaker beliefs. On one of his
releases from prison after a two-year spell, 'many of my neighbours came running to welcome me home'. Indeed, in 1665, a situation reminiscent of pure
farce arose when the priest spent an evening searching for the tithingman and
the village constable to break up a Quaker meeting at Sansom's house. He
failed to find them, because they were at it. This same priest was responsible
for an event which reveals more of Sansom's assumptions about literacy than
any other. In 1668, he embarked on a public tirade against Sansom, at the
Court Leet of Boxford and Westbrook, when he accused him of denying the
Trinity and the Sacraments, and

> made a long clamourous speech against me, using many bitter,
> reviling words. And not satisfied with that, he in his fury with his
> own hands plucked my hat from my head two several times, in the
> presence of all the people . . . thus he spent much of the time until
> he went to dinner, endeavouring . . . to make me a gazing-stock to
> the whole assembly.

Oliver Sansom was very upset, obviously partly because the Leet contained
'the chief men of three or four parishes'. He objected to being made a spec-
tacle in front of such a group. His immediate redress to re-establish his credit
and defend himself was to write a paper of rebuttal. 'This little Paper, I
fastened to a post in the middle of the great hall where the court was kept,
that it might be seen and read of all those present.' He took it down after 'it
had stuck there some time and was pretty well viewed'. His implicit assumption was that 'the chief men of three or four parishes' could, and did, read, so
that his paper of defence was as good a means of answering the charges against

himself and re-establishing himself in their eyes as the speech he apparently lacked the opportunity to make.[28]

John Whiting of Naylsey in Somerset was born in 1656, the son of a convinced Quaker yeoman 'having a competent estate in the same parish, where my ancestors lived for several generations'. Despite the early deaths of his father, his mother, and then his stepfather, this estate was evidently considerable enough to keep John at school. He does not tell us at what age he left. He was certainly still there at twelve and may have been there until fourteen. He went to grammar school, along with the sons of the local minister, but there was never from his writing any suggestion of his going on to university. At nineteen he left his guardian and took up active farming, which was frequently disrupted by imprisonment for his beliefs.

Whiting's autobiography is in itself the most compelling piece of evidence that he shared the assumption of that other yeomen, Oliver Sansom. Unlike all but a very few of the autobiographies, it is a piece of work of which parts can still be read for their intrinsic interest. Whiting was a sober, shrewd and perceptive observer. He noted his own reactions as a child when his conscience impelled him to put Quaker beliefs into practice and 'the plain language also cost me very dear, it was so hard to take it up, that I could have gone miles about rather than to have met some of my relations to speak to them'. He noted the shocked reactions of the prisoners who watched Jeffries's retribution for Monmouth's rebellion, and recorded 'they forced poor men to hale about mens quarters like horse-flesh or carrion, to boil and hang them up as monuments of their cruelty'. He inserted potted biographies of the other Friends he talked about, and they frequently come off. His gossip is interesting too, as when he wrote of a proclamation from Elizabeth Bathurst's pen in 1679: 'This treatise was so extraordinary, both for depth of matter and expression that some would not believe it was written by her, being but a weakly maid, though it was known to be her own writing.' His considering, unhysterical cast of mind comes through very clearly, and it is no surprise that he continued to hold local office in his parish, where he was overseer of the poor in 1679, despite his Quakerism, which had first cut him off from his peer group when he reluctantly gave up playing with the other boys after school at night when he was twelve.

Although the quality of his autobiography is the best testimonial for John Whiting's education, there is plenty of other evidence in it for the importance that reading held for him. Of course, he read 'the scriptures of truth, which I diligently read as well as fireside books' as a boy. He also produces evidence on the remarkable degree of organization reached by the Quaker book trade. In one of his imprisonments he remarked incidentally, 'I had a parcel of friends books, etc., come down from London, as I used to have . . . and the carrier left them, as he used to do for me, at Nerberryinn.' His reading spread wider than the Bible and sectarian propaganda though; he refers to Eusebius, and to Bishop Burnet.

All the autobiographers touched on so far were without benefit of university education. Another third of those who identified both their social backgrounds and their educational experiences did go on to university. Most, though not all, of them came from more prosperous yeomen, small gentry, merchant and ministry backgrounds. I have not considered them here, because their experiences are more familiar[29] than the struggle to acquire basic literary skills displayed by the poorest autobiographers. These boys appear from the worm's eye view of the humbler autobiographers as an educational élite. But to summarize their circumstances as 'prosperous' or 'privileged' is of course relative. To the Chubbs and Tryons of seventeenth-century society, they were indeed privileged; but the plight of Henry Jessey, who in 1623 at Cambridge had 3*d*. a day for his 'provision of diet' and spent some of this on hiring the books he could not afford to buy, demonstrates just how relative this 'privilege' was. The most succinct description of the physical difficulties of finding privacy and quiet in which to work which were suffered by boys from humble background acquiring an education is provided by Thomas Boston. His father, who was a maltster, could put him through grammar school; but at the end of it Thomas spent two years trying to find notarial work, or raise the fees for university somehow. In that time he battled to keep up his Latin, and re-read his Justinian 'the malt-loft being my closet'.

The general impression given by the autobiographers is that boys from non-yeoman backgrounds quite frequently had a year or two's sporadic education, but it was often broken off before seven either by family needs or demographic mishap. Those boys who were fortunate enough to be supported at school until fourteen divided into two groups. Some went into apprenticeships; some to the universities as an apprenticeship to the Church, or to teaching. The latter almost all came from yeomen, or more prosperous families.

Oxford and Cambridge had nothing to do with the 'literate' worlds of the Yorkshire labourers Langdale and his friend Hewson, and the Wiltshire labourer Stephen Duck, the Gloucestershire shepherds who taught Tryon to read, the Bedfordshire small craftsman, John Bunyan, whose tastes in reading changed, the urban artisans with rural educations, Tryon, Chubb and Crouch, and the more assured and confident Berkshire and Wiltshire yeomen, Sansom and Whiting. Much more important, only Langdale, Sansom and Whiting amongst them owed anything to the grammar schools. The picture they jointly convey is one of a society in which a boy even from a relatively poor family might have a year or two's education up to six or seven. If he was at school until seven he could read, if he was at school until eight or at the latest nine, he could write. Either way he would be able to make sense of whatever cheap print the pedlars brought within his reach. Either way, his mental environment had undergone an enormous and very important change.

There is, of course, no real conflict between recent work stressing the social restrictiveness of grammar and university education in Tudor and Stuart England and the glimpses the autobiographers give us of the spread of elementary skills, particularly reading, amongst the very humble. Yet emphasis on the first, however well justified, gives an incomplete picture unless it is tempered by the second. It is particularly incomplete in view of the likelihood that boys below the level of yeomen were quite likely to learn to read, since reading was taught at an age when they could earn little, whereas writing was commonly taught at an age after the meaningful earning lives of such boys had begun. An account of 'literacy' based on the only measurable skill, the ability to sign, necessarily omits this possibility that reading was a much more socially diffused skill than writing. Since the psychological and social changes brought about by the spread of reading skills were very great, the evidence of the humbler autobiographers of their acquisition of reading skills ought to be taken into account, if a balanced picture of the effects of the combined spread of cheap print and elementary education in the sixteenth and seventeenth centuries is to be obtained.

Additional note on the influence of 'literate' women

'Literate' by definition implies the ability to write. It seems quite likely, however, that many schooldames taught reading who could not themselves write, and who also escaped the episcopal licensing procedure. Bishop Lloyd compiled a very detailed shorthand survey of the small market town and parish of Eccleshall in Staffordshire in which he himself had a seat, between 1693–8. It contained the names of no less than one man and five women from whom he described as 'schoolteachers,' as well as a visiting 'writing master' who came twice a year for six weeks. (Transcripts of the Survey of the Township of Eccleshall, 1697, and the Parish of Eccleshall, 1693–8, compiled by N.W. Tildesley (1969) in the William Salt Library, Stafford.) Not a single one of these people appears in the diocesan records at all, although Eccleshall is, admittedly, a peculiar. (I am much indebted to Dr Alan Smith for this information.) Four of the five women were wives of day-labourers and of small craftsmen. This is a social group of women who have completely escaped observation. They may have played a very important part in preliminary education, as the frequency with which authors, from Dr Johnson down to Oliver Sansom and James Fretwell, refer to their schooldames who taught the first steps, shows. This runs counter to David Cressy's suggestion that 'since women were rarely educated themselves, it is unlikely that they played a great part in expanding the literate public' (*thesis cit.*, 179–81). The autobiographies do contain a number of examples of mothers teaching reading, however. They included mothers like Benjamin Bangs' mother, daughter of a Hertfordshire clergyman married to a Norfolk yeoman, who was left widowed with nine children in the mid 1650s. She was obliged to sell the farm as soon as the oldest children were old enough to be put to service, but the youngest three she kept at home 'under her Care and Instruction . . . We were all indeed indifferently well brought up both in reading and writing; and although we of the younger sort were most behind, yet we were able to signify our Minds to one another by our Pens'. Benjamin Bangs, *Memoirs of the Life and Convincement* (1757). Of more interest socially than this example of a woman spreading literate skills downwards socially through demographic accident are those of women who could not themselves write, who deliberately fostered reading skills. Oliver Heywood's mother, wife of a Lancashire fustian-weaver, seems only to have been able to read. As a young girl after her conversion in 1614 she 'took her bible with her and spent the whole day in reading and praying'. Later her son went with her to Puritan exercises and sermons. Afterwards he wrote, 'was in some measure helpful to her memory by the notes of sermons I took'. He regularly sent her notes of sermons when he went up to Cambridge, and as an old woman she meditated on these: 'it was her constant course in the night when she lay waking to roll them in her mind, and rivet them there'. She took great pains over her children's education: 'She was continually putting us upon the scriptures and good bookes and instructing us how to pray . . . ' and this work extended outside her own family. 'It was her usual practice to help many poore children to learning by buying them bookes, setting them to schoole, and paying their master for teaching, whereby many a poore parent blessed god for help *by their children reading*' [my italics]. *The Rev. Oliver Heywood, B.A., 1630–1702: His Autobiographies, Diaries, Anecdote and Event Books* ed. J. Horsfall-Turner) (1882), I, pp. 42, 48 and 51.

8   THE HISTORY OF LITERACY IN SWEDEN*

Egil Johansson

The reading tradition in Sweden and in Finland

It has been difficult in the past to make the history of Swedish literacy known and accepted in other countries. A typical statement on this matter was made by Carl af Forsell in his *Statistik över Sverige* (*Swedish Statistics*) 1833, which is full of useful information:

> Most foreign geographies and statistical works, e.g. those of Stein, Hassel, Crome, Malte Brun and others, maintain that the lower classes in Sweden can neither read nor write. As for the first statement, it is completely false, since there is not one in a thousand among the Swedish peasantry who cannot read. The reason for this is principally the directives of Charles XI that a person who is not well acquainted with his Bible should not be allowed to take Holy Communion and that a person who is not confirmed should not be allowed to get married. One might nowadays readily add that, in order to be confirmed, everyone should be able to prove that, besides reading from a book, he also possessed passable skills in writing and arithmetic. Even if in other respects the cottage of the farmer or the crofter gives evidence of the highest poverty it will, nevertheless, nearly always contain a hymn-book, a Bible, a collection of sermons and sometimes several other devotional manuals. The English Lord Chancellor, Brougham, said in Parliament on May 1st 1816, that in the previous six years 9765 couples had been married in Manchester among whom not a single person could either read or write. According to the *Revue Encyclopedique* of October 1832, 74 adolescents out of a hundred in the northern departments of France could read, whilst in the western ones it was 12 out of a hundred, and in the whole country only 38 out of a hundred.

Af Forsell rejects indignantly foreign opinions about the low status of literacy in Sweden at the same time as he strikes back by referring to low figures for England and France. The problem is still of interest. It is still difficult for

*Reprinted from Egil Johansson, 'The History of Literacy in Sweden, in comparison with some other countries', *Educational Reports, Umeå*, No. 12, 1977 (Umeå, Sweden: Umeå University and School of Education, 1977), 2–42, by permission of the author.

foreign observers to understand what has happened in Sweden, owing to the special nature of the Swedish and Finnish reading tradition.

Firstly, the ability to read gained ground much earlier than the ability to write, whereas these two abilities have followed each other closely in most other countries. Secondly, people were persuaded to learn to read by means of an actual campaign initiated for political and religious reasons. in the reign of Charles XI the Church Law of 1686, for example, contained a ruling concerning general literacy.

Thirdly, this reading campaign was forced through almost completely without the aid of proper schools. The responsibility for teaching children to read was ultimately placed on the parents. The social pressure was enormous. Everybody in the household and in the village gathered once a year to take part in examinations in reading and knowledge of the Bible. The adult who failed these examinations was excluded from both communion and marriage.

These are the distinctive features that af Forsell points to as being traditionally Swedish. He hints, moreover, by referring to the large number of books, at the literate environment in these poor households. His statements are, of course, too optimistic in their generalizations about the ability to read as a whole. But his argument is typical of the dilemma, which still prevails, of presenting the Swedish tradition internationally.

This dilemma is such as to make one more voice necessary. This very distinctive reading tradition was, as it happens, also observed by foreign travellers. The Scottish evangelist, John Patterson, writes about his trip to Sweden in 1807–8:

> From Malmoe I paid a visit to my friend, Dr. Hylander, in Lund, made the acquaintance of the bishop and some of the professors, and enlarged my knowledge of Sweden. As Dr. Hylander had a parish not far from Malmoe, I one day went with him to attend an examination of his parishioners. It was held in a peasant's house, in a large hall, where a goodly number were collected. The people, old and young, answered the questions put to them readily in general; those who were deficient in their knowledge were severely dealt with, and exhorted to be more diligent. On the whole the exercise was calculated to be useful. It was a pleasing circumstance that all could read. Indeed, this may be affirmed of the inhabitants of all the northern Protestant Kingdoms; you seldom meet one above ten or twelve who cannot read, and the most of them write their own language; yet at the time now referred to there was nothing like what we have in Scotland, a provision for the education of the people by means of parochial schools. The parents were the teachers of their children, till they reached the age of fourteen or thereabouts, when they attended the pastor or his assistant, to be prepared for confirmation and being admitted to the Lord's Supper. And as no person can be

confirmed till he can read and repeat his catechism, or, until confirmed, can give his oath in a court of justice, or get married, a great
disgrace is attached to not being able to read; indeed, one who cannot read is nobody in the eye of the law. This state of things has its
advantages, as far as education is concerned; but, alas! it has its disadvantages, as it admits all to the enjoyment of religious privileges,
and thereby tends to make a nation of religious formalists. After the
examination was over, all the heads of families sat down to a sump-
tuous dinner provided for the occasion, and which gave me a little
more insight into Swedish society among the peasantry. I was much
pleased with the whole, and thanked my friend for the opportunity
then offered me of seeing more of the people.

Patterson commented approvingly on education for the masses in Sweden.
The ability to read was a general accomplishment. School instruction did not,
however, exist in the same way as in Scotland. Parents were instead responsible
for the teaching of their children. The result was supervised by means of a
system of examinations held by the clergy, which, however, according to
Patterson, led to a certain degree of religious formalism. Thus, the various
features of education for the masses in Sweden were also observed by
Patterson.

Another traveller, the German ecclesiastical historian Friedrich Wilhelm
von Schubert, had the same impressions as Patterson during his tour of
Sweden and Finland in 1811. He observed that the ability to read gained
more ground after the first decade of the eighteenth century. Von Schubert
has, as a matter of fact, presented one of the most detailed descriptions of
the custom of church examinations in Sweden and Finland.

The reading tradition in Sweden and Finland is also a problem for af
Forsell's successors in the field of statistics today. The difficulty of comparing
Sweden and Finland with other countries has, in reality, increased over the
years.

Since the Second World War the accepted model has been to regard it as
necessary that reading and writing should follow each other closely, that
formal school instruction should be almost the only conceivable teaching
method, and that economic models should provide us with a decisive explanation of a functioning literate environment. A general ability to read in a
poor, pre-industrial, agrarian, developing country like Sweden or Finland
seems a sheer absurdity. The notion that the ability to read gained ground
much earlier than the ability to write is completely foreign to this approach.

A typical expression of this contemporary outlook on the ability to read
is given in the treatment of literacy in the Finnish censuses of 1880–1930.
The figure for the adults who could neither read nor write was, according to
these censuses, constantly lower than two per cent. These figures constituted,
as late at the 1930s, no major problem for the statisticians in the League of

Nations. They quoted the number of illiterate people in Finland in 1930 at 0.9%.[1]

The Finnish authorities were, however, already at this time worried by inquiries about the meaning of these figures. As a result of this, the next census included unfortunately no information about cultural attainment because of obscurities when making international comparisons.

After the war UNESCO's statisticians were even harsher.[2] Those who were only able to read were classified as illiterate. The figure for the number of adult illiterates in Finland in 1930 was thus 16 instead of 1 per cent. For earlier periods, this figure was much higher. It was 29 per cent for 1920, 45 per cent for 1910 and 61 per cent for 1900. The corresponding figure for 1880 was as high as 87 per cent. The contrast is glaring in comparison with Patterson's and von Schubert's observations of the Swedish and Finnish educational tradition.

But these contemporary UNESCO observers were also uncertain about the interpretation and use of the Finnish figures. An argument with the Finnish statisticians was described in a report published in 1957. Both sides were equally confused. The Finnish group tried to include those who were only able to read with those who were able to write even if they had not been passed by the clerical examiners.[3]

Such an adjustment to the contemporary definition of literacy need not, however, necessarily be the only way of escaping the dilemma of the Finnish figures. The way out of this dilemma might instead be to accept the reading traditions on Sweden and Finland as historical reality and then adjust the concept of literacy according to that. This alternative has been attempted in this chapter.

Theoretical starting-points: two patterns of analysis

Thus, to make a population literate requires some form of organized instruction or a number of literacy campaigns. This is true of all times and all countries. The ability to read and write became universal in the West only during the final years of the last century after the consolidation of compulsory schooling. The same result is aimed at in the developing countries today by means of large-scale literacy campaigns.

Such *purposeful educational measures* always follow a typical pattern. The breakthrough of literacy is characterized by great differences — education gaps — between the age groups. The younger ones are, to a larger extent, subject to teaching. The total literate growth is concurrent with the changeover of generations. The illiterate generations die away. The coming generations are made literate by means of education. The population will thus gradually become literate. This pattern is typical both of the past and of today and is the result of strong teaching measures. It is also, of course, part of this pattern that in the end there are no noticeable differences between occupational groups, sexes, town and country, etc. All this is obvious. The observations indicated are, nevertheless, extremely useful for testing and defining various stages of literacy in a population.

This first pattern, however, gives place continually to another, which is characterized by prevailing differences amongst a population as regards *the demand and need for* literacy. These differences are principally defined by social and economic conditions. Differences primarily appear between various occupational groups. Some occupations are very dependent on active literacy. A literate environment is obtained in these occupations without any particular teaching campaign. The teaching requirements are supplied through private or limited social initiatives. Characteristic features appear here, too, with differences remaining to the very last between occupational groups, sexes, town and country, etc. To trace and observe this pattern as well has proved to be profitable when analysing the development of literacy.

For want of better terms I usually call the two patterns of analysis *push-* and *pull*-patterns. The former is explained by means of systematic teaching measures irrespective of, e.g., regional and social differences. The spontaneous learning motives are in the latter case explained by just such differences in environment as have been mentioned above.

Both patterns of analysis will be used below to analyse the historical source material for Sweden and Finland.

The European background

Several factors helped to pave the way for a more widespread reading ability in Europe from the sixteenth century onwards. Printing made it technically possible to produce books. The growth of nation states accentuated the need for books which would be available in the various national languages. But it was the Reformation which stimulated the popularization of reading. The individual was now expected to acquaint himself with the words of the Scriptures in his own native language.

These events are illustrated, for example, by the rapidly increasing number of translations and editions of the Bible. From the earliest history of the Church there had been versions of the Bible in about ten of the ancient civilized languages, among them Greek, Syrian, Coptic, Latin, and Gothic. In the late Middle Ages, attempts were made at translating the Bible into the western national languages. These translations were most often based on Latin. The art of printing and later the Reformation increased the importance of these translations. The Bible was printed in its entirety in German in 1466, in Italian in 1471, in French in 1487, in Dutch in 1526, in English in 1535, in Swedish in 1541, and in Danish in 1550. By this time the New Testament and other parts of the Bible had, as a rule, already been translated and printed.

Luther's version of 1543 of the complete Bible from the original languages, Hebrew and Greek, appeared in no less than 253 editions during the lifetime of the translator.

To start with, the translations of the Bible were important principally for church services and sermons. It was not until the seventeenth century that the ability to read, which had been aimed at by the reformers, gained more ground among the masses. Thus, a clear difference rapidly appeared between Protestant and non-Protestant Europe. Whereas in Catholic and orthodox Southern and Eastern Europe there were still very few people who could read – less than 20 per cent – there was a dramatic increase in Protestant Central and Northern Europe. An intermediate position was held by Northern Italy and parts of France with a certain literate tradition since the Middle Ages, at least in the commercial towns.

The ability to read was perhaps most widespread in Iceland with its unbroken literary heritage. But figures for England, Scotland, and the Netherlands also show that many people were able to read in these countries as well, perhaps more than 50 per cent. In Protestant Europe it can be estimated that about 35–45 per cent of the population could read at the turn of the century in 1700.[4] The reading campaign was now in full swing in Sweden and in Finland as well. This campaign was, as a matter of fact, carried out very thoroughly in these two countries, which will be shown in the following.

The world of the 'Hustavla'

The full emergence of the Reformation

Trends in Sweden corresponded closely to those in Europe. Here, too, the Reformation had led to demands for popular education. More of the Scriptures were now supposed to be read and known in church and at home. Oral instruction could not, however, by itself fulfill the increasing requirements for knowledge during the seventeenth century. Reading from a book was now an indispensable skill for everybody. Sweden did not in this respect, differ very much from other Protestant countries.[5]

The ideas of the Reformation were, in reality, put into effect by the united efforts of the whole country. The work of national reconstruction was followed up during the seventeenth century by an extensive education of the people, which showed itself in various kinds of laws and regulations; for the dioceses this took the form of resolutions from clerical conferences and diocesan regulations, and for the whole country there were ecclesiastical and parliamentary resolutions. A number of proposals concerning Church law regulations for popular instruction were brought up. They led to the Church Law of 1686 which clearly manifested the development.

The Church Law contained rulings about general literacy. It said, e.g., that children, farm-hands, and maid-servants should 'learn to read and see with their own eyes what God bids and commands in His Holy Word'. The expression was typical of the Reformation. Every individual should 'with his own eyes' see and learn the meaning of the Bible. The object of this reading was to make the individual conscious of Christian faith and life, the latter being most important. Christian life would demonstrate faith in a social order combining every aspect of existence in what has been called 'the world of the "Hustavla" '.[6]

The world of the 'Hustavla'*

The collection of words from the Scriptures in the 'Hustavla' lay down the guiding principles for the whole society, for clergy and parishioners in the spiritual or teaching order, for the authorities and subjects in the political order, and for master and servants in the household or the economic order. Everybody was given duties and rights in a reciprocal system where everyone had to fulfill his obligations.[7] Figure 8.1 is an attempt to illustrate the social outlook of the 'Hustavla'.

Everybody lived, according to the code of the 'Hustavla', in a three-dimensional system of social relations. The figure can be made concrete by means of the following examples.

1. The king was sovereign in the political, listener in the spiritual, and head of the family in the economic order.
2. The clergyman was correspondingly subject, teacher, and head of the family.
3. The master was subject in the country, listener in the congregation and head of the family in his house.
4. The rest were, generally speaking, subjects, listeners, and household members.

The system was, thus, strongly patriarchal. The father figure recurred in the home, in the congregation and in the national economy. The master with his family, the vicar with his parishioners, and the father of the people with his subjects made up the same pattern of joint responsibility and reciprocal obligations.

But this interplay also had its tensions. The ideological and political responsibilities did not coincide. The Church guarded its sole right to teach and instruct. The king was, in church, only a listener, however distinguished

---

*The 'Hustavla', (a religious plaque which was hung on the wall), was a supplement to Luther's *Small Catechism*. It consisted of specific Bible verses arranged according to the traditional, Lutheran doctrine of a three-stage, social hierarchy – *ecclesia* (church), *politia* (state), and *oeconomia* (home or household). These selections of Scripture outlined the Christian duties and obligations which each stage in this hierarchy owed to the others – i.e. priests/parishioners (teachers/pupils), rulers/subjects, heads of families (parents)/children and household servants.

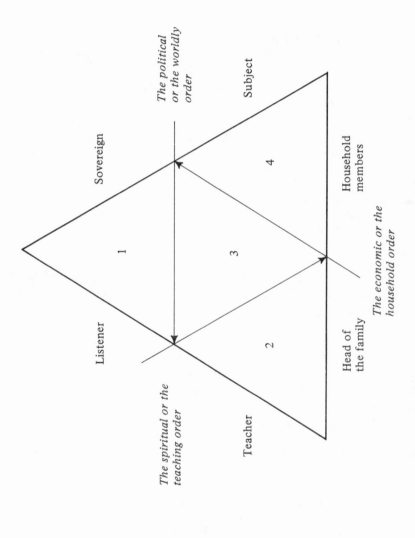

Figure 8.1 Outline of the three fold interplay of forces in 'the world of the "Hustavla" '.

he might be. But it was exactly in his capacity as the most distinguished of members that the king tried to assert the influence of the State over the Church. One sees this tension in the ideas of the Reformation with regard to the spiritual and the worldly domains. Both were of God. The worldly domain was God's indirect or 'improper' means of maintaining the social order with the help of laws and authorities. The spiritual domain was God's direct or 'proper' influence by means of his word on the individual so that a 'new individual would daily prove himself', in the words of the Catechism.[8]

The tension in the household order was abolished. The head of the family was both sovereign and priest in his house. He was the teacher and the up-bringer, influenced by the activities of the teaching order in the parish.

The spiritual or the teaching order

The activities of the spiritual or teaching order were to a large extent determined by the lives of the Church and the parish. The bishop, assisted by consistory and rural deans, ruled the dioceses. Locally, the clergymen served as parish 'teachers' by means of their sermons, instruction, and examinations. This spiritual education was supplemented by the healing of souls and church discipline. It was the duty of the parishioners as 'listeners' to become more and more acquainted with the message of the Church and put it into practice. The divine service was increasingly used as a means of education. Sermons on the Catechism, e.g. in dialogue form between parish clerk and clergyman, were one way of improving collective learning. Questions on the sermon with the parishioners sitting on their benches, or gathered in the sanctuary together with the other members of their district was another way of teaching and checking the learning process at the same time. Those who failed their exam-inations could be excluded from Communion and thus from the right to marry, since sufficient knowledge and understanding of the Scriptures was of fundamental importance for the household order as well. The duties of the clergymen were consequently extended to include calling on the parishioners in their homes and yearly examinations.

The economic or the household order

The economic or the household order functioned within the villages and in the homes. The quotations from the Bible concerning the mutual dependence between husband and wife, parents and children, master and servants took up most of the space in the 'Hustavla'. Except for the purely economic functions of work and everyday life, the household was also, just like parish life, characterized by sermons and instruction. Psalm-book and Bible texts were supposed to be used daily at family prayers. The older members of the family were supposed to give the children a programmed education, based on the Catechism. The clergyman was a teacher in the parish and the master was in a corresponding way supposed to be responsible for devotion, instruction, and examination in his house. He had also the authority to bring up children and servants with 'a reasonable amount of chastisement'. The congruence between the teaching and household order was striking. Home life was strongly influenced by congregation life on workdays and holidays alike.[9]

Church services and instruction went side by side in the village. This was at least true of Norrland with its vast woodlands, where the villagers gathered for prayers and reading on Sundays when they did not attend church. The meetings alternated from house to house as did most often the task of reading the texts and sermons. Detailed directions are given in a separate church ordinance for Norrland, dating from the beginning of the seventeenth century.

> Likewise on Sundays or respective holy days in the Church year the clergy shall hold the daily lessons, together with Holy Scripture and Christian prayers and psalms, and also examine and instruct young persons. Residents of the outlying villages shall come to the homes of individuals who are already able to read and thereby hear the lessons and devotions which such persons are required to read aloud to them.

The ordinance also stated that 'all young boys, who might be thought capable of reading from a book, shall come to the church and there learn to read and sing'.

Such village reading is known from the early seventeenth century. It formed the basis of the well-known so-called 'reading movement' which at times came to be opposed to new books and new regulations within the Church. From this we get a documentation of the social environment in villages and homes which developed in the world of the 'Hustavla'.

The political or the worldly order

Political life in its popular form was shaped within village communities and parishes. Within the village there were the village council and the village assembly, meeting a couple of times every year to decide upon the common interests of the village, such as sowing and the harvest, the tending of cattle, fencing, the management of forest-land and mills owned in common, etc. The village community came together at the annual village feast and at weddings and funerals where the villagers always turned out in full force. The yearly examinations and examination feasts fitted well into this tradition.[10]

An extremely old form of popular self-government was preserved at the parish meetings, where the parishioners, gathered under the guidance of their vicar, made decisions about common problems such as church building, poor relief, and popular instruction. The life of the individual was also taken up at the parish meetings, where there was a local administration of justice, something unique to Sweden. Trials could be held for such misdemeanours as Sabbath-breaking, swearing or drunkenness. Particular care was taken to watch over public morals with, among other things, regulations concerning betrothals and marriages. Marriages had to be contracted publicly in church. New households had to be sanctioned by the parishioners.[11]

Six or twelve representatives were chosen to carry out the resolutions of the parish meeting and to watch over general order. They were, together with the local vicars and the church-wardens, the governors of the parish. They were supported by elected supervisors in the outlying villages.

The parish assembly most often also chose the vicar, even if he then had to be appointed by the bishop or the king. It also appointed electors for the general election of representatives from the peasantry to the Swedish Riksdag (Parliament). The electors came together according to jurisdictional districts (in Dalarna within the country administrative division and in Norrland within the assize division) and appointed the representatives from the peasantry to the Swedish Riksdag for the parliamentary sessions every three years. The number of members from the peasantry was about 150 at every Riksdag during the seventeenth and eighteenth centuries. There was a rapid turn-over of representatives. About one third were chosen for one parliamentary session, another third were chosen for two, and only 10–15 per cent were chosen for five parliamentary sessions or more. These figures apply to the latter part of the eighteenth century.[12]

Some 80 representatives for the burgesses were elected in the towns in a corresponding way by the magistrates and the burgesses. The ecclesiastical estate was made up of the bishops and of elected clerical representatives, 51 members in all. The nobles, on the other hand, had personal representation for their class. Some three hundred nobles could be assembled at the same time for proceedings in the Riksdag.

Each of these classes or estates, however, cast only one vote when all the estates voted. The power of the peasantry to assert their position increased, and this has been partly explained by the fact that more and more of them were learning to read. This was the way power was divided between subjects and the authorities in the political order from the village community to the Riksdag in the world of the 'Hustavla'. The increasing book-learning provided important inner strength for all the functions of society.

The reading campaign around 1700

The functional need for reading ability. Books
Persons in the world of the 'Hustavla' required deep ideological insight in order to be able to function properly. The liturgy and instructions concerning devotions and continued education in church and at home were taken up principally in the Psalm-book.[13]

Ever since the first editions in the 1530s the Psalm-book contained, besides psalms, the Bible texts of the ecclesiastical year, the Catechism with Luther's explanations, the 'Hustavla', and prayer for home and church.

The Psalm-book of 1695 contained 413 psalms, some of them very long. The first 21 psalms were 'catechetical psalms', corresponding to the five articles of the Catechism. Then followed psalms 22–112 with biblical motifs from the Book of Psalms, and from the texts of the ecclesiastical year in psalms 113–215. The remaining half of the psalms were didactic psalms for everyday life, morning and evening psalms, etc. One of the most noteworthy psalms was number 260, 'The Golden ABC'. Each of the 24 verses began in turn with the letters of the alphabet.

After the psalms in the Psalm-book of 1695, followed the texts of the ecclesiastical year, the Small Catechism, the 'Hustavla', the Athanasian Confessional Creed, David's seven Penitential Psalms, prayers for everyday use, and the regulations for baptism, marriage, and congregational services. The volume also included a long and penetrating discourse on how to interpret and obey the Christian doctrine.

This Psalm-book appeared in at least 250 editions and in 1.5 million copies up to the introduction of the new Psalm-book in 1819. The parishioners were recommended to sing from the book in church. The rhythm was marked by this. Long pauses between the verses were supposed to allow time for reading the next one. These pauses in church music were later to puzzle music theorists.[14]

More widespread than the Psalm-book were the special editions of the Catechism including the ABC-book, the text of the Catechism, Luther's explanation, additional expositions with questions, answers and words from the Scriptures. A number of editions of this kind were circulated during the seventeenth century with an ever increasing content.

Most widespread was the Catechism of 1689 with the expositions of Archbishop J. Svebilius. It included the text of the Catechism, Luther's explanation, Svebilius' expositions (including 303 questions and answers, and Scriptural passages), daily prayers, the 'Hustavla', the seven Penitential Psalms, additional questions for young people, bridal couples, and finally J. Arndt's rules for Bible-reading in the home.

Both the exposition in the Psalm-book mentioned above and the references in the Catechism to the Bible reader stressed the importance of active and engaged reading and its application to life.

The Catechism was regarded both as a book of devotion and as a compilation of Scriptural content. The Bible editions themselves were too expensive. It was not until the nineteenth century that the Bible became a common feature in the home.

The initiative from above

The Catechism and the Psalm-book became the most important works in the household during the seventeenth century. They manifested, together with the Church Law of 1686, the edicts, which applied to everyone, stipulating a fully developed Church education for the masses.

There were also, apart from the Church Law, other ordinances applicable to the whole country. A royal degree of 1723 constrained parents and guardians to 'diligently see to it that their children applied themselves to book reading and the study of the lessons in the Catechism'. Neglect could lead to payment of fines used for 'the instruction of poor children in the parish'. Such penalties give a good picture of the initiative from above on a central level. It was in the dioceses that theory became practice.[15]

The Conventicle Edict of 1726 had a similar significance. It was best-known for its prohibition of the pietistical conventicles with their devotional meetings outside the confines of the family household. Such spontaneous meetings were in themselves signs of increasing commitment to individual reading and devotion. But they were not to be included in the instruction in the teaching and household order. In the place of such conventicles, the edict recommended and stressed regular family prayers in the home, but only for the family household.

Popular instruction was also often prescribed at diocesan level, in diocesan decrees and in resolutions passed by the clergymen's assemblies. Instruction was to be organized by the diocesan authorities. The local responsibility was placed on rural deans, vicars, and parish representatives. The initiative from above was completed by long and harsh examinations by the bishop and the rural dean at their visitations in the parishes. The recurrent instruction and examinations of the clergy enabled the Catechism to spread to the villages and homes.

The horizontal diffusion

The reading ability campaign in Sweden was carried through almost completely without the aid of proper schools. There were 'school masters' in the parishes in, e.g., Skåne and Gotland. The parish clerks and other assistants were also in some parts of the country made responsible for the instruction of the children. But the main responsibility lay with the parents in the home. This, too, was one of Luther's original ideas. The master was, in the household order, responsible for education in the same way as the clergyman was in the parish. The idea of the 'general priesthood' made the household order into something of a teaching order as well.[16]

A number of ABC-books with instructions for learning were published during the seventeenth century.[17] Behind these instructions one finds the pedagogic ideas of Wolfgang Ratke and Amos Comenius. Ratke's *Didactica* was translated into Swedish in 1614. Comenius' first Swedish version of *Didactica Magna* appeared in 1641 and *Orbis Pictus* in 1683. Ratke and Comenius were both consulted about the educational problems in Sweden. The latter also visited Sweden twice in the 1640s.[18]

The reading instruction recommended in the ABC-books was the synthetic alphabetic method. The children were to learn the names of the letters first and then gradually learn to combine them into syllables and words. The following instruction at a visitation in Norrbotten in 1720 provides a good illustration of this form of instruction.

> The Rural Dean admonished the parish organist and others in the congregation involved in the instruction of young people to inculcate a firm knowledge of the lettered alphabet before proceeding with lessons in spelling. In like measure, they should not begin with basic reading before they have instructed the children in the correct and proper art of spelling. Furthermore, they should not impose any memorization exercises on the children before each is able to read directly from all books used in instruction. With respect to the first exercise in memorization, they should take heed that the children do not add or remove any letter of the written text but rather that they faultlessly follow each letter verbatim. Similarly, a child should not be allowed to recite the second lesson before the first is securely fastened in his memory. From the very beginning the children shall have become accustomed to reading clearly and diligently and to making firm observance of each sentence to its very end. Furthermore, they shall have become fully aware of the text which they are reading and heed its utterance as if they heard it spoken by another. In this manner the children should gradually acquire a firm grasp of the textual meaning and content and be able to articulate such in words other than those given in the text. In like measure, they shall answer with their own words to the questions posed them in the text.

The instruction is typical. It corresponds well to leading thoughts of the time. Learning should pass from what was concrete for the eye, via memory, to a complete understanding and application.

It was possible to spread reading ability and catechetical knowledge horizontally because of strong social pressure. It was important to make progress within households and village communities. Those who were already able to read were supposed to instruct those who could not. Successes and failures became known at the recurring examinations.

But it would be wrong to say that everything was a matter of compulsion in the Swedish reading campaign. Family prayers and village reading led many people to feel a need for religion. One sign of this was Pietism, that was just breaking through. Another were the 'readers' in Norrland. Insight into both the difficulties and successes of the campaign is obtained from the Church examination registers, forming part of the most noteworthy heritage from the time when Sweden was a major European power in the seventeenth century.

The Church examination registers[19]

Popular instruction as organized by the Church has been extremely well documented in Sweden and in Finland. Progress in reading and Catechism knowledge was noted in special examination registers. The existence of these sources is in itself a strong verification of the above-mentioned campaign. It will be convenient to divide up the oldest examination registers on the basis of dioceses and deaneries as a first illustration, since popular instruction was enforced vertically from the dioceses, via the rural deans and the vicars, and thence out to the people (Figure 8.2).

The dioceses differ considerably from one another. The diocese of Västerås has the oldest examination registers. Some of them date back as far as the 1620s. From this decade there are at least some examination registers still extant for every deanery in this diocese. In the surrounding dioceses, Karlstad, Strängnäs, Uppsala, Härnösand, and, in the south, in Växjö and Visby, examination registers have been preserved for most of the deaneries since before 1720. The work in connection with the Church Law of 1686 is clearly reflected in the many registers from the 1680s. In the dioceses of Linköping, Kalmar, Skara, and Göteborg there are examination registers dating from 1750 for the majority of the deaneries. The diocese of Lund is the exception, with a very early series of yearly so-called Catechism registers from the 1680s and a considerably later collection of actual examination registers. The latter are in reality so recent that the last 25% of the deaneries only have examples from the nineteenth century. These sources consequently illustrate the date of the origin of the oldest preserved examination register for every deanery. This indicates the pace of the enforcement of popular instruction, where diocese and deanery make up hierarchic units. The difficult historical problem of judging to what extent the preserved source material is also the original one and the oldest, is to some degree made easier because of these figures.

Some idea of the proportions of the historical problem with the archives can be gained by examining how the oldest preserved examination registers are distributed over the parishes (Figure 8.3). The order between the dioceses is the same. The majority of the parishes in the diocese of Västerås have examination registers dating back to before 1750. The other dioceses have examination registers from the latter part of the eighteenth century and the diocese of Lund from the beginning of the nineteenth century. As for the parishes, the diocese of Lund once again has Catechism registers which are well ordered and date back to the final decades of the seventeenth century. These registers were, however, used at only one examination. New ones were made up for every new examination. They have been preserved and there is a wide distribution over the parishes.

The Church examination registers were, on the other hand, used for many examinations, sometimes over many years. They were taken along on exam-

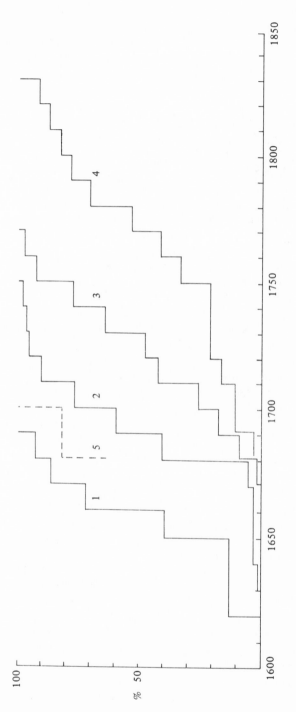

Figure 8.2 Percentage of deaneries in various dioceses within which at least one Church examination register is known to have been begun, at various points in time. (For the diocese of Lund a second line gives special catechism registers.) Urban areas excluded (N = 170).
1. The diocese of Västerås (N = 15)
2. The dioceses of Härnösand, Uppsala, Strängnäs, Karlstad, Växjö and Visby (N = 77)
3. The dioceses of Linköping, Kalmar, Skara and Göteborg (N = 54)
4. The diocese of Lund (N = 24)
5. The diocese of Lund, Catechism registers (N = 24)

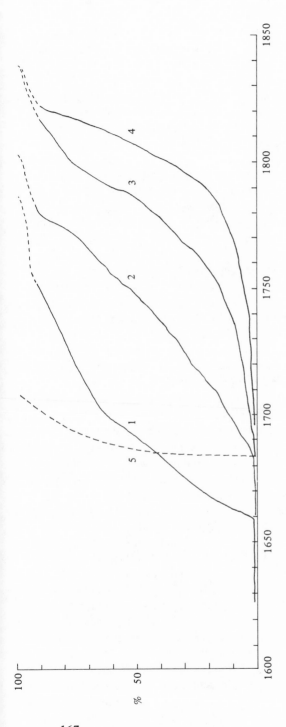

Figure 8.3 Percentage of parishes in various dioceses in which a Church examination register is known to have been begun, at various points in time. (For the diocese of Lund a second line gives special catechism registers.) Urban areas excluded (N = 2373). For grouping of dioceses 1—4 and 5, see Figure 8.2.
Sources for Figures 8.2 and 8.3: Files for the Church archives. Division of deaneries and parishes according to the 1805 deanery tables.

ination rounds which were often very long in the more extensive parishes of the country. They were subject to hard wear, damp, and fire damage, and ran the risk of getting lost in many different ways. It should also be noted that in the beginning the examination registers, did not have the same status as the older Church records, such as the registers for births, marriages, and deaths. It was not until the eighteenth century that their official importance increased as bases for census registration and as sources for the work of the Old National Central Bureau of Statistics, after 1749.

It is still uncertain to what extent the original examination registers have actually been preserved. Extensive studies are required to reduce this uncertainty. The already existing surveys nevertheless confirm the activities of the clerical authorities for a more widespread popular education after the end of the seventeenth century. An examination register from Tuna in Medelpad will be taken as a typical example of this.

An example: the reading campaign in Tuna in the 1690s

The Church Law of 1686 led to the setting up of organized examination registers in an increasing number of parishes. Tuna in Medelpad is one of them. Its oldest preserved examination register extends over the years 1686–91 (Figure 8.4).

The parish was at this time divided into six examination districts (rotes). The first pages are, unfortunately, missing in the register. The first district is, therefore, not complete and is omitted from the following analysis. 397 persons over the age of six are noted in the other five districts. The youngest children are not noted until they have been examined. This is already an illustration of the examining function of the register. The parishioners are arranged according to district, village, and household. The social position is stated for every individual within the household: husband, wife, son, daughter, maidservant, farmhand, lodger, etc. Age, reading marks, and Catechism knowledge are, together with names, noted in special columns. The latter take up most of the space with ten columns for various types of knowledge: the words of the text, Luther's explanation of the five articles, prayers, the 'Hustavla', and specific questions. It is typical that these last three or four columns are never filled in this first register even if they are always drawn up. They indicate the increasing knowledge of the Catechism acquired because of an increase in reading ability. They bear witness in their own way, to an intensified teaching campaign. Reading and Catechism knowledge are noted with judgements in plain language, e.g. 'intet' – *cannot* read, 'begynt' – has *begun* to read, 'lite' – can read *a little*, 'någorlunda' – can read *acceptably*, and 'kan' – *can* read. '*Cannot* read' and '*can* read' are presented separately in the following tables. 'Has *begun* to read' is the most frequent of the other marks. It was used principally for children and young people. As regards Catechism knowledge, this report only indicates the number of Catechism items that had

Village	The fourth district: Farmer, Wife, Children, Servants	Age	Can read from a book	Simplic. partes Catech.	Dialogus cum explicatione	Symbolum cum explicatione	Orat. Dom. cum explicatione	Baptism cum explicatione	Sac. Caena cum explicatione	Confession of sins	Prayers	The 'Hustavla'
Alstad	Jacob Eriksson	62	Can	Can	Can	Can	Can	Can	Can			
	(Wife) Ingeborg Eriksdotter	40	Cannot	Can	Accept	Badly	Can	Can	Can			
	(Son) Erik Jacobsson	14	Begun	Can	Can	Can	Can	Can	Can			
	(Daughter) Britta Jacobsdotter	16	Begun	Can	Can	Can	Can	Can	Can			
	(Son) Jacob Jacobsson	10	Begun	Can	Can	Can	Can	Can	Can			
	(Daughter) Karin Jacobsdotter	12	Begun	Can	Can	Can	Can	Can	Can			
	(Daughter) Anna Jacobsdotter	7	Begun									
	(Aunt?) Elin Eriksdotter	66	A little	Can	(died)							

Figure 8.4. The family of Jacob Eriksson in the parish of Tuna in the fourth examination district and in the village of Alstad. Page 12 in the Church examination register for 1688–91. The family includes parents, five children, and an elderly lodger, probably an aunt. The columns indicate age, reading ability and, on one hand, knowledge of the words of the Catechism (Simplic. partes) and, on the other, knowledge of the five articles together with Luther's explanation (cum explicatione). Room is also left for confession, prayers, and the 'Hustavla'. At a later examination (in the Church examination register for 1696–98) all children, except Anna, have been given higher grades in reading in that 'begun' has been altered to 'can' read. Source: Tuna, Medelpad, Church examination register 1688–91, p. 12.

169

been learnt. A sketch of the material is presented in the following table (Table 8.1).

A total of about three quarters of the population were given reading marks ('begun', etc., or 'can'). Reading and Catechism knowledge are highly correlated. Most of those who got a high score in memorization also had high reading marks. The reverse is, on the other hand, not equally clear. The highest score in reading is not necessarily an indication of the highest degree of Catechism knowledge. This illustrates the previously mentioned order of learning. Reading was supposed to precede memorization.

This observation is even more obvious for those who have no marks. 19 persons have no reading marks and for 61 persons there are no notes for Catechism knowledge. Of these, 14 persons have no marks whatsoever. They have perhaps never been examined at all, since five of them are six-year-old children, whereas four of them are over sixty years of age. Only one of the two marks is missing for 52 persons. 47 of these were examined in reading, but not in memorization. The reverse applies only to five persons. This is also a proof of the high priority given to reading instruction. The fact that several persons were given the mark *'cannot* read' does not contradict this. Quite the contrary. Reading from a book was given most attention and emphasis at the examinations. This was the typical situation of teaching and examination just before the break-through of reading in a parish. It becomes clearer when the two marks are divided according to age. Twelve persons are omitted from this and the following tables, since there is no information concerning their age (Table 8.2).

All the dramatic events in a newly started reading campaign are depicted in the table. It is clear from the column for 'cannot' that nearly half of the oldest cannot read and one fifth of the middle generation cannot read, whereas almost no one in the youngest group is illiterate. The learning process in itself is indicated in the next column, 'begun', etc. Most of the youngest are in the midst of the process of learning to read. On the other hand the time for learning has passed for the oldest ones. They either lack (*'cannot* read') or possess reading ability (*'can* read'). Their results may, nevertheless, give us an idea of the preliminary stages in the reading campaign. Knowing how little reading ability changes at a mature age, the oldest persons provide an indication of the number of people who were able to read, e.g. a quarter of a century ago. That is, they represent reading ability in the 1660s, which at that time would have been approximately 40 per cent and would thus have increased in the 1690s to over 70 per cent. The youngest children have not been included. Such a calculation also illustrates the dramatic change to a purposeful campaign for reading ability. The picture becomes even clearer when the material shows how the earlier Catechism memorization is outdistanced by reading. A division of Catechism knowledge according to age will, however, be presented first (Table 8.3).

Table 8.1. *Reading marks and Catechism knowledge in Tuna in 1688–91 (N = 397)*

Columns about memorization (Catechism item)	Reading marks				
	No note	'Cannot'	'Has begun' etc.	'Can'	N
6–8	1	12	27	74	114
5	1	21	35	52	109
1–4	3	30	37	43	113
No note	14	20	20	7	61
Total	19	83	119	176	397

Table 8.2. *Reading marks in Tuna 1688–91 related to age. Percentage figures (N = 385)*

	Reading marks					
Age	No note %	'Cannot' %	'Has begun' etc. %	'Can' %	Total %	N
Age > 60	9	43	7	41	100	(42)
51 – 60	0	47	13	41	100	(32)
41 – 50	5	35	20	40	100	(40)
31 – 40	0	21	37	42	100	(43)
26 – 30	3	20	31	46	100	(39)
21 – 25	2	13	22	63	100	(59)
16 – 20	3	16	26	55	100	(38)
11 – 15	2	2	46	50	100	(50)
< 11	12	5	62	21	100	(42)
Total %	5	21	30	44	100	(385)

It is conspicuous how evenly the Catechism items are distributed over the age groups, apart from the youngest who, so far, have not shown a very large amount of knowledge. For half of the youngest there is no note at all. The same is true of one quarter of the oldest persons. The table gives an impression of stagnation. This shows how far the old education standard had reached with mainly oral instruction and memorization. Only three persons (1%) have gone beyond the old standard of Luther's explanations. These three belong, typically enough, to the younger generation. More people are waiting to learn all the articles of the Catechism. Some of the ten columns, drawn up in the

Table 8.3. *Catechism knowledge in Tuna 1688–91 related to age. Percentage figures (N = 385)*

Age	No note	1	2	3	4	5	6	7–8	Total %	N
Age > 60	24	0	7	7	7	29	26	0	100	(42)
51 – 60	6	6	0	16	9	41	22	0	100	(32)
41 – 50	8	3	15	8	5	30	33	0	100	(40)
31 – 40	12	2	0	9	7	28	42	0	100	(43)
26 – 30	13	5	13	8	10	33	15	3	100	(39)
21 – 25	10	5	10	3	12	27	30	2	100	(59)
16 – 20	8	0	8	16	8	24	37	0	100	(38)
11 – 15	4	8	14	6	14	22	30	2	100	(50)
< 11	48	5	2	0	5	21	19	0	100	(42)
Total %	15	4	8	7	9	27	28	1	100	(385)

The "Number of parts of the Catechism" heading spans columns 1 through 7–8.

examination register (Fig. 8.4), are waiting to be filled in. But this requires a more widespread and more widely used reading ability. This process has begun, as becomes quite clear when reading marks and Catechism knowledge are put together in age groups (Table 8.4).

Here, too, the older and the younger differ a lot from each other. Among the oldest, both those who are able to read and those who are not able to read have marks in Catechism knowledge (Table 8.4). If one examines the number of Catechism items one will, however, discover a difference in that those who are able to read among the oldest persons also have a more extensive knowledge of the Catechism. For example, in the age group 41 years and older, 32 persons got the highest Catechism score, i.e. a note for 6 items. Three quarters of these 32 persons are also able to read. Those having marks in both reading and Catechism in the age range 16–40 are as many as 77 per cent. In the second youngest age group they are as many as 94 per cent. The children, 6–11 years, finally, once more illustrate the progressive educational campaign. Nobody obtained marks in memorization first, whereas 31 per cent have, on the other hand, obtained marks in reading first. A more detailed table strengthens these impressions (Table 8.5). Five out of the eleven children in the 6–7 age group neither got marks for reading nor for the Catechism. They are here, just as in Table 8.4, regarded as not able to read. The sequence of learning is here clearly illustrated. It passes from 'has begun' reading to catechetical knowledge; one cannot come to the latter without the former.

A typical feature of the patterns of analysis has, thus, been found in the material for Tuna. The sudden advent of the reading campaign is seen in the educational gaps between the older and the younger generations. Another

Table 8.4. *Reading marks and Catechism knowledge in Tuna 1688–91 related to age. Percentage figures (N = 385)*

| | No note in Catechism knowledge | | Catechism knowledge | | | |
	Not able to read	Able to read	Not able to read	Able to read	Total %	N
Age						
> 40	11	2	36	51	100	(114)
16 – 40	6	4	13	77	100	(179)
11 – 15	2	2	2	94	100	(50)
< 11	17	31	0	52	100	(42)
Total %	8	6	17	69	100	(385)

Table 8.5. *Reading marks and Catechism knowledge in Tuna 1688–91 related to ages 6–13 (N = 68)*

| | Reading marks | | | | |
Age	'Cannot' No notes in Catechism	'Has begun' No notes in Catechism	'Has begun' 1–8 items in Catechism	'Can' 1–8 items in Catechism	Total N
12–13	0	0	8	12	20
10–11	2	3	9	8	22
8–9	1	5	7	2	15
6–7	5	5	1	0	11
Total	8	13	25	22	68

typical feature is that differences between the sexes, for example, become less obvious. The reading mark 'can' was obtained by 54 per cent of the men over 50 and by 33 per cent of the women. The corresponding percentage figures for the youngest, 20 years and younger, are 44 and 41 per cent respectively. A levelling-out is in progress. Women often have higher scores than men later on in the eighteenth and nineteenth centuries.

The increasing number of women who were able to read directs our thoughts to home instruction as it is depicted in literature and art, with either the mother or the father instructing the children in the home. To what extent did the children in Tuna have literate homes as early as the 1690s? A sample in the third and fourth examination district provides an answer to this question. Out of 16 families with children who were 16 years old and younger there is only one family where both the parents are illiterate. Both parents are able to read in ten families. It is hardly possible to discover any difference in the children's standard of reading, since this is more likely due to age, as has already been indicated. The newly started reading campaign is thus further confirmed. It was possible to fulfill the demands placed on all the younger people to learn and use the printed word provided that the required pedagogic measures were taken.

Reading ability in Tuna was tested primarily with the aid of the first pattern of analysis, starting from purposeful educational measures. The development of reading is characterized by obvious differences in grades between the generations. It also appeared in its pedagogic aspect with, principally for the children, an intensified learning to read stage preceding Catechism knowledge.

The second model of analysis with differences in environment, e.g. between families, has already been suggested. A knowledge of the letters of the alphabet, however easy it may be to acquire, does not spread spontaneously within a given environment. The generation gaps and the differences between the sexes among the older people also suggest this. Instruction and learning had to be provided, though not necessarily at great cost and in large quantities, but to a sufficient degree to make the basic skills of reading functional in an environment which was becoming more and more literate.

Systematic studies of the reading campaign

The Church examination registers provide an enormous field for research. The research has, however, in spite of many sporadic efforts, not obtained a firm grasp of these sources with regard to their contents and usefulness for the judgement of the distribution of reading ability. The development of methods has taken two directions within the project. The first is an integrated system of information, keeping together the total amount of information in the Church archives of a certain parish over a long period of time. This method has been adopted and fulfilled in the interdisciplinary project, *Demografisk Databas* (Demographic Database).[20] The other method that has been developed within the project aims at structuring and organizing the varied notes on reading ability and Catechism knowledge in the examination registers.

The distribution of reading ability is seen as a centrally directed campaign. On the basis of this, certain hypotheses are made, in their turn leading to a defined methodology for the use of the sources. The contents of the examination register for Tuna were described in detail in the preceding section. It was, among other things, stressed that the age distribution of literacy is an important indicator of the pace of change. Change can, thus, best be seen through a comparison *between* the generations. All the youngest become literate. Many of the oldest remain illiterate. But as the older people die away, there are a growing number of literate persons in a population. Earlier differences in reading ability between the sexes, between different social groups, between town and country, between various regions, etc., also at the same time become less pronounced. The earlier characteristics of reading ability in the West thus disappear. This reading ability used to be very low and was largely preserved by the immediate economic and cultural needs of the community.

Two different patterns of analysis thus become evident. In the first one, the age distribution is decisive for the analysis. The generation gaps will be the most expressive factor. The social gaps provide the explanations in the second pattern. It is, nevertheless, of vital importance to take both patterns of analysis into consideration in every examination. They always complement each other. They are, of course, equally valid for the studies of the educational explosions of today.

These observations lead to the hypothesis that the reading marks in the examination registers in their initial stage are primarily to be correlated with the year of birth. This leads to a very simple methodology. The marks are distributed on birth cohorts, irrespective of when the examinations were carried out. This means that the same 'generations' can be compared in different registers and between different parishes. The methodology will consequently also allow a certain amount of prediction of the past and the future on the basis of the time for a certain examination.

The methodology can be illustrated with the results from some preliminary studies. Table 8.6 presents reading ability in Tuna, Möklinta, and Skellefteå c. 1700. The years of birth for Möklinta are given in the examination register. The indications of age have, for Tuna and Skellefteå, been converted into years of birth. The total number of people who could read in the three parishes was, according to the registers, somewhere between 66 and 85 per cent. The results will, if distributed by decades of birth, show a great degree of similarity. Generation gaps can be discerned, with marked leaps in the process. A graph illustration (Figure 8.5) is even more explicit. The time axis indicates the measurements and the time of birth for the individuals. The curves represent a projection for every cohort back to its decade of birth. There is a great degree of similarity between the three parishes. The difference in time between the first and last measurement is still as great as thirty years. The advantage of this methodology is obvious. It will now be possible to make comparisons between various times and areas.

The methodology can be taken even further if there are results for several measurements in the same parish. Age, for example, is indicated in the Catechism registers for 1702, 1731, and 1740 for Skanör. The total number of persons able to read increases during this time from 58 to 92 per cent. The difference in 1702, with 67 per cent for the men and 49 per cent for the women, has been completely levelled out by 1740. The women have, by this

Table 8.6. *Reading ability in Tuna 1691, in Möklinta in 1705, and in Skellefteå in 1724 related to year of birth. Percentage figures (N = 385, 1410, and 1489 respectively) Source: The Church examination registers.*

	Reading ability		
Year of birth	Tuna 1691 %	Möklinta 1705 %	Skellefteå 1724 %
−1619	–	21	–
1620−29	48	27	–
1630−39	54	36	–
1640−49	60	53	48
1650−59	79	61	58
1660−69	81	65	69
1670−79	90	80	79
1680−89	83	89	86
1690−99	–	89	92
1700−10	–	–	97
Total	74	66	85

time, even out-distanced the men to a certain degree with 93 per cent of the women and 91 per cent of the men literate respectively.

The result, however, becomes even more remarkable when reading ability in Skanör is projected back and forth in time on the basis of the different measurements. In Figure 8.6 the three results for 1702, 1731, and 1740 are related back in time to the respective periods of birth, and also between the measurement dates, to composite age groups common to all three. The total increase in reading ability is drawn as a line between the measurements. The slope of the line corresponds to the retrograde projection of reading ability distributed on birth cohorts. Such a projection anticipates apparently fairly well the total reading ability some thirty years later. The simple conclusion is of course that the total reading ability of a population at a certain time is represented by the reading ability of the middle generation. This obvious rule of thumb is just as useful for the ample census material of later times for reading ability. The intensity of the education of older people must of course also be observed, since it can affect the validity of the rule.

Another confirmation of the usefulness of the method is finally given in a projection of reading ability for the birth cohorts in Tuna, Möklinta, and Skellefteå. The shaded area in Figure 8.5 indicates such a projection. In other words, it indicates the total growth of reading ability in the three parishes.

Such projections of birth cohorts need not of course be used when there is a fairly long series of measurements for the same parish. This is, however, not

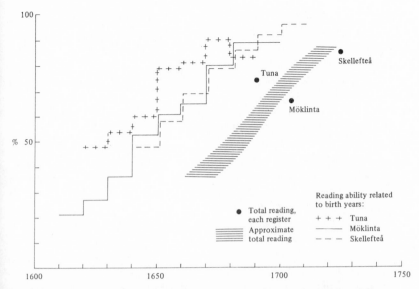

Figure 8.5 Reading ability in Tuna in 1691, in Möklinta in 1705 and in Skellefteå in 1724 according to the Church examination registers. In total (74, 66 and 85 per cent respectively) and related to date of birth. Percentage figures. (See also Table 8.6.)

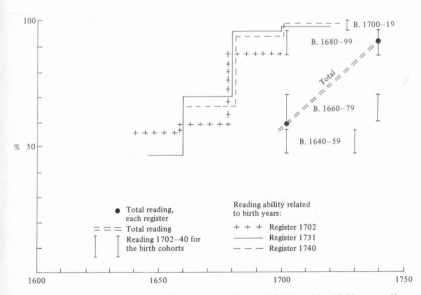

Figure 8.6 Reading ability in Skanör in 1702, in 1731 and in 1740 according to the Catechism registers. In total (58, 81 and 92 per cent respectively) and related to date of birth. Percentage figures

often the case because of gaps in the material. The methodology described above is then a useful complement. It is being tried out on a sample of parishes and examination registers for the whole country.

The reading campaign in the Dioceses of Västerås and Visby. Part results for a sample of parishes from the whole country

The hypotheses and the methodology presented above have created opportunities for decisive research work on the hitherto completely confusing material of the Church examination registers. The project has been awarded grants which have made it possible to plan and carry out a systematic study of a random sample of examination registers from parishes over the whole country. The parishes in every deanery have been arranged and numbered according to the deanery tables of 1805. One or two parishes for every deanery have then been selected with the aid of a table of random numbers. A division has been made into town and country parishes. Only the country parishes have been worked on so far; this is also where 90 per cent of the population lived up to the middle of the nineteenth century.

Because of the differences between the dioceses, the sample was processed diocese by diocese. The result for the diocese of Västerås will be our first example (Figure 8.7). The fifteen deaneries in the diocese of Västerås are each represented by a parish chosen at random. The earliest register with both reading marks and information about age, has been studied for every parish. There is, unfortunately, information about age in only six of the parishes before 1750 (Figure 8.7), but after 1750 the number of measurements increase. In seven parishes the first useful registers have been checked against later registers. This means that a total of 23 examinations can be presented. The sources of error are, of course, numerous. There are, for example, some obscurities in a number of registers. That is why the doubling of some registers mentioned above has served as a check-up. Great pains have been taken to avoid the same persons appearing several times at any one measurement. That is why, if possible, only the last examination in every register has been studied.

Since some parishes in the diocese of Västerås were very densely populated, a sample of persons has been made within the registers. This, too, has been made at random. The total population will, of course, be brought into the final report. The result for the diocese of Västerås seems to be unambiguous. Both the notes for separate examinations and a projection of the birth cohorts by two or three decades illustrate a very distinct reading campaign c. 1670–1720. The conclusions are verified in many ways, e.g. by the contemporary examination documents and by biographical data. They have also been verified in literature.[21]

There are also results for the diocese of Visby, although the examination registers studied for this diocese are much more recent – from 1750 onwards. The result is, nevertheless, comparable to the result for Västeras. All exam-

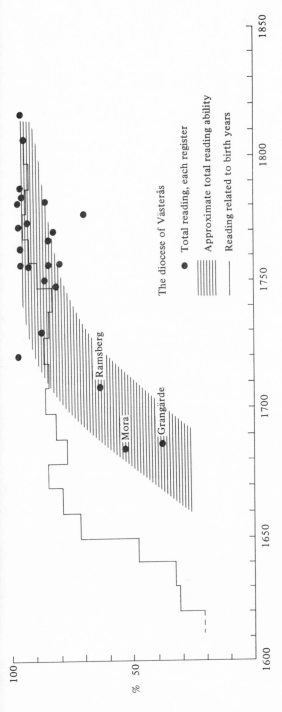

Figure 8.7 Reading ability in the diocese of Västerås according to the Church examination registers in a random sample of parishes. In total and related to time of birth. The population is about 15 years of age and older. Sample: 15 parishes, 23 Church examination registers. Percentage figures ($N = 4371$)

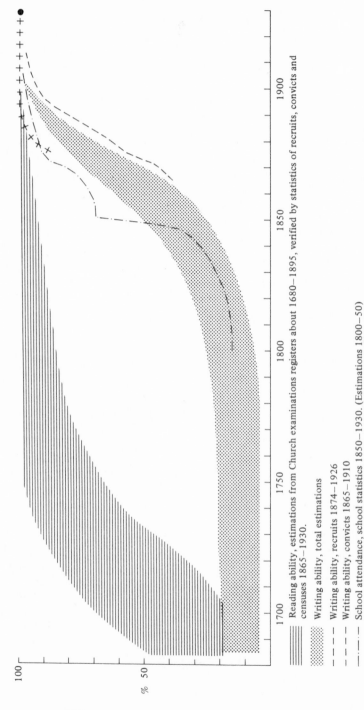

Figure 8.8 Reading and writing traditions in Sweden about 1680–1930. Preliminary results of current research. Population about 10–15 years of age and older. Schoolchildren about 6–15 years of age. Percentage figures.

	Reading ability, estimations from Church examinations registers about 1680–1895, verified by statistics of recruits, convicts and censuses 1865–1930.
	Writing ability, total estimations
– – –	Writing ability, recruits 1874–1926
– – –	Writing ability, convicts 1865–1910
– · –	School attendance, school statistics 1850–1930. (Estimations 1800–50)
●	Total reading and writing ability 1930. Census. Population 15 years of age and older.

ination registers in the selection show a total reading ability of more than 80 per cent. A retrograde projection of birth cohorts also indicates a high degree of similarity with the diocese of Västeras. The conclusion is that the actual reading campaign took place before 1750 in Gotland as well, which can also be tested on some registers from the beginning of the eighteenth century. These registers do not appear in the sample for the diocese of Visby.

These preliminary conclusions must now be tested and tried out for other dioceses as well. But at least they demonstrate the suitability of the programme by means of a sample for the whole country. The results must, of course, also be combined with other contemporary source material. They must also be compared to other relevant research results, e.g. in literature and in anthropology. The quality of the reading acquired as a result of the Swedish literacy program must also be studied. Later in the program, when the reading ability acquired in the initial campaign was to be consolidated, and deepened, in the population, the quality of reading came to be the subject of detailed markings in the examination records.

Summary of the spread of literacy in Sweden

The project has so far presented a general survey of the spread of literacy in Sweden. This can be visualized by means of a figure (Figure 8.8). The shaded areas indicate hypotheses about literacy. The hypotheses concerning reading are primarily based on the Church examination registers. The hypotheses for writing are based on school statistics and on the information concerning literacy of convicts and army recruits, and the census of 1930. These sources also verify the big difference between reading and writing till well into the nineteenth century.

This difference is, in reality, very important. It must be regarded as an established fact that general reading was achieved without formal school attendance. Swedish home instruction was so successful that those who only received home instruction were, in reality, regarded as able to read in the official statistics. This cannot be explained without returning to the rigorously controlled reading campaign, which started two centuries earlier.

The final stage of home instruction can easily be tested even today. Old people can tell you about parents and relatives who almost certainly could read printed letters but, on the other hand, could not write more than possibly their own names. These people had, as a rule, never attended school. Such 'illiterates' also exist in literature, e.g. Ida, the wife of *Raskens* in the novel by Vilhelm Moberg of the same name, or the father of Ivar Lo-Johansson, 'Analfabeten' (*The Illiterate*).

If this difference between reading and writing in Sweden is accepted, it will facilitate the use of the Swedish material when comparisons are being made with other countries.

Some conclusions

The history of Swedish literacy provides some experiences that can also be applied to the problems of the current literacy debate.

1. The two patterns of analysis have been quite useful. The first evaluates strictly controlled mass campaigns with a political or an ideological background designed at a rapid pace and increase to bring about widespread literacy. According to the second pattern of analysis permanent differences are observed between sexes, occupational groups, town and country, etc., which reveal that economic needs are what primarily direct the events.

2. But this also contradicts the modern opinion that literacy is primarily (and solely) part of the so-called modernization process, where industrialization, urbanization, political participation, etc., make up the inevitable framework. To accept an early reading tradition in a pre-industrial, agrarian, developing country like Sweden is an important contribution towards dissolving some of the most difficult problems in this formula for Western modernization.

3. This formula also states that reading and writing always follow each other closely. The acceptance of the Swedish and Finnish material will release the literacy debate from one of its most difficult positions. A modified literacy concept must then be taken seriously with revaluations of functioning semi-literate environments.

4. This early reading tradition in Sweden also strongly emphasizes the importance of engaging the whole population in the literacy process. An informal learning process where everyone helps everyone else is cheap and provides effective co-operation between home and school, where the home and the family provide the primary educational context.

5. The Swedish material also stresses the importance of the political will for the literacy campaign. This was also strongly emphasized, e.g., in the Declaration of the Persepolis Literacy Conference in 1975.

6. Warnings were also issued in Persepolis against the so-called postliterate problem in the West. The gravity of these warnings has made itself felt in Sweden, too. A modern society does not spontaneously maintain literacy at the highest level. New directions for emphasizing the basic skills of reading and writing must be issued in the schools.

7. Finally the Swedish tradition illustrates the fact that the ability to read must not be an end in itself. 'To read the word or to read the world' was a striking theme in Persepolis. Everything was, in the Swedish tradition, concentrated on comprehending, understanding, and putting the word into practice in everyday life. Reading was not to be an end in itself; it was instead a question of experiencing the total environment of life and society. 'To read the world of the Word' could be the surviving message of the old Swedish reading tradition.[22]

9 LITERACY IN EARLY AMERICA 1650–1800*

Kenneth A. Lockridge

This is a report on the conclusions reached in a monograph on *Literacy in Colonial New England* (1974), and a commentary on those conclusions in the perspective of recent research on literacy in early modern Europe.[1]

The general theme to keep in mind is that, on both sides of the Atlantic, religion was the major force in teaching men and often women to read. When the religious impulse also led to a system of schools, most men but rather fewer women also learned to write and possibly to reckon. In the absence of such systematic schooling, writing and probably also mathematics were called forth chiefly by the requirements of commercial exchange and by the legal regime associated with these. These requirements varied in strength from occupation to occupation, from area to area, from nation to nation, and over time. During the sixteenth, seventeenth, eighteenth, and early nineteenth centuries both religion and the demands of exchange were raising the levels of all types of literacy whether suddenly or almost imperceptibly. Throughout the western world thereafter, these and perhaps other forces led to the introduction of systematic public education which provided essentially universal schooling in all basic literacy skills.

I

To summarize the results concerning *Literacy in Colonial New England* circa 1650–1790:

In the first place it seemed that signatures on legal documents were a reliable measure of literacy. As has been argued elsewhere, signatures probably run rather above the level of mathematical skills, a little above the level of writing, and correspond most closely with fluent reading, though they by no means include everyone capable of reading. Signatures should vary in parallel with major variations in the levels of these literacy skills. Nothing in the sources for New England indicated any major exceptions to these assumptions.

It also appeared that the level of signatures among persons making wills was a fair approximation of the level of signatures among the general population. Careful and independent estimates indicated that the weaknesses of old age, which tended to lower the signature level of persons leaving wills,

*Reprinted from Kenneth A. Lockridge, 'Literacy in Early America, 1650–1800', by permission of the author. (A French translation appeared in *Annales: e.,s.,c.* 32 (1977), 503–18.)

were very closely counterbalanced by the high wealth and occupational status of these same persons, which tended to raise their signature rate to an equivalent degree. Hence signatures on wills should correspond to the signatures and so to the literacy of the general population.

Wills also represented a relatively constant sample of the population in all areas of America; they provided much the richest additional information of any source of signatures; and they corresponded to comparable sources of signatures across the Atlantic. Wills were, therefore, the best of a mixed lot of sources for the study of early American literacy. They did grievously under-represent women, so the conclusions derived from them were limited chiefly to male literacy. In diverse counties containing over one third of the population of New England, all wills for the years 1650–70, 1705–15, and 1758–62 were sampled, with additional samples including the years 1785–1795. The total number sampled was over 3000.

The signature rate for men in early seventeenth-century England was probably not much over 40%. The signature rate among the men who settled New England and who left wills there between 1650 and 1670 was over 60% (Figure 9.1). It seemed evident, therefore, that the migrants to New England came from more literate areas of England or from more literate segments of the population or both.

Thereafter the male literacy rate in New England should have risen further, since after 1650 most New Englanders lived under laws requiring all but the smallest communities to maintain a reading-and-writing school and requiring larger communities to maintain also a grammar school. These laws arose quite explicitly from the imperatives of the protestant religion as interpreted by the Calvinistic Puritans who had undertaken the migration to New England. In the laws, 'Satan' was the avowed opponent. To create such schools, as migration permitted the Puritans to do, was to hold off the deadly ignorance emanating from the Devil. But, as of the generation born in New England and dying there around 1705–15, the schools had not made much progress against Satan. The signature rate had been maintained at 60% but not raised significantly. The reason seemed to be that a large minority of the scattered population lived in communities small enough to escape the school laws, legally or otherwise. Also, men perhaps saw no pressing need for literacy. Whatever the reason, each locality within New England tended to maintain that exact level of partial literacy with which it had been endowed by its original sub-stream of migrants. Within each area, the differences in literacy between the various occupations and degrees of wealth remained as sharp as they had been among the English migrants.

The real increase in literacy came in the subsequent generations, as the cohort dying circa 1760 showed over 80% male signatures and the cohort dying around 1790 reached 90% (Figure 9.1). The schools seem to have been behind this improvement, since it was generally only men who went to these

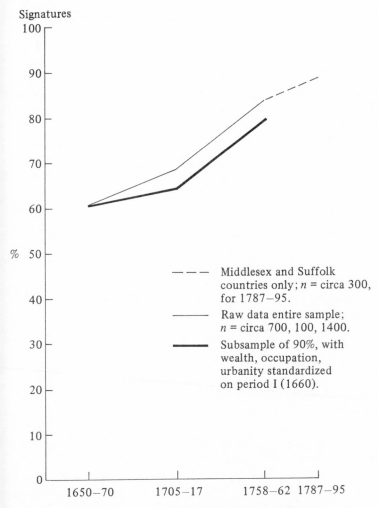

Figure 9.1 Male signatures on New England wills 1650–1795
Notes: 1. Signatures are on the vertical axis in all graphs.
  2. The number of cases in the sample is rounded off in all graphs.

public reading-and-writing schools, and it was only men whose signature rate improved.[2] In the one region with a weak school law, New Hampshire, male literacy rose more slowly than elsewhere. Moreover, it is difficult to conceive of a pattern of home education which could have accomplished this rise in male signatures. Home education could have contributed substantially only if a large proportion of fathers taught their own and perhaps other mens' sons, but not their own or others' daughters, to write. Generally no such mechanism has been detected behind sharp rises in writing skills anywhere in western

society. To the contrary, such rises are everywhere associated with systematic schooling.

A correlation emerged between the rate and degree of increase in male literacy in the various counties and the population density in those counties. This suggested that increases in the proportion of persons living in communities too large to evade the school law and large enough to be able to pay for a school had led to increased availability of schools and so in time to higher male literacy.

More than availability may have been involved, for it is often assumed that increasing population density entails greater commercial and legal sophistication and a greater demand for writing and for mathematics. It was difficult to say whether this added force played a role by increasingly encouraging New England men to send their sons to school. What seemed clear, particularly from two large counties where there was no upward shift in the pattern of wealth or of occupational status during this period and where the full rise in signatures nonetheless took place, was that neither the expectation nor the reality of improved socio-economic condition was involved in the massive rise in literacy in New England in the mid eighteenth century. If economic pressures were involved, they probably smacked more of the increasing necessity for literacy in order to maintain one's place in the world, or of an increasing need to have literacy to move into any vacancies in the next rung of a relatively fixed social hierarchy. Data from elsewhere in early-eighteenth-century America implied that even these forces were not raising literacy there, so it appeared doubtful that any economic forces played a primary role in the rise in literacy in New England.

Recent Swedish research had suggested that in such a society the influence of population density in improving educational coverage was primarily through increasing simple proximity to and availability of schooling. It seemed likely that this was the case in New England, and that crossing a minimal threshold of population density removed an artificial handicap to the availability of schooling. At most the evolution away from the unusually scattered population and small villages of the seventeenth century may also have restored a more normal sense of the functional usefulness of and need for literacy, and so contributed somewhat to providing the Church a viable social context for its mission. To these degrees and possibly to these degrees alone the Protestant state schools required assistance in achieving universal male literacy.

In this perspective, religion, in the form of an intense, widespread, and relatively uniform Protestantism of sufficient influence to persuade the state to require systematic formal schooling, was the essential force behind the rise to universal male literacy in New England. Once the diffuse population of the first generations ceased to impose a handicap, this force made schools widely available. Given availability, some, perhaps ever more men sent their sons to school out of practical motives, as men would have done had school been available in other more or less normally evolving societies of the time. Yet only wide availability made this possible in New England, and behind availability, throughout the colonial period, was the law and behind the law was the Church. Furthermore, the same Protestant spirit embodied in the schools was probably for a long time a major force in sending men's sons to the schools. Right through the eighteenth century, the books listed in men's inventories remained overwhelmingly religious in character,[3] and a clear majority of charitable bequests in these wills continued to go to religion. Religion, then, as well as any subtle social evolution, sent men's sons to the schools.

The motive behind such Protestantism, whether or not it added schools and so writing to its programme, was that men and often women should learn to read the Word of God. One might ask whether this heavily Protestant literacy or rise in literacy transformed the lives of men. It did eliminate most regional, occupational, and class differences in literacy, no small event in a world otherwise marked by a series of reinforcing hierarchical distinctions. On the other hand it did not reduce the most notable of these distinctions by making ordinary men richer or by raising the occupational status of more than a few. Nor did it raise women's ability to sign. And there was positive if controversial evidence that literacy both before and after its rise did not entail new, more generous, abstract, widely aware or innovative social sympathies. Except in very rare cases, the charitable attitudes of literate men and women, as reflected in the gifts they left in their wills, remained fully as cautious, personalistic, localistic, pious, and alleviative as the charitable attitudes of illiterates. This evidence is not surprising in view of the expressed intentions of the Church and the nature of the society.

After nearly universal male literacy was reached, in the generations educated following the middle of the eighteenth century, the motives for maintaining the school system and high literacy may have begun to partake ever more of increases in economic necessity and, eventually, of rising economic opportunity. The latter sort of literacy may have been associated with more outgoing, constructive, and optimistic attitudes. Yet there is no evidence of any social developments sufficient to raise substantially the level of literacy in other colonies during the later eighteenth century, so it is uncertain whether late eighteenth-century New England ever generated secular forces strong enough to maintain its almost universal literacy. In the nineteenth century the increasing commercial, legal, and political sophistications of modern society raise the question of whether that universal literacy which was then sustained in New England and achieved elsewhere, even with such secular motives behind it, was enough to enable men to meet the functional needs of new times. This evolving 'literacy gap' may have left literate men behind, and later literacy may have brought only frustration. One might well wonder whether, for the mass of people, there was ever a 'liberating' literacy in New England.

The best comparison for colonial New England seemed to be with Sweden and Scotland, two other areas with an intense, wide, uniform Protestantism where likewise the state was prevailed upon to encourage systematic education. This took the form of priestly examinations in Sweden and of schools in Scotland. With New England, these societies stood out among the western nations of the early modern era for the rapidity, breadth, and peak of their rise in literacy. As of the end of the eighteenth century such areas alone could claim to have reached universal literacy in any respect. This seemed to say a great deal about the power of religion, particularly in this form, as compared with other cultural or with environmental or economic influences on literacy. State—Protestant education achieved what other forces could not, and to some degree, considering the nature of society in New England, lowland Scotland, and Sweden, it achieved this largely on its own. What this kind of literacy entailed was uncertain save to say that more men read the Word of God. All the evidence was that literacy, like other innovations of Protestantism, needed a long time and another context to achieve its full implications.

Since *Literacy in Colonial New England* appeared, two years ago, students of literacy in early modern Europe have brought forward information which calls for some comments though perhaps not for major changes in this picture.

Signatures still seem to hold up well as a measure of male literacy, subject to the qualification that as many as half of men who made marks could probably read and possibly a minority could read well. Such allowance was made in the book and the estimates of total illiteracy were accordingly reduced. What is new is the way this proportion of male readers-only seems to vary, from nearly 100% of men who could not sign in Sweden through the 30—50% estimates for Anglo-America down to around 10% for early nineteenth-century France. These variations are associated with the way reading was taught in each nation, from the conscious promotion of reading and reading alone throughout Sweden, to the stress on reading sometimes followed up with writing in England, perhaps because the English economy demanded writing more than in Sweden, through the routine sequence of reading-and-writing in the New England schools, to the deliberate attempt at least in nineteenth-century France to teach reading and writing simultaneously. Despite these variations, signing still seems to have correlated more or less well with the level of fluent reading, even in Sweden where this would be least expected. The new evidence also shows that signing correlated closely with the ability to write. In these respects the measure performs as expected.

Wills, too, seem to hold up fairly well as a sample 'representative' of the population. Daniel Scott Smith has found that, in one New England town, two thirds of the most wealthy 40% of men left wills while only one fifth of the next 40% left wills and a mere one fourteenth of the least wealthy 20% of men.[4] Treating the sample of New England wills in this perspective and weighting the wills of the less wealthy to convert the sample into a facsimile of the total male population results in aggregate literacy rates on the order of 15% (*c.* 1650–70), 17% (1705–15), and 5% (1758–62) lower than in the raw sample. These estimates of bias are extraordinarily close to the downward adjustments for wealth and occupational bias used in the book. The differences in the estimates are so small and contingent that it would be pointless to play with them. The only potentially significant difference is that Smith's estimates would emphasize, even more than the book, the relative lack of progress in literacy before 1705–15 and the sharp relative increase in literacy thereafter.

The opposite bias, by which old age artificially reduced the ability of men to sign, seems to have been about the same among David Cressy's group of contemporaneous Englishmen as it was estimated to be among the men leaving wills in seventeenth-century New England. These Englishmen had about the same level of literacy as the New Englanders, so presumably about the same degree of need to acquire and to retain the skill. Their signatures on depositions show that 12% of them forgot how or were unable to sign their names after they passed 60 years of age. The initial estimate for the downward bias of age in New England was a little higher, at 15%, because of a minor tendency of rising literacy to leave older men relatively less literate, an effect controlled out of the English data and which eventually disappears from the New England data.[5]

The new evidence thus reaffirms the conclusion that the biases of wealth and of age were of nearly equal and of declining effect, and wills still seem to approximate the literacy of the population. In English wills these opposite biases seem at first to tip slightly in favour of the reducing effects of age, as the raw signature rate in wills had to be raised to match the higher signature rate found in more random documents and presumably in the population. On second glance these English 'random documents', depositions among them, appear to have a small but significant wealth bias of their own, which means that their signature rate should be reduced to somewhere near the level found in wills in order to meet the rate in the presumed general population!

The new methodological evidence does not, therefore, substantially alter the shape of the literacy line established for colonial New England, women partially excepted.[6] Neither does it change the analysis of the causes behind these lines, although here, too, there are comments to make.

I had noted that only 33–40% of Englishmen born around 1600 were literate, whereas of the men who migrated to New England 60% could similarly sign their names. Swedish research had seemed to confirm this sort of positive selection for literacy among long-range migrants, but had not predicted such a strong effect. An effort to explain this phenomenon leads into a tangle of speculations concerning the relationships between literacy, occupation, Puritanism and migration.

One could assume that men who could read were more likely to become Puritans, particularly artisans and yeoman-farmers. The migration to New England was, therefore, weighted toward occupations in which men could read and also incidentally could sign and indeed write. Yet it would be difficult to project a migrant stream in which more than 45% of the men could sign, merely on this basis of selection, since the migration manifestly contained a heavy admixture of English husbandmen, many of whom could read but only 25% of whom could sign.

Further selectivity, and the actual 60% signature rate of the male migrants, might be explained in terms of the fact that *within* these areas and occupations Puritanism *also* selected for those men who could write. The problem is that, while generally Protestantism and specifically Puritanism selected for readers, and sought to create readers, the religion did not of itself require or widely foster the higher skills reflected in signatures. Only where a uniform radical Protestantism influenced the state to create systematic schooling, as in New England, were this religion and writing skills closely associated over a wide area. Hence there is no reason to believe that Puritanism affected specifically those men who could write within the areas and occupations most likely to receive it.

A Puritan migration is, however, another matter. Margaret Spufford has shown that letters could serve as an instrument of discipline among English sectarians, and the groups most likely to migrate were possibly those most disciplined into a group identity, and in best contact with the leaders of the Puritan movement. This most definitely entails a selectivity for signature-literacy among the male migrants, though it cannot be known whether this effect would be enough to account for the 60% rate among the migrants to earliest New England. Surely some allowance must be left for 'pure' migration effects, such as those found in Sweden, where more literate persons tended to migrate for reasons having to do solely with the secular necessities or psychological structure of long-distance migration.

Virginia may cut the Gordian knot, for the signature rate of male migrants to Virginia dying circa 1650—70 was nearly 50%. This suggests that at least some of the literacy superiority of contemporaneous migrants to New England was a migration effect having nothing to do with the selectivities of Puritanism or specifically of Puritan migration. This in turn is confirmed by further research in Sweden indicating that long-distance migration could easily explain an increased level of writing-literacy of this order of magnitude.

The mechanism used to explain the delayed but substantial later increase in male literacy in New England seems to remain valid. Swedish evidence continues to support the notion that schools and the availability or proximity of schooling were of crucial importance creating mass writing skills. In Västerås diocese early in the nineteenth century, Torsäng, a parish with a school founded in 1758, rose from perhaps a 30% male signature rate circa

1800 toward 50% by 1825 and on to 80% by 1850. A nearby parish with similar economic characteristics, but no school, remained around 33% male signatures until just after 1850, when it rose slowly to over 40% signatures. A notably poorer parish likewise without a school did about the same, moving from 26% to 33% signatures over the same period. Within Torsäng, as later within the northern parish of Bygdeå, children's proximity to the school was probably more closely associated with school attendance than was their fathers' occupation. The importance of simple availability probably explains why Sweden later went from the lowest level of writing skills in western Europe to among the highest, following the establishment of a universal system of local schools in the middle of the nineteenth century. Except for populations as scattered as that of earliest New England, where schools could not easily be made available, it was possibly true throughout much of western history that to make schools available was to make reading and writing universal almost regardless of other conditions.[7]

Schools and availability notwithstanding, it is clear that already in the seventeenth, eighteenth, and early nineteenth centuries economic expectations, aspirations, or more likely necessities often played a significant role in raising the level of male signatures. The close association between occupational needs and signatures found in early modern England appears in attenuated form somewhat later in Sweden. In both countries this association could produce nearly universal literacy in certain commercial (not industrial) centers, either because these cities recruited literate men from the countryside, or because they produced their own. The small trading city of Västerås, for example, showed more than 90% male signatures already in 1800 and the rate rose thereafter. And in England and even in Sweden this kind of association appears to have been behind a slow long-term increase in male signatures even outside the cities. As literacy became useful or necessary to certain occupations, they rose toward quite high levels, raising the average even though literacy remained otherwise low. Artisans and yeomen farmers thereby raised England to over 60% male signatures between 1550 and 1750, and a similar pattern was probably what was raising the rate of male signatures among independent farmers in school-less parishes of Västerås diocese gradually toward the same levels, a century later.

Such a force may have contributed to the rise in literacy in eighteenth-century New England, but there is still reason for caution. The English evidence reaffirms that the force at work was not so much economic opportunity as the increased necessity for literacy within the existing society, born of changes in the modes of economic exchange. Also, this was a relatively weak force, which operated slowly. And there is a hint in the level trend of English signatures from 1750 to 1795 that the 60%+ rate reached by the former date had temporarily saturated this structural demand for literacy. If a 60% rate saturated the more developed English economy and society, and incidentally seems to have been all that the rest of colonial America could sustain, the economy of colonial New England must have been oversaturated by a literacy which began at 60% and rose to 90%. Hence it is doubtful that the sharp final rise to universal literacy in New England was evoked or entirely sustained by such economic demands.

It is possibly still true that crossing a minimal threshold of population density early in the eighteenth century may not only have made schools more available but also restored a 'normal' awareness of the practicalities of literacy and so have helped send many men's sons to the newly available schools. But it is impossible that this rather less dramatic interaction could have raised literacy in New England to universality without the schools, and in the end only religion, its schools, and perhaps also to a degree its motives can account for the initial universality achieved in New England. The attitudinal associations of a colonial New England literacy which was so largely Church-inspired, and which rose in the absence of substantial upward economic mobility or dramatic social change, still seem rather likely to be conservative. Or, it still seems unlikely that in such a context literacy would be found associated with new attitudes.

Possibly, too, among the generations educated after the middle of the eighteenth century, economic necessity did replace religion as a motive sustaining a significant proportion of this universal literacy, though by no means all. This would be consistent with recent analyses of the evolution of New England society. But there remains the question of what new attitudes were associated with a mentality of necessity. Data on charitable bequests from English wills, cited in the book, suggested that the answer is 'none'. At best the cheese-paring 'rationality' of the cartoon Dutchman. And such attitudes, and any new attitudes associated with a much later literacy evoked by economic opportunity, must be placed in the perspective of a functional literacy which may have dwindled steadily in the face of evolving social complexities.

In the largest perspective the New England literacy achievement remains unusual but not unique. I would probably now associate New England more closely with Prussia, and perhaps other German states, than with Sweden, whose educational miracle seems to have been confined largely to reading. The fact remains that New England, parts of northern Germany, and perhaps Scotland were clustered alone at or near universal male signatures by the end of the eighteenth century. Their common feature was a low degree of social development coupled with an intensive, widespread, and uniform Protestantism which prevailed upon secular authorities to encourage systematic schooling.

We must not overstate the uniqueness of this milieu in fostering literacy. The north-east *départements* of France had approached 70% male signatures by the end of the eighteenth century, for a variety of reasons having little directly to do with Protestantism or with systematic state-schools. Nonetheless, the unique universality and unprecedented rate of advance of male signature-literacy in New England, in 'Prussia', and in Scotland mark out intense state-Protestantism and its schools as the most powerful force for literacy in the early modern era. And the lesser but substantial achievements of the North of England, where male signatures rose to 75% by 1800, the early advent of universal reading for men and women in Sweden, together with the substantial increase in reading-only in England and in much of the north Atlantic world between the sixteenth and nineteenth centuries, must be attributed at least in part to a more generalized Protestantism. The immediate 'modernity' of the associations and uses of literacy acquired in such contexts remain open to a very strong scepticism. Literacy in much of 'early modern' Europe was possibly more early than modern.

II

Literacy in Colonial New England then took up literacy in the rest of colonial America. Other scholars had suggested that a force or forces more or less unique to the new environment might have created a near universal and liberating literacy everywhere in America. This did not appear to have been the case, and without the special religious intensity and uniformity which culminated in state-sponsored schools in New England, the rest of early America had a literacy profile similar to that of England.

The sources used were wills from Pennsylvania, as reported by Alan Tully, and particularly from Virginia. English wills were sampled in Norfolk, Gloucester, Kent, and Yorkshire. The measure was signatures.

Male signature rates in the rest of colonial America appeared to have begun at a level significantly above that in England, and to have risen to 60–65% by the early eighteenth century, a rate still a bit above that in England (Figure 9.2). The evidence was that migration explains this marginally better achievement. A very large proportion of men leaving wills in this period were of foreign origin and education, chiefly English, and the records of migrant literacy point to an immigration at least as literate as its places of origin and increasingly literate.

Thereafter the trend of male literacy remained in the neighbourhood of 65% right up to the end of the eighteenth century. Indications were that the Germans and Scots–Irish who arrived in such large numbers in the middle of the century showed about this same level of literacy, so the trend of indigenous male literacy could have been no more than stagnant. Data from older Virginia counties which had little immigration confirm this impression of stagnancy. Generally not even the Pennsylvania Germans, with their relatively frequent local schools, were able to raise literacy higher. In the absence of systematic schooling of the New England sort, literacy remained where the immigrants had brought it, and roughly equivalent to the level in England. This does testify to some functional need for literacy, whether

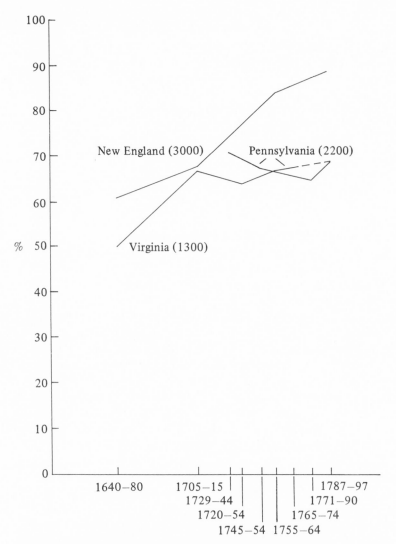

Figure 9.2 Male signatures on wills: Raw data
Notes: 1. Virginia data from P.A. Bruce, *Institutional History of Virginia in the Seventeenth Century* (New York, 1910), show circa 60% male signatures 1640–1700.
2. Virginia samples range 150–350.
3. Western countries are added to Virginia sample in proportion to their growing share of the population.
4. Pennsylvania data from Alan Tully, 'Literacy Levels and Educational Development in Rural Pennsylvania, 1729–1775', *Pennsylvania Magazine of History and Biography* (1973), except for 1790s sample.

religious or practical or both, but also to the absence of any unusually powerful 'American' educational forces able to raise literacy higher.

In such a context literacy prevailed among the most wealthy groups and among certain occupations, but remained a minority experience for the lowest third of male society. Literacy therefore continued to re-enforce the other distinctions which made society hierarchical, and mass illiteracy remained a reality, with as many as 25% of men in these parts of America ablebodied but totally illiterate. This was of course also the pattern in England. The lot of women was the same as in New and old England; though only a minority could write, the influence of a generalized Protestant culture probably meant that a majority could read.

There was no evidence in the charitable bequests in the Virginia wills that this less dramatic literacy environment raised literate men's minds from that personal, the local, and the passive worldview which had endured among literates and illiterates even in New England, and which could be found also in the wills of literate and illiterate Englishmen. And in these other colonies, as elsewhere, there was a question of whether any degree of basic literacy would enable men to meet the coming demands of modern society. If literate men were 'liberated', the evidence was lacking.

It appeared, then, that two thirds of America met the Revolution with a literacy which was stagnant, incomplete, socially hierarchical, and, *en masse*, intellectually passive. This is neither scandal or surprise, since no more in America than in England was there any force other than the schools of state-Protestantism which could revolutionize the level of literacy, and even that force perhaps could not immediately revolutionize its implications.

So it seemed as the manuscript of *Literacy* went to press. The main revisions to this part of the picture concern the relative power of the lesser and possibly largely economic forces affecting men's literacy in 'the rest' of colonial America (hereafter simply 'America') as compared with the power of similar forces in England. These forces alone were not enough to raise male literacy significantly above two thirds in America or in England, but they did create variations in literacy rates between occupations and between wealth-groups, and the net product of such forces in each culture was the pattern of relationship between literacy and these other social distinctions within each culture.

I had suggested, in the first place, that among the great mass of farmers and artisans literacy appeared to be lower in America than in England, possibly implying a lesser economic need for literacy among these occupations in America (Figure 9.3). (In this perspective the slightly higher overall literacy of America was chiefly the result of leaving behind much of that heavily illiterate class of labourers which so reduced the otherwise higher English literacy figures. And this American advantage turns to a deficit once the slaves who took the labourers' place are included in the figures.) At the same

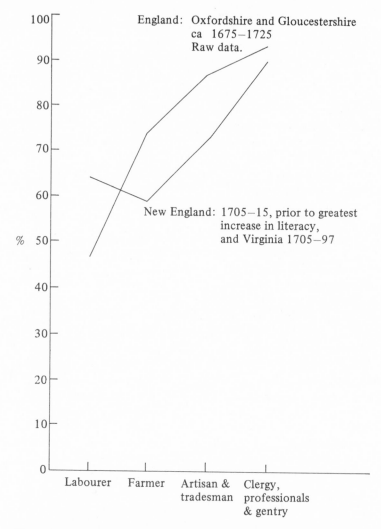

Figure 9.3 Signatures by occupation: New England vs England 1700–25
Note: English data from Lawrence Stone, 'Literacy and Education in
England, 1640–1900', *Past and Present*, 42 (1969), 61–139.

time there was a hint of a closer relationship between literacy and the upper
middle and higher levels of wealth in America as compared with England
(Figure 9.4). In retrospect, this does not seem to be because in America
fathers in middle and higher wealth groups were better able to purchase
literacy for their sons. Rather, it suggests that, while the farmers and artisans
in America did not so often require literacy for successful functioning, those

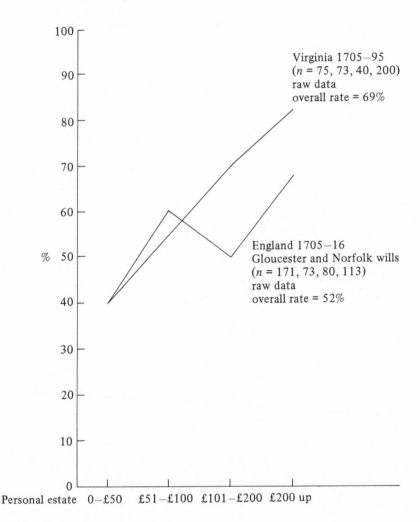

Figure 9.4 Male signatures v. wealth in Virginia and in England
Note: The relationship of literacy and wealth is constant in eighteenth-
   century Virginia, hence 1705–95 data are used to enlarge the sample.

who did become literate were a little more likely to become rich than was the
case in England. This further suggests that, while in England a man could be
illiterate and rich because he had inherited some wealth, in America there
was a somewhat higher proportion of well-off men who had earned their
wealth in part through knowledge and effort. This paradox leaves us with
a relatively illiterate American lower middle class, the vast majority, but

also at least a few examples of the classic new world gentleman in rolled shirtsleeves.[8]

Yet these are only marginal effects in an overall picture which still looks fundamentally the same in America and in England. In both areas a step up in occupation or in wealth was associated with a higher probability of literacy for reasons having most to do, from the evidence, with enduring economic necessities. While it helped to have literacy to maintain one's position, or to move up into a vacancy in the next run, these necessities were not increasing in a revolutionary fashion in the first decades of the eighteenth century. In any event there were no systematic schools available to respond to increasing necessities. Hence there was no great increase in measured aggregate literacy and in neither society was the social structure of literacy transformed as it had been in New England.[9]

Indeed, the more one fiddles with the evidence, the more similar Virginia and England appear. Consider as an example the possibility of adjusting for the way the biases of age and of wealth separately affected each distinct wealth or occupational group studied in the American wills. The book did not do this because so many contingencies were involved, but the apparent consequence of calculating separate adjustments for each group is to reaffirm the basic similarities in the Anglo-American literacy environment. For the net impact of such adjustments is to raise the literacy of the middle American occupations, the farmers and artisans, a little closer to that of the gentry, merchants and clergy, while leaving the lowest occupational groups relatively lower in literacy than appeared previously. The result is a literacy spectrum like that which has recently been elucidated for eighteenth-century England, in which the nearly total literacy of the top of society was approximated among yeomen and artisans, leaving an immense gap down to the husband-men and labourers of whom the great majority remained illiterate. And, again, the fact that there were relatively few husbandmen, marginal or renter farmers, or labourers in mid-eighteenth-century America was compensated for by the black men who took their place. The result of a closer look at the data is, therefore, more than anything else an increased emphasis on the basic similarities in the literacy environments of eighteenth-century America and eighteenth-century England. The differences mentioned earlier endure, but appear even more minor.

III

The differences between New England and the rest of the colonies make it difficult to compare early American literacy to literacy elsewhere. The best way is to present the spectrum of literacy of populations of roughly similar size in America and in Europe as of 1800. This would show New England, possibly matched by Prussia and other north German states, followed closely by Scotland, those followed in turn by the North of England and by the north-east of France, then the rest of America excluding slaves, with Sweden's read-little-write profile inserted somewhere, then the rest of England, the rest of America including slaves, and the various other regions of France at ever lower and less well-determined levels.

The reasons for this hierarchy have been suggested throughout this essay. It becomes clear that the most interesting areas to study are not simply those where Protestant schools 'pushed' (to borrow a term from Egil Johansson) literacy toward universality but those areas in England and in France where a complex of lesser forces did much to 'pull' literacy to a fairly high level. It is here that we must also look for the attitudinal associations of literacy, though here also it might be unwise to expect too much, if the primary motive evoking literacy here was the desire to maintain one's position under changing and perhaps ever more difficult circumstances.

That desire, moreover, would have affected all men to some degree, not merely the fathers of literate sons or the literate sons alone. In this respect one final pattern in the evidence from New England and above all from Virginia and from England is most suggestive. While the attitudinal profile of charitable gifts in all three areas remained heavily personal, local, and pious among both literates and illiterates, in all these areas there was a sharp decline in the frequency of charitable giving among literates *and* illiterates. No change in the law affecting bequests caused this diminution of giving, for the law remained in the framework established under Queen Elizabeth. Nor does the charitable impulse appear to have shifted instead to 'living' gifts granted before the last will and testament was drawn up. Rather the decline in charitable giving seems to reflect a declining interest in the needs of society, as the state took over functions once left to voluntary action, and as men withdrew their private resources from society to focus these instead on themselves and on their families.

It is this phenomenon which I set out to study, before moving off to study literacy through the wills. More work must be done to ascertain whether a sense of pressing necessity or of potential self-betterment lay behind this new focus on the self, though from all the evidence it was both. For purposes of this paper, the implication is plain. Such changes as were taking place in the attitudinal structure of western man were not exclusively or even very heavily associated with literacy. Nor, of course, were these changes found only in early America. Nor, above all, did the new man emerging seem to be as socially optimistic, emphatic, outgoing or constructive as some have suggested. In this perspective (in areas where the church did not push literacy), higher literacy appears as an epiphenomenon of a broader movement toward a mentality which involved the careful husbanding of every resource in a western society ever more crowded, commercial, and complex.

But at this point the story becomes not the story of literacy, which itself had perhaps fewer implications than might be thought, and not the story of America, which was simply a part of western society, but the story of that peculiar, eventually powerful, yet somehow 'limited' 'individualism' which was the distinctive product of the early modern era. While this had revolutionary implications for man's fate, it did not necessarily revolutionize or still less broaden human consciousness, nor through literacy nor otherwise did it necessarily bestow that entire competence for which men strove.[10]

In the course of the sixteenth, seventeenth, and eighteenth centuries, then, millions of men and women in Europe and in America were led to pick up the potentially radical tool of literacy, often for reasons deeper than its ever greater availability. But it could be wrong always to associate the social forces moving them with progress or with upward mobility. There is evidence for a more sceptical and pessimistic account of the social forces behind this new instrument. Moreover, until the nineteenth century no social forces alone but only religion and the availability it brought could push this mass literacy to universality. Both in the presence and in the absence of this religious push, a measure of attitudes so sensitive that even in a biased sample it should show some attitudinal impact from literacy, shows virtually none. This is consistent with current scepticism concerning the degree of functional adequacy and of attitudinal liberation among the mass of modern literates.

Literacy could be seen, in fact, as an epiphenomenon of a larger and more subtle struggle for individual adequacy in the face of social changes which we hardly understand and which might conform only loosely to certain conceptions of modernization. It is this essential event which *Literacy* sought to regain from the American historians and from the more single-minded exponents of a modernizing and transforming literacy. Rising literacy, like the declining fertility of the nineteenth century, is chiefly a monument to our ignorance of the deeper processes of human history.

10   DIMENSIONS OF ILLITERACY IN ENGLAND 1750–1850*

R.S. Schofield

Recently an increasing number of economists have begun to consider education as a process of human capital formation, and to view expenditure on education in terms of private and social investment.[1] This perspective leads naturally to the question of the contribution of education to economic growth, and economists of education have not been slow to appreciate the relevance of the English experience during the eighteenth and early nineteenth centuries.[2]

Unfortunately, the study of education in this period is much less advanced than the study of economic growth. Most accounts rely on inferences drawn from the history of the development of educational institutions and from the history of the popular press, buttressed by a few contemporary and modern studies of the literacy of a limited number of groups. The present consensus is that educational opportunities expanded during the period 1750–1850, so that by 1840 between 67% and 75% of the British working class had achieved rudimentary literacy. Some writers believe that the growth in the middle of the period was not great, and point to a halt in educational advance at the turn of the century,[3] while others have discerned a particularly rapid growth in literacy in the first few decades of the nineteenth century.[4] All agree that there was considerable variation: regionally, between town and countryside, and between different occupational groups.

International comparisons of modern literacy rates and stages of economic development suggest that a 40% literacy rate may be a minimum threshold, and an increasing literacy rate a necessary condition, of economic growth.[5] The evidence at present available shows that England had crossed the 40% threshold by 1840, but it is not yet clear whether or not this had happened before 1750. However, the apparent coincidence of economic growth with a rise in literacy during the period seems to confirm the usefulness of regarding education as an investment in human resources, which brings both direct economic benefits in the form of increased productivity, and indirect economic benefits in the form of the replacement of a traditional set of values by another set, sometimes characterized as 'modern', or even 'rational'.

*The research underlying this paper is supported by the Social Science Research Council.

Reprinted from Roger S. Schofield, 'Dimensions of Illiteracy, 1750–1850', *Explorations in Economic History*, 10 (1973), 437–54, by permission of the author and the publisher, Academic Press, Inc., © Academic Press., Inc. 1973.

In this paper I shall avoid the larger cultural issues raised by this last proposition. Instead, I shall review the present evidence for the course of literacy in the period 1750–1850, present some fresh evidence, and suggest some implications for the relationship between literacy and economic growth in the period.

I

Arguments from changes in the volume and nature of popular publications to changes in the level of literacy enjoyed by the population at large are particularly insecure. First, there is no necessary relationship between the volume of production and the size of readership, because the number of readers per copy cannot be assumed to have been constant either over time or between publications. Second, changes in both the volume and the nature of publications may have been influenced by many factors other than changes in the level of literacy: for example, technological innovations such as the steam press, or changes in fiscal policy such as the many different rates of stamp duty charged in newspapers in the eighteenth and early nineteenth centuries. But arguments from the increase in educational facilities (the founding of the Charity Schools in the eighteenth century, the Sunday Schools in the 1780s, and the monitorial, industrial, and workhouse schools in the early nineteenth century), although frequently advanced, are also fraught with danger. Some of these schools, notably the Charity and the Sunday schools, were more concerned to impart a moral and religious training, and for them instruction in literacy was a secondary consideration. All schools had great difficulty in securing attendance. Early nineteenth-century surveys showed time and again that the number of children enrolled at school was no guide to the number actually receiving instruction.[6] This was partly because, with the exception of the Sunday schools and some of the institutional schools, fees had to be paid, for despite the large number of ostensibly free schools very few genuinely free places were available. Education was therefore in direct competition with other goods for cash expenditure. It was also in competition with earning capacity, for the early nineteenth-century surveys also show that even in the case of free schools attendance slumped when employment was available.

Thus, the difficulty with indirect measures of literacy, such as the volume of popular publications and the supply of education, lies in the intervention of other variables; but direct measures of literacy also have their drawbacks. The early nineteenth century, particularly the 1830s and 1840s, witnessed a rash of educational, cultural, and moral surveys, made by a wide range of interested parties, many of which investigated the ability of different sections of the population to read and write, often in considerable detail.[7] Unfortunately, the restricted date span precludes their use for a study of literacy over a long period, and their great variety and frequent inexplicitness about the standards of reading and writing being measured make comparisons between them difficult. This is the same problem facing the student of literacy rates in the developing world today, who finds on closer inspection that 'able to read' has been defined and measured differently in each country. Indeed, most modern investigations, like most of the early nineteenth-century surveys, rest on answers to questions about literacy rather than on direct tests. Thus, they measure people's beliefs about their literary abilities as expressed to a stranger, not the existence of these abilities. Clearly, if literacy is associated with high status, the dangers of misrepresentation are considerable.[8] For example, in a survey of literacy in East Pakistan in the mid-1960s a sample of rural cultivators was asked whether they could read a newspaper. Fifty-seven percent claimed that they could, but subsequent testing revealed that 15% in fact either could not read at all or could only stumble through the text without comprehension. The level of ability amongst the 42% who really could read also varied widely: about a half of them could only read slowly but with comprehension, while a half (or 22% of the sample) could read fluently.[9] In England in the period 1750–1850, as in East Pakistan in the mid-1960s, there was a wide range of reading ability, and in such a situation the proportion of the population reported as being 'able to read' clearly depends on the level of skill taken to comprise reading ability.

Ideally, therefore, measures of literacy should be both standard and direct. For pre-industrial England in the late eighteenth and early nineteenth centuries there is only one measure which satisfies these two conditions: the ability to sign one's name. Although at first sight this is not a particularly meaningful literary skill, it has the advantage of giving a fairly 'middle-range' measure of literacy in this period. This is because, ever since the sixteenth century, school curricula had been so phased that reading was taught before writing, and the intermittent nature of school attendance thus ensured that large numbers of children left school having acquired some reading ability, but little or no ability to write. In this period, therefore, the proportion of the population able to sign was less than the proportion able to read and greater than the proportion able to write. Early nineteenth century evidence suggests that the proportion of the population claiming a basic level of reading ability may have been half as much again as the proportion able to sign, and that the proportion able to sign roughly corresponded with the proportion able to read fluently.[10] It also confirms that more people could sign than could write, but this was occasionally denied in the early nineteenth century, for the advocates of state education used the proportion of spouses unable to sign the marriage register as a stick with which to beat the defenders of private education, who consequently made valiant efforts to discredit it as a measure of literacy. Their argument was that many people who could write were inhibited from signing their names by the solemnity of the marriage ceremony or out of feeling for an illiterate spouse. However, such people would presumably have been accustomed to holding a pen and would in consequence have made firm marks. Yet the numbers of such marks in the marriage registers are very small, and are unlikely to have had more than the most marginal effect on literacy rates based on the ability to sign. Another, and contrary, objection which is sometimes brought against the use of marriage register signatures as a measure of literacy, is that some people signed who could neither read nor write. Children today may be capable of this trick; but it is *a priori* unlikely in pre-industrial England, given the phasing of instruction in reading and writing, the lack of writing materials in most homes, and the very few occasions in a lifetime in which a signature or mark was required. In practice, such a signature would be ill-formed through inexperience of both pen and letters, but such signatures are rare in this period.

A further advantage of the ability to sign as a measure of literacy is that it is available for a large number of people and thus makes possible comparisons both over time and between residential and occupational groups. The source for this wealth of information is the series of marriage registers kept by the Church of England, for since 1754 the law recognized as valid only those marriages which were registered in the Anglican registers and signed by the parties and two witnesses.[11] The register evidence therefore relates to the 90% or so of the population who were ever married, and measures their ability to sign largely when they were in their mid-20s, some 15 or so years after leaving school.[12] For the period from 1839 to 1914 the Registrar General has published in his *Annual Reports* the numbers and proportions of men and women able and unable to sign their names.[13] Figure 10.1 shows the national annual illiteracy rates (percentages unable to sign) of men and women over this period, plotted on a semi-logarithmic scale to facilitate comparison of rates of change at different periods. The achievement of the second half of the nineteenth century is remarkable: the percentage of men unable to sign fell from just over 30% in 1850 to 1% in 1911, and the percentage of women unable to sign fell from just over 45% in 1850 to 1% in 1913. The fastest rate of improvement was amongst those marrying after about 1885, or leaving school after about 1870. The improvement between about 1850 and 1885 (i.e., school-leavers between about 1835 and 1870) was less rapid, and the rate of improvement between 1840 and 1850 (school-leavers of 1825–1835) was markedly slower still.

Since the marriage register evidence is available from 1754, it should be possible to extend the Registrar General's series back another 85 years. An informal attempt to do this was made as early as 1867 by a member of the Royal Statistical Society, who collected information from 26 rural and 10 urban parishes for three periods: 1754–1762, 1799–1804, and 1831–1837.[14] This tiny and haphazard sample of 36 from a population of some 10,000 parishes features in most modern discussions of the course of literacy

Percentage unable to sign

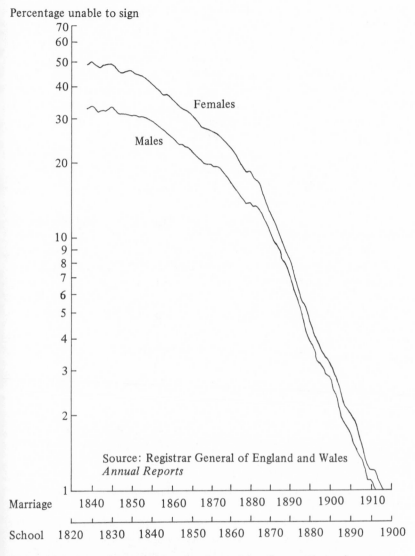

Figure 10.1 Annual percentages of males and females unable to sign at marriage, England and Wales, 1839–1912

during this period. Since 1867 a number of local studies have been made,[15] and signatures and marks in other sources, such as wills and marriage licenses, have been used to supplement the marriage register material. These sources, however, present considerable difficulties; wills were commonly made *in extremis* and consistently overstate the percentage unable to sign, while marriage by license was attractive not only to high status groups but also to the more literate in each status group, so that evidence drawn from marriage licenses consistently understates the percentage unable to sign.

One aspect of literacy in this period which is quite clear from the Registrar General's figures based on the marriage registers is a marked geographical variation in the percentage unable to sign. In 1839, the first date for which these figures are available, the metropolitan area of London is the most literate 'county', with 12% of males unable to sign, followed closely by three counties near the border with Scotland, all with under 20% unable to sign. The next best group, with 20%–30% unable to sign, comprises a string of counties on the northeast coast, together with Devon and Dorset. The worst two groups, with 40%–55% unable to sign, are Wales and the West Midlands with Lancashire, and a belt of counties stretching from East Anglia through the home counties to Wiltshire. The midland and most of the southern coastal counties comprise an intermediate group, with 30%–39% unable to sign. Thus in 1839 the proportion of males who were illiterate at marriage was three times higher in Bedford and Hertfordshire than in Northumberland, Cumberland, and Westmorland. But the Registrar General's figures for Registration Districts, which are available from 1842, show that local variation within a county was even greater than this. Thus, the national estimates of illiteracy for the period before 1838 presented in the current literature, which are based on very small numbers of parishes, are subject to large sampling errors, and accordingly little confidence should be placed in them.

II

The task of obtaining trustworthy figures and of studying this extraordinary variation in illiteracy rates can only be achieved either by making a full enumeration of all marriages registered between 1754 and 1838, or by drawing a properly designed sample. The first alternative is scarcely practicable, if only because the marriages are recorded in 10,000 parish registers, most of which are still lodged in the parish chests. This geographical constraint also makes it sensible to sample marriage registers rather than individual marriage entries. Accordingly, I have drawn a random sample of 274 parishes, a figure which was calculated to produce national estimates with a standard error of about 2%, taking into account a rather strong parish clustering effect. Figure 10.2 shows the national estimates of the percentages of men and women unable to sign in each year during the period 1754–1840. The 274 parishes produced about 1,300 marriages annually in the late 1750s rising to about 2,900 in the late 1830s. The effect of clustering on the variance of the sample estimates was greater than expected, and the standard error of the estimates in most years was about 3%. The sampling error lends a tremor to the lines on the graph, but the trends are nonetheless clear.

The percentage of women unable to sign was just over 60% in the mid-

Percentage unable to sign

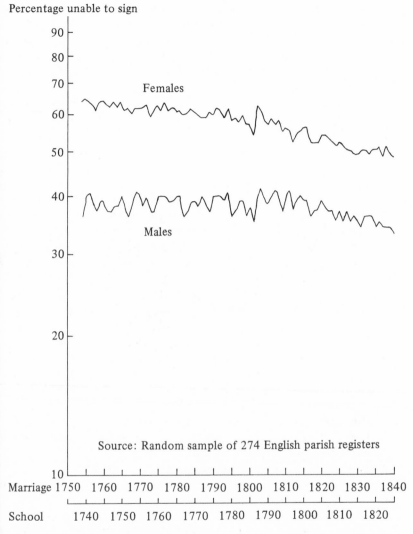

Figure 10.2 Estimated annual percentages of males and females unable
to sign at marriage, England 1754–1840

eighteenth century, and improved slowly to fall to just below 50% by 1840.
The rate of improvement after 1800 was noticeably faster than before this
date, but at no time was it particularly rapid. Allowing for a 15-year lag
between schooling and marriage, the quickening of improvement in female
illiteracy dates from about the mid-1780s and may possibly be connected
with the development of Sunday School education at this time. Male illiteracy,
however, followed a somewhat different course. Far from falling throughout

this period, as present accounts lead one to expect, it remained more or less stable for 50 years. Just under 40% were unable to sign until about 1795. The percentage then fell toward 1800, but rose toward 1805, and then fell again at a similar rate to that of the women to around 33% in 1840. The turning point is a little less clear for males, but it was probably between 1805 and 1815. If we assume that entry into the labor force may be taken to be the age of leaving school, then some point in the 1790s marks the date around which the literacy of entrants to the labor force may first be said to be increasing since 1740. Despite differences in scale, a comparison of Figures 10.1 and 10.2 brings out the marked contrast between the relative stability of both male and female illiteracy in this period, and the dramatic fall in the later nineteenth century.

National figures, however, as we have already observed, summarize and conceal wide variations. Ultimately, the sample results will show how far regional experiences differed from the national trend. But geographical location is only one of many factors which affect illiteracy rates. Others probably included the availability of schooling, and a wide variety of social and economic variables; for example, the concentration of land ownership, the dispersion of settlement, and the occupational structure of the community. Unfortunately, information on all of the many factors likely to have influenced the local development of literacy in each parish during the period is unavailable, and the best that can be achieved is evidence for some social and economic characteristics of the sample parishes at some points during the period. An investigation has been begun into how far these characteristics, either singly or in combination, can explain differences in the levels of male and female illiteracy, and differences in changes in these levels. No results are yet available for discussion, but the imperfections of the indicators which can be used make it likely that the proportion of local variation which can be explained in this way will always be small.

In the meantime something of the nature of this local variation, however, can be appreciated from a superficial examination of Bedfordshire, the worst county in England for male illiteracy in 1839, with 55% unable to sign compared to 33% nationally. A full enumeration has been made of all marriages registered in every parish in Bedfordshire in the period 1754–1844, and this has revealed an astonishingly varied picture of parishes with different combinations of high and low male and female illiteracy, and of improvement and deterioration in illiteracy rates. Overall, the decadal illiteracy rate in Bedfordshire for males deteriorated from 54% in 1754–1764 to 60% in 1795–1804 and then improved, with a setback in 1825–1834, to return almost to its original position (55%) in the final decade studied, 1835–1844. The female illiteracy rate was higher throughout; it began at 72% in 1754–1764, and behaved similarly to the male rate, though it deteriorated less in the late eighteenth century, and it improved earlier and more substantially to reach

67% in the final decade, 1835–1844. But not all the parishes in the county had this average experience, and so far as male illiteracy is concerned two extreme groups can be discerned: 14 parishes in which the male illiteracy rate fell by more than 10%, and 24 parishes in which it rose by more than 10% over the period. The divergent decadal male illiteracy rates for these two groups, particularly marked after 1775–1784, are shown in Figure 10.3. At the level of the individual parish female illiteracy rates in general moved parallel with the male rates, though there were some parishes in which increases in male illiteracy of more than 10% were accompanied by falls in female illiteracy.

These two extreme groups can be compared on a number of geographical, social, educational, and economic characteristics. There was little or no difference in the geographic location of the members of the two groups, nor was there any difference either in their rate of population growth or in their *per capita* expenditure on Poor Relief in the 1780s. Some of the remaining differences were weak; but, on the whole, parishes in which illiteracy *declined* by more than 10% over the period were more likely to have had an ordinary day school, but not a Sunday school, a wider dispersion of land ownership, a higher percentage of inhabitants in non-agricultural occupations, and to have expended less *per capita* on Poor Relief in the 1830s than had parishes in which illiteracy increased over the period. The parish which experienced a marked increase in illiteracy therefore tended to be predominantly agricultural, dominated by a single landlord, with little or no schooling available, and a high *per capita* expenditure on Poor Relief in the 1830s. I have reported these results informally because the small number of parishes used in the summary survey means that some of the results are barely significant statistically. There was also, naturally, considerable interaction between the social and economic variables, for example, between landlord domination and low or negative population growth, and clearly the subject of local variation in illiteracy rates deserves a more sensitive and complete exploration.

One outstanding feature of the Bedfordshire evidence was the experience of market towns, for in every case illiteracy declined during the period. This was also true of market towns throughout the country, and suggests that the relationship between illiteracy and occupation would repay investigation. Unfortunately, the opportunities to do this systematically are limited, for relatively few marriage registers give occupations consistently until the mid-nineteenth century. Table 10.1 shows the illiteracy rates for a number of occupational groups taken from a sample of 23 parishes whose registers give occupational descriptions throughout the period.[16]

This occupational hierarchy is one of the most consistent features of illiteracy in the past. It is to be found in all regions and at all times, regardless of the level of illiteracy. Naturally the differences between occupations vary, and sometimes categories, particularly some of the trades and crafts, exchange

Percentage unable to sign

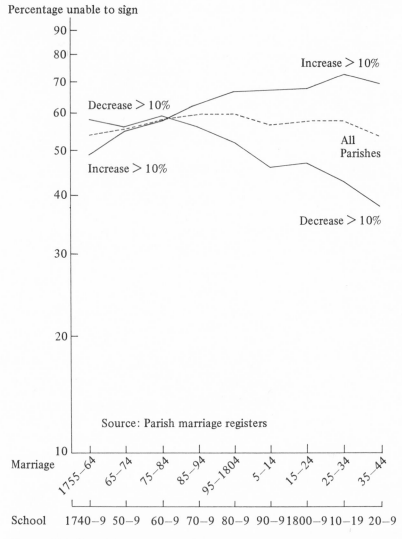

Figure 10.3 Decadal percentages of males unable to sign at marriage, Bedfordshire, distinguishing parishes in which percentages increased and decreased by more than 10%

places. The common-sense interpretation of this hierarchy would seem to be that literacy had a different functional value in each of the occupational groups. For example, long before the mid eighteenth century the subculture of the social élite presupposed literacy, and literacy was also essential to the economic functions of men in the professions and official positions. These groups, that is, needed to be literate in order to fulfill their economic and

Table 10.1. *Illiteracy by occupational group, 1754–84 to 1815–44*

	1754–84		1785–1814		1815–44	
	Sample size	%	Sample size	%	Sample size	%
Gentry and professional	68	0	170	1	204	3
Officials, etc.	20	0	43	5	94	2
Retail	19	5	94	10	150	5
Wood	137	16	361	17	448	11
Estate	29	17	66	18	87	30
Yeomen and farmers	97	19	262	18	315	17
Food and drink	57	19	189	18	277	18
Textile	41	20	83	39	38	16
Metal	60	22	170	29	301	19
Leather	78	23	232	30	320	22
Miscellaneous	81	30	129	32	130	25
Transport	154	31	462	38	549	30
Clothing	63	35	112	21	135	14
Armed forces (non-officer)	180	41	773	51	122	32
Husbandmen	665	46	560	56	123	52
Construction and mining	146	51	352	47	499	38
Laborers and servants	192	59	596	65	1,632	66
Unknown	37	24	130	25	19	26
All	2,126	36	4,784	39	5,443	35

social roles. But others did not, for even in the mid-nineteenth century literacy was by no means indispensable in the social and economic life of large numbers of laborers. In the middle ground of different trades and crafts the superiority of occupations involving commerce and contact with the public (retail food and drink) over occupations involving heavy manual labor (construction and mining) also makes sense in terms of literacy having a different practical value to different occupational groups. Indeed, since schooling in this period involved direct cash expenditure as well as forgoing earnings, the practical utility of literacy would have been a powerful argument either for or against investing in education. For some groups the costs of this investment exceeded perceived benefits. Even in the more literate world of the late nineteenth century the abolition of school fees still left the 'costs' of lost earning power to be borne, and universal investment in education was only achieved under the compulsion of the law.

III

In the late eighteenth and early nineteenth centuries a decision to invest in education was a decision to invest in the acquisition of literary skills: the ability to read and, at further cost, the ability to write. For it was primarily these two skills that were taught in the elementary schools; arithmetic and substantive knowledge were offered later, and required a further cash outlay. The acquisition of literary skills, or literacy, might be desirable for three reasons: because it was essential for participation in the life of a particular social group, because it was essential for acquiring skills, or new skills, relevant to a particular occupation, or because it would lead to upward social and economic mobility. It is by and large true that in the late eighteenth and early nineteenth centuries the literate occupations had higher status and were better paid; but the early nineteenth-century educational surveys show that both the subjects children studied and the length of time they stayed at school depended on the occupation and status of their parents, which suggests that the prospect of upward mobility for their children did not lead many working class parents to invest heavily in education.[17] How far literacy was necessary to men and women in order for them to participate fully in different walks of life in the late eighteenth and early nineteenth centuries is a large question. Literacy was clearly widespread: a majority of the population could read, and in the early nineteenth century there is plenty of evidence of a literate culture amongst large sections of the working class. The fall in the illiteracy rate amongst women from 64% in 1750 to 50% in 1850 suggests that literacy became a more important component in the life of women during the period. On the other hand, male illiteracy remained constant until the decade 1805–1815. More remarkably, Table 10.1 shows that in many occupations illiteracy actually rose during the later eighteenth century and that in the early nineteenth century some occupations were still less literate than they had been in the mid-eighteenth century.

Perhaps no great emphasis should be laid on these figures, for they come from a small number of parishes for which information on occupations is available throughout the period. Yet they at least suggest the possibility that for many males in a variety of occupations literacy did not become more essential as a cultural skill during this period. They might also suggest that, with the conspicuous exception of the clothing and construction trades, literacy may have been no more essential for acquiring economic skills and techniques in the early nineteenth century than it had been in the mid-eighteenth century. Yet technical developments involved thousands of people in learning a multitude of new practical skills. An attempt was made in the eighteenth century to provide practical instruction for the poor in Charity Schools, but although this scheme proved to be greatly to the tastes of the times, it had to be abandoned as uneconomic.[18] For most children in the late eighteenth and early nineteenth centuries, school remained a specialized institution for the instruction of literary skills. Consequently, few children were regular in attendance, and few remained at school for more than 1½ years.[19] Practical economic skills were therefore learned within the context of the household and work-group, as part of a comprehensive process of socialization, of which apprenticeship is a well-known, but formalized example.

Thus, insofar as economic growth in this period entailed the acquisition of a large number of practical skills by a growing proportion of the population, developments in literacy and education were probably largely irrelevant to it. And, insofar as economic growth resulted from the increased productivity of labor brought about by the shift from domestic to factory production, literacy and education were also probably largely irrelevant, for many of the new industrial occupations recruited a mainly illiterate work force, so much so that many industrial communities were markedly more illiterate than their rural neighbors.[20] This contrast has been attributed to a collapse of education in these rapidly growing urban areas, but a large proportion of the work force had moved to these towns after having been educated elsewhere. Thus, urban migration in this period was not only occupation-specific; it was also literacy-specific. This is made clear by the opposite effect, namely, the superior literacy of market and county towns over the surrounding neighborhood. For these communities contained a high proportion of occupations concerned with distribution and exchange, which required the ability to keep the records, and thus presupposed literacy. Indeed, such an intersectoral shift in occupational structure accompanying economic growth may perhaps account for the positive correlation between literacy and economic development in present-day economies.[21] Inferences sometimes drawn from this association are that an illiteracy rate of about 60% is a threshold above which economic growth is unlikely, and that an improvement in literacy is a necessary precondition or concomitant of economic growth. The English experience in the century from 1750 to 1850 may perhaps be taken to cast some doubt on the utility of positing universal relationships between literacy and economic growth. Although it is true that the national male illiteracy rate had crossed the 60% threshold before 1750, the female rate only crossed it definitively around 1795, and female illiteracy was very high in areas of high female industrial employment; for example, it was still 84% in Oldham in 1846.[22] Nor does the static nature of male illiteracy both nationally until the decade 1805–15, and in several occupational groups until the mid-nineteenth century, lend much support to the notion that an improvement in literacy necessarily precedes stability, and the marked contrast between the literacy of commercial classes and the illiteracy of much of the industrial labor force, suggest that for England, at least, the usual causal relationships between literacy and economic growth might profitably be reversed. In this alternative perspective the reduction in illiteracy in nineteenth-century England would appear more as a cultural change brought about by economic growth than as one of the causes of growth.

11   THREE CENTURIES OF CULTURAL CROSS-FERTILIZATION: FRANCE*

François Furet and Jacques Ozouf

So, literacy is not schooling, and the history of the school by itself will not suffice to give a full account of the literacy process. Yet if this central link has so often been held self-evident, and if it has served as the common sub-soil implicit in so many of the struggles in the nineteenth and twentieth centuries, this is because through it the French have shared in an interpretation of their history. Marx, in 'The Holy Family', characterized this interpretation as the 'illusion of politics': the conviction that all change flows from the conscious action of people, and that human destiny is therefore in the hands of educators and legislators. It was hardly surprising then that the school, as the focus of such voluntarist belief, became the strategic fulcrum for the fashioning of minds, and a central issue in political struggle.

It was the French Revolution which brought the conflict to a head, but it was not at the origin of the issue. For from the very beginning the Catholic Church had viewed the school as an instrument of social and intellectual control and, consequently, as a source of power whose exercise must be neither abandoned nor even shared. When the monarchic state intervened, at the end of the seventeenth century notably, it was not so much to demand its portion as to set the seal, at the expense of the Protestants, upon the concept of a Catholic school whose task was to extirpate heresy once and for all; its intention was to place throughout the kingdom, down to the tiniest parish, a schoolmaster representative of the Revocation of the Edict of Nantes. A century before the Revolution, then, the school lay at the heart of religious conflict, the instrument of either one party or the other. So there was little new in the fact that the revolution in its turn should have made it its standard against the old world, focusing upon it its hopes of changing the minds of men; it turned the Church's own weapons against it, its educational beliefs and practices, for all were agreed that the minds of the young were utterly malleable, and that therefore the school could never be neutral. The Republic wanted its school to be republican, and for a century and a half crystallized around it the main thrust of its battle with the Church.

Two sorts of confusion arose thereby. For a start, the history of the school,

*Reprinted from *Reading and Writing: Literacy in France from Calvin to Jules Ferry* by François Furet and Jacques Ozouf, by permission of the publisher, Cambridge University Press, © Cambridge University Press 1982. First published in French by Editions de Minuit © 1977. Translated by Rupert Swyer.

over-burdened with ideological and political significance, has always been regarded as central to the history of the literacy process: people have either viewed it as the victory of enlightenment over obscurantism, or alternatively as that of the Church beset by republican persecution. As for the history of literacy itself, which has been a long, slow process of evolution and putting-down of roots, subject to a high degree of social inertia, people have confused it with the history of ideas about the school and its ideological role: but these clearly do not proceed at the same pace, nor are they subject to the same gravitational pulls.

Our inquiry only becomes meaningful if it has managed to set this history back on its feet; if it has succeeded in focusing attention on the literacy process itself, as a gateway to written culture; if it has restored to society herself the chief credit for this change. The Church, the State, the School are mere dramatis personae or agents.

The sequence of events, as shown in the first place by Maggiolo's survey, and as polarized by our supplementary surveys, by and large reveals – regardless of local or regional variations – a series of trends that are utterly independent of big political events, including the most important one, the French Revolution. The great battle that was then joined between Church and state for control of the schools appears to have had no decisive (nor even a particularly noteworthy) impact on the evolution of literacy scores. The reason for this, as we have seen, was that decisions taken by the Revolutionary Assemblies wrought no lasting change in the traditional school system, and still less so the periods of terror in 1793 and 1797, whether Montagnard or Fructidorian. But it is also proof that this school system, far from being an institution imposed upon society from above, was on the contrary the product of social demand for education, swelling in step with the gradual spread of a cultural model. This demand germinated and burgeoned in institutions other than the school – such as the family. In the last resort, also, it determined the distribution of schools, their type, their methods and their curricula. By the time, a century after the Revolution, Jules Ferry fulfilled the Jacobin dream by establishing the republican, secular, free and compulsory school, the French were practically fully literate. The reason was that, in the previous two or three centuries to which it was – unwittingly and unwillingly – heir, the communities of France had founded, run and financed schools of their own.

Which is why both the chronology and the distribution of the French literacy process are dependent less on the evolution of the school network than on the social history of France. The consequences of this are many and heavy. The obligation to gain admission to written culture was democratized first by protestantism, and subsequently by the Counter Reformation; but more than a condition of salvation, and for much longer, it represented the key to entry to the cultural model of the upper classes. Wherever we look, in every period, social stratification presides over the history of literacy. By the seventeenth century, the elites of the old kingdom of France could read, write and count, while the peasantry was still massively illiterate. Most of the spectacular progress made in the eighteenth century occurred among the middle ranks of the old society: merchants, shopkeepers, artisans, tenant farmers and rich peasants. Wage-labourers, especially in the countryside, formed a kind of residual though substantial stock, undented by progress in the surrounding milieu. It was only in the nineteenth century that they too became caught up in the general movement towards universal literacy, the timing of the process keeping pace with its gradual 'trickling down' through society.

The opposition between town and countryside, from this point of view, refers to much the same state of affairs: the reason why the towns achieved literacy earlier was that their population contained more lawyers, merchants, artisans, and fewer peasants or journeymen. So much so that in the nineteenth century the mushrooming towns that grew up as a result of 'English-style' industrialization suffered a drop in average literacy rates owing to the massive influx of new wage-labourers. The *ancien régime* town, on the other hand, growing up and reigning over its peaceful countryside as market town and administrative centre, taking pride in its law-courts, its high school and its seminary, was a pole of literacy *par excellence*: not only because by definition it contained more 'bourgeois', in the old sense of the term, here foreshadowing the other, but because as a result of this they wielded greater influence over the rest of the population. The smaller towns, with a literate elite, thus enjoyed a decisive advantage: the elite was more important than elsewhere, and the example it set was visible to everyone. The urban history of the literacy process shows just how much importance old French society attached to admission to written culture, several centuries prior to the triumph of industrial capitalism. Seen from this angle, the French Revolution merely celebrated one of the great certainties of the *ancien régime*.

The final angle from which social development conditioned the literacy process was that of regional disparities. The maps included in *Lire et Ecrire*, which illustrate a France divided in two, reiterate and partially transpose the geographical distribution of social inequalities and disparities in socio-occupational structures. But they show too that the literacy process by and large conformed to the laws of uneven economic development:[1] literate France was, both globally and in detail, the openfield France, with high farm productivity and well-to-do villages and peasant communities. The spread of literacy was born of the market economy, which contributed to the division of labour and to the growth of written communication, from the pinnacle of society downwards. The great religion of the Book, Protestantism, soon to be joined by the Counter Reformation, could probably have made do with a modicum of reading ability on the part of the faithful, as in Sweden. But the market economy, backed by and relying upon the machinery of the centralized state, expanded the role of writing as a necessary condition of modernization. In fact, the true subject – and the mystery – of our inquiry is the transition from the religious to the 'modern' age.

So the descriptions and analyses contained in *Lire et Ecrire* lead us less to a conclusion in the true sense than to further questions. For something lies beyond the language of figures and maps, namely the questions it enables us to ask.

The literacy process: what a deceptive term that is if taken to imply a beginning – when no one can read or write – and an end – when everyone can! Down the two or three centuries whose history we have sought to reconstitute, what it suggests rather is a process in which, between the seventeenth century and the 1914–18 War, French society entered into written culture. But this long underground history is not the story of some radical substitution of written for oral culture. For writing had pre-existed this collective acculturation; the oral tradition, meanwhile, has survived right into the middle of the twentieth century.

Probably the most useful concept in seeking to understand the point at issue is that of restricted literacy, as defined by the English anthropologist Jack Goody.[2] What happened in France between Louis XIV and Jules Ferry is not, properly speaking, the spread of literacy among the French people, rather it is the transition from restricted to mass literacy. The reasons for restricted literacy may be chiefly technical, as in China, where non-phonetic writing was so difficult to learn and master that a small number of literati enjoyed a monopoly of it. Mostly, though, it is rooted in privileges relating to the handling of some sacred text by a specialized clergy trained for the purpose: the job of the masses here is to listen and commit to memory. In either case, however (technical or religious), the fact of having a monopoly over writing gave its possessors immense political and social power.

Now the civilization of the Christian middle ages was characterized by restricted literacy. It was associated with a book-centred religion, whose sole depositees and interpreters were the clergy; it was associated too with mass preaching, aimed at the ignorant crowd, which was expected to listen, memorize and chant: writing, that secret of secrets, that language for initiates, that power of the clerks, existed solely for translation into the oral register. Scarce, fragile, confidential, it was inseparable, even for those who knew how to write, from the complementary exercises of memory and eloquence, as can be seen from the way rhetoric was taught in the middle ages. For the dominance of writing had not yet become the dominance of administrative rationality, which was then in limbo; it was still that of belief, which summoned up collective emotions, interpersonal and concrete transmission of the message: a dominance in which the book was still contaminated by commentary or litany, voices, or the murmur of men.

The history of the introduction of written culture to Tahiti,[3] as described by the members of the London Missionary Society at the beginning of the nineteenth century, is a perfect illustration of the functions performed by this culture in the history of Europe, of its chief agents, and of the mechanisms by which it established itself. This tardy, exotic laboratory for a transplanted European culture offers us a caricature of the brutal import of writing into the Society Islands by the West, which the local authorities acquiesced in under pressure. In those waxworks of European history, the colonial institutions, we can just about make out the strange features, distorted by their extension in space and their contraction in time, of a civilization that seems natural to us because familiar.

The first missionaries sent out by the London Missionary Society settled in the Island of Tahiti in 1797, under the protection of King Pomaré I, whom they backed against his rivals. By 1805, Tahitian had become a written language, thanks to their intercession: a letter from the Roman alphabet was attributed to each sound to simplify learning, so that to spell a word was to pronounce it. Writing thenceforward became the twin banner of power and Christianity against oral culture and the rivals of the Pomaré dynasty. After his victory in 1815, Pomaré II founded a Catholic kingdom, whose subjects embraced the new religion. The book having been the vehicle for this conversion, the missionaries set themselves up as printers and schoolmasters; the press established in 1817 published all the books required for this dual process of literacy and catechization: spelling books, selected readings from the Old and New Testaments, uplifting stories from the Scriptures, religious booklets, sermons, prayer books. At the same time as being a vehicle for Christianization, written culture also served as an instrument for the regulations, laws and codes inseparable from the 'civilization' of these islands. A touching 'European-style' family occasion took place in 1824, when the English missionaries who had organized the accession of Pomaré III, aged four, placed the crown upon his head, Bible in the right hand, legal code in the other. Lo and behold, writing was queen of the isles!

The missionaries seem to have been surprised by the aptitudes, and above all the extraordinary memories, of their new catechumens: in one year, adults learned to read the New Testament fluently, and were able to quote whole chapters by heart. The performance was an ambiguous one, though, for the pupils recited rather than read: some knew their spelling books thoroughly, but held them upside down; they all loved the hymnals, with their familiar metrical forms. In a word, the transition from oral to written culture occurred, in the first place, through memorization. Learning by rote was the heart of the old system of education, and it could serve as a useful stepping stone to the new one. The Tahitians reveal the same ambiguous ability to 'read only' as characterized the literacy process in Europe. It is all the easier to spot here for having been introduced abruptly from without, imposed from above, with the result that written culture enjoyed even greater prestige here than among French peasants in the eighteenth and nineteenth centuries. It is more than just a sign of upward social mobility: it represents the superiority of the colonial world over the world of the natives. Which accounts for the excessive devotion to the book, for the crush of local inhabitants around the printing presses, those flotillas of canoes laden with cargoes of learning, and, in many cases, probably, a symbolic simulation of reading, which was indispensable for the appropriation of the new object.

To this extent, 'reading', based on memorization, of religious texts amounted to no more than a veneer of colonial Christianity, coexisting with the more permanent traditional oral culture, which still held sway in the minds of the people. At this basic level it did not even imply a gradual transition towards another cultural world: rather it was the instrument for the substitution of one form of worship for another, of one form of domination for another, in which writing was worshipped as an image of secrecy, not of learning. Which probably explains why it was reversible, not as in European history: the work of the missionaries in the Society Islands apparently did not survive the demise of the Pomaré dynasty, and an amateur anthropologist who visited the islands twice, in 1829 and 1830, the American consul 'to the Oceanian islands', recorded the 'retrograde' movement of the natives, their rapid backsliding from 'civilization' to their 'primitive state'. There were, to be sure, churches and schools in Tahiti, but no society to want or found them.

It was in the Renaissance that the European West rediscovered the conditions that had made possible the miracle of Greece and Rome, namely the phonetic alphabet, and the absence of a religious monopoly with a unique book. Even so, the advantages which Graeco-Roman civilization derived from the tolerance of its priests tended to be mirrored in Europe by competition, rather, among its clergy: once the book was open to more than one interpretation – although remaining, by mutual consensus, the key to salvation – the faithful now found themselves called upon to judge for themselves. Whereas Erasmian humanism had produced a secularized version of a culture revitalized by the model of Antiquity, for the use of the elite, Protestant heresy, on the other hand, democratized writing for the masses. The dissipation of the secret of the clerks spelled the end – in the long run – of a restricted literacy society. Paradoxically, writing came to western Europe through religion, and doubtless throughout the learning process it retained its superstition of Latin, the language of the Church.

As early as the end of the sixteenth century, the post-Tridentine Catholics agreed with their Protestant rivals that literacy ought to be universal. That was the great revolution, the dividing line between two epochs, two kinds of relation between individuals and the written word. Beforehand, in restricted literacy society, the text had been sacred, it contained the truth. To approach it demanded endless coded study: because it was constantly repetitive, like some interminable genealogy, whose enigmas the scholar strives to decipher in order to winkle the truth out of them. In material terms, writing was a copyist's art, a form of drawing, a collective exercise in symbolism, in the same way as reading was an exercise in chanting. Recopying and repetition illustrate writing's dependence on the oral tradition; the role of the former was merely to pin down the latter and prevent it from getting lost. But things were very different once everyone was able to read and write. The individual's relation to the written text underwent complete transformation: the function of the cultural mediator had no further justification, and from having been collective, the conditions of communication became individual. Writing now concealed an 'I' and no longer a 'he'; reading revealed a content, and no longer a mere remembrance.

This mutation – of which the invention of printing merely furnished the technological condition – was thus inherent in the heresies of Protestantism, which from the moment of their victory introduced pluralism into reading (i.e. turned it into an individual exercise). In fact, though, this did not happen quite as swiftly as the principle suggests. All it did was to usher in a period in our history during which the whole of society made its entry into written culture. It did so at very different paces, and had to overcome lengthy resistance on the part of traditional culture, which was founded on speech. The information we have gathered perhaps allows us to advance a number of hypotheses on these long centuries of cross-fertilization between the oral tradition and the written word.

For a long time, the distinction between reading and oral communication was unclear. In the school curriculum it was merely the first, quite distinct, step in the literacy process: the most universal, but also the most rudimentary. This reflected the Church's long held view of reading as, principally, the means of ensuring collective celebration of Church ritual. Reading, which was learned first of all in Latin, either in school, church or at home, only gradually became dissociated from the act of memorization; where it was not associated with ability to write, it amounted more to a mnemonic for an illustration than a means of deciphering a text. It did not change the individual's relation to culture: it confirmed it. Morally speaking, it was innocent, confining itself to the reception – generally collective (i.e. public) – of the divine message. It implied neither the autonomy of the individual, nor the obligation to exercise at least a modicum of intellectual freedom, nor again the beginnings of an inner break with the restraints of the community. Writing means being able to communicate in secret, individual to individual. Reading by itself is merely a passive activity: the fact of receiving the message does not really ensure admission to the new cultural circuit. This is presumably what a peasant in the Quercy was trying to say when he told the author that until recently many of the girls in his canton had been able to read only, not write: 'The nuns didn't want them to be able to write to their sweethearts.'[4]

Insofar as residual data for the nineteenth century allow us to assume, it is quite probable that there was in ancient France, and especially in that part of France where the school was least securely established, a very widespread semi-literacy based on reading, organized by the Church and in the home, and chiefly intended for girls: this phenomenon would tend to be evidence of religiosity rather than of any concern for modernization. Until sometime in the nineteenth century this rudimentary, lopsided, education did nothing to alter the traditional means of communication among the rural population: this concession on the part of the Church to the spirit of the times served to consolidate the power and the prestige of written religion over these regions and folk with their oral culture.

In 1709, a Mister Jean-Baptiste de Guigues, priest at Tourettes, in the diocese of Vence, was accused by the officiality of owning Jansenist books and of allowing his flock to read them.[5] In fact, several witnesses testified that the priest lent his books not only to men but to women also, far more of whom were implicated in the case. Honnorade Isnard, 'wife of Etienne Curel, labourer on the land', had read *la Vie mystique de Jésus Christ, l'Instruction à la pénitence* and *la Conduite chrétienne*, which de Guigues had lent her. She had read the services written by the priest on the grandeur of Jesus, the Child Jesus and the name of Jesus. Among these devout women was a schoolmistress, Louise Gazagnaire. She had read two volumes of the *Testament nouveau avec des Réflexions* and *Savoir sur l'Epître de saint Pierre et sur l'Evangile de saint Jean*, belonging to the lady of Tourettes and lent by de Guigues. She too had read the priest's services. Yet she was unable to sign her name. Indeed, none of the women who gave evidence at the trial were able to sign their names. Thus Jansenism, that learned devotional form, with its bookish refinement, trickled down to the lower classes through reading, whose sole purpose was to receive the word of God. Men and women who could not read listened to others reciting it, or learned to chant it from memory. This was the function of the 'social evenings' so heavily criticized at the priest's trial; far into the night, the 'congregation' of women in the parish would gather at Louise Gazagnaire's. They often sang or chanted until midnight, 'which created a big scandal in the neighbourhood'. It was at these meetings, according to one witness, that de Guigues would hold readings of Amelot's *le Nouveau Testament* and *l'Imitation de Jésus Christ*.

Another witness stated that these social gatherings had taken place prior to the arrival of the Jansenist priest, and we have every reason to think that in the France of the past they often served as a place of religious socialization, for women especially. Through them, books were annexed to the tradition of community culture, based on rote learning and oral communication.

Writing represented modernization, modernity. What transformed the act of reading into a silent, internal, individual exercise was the conquest of writing. Without writing reading was powerless to withstand the group pressures which the oral tradition exerted on the individual. Alone, the democratization of the art of writing paved the way for a new kind of relation with the social and natural world, thereby transforming the conditions of reading. It was this that triggered the transition from 'restricted literacy' to general literacy (in the two senses of intellectually complete and socially widespread). To be sure, this transition did not occur in the space of a single generation, nor even in one century: in the case of France it took three centuries, and dating is made all the harder by the fact that the spread of general literacy throughout society long assumed the features of the previous period, that of restricted literacy. For example, until the French Revolution, most people learned to read in Latin. Again, right up to the mid nineteenth century, the technique of writing retained its bewildering formal complexity, with the variety of handwritings testifying to its status as a rare and learned art.

For the spread of writing presupposed the divulgence of a corporate secret, an exclusive form of power: that of being able to communicate beyond the control of the group, i.e. beyond the control of tradition. The upshot was that the whole of society now gradually found itself splitting into autonomous units (or at least units more or less independent of the collective voice, which is the wisdom of the ages). This transformation of the dominant mode of communication even modified the social fabric itself, breaking up the group in favour of the individual. Oral culture was public, collective; written culture is secretive and personal. It is a great silence, inside which the individual carves out a free private space for himself.

It establishes a new relation between time and space, for the benefit of those able to master its economy. Indeed, specifically historical sensibility begins with writing. Before, no one ever records the sequence of men and events; it is viewed exclusively through an original matrix, which is assumed to reproduce the same thing over and over again, as though the present was at all times absorbing all of the past, in an endless process of repetition. By setting down on paper markers to record the passage of time, births and deaths for example, writing frees individuals from the tyranny of the present; it enables us to establish the 'pastness of the past' (J. Goody). This activity, which is infinitely more abstract than speaking or listening, also detaches the writer from what he is writing: time can be related. It is the present which, in a sense, has ceased to exist, since even the thing that pins it down constitutes a past.

This transition from repetitive time (i.e. non-time) to linear time in individual consciousness is accompanied, in the group, by the preservation and selective appropriation of this past through writing: archives contain what amounts to its *available* memory, as distinct from the real memories of its different members, whereas oral culture indiscriminately mingles both sorts of memory handed down by word of mouth, from one generation to the next, of the secret of the community's origins. This process of transforming the past into a heritage by means of writing thus establishes the difference between history and religion: the group possesses a specific time of its own, which is punctuated by identified and recorded events.

Of course, this time, though pinned down and appropriated by the written word, may yet remain religious in character, created and governed by a transcendental being such as the biblical God. In that case it serves as a universal, model time, a tale of the Beginning written down once and for all, around which all particular histories of humanity revolve. Even so, it is still *history*, in other words, a vehicular time open to the creative, cumulative activity of mankind and his societies. It helps us to distinguish the past from the beginnings, and consequently from the present: in a word, it constitutes that present.

The written word is in that case the legatee of this past. It allows it to exist both in terms of the ego and in terms of the group. The archivist and the historian are its specialist guardians, but in fact every member of the community can have access to this collective memory, which is both more reliable and above all older than their own. The recording of events, the fact of relating them and celebrating them, tends to supply the group with a foundation that is simultaneously secularized and particularist. Now comes the time of the history of the City, which in Europe's case was to become the history of the nation. Even when much in this history has come down from the oral tradition or mythology, it is obliged, merely because it is written down, to rationalize the passage of time. Herodotus paved the way for Thucydides.

In the process, the written word binds the individual to a human entity vaster than the group with which he shares the community's oral tradition. Face-to-face discussion presupposes close neighbourliness, whereas the written word multiplies and standardizes information for an intellectually individualized, geographically scattered, world. It would be more accurate to say that the first thing the written word did was to break down relations between the individual and the fragile group formed by oral communication, transferring those relations to a broader, different community. Speech is no longer inseparable from the empirical moments out of which it springs; it is abstract, general, cumulative, presupposing a minimum number of recipients capable of understanding it at its level of abstraction, generalization and knowledge. What now underwrites inter-individual relations is no longer the immemorial utterances of old men, acting as guardians of local jurisprudence, but the dual authority of the market and the state, sealed in writing and embodied in contract and law. As money is the general equivalent of commodities, so the contract is the general form given to the will of the individual. For two groups to exchange goods or women, all that is needed is for them to live stably in geographical proximity, and for there to be an oral tradition between them, regulating these exchanges, which are programmed for the two communities. But for two individuals to perform the same operation, they first need to exist as such, i.e. as free, abstract units, acting in their own right: freed from group and geographical constraints, and founders of a new code to regulate the market in individual wills. The written word is alone capable of pinning down the *particular* terms agreed upon in discussion, the signature of each contracting party guaranteeing performance. Witnesses, those depositees of agreements concluded, cease to exist save at marriage ceremonies: the group likes to keep an eye on exchanges of women. But the exchange of goods is consigned to the secrecy of the contract, which is constitutive of free and equal individuals, in other words, of the market. To sign one's name is to step over the frontier.

The other guarantee backing inter-individual dealings is the state. But the state too is the written word. A contract is meaningless except in terms of the law. Without writing, after all, there can be no general law sufficiently abstract to be applicable to the multitude of different cases imaginable. Without writing, all that would remain would be tradition, or custom, preserved and handed down by old men, whose knowledge derives not from what they have learned but from what they have seen: they are the collective memory of the group's experience. Now when this tradition or custom is consigned to paper, through the intermediary of the notary (for private law) or the lawyer (for public law), it escapes simultaneously both the concrete experience and the arbitration of the old: it hands down principles and doctrine, of which juris-prudence is an illustration. The written law is an abstract universal. The emergence of the state is the fruit of the obedience and even the respect due to it.

When it comes to obedience, the state has the means to constrain people to it, the means of bodily violence being the most blatant of these. Writing is another, though more subtle, and perhaps more fundamental: it is the written word which establishes direct communication between state and individual, 'liberated' from the tyranny — or the protection — of the group; it is through the written word, as it short-circuits the barriers erected by the oral com-munity, that each subject or citizen is recorded and defined by his social co-ordinates: born on such-and-such a date, of this father and that mother, in the town of X, occupying some specific profession, and so on. The tax rolls were the first manifestation of this political individualization; this was the condition of state rule, which is probably why, independently even of the monetary contribution which it heralds, this so often aroused the hostility of traditional communities, from the parish to the assemblies of the nobility.

At a later phase in the development of the state, the accumulation and storage of these written biographical traces made possible the process of statistical aggregation, which is a method of envisaging the collective through, and on the basis of, the individual. This is a central paradox, one that has always been crucial to European political philosophy, and statistics are the modern state's operational response to it, its thirst for knowledge being inseparable from its desire to manipulate people. It was the abstract thought of distinct individuals which supplied the intellectual groundwork for statistics, and it was the fact that these individuals were themselves recorded and noted down which made the operation technically feasible; statistics then organized them into comparable, interchangeable units, henceforward subject to calculated probabilities (this speciality too made its appearance around the same time), in other words, definable in terms of what is identical in their behaviour and roles. The outcome was a mechanical vision of society, subject precisely to the laws of its constituent mechanism: no longer a group consciousness, but a form of knowledge-cum-domination.

Seventeenth-century English political arithmetic, Prussian political arithmetic in the eighteenth century and French mercantilism in the same age, were both doctrines of national might and head-counting techniques: the strength of the modern state was measured in terms of the number of its subjects. From this, military strength was derived, of course, but it was rooted in economic and monetary wealth: the counting of men and their income yielded a tax base and thus defined the resources of the state. Before becoming one of the values of our civilization, the individual was an accounting unit; more important than the honour accorded him by society is the fact that he is manipulated by the state; before representing the image of freedom and equality in the form of inner consciousness, he is first defined externally by his measurable characteristics and by what he shares with all his fellow men. The egalitarian function of state centralization precedes the egalitarian religion of individualist philosophy. The former imposes the written word through obedience to the temporal power, whereas the latter internalizes its implied values.

This is because it is not enough merely to obey the written law; it demands respect as well, in other words internal acceptance. Now this, however, is only lastingly acquired through a minimum of access to the intellectual world that makes the very notion of law meaningful. At the simplest and most factual level, 'ignorance of the law excuses no man', which implies a minimum of literacy; in any case, in his everyday life the individual is increasingly hemmed in by the state and its laws, so much so that ignorance is turning into a kind of social handicap. Even when, being unable to read or write, the individual cannot know the law, he must at least internalize the spirit of it, and however ignorant he may be he must submit to this new form of socialization: the secret of good conduct soon passed out of the hands of the old — who had been its trustees because they had lived through so much — and into those of the schoolmaster, the notary, the magistrate — because they had read everything. The parish priest, who represents a kind of half-way figure between the oral tradition and writing in our history, gradually ceased to embody written civilization as the triumph of the latter spread. General literacy claimed two victims, the parish priest and old people, by robbing the former of the secret of his prestige and the latter of the utility of his memory.

What they lost was reinvested in the abstract community, and in the state, its symbol: what we now call 'politics' — i.e. the sphere of dealings between individuals and the state, and of the struggle for power as such — does after all presuppose the existence of a broadly dominant written civilization. In oral or restricted literacy societies, politics never manages to establish organizations of its own: struggles for power do take place, but they are waged by traditional communities according to their own view of themselves based on oral consensus, and hence enveloped in religion or rooted in changeless tradition.

By placing the individual in his social context, the generalization of writing threw up a new problem, that of how to integrate the individual into the collectivity, posing this as a distinct, abstract question: it substituted ideology for religion, assuming we are prepared to apply the word ideological to the new manner of envisioning society in secularized terms, in such a way as to re-establish a correspondence between individual and society in written culture. Ideology is a representation of social life in terms of the historical action of individuals; it presupposes the collapse of the traditional community and of oral transmission of information. It re-places the individual in a new vision of society by means of representations or values of written culture, which society is then supposed to incarnate, attain or accomplish through the free activity of its members.

Lawrence Stone[6] notes that the three great revolutions of modern times, in seventeenth-century England, in France at the end of the eighteenth century and in Russia at the beginning of the twentieth, all coincided with a moment at which half the male population had achieved literacy. If we are to read into this similarity anything other than coincidence, then it is precisely the fact that as a modern political phenomenon revolution is characterized by the emergence of a new kind of relation between state and individual, going hand in hand with the development of written culture: this relation is confirmation both of the autonomy and of the importance attached to the individual as the basis of the new political civilization, and of his egalitarian integration into the nation-state through the agency of ideology. From these two standpoints, destructive and reconstructive, disintegrating and reintegrating, it presupposes that writing is widespread in the population: how, for instance, could we conceive of the explosion and the dissemination of Jacobinism between 1789 and 1893 without this prior acculturation, or without the availability of this means of transmission.

Of course, this is not to say that Jacobinism was confined to the literate section of the population: there are a certain number of 'bridges' between oral and written culture, such as the reading of newspapers in public, by members of the *clubs populaires* — but this is tantamount to saying that a phenomenon such as Jacobinism was an expression of an already-dominant written culture even among the masses. It was a culture that was at great pains, moreover, to repress minority languages as symbols of the past, as symbols of an impoverished form of communication, of a community that was not 'national'.[7]

By modifying the system of communication and the transmission of information, writing thereby transformed social relations in their entirety; at the same time, it was through it that the new relations became firmly established. The notary's deed, or the deed merely made official by a commissioner for oaths, is to the private sphere what the constitution is to the public: it institutes rights, property and status, and stands guard over them. It supplants ritual in celebrating the events of people's lives: one's signature, crucial evidence of ability to write, now bears witness to the big moments in life and is the sole guarantor of their permanence. The traditional wedding ceremony, for instance, with its carefully coded exchange of gestures and words, tends to be supplanted by the bridal couple's signatures; the participation of the community in the event, and its sanction, gradually gives way to the symbolic presence of witnesses. The marriage 'deed', once a collective representation, has become a slip of paper. It is as if in literate societies writing played the part performed by collective rituals in oral civilizations: it incarnates the very existence of that society, endowing it with foundations in a specific space–time which thenceforward dominates all social behaviour.[8] It is significant, from this point of view, that it was the French Revolution which most intransigently insisted on the benefits of written culture as opposed to the pernicious influence of oral tradition: this belief, which the Revolution bequeathed to republican generations throughout the nineteenth century, is part and parcel of its constituent ideology, according to which its function is to wrench communities from their past in one tug, in order to point the way to *another* future. The written word is conceived of as instrumental in breaking with the everyday life of the *ancien régime* and as a means of instituting new customs and habits, which alone might assure the long-term survival of the public weal embodied by the Revolution.

This conception, which was inseparable from that of Jacobinism as a 'life-renewing' force, was particularly clearcut in the Directoire period, when it shone forth in all its institutional transparency: the Jacobins no longer enjoyed the dynamic, organized support of the 'clubs populaires', and to counter the royalist upsurge they were obliged to lash the Revolution to whatever mooring point – legislative or imaginary – they could find in the institutions. As witnessed by the report submitted by a deputy for Maine-et-Loire to the Council of the Five Hundred, J.-B. Leclerc, on 16 Brumaire, Year VI. This was just after the 18 Fructidor: its aim was to wean citizens away from the bad habits upon which the royalist reaction fed; to put a stop to what he termed 'this retrograde development', the rapporteur proposed to intervene in the 'private morals' of the citizens, i.e. in their family life, by instituting a 'family book' which would serve both as its written memory and as an instrument for the celebration of a private cult, guaranteeing public morality.

The family book (or album or commonplace book) was to contain certificates of birth or adoption, civil registration, marriage, guardianship, wardship, and death. These certificates would accumulate in the natural order of the events they were supposed to record, and would be separated by a blank space to be filled in by lists of prizes won on different occasions, either in the state schools or public festivities. There would in addition be room for a record of occasions when one had acted as witness in a marriage, an adoption or any other civil deed, as for those when one had the misfortune to lose a child, a relative or a friend. There would also be space to mention public offices held, either by election or by governmental appointment. These records entered into the family book would differ from official records in the sense that they would concentrate on the moral aspect of events marking the chief moments in life, not forgetting the purely civil forms in the case of the most important occasions, knowledge of which is necessary to facilitate settlement of family interests and disputes. This book would be brought out at all occasions connected with the civil register, and each deed would be authenticated by the same signatures as those required for the public records. There would be very stiff penalties for forgeries or the entering of information other than that prescribed by law, as well as for deliberate damage to or defacement of a family book, whether one's own or someone else's: everything, even mere disrespect for this institution, was to be severely checked.

On the death of the two spouses, the book would pass to their eldest child, or to their closest heir. Its preservation was to be a sacred duty. Its owner would be bound to communicate it to all other members of the family, and these would be entitled to sue in the event of refusal, damage, defacement or forgery; he would also be duty bound to present it to the magistrate—inspector of public schooling, who would be empowered to lay charges against anyone breaking the laws relating to this book.

Nobody could apply for civil registration without a family book, nor could anyone be entitled to one until deemed fit to own one by his education and his morality. Immediately after the civil registration ceremony, the individual's birth certificate would be entered into the book, along with any prizes he might have won, the book thereafter accompanying him through all the events of his life.

Thus the institution of a family record would perform a function at once civil, moral and political. It would contain the civil records (birth, marriage, etc.) as well as deeds relating to the interests of the family, so as to furnish each family with precise information about itself. But it would relate this private history in moral terms, so that the record of it might serve as an example and a matter for celebration. Lastly, it would at all times serve the Republic, since this instrument of what Leclerc termed 'domestic surveillance' also helped to ensure public morality. As an infallible substitute for individual recollection, as the principal repository of virtue, elevated into a ritual, the written word was given the task of reconstituting republican society from its basic units upwards; the family had become the focus of the beneficial commemoration which this made possible: unable to contemplate a collective past sullied by the Terror, the Republic now envisaged a future founded upon these archives of private virtue.

The written word is, simultaneously, the basis for the new morality, i.e. respectability, the means through which it is perpetuated, and the means whereby the 'familial' may be re-aggregated with the 'social', through shared celebration. The 'lonely crowd'[9] of families thus rediscovers communion with the Republic through a book that recounts its virtues.

The Thermidorian dream of using this family book of examples to build an entirely new and utterly good society was merely a transposition into family terms of the Jacobin belief in the virtues of written culture: for the men of '97, as for those of '93, the dichotomy between oral and written was coterminous with the temporal opposition between old and new, barbarity and enlightenment, good and bad behaviour, which gave meaning to the revolutionary upheaval and to the order it was now creating, whether transmitted through the school or through the family. In both cases, writing was the lever and symbol of the advent of civic and private virtue, and at the same time an instrument of republican surveillance.

The elements of this ancient belief date back to Protestantism, before the Catholic Reformation took them over, until finally, in a secularized, radicalized form, they emerged as the favoured breeding ground of republic mythology. For only the written word lent plausibility to the idea of a complete break with the past, following the example of the revolution itself: an end to tradition, the emergence of a humanity reconciled with reason and morality. However illusory, this should not blind us to its constant, profound insight, namely that the spread of writing throughout the entire nation had generated a new tissue of social communication, subjecting people's behaviour to the arbitration of a new 'reason'. Stendhal, an attentive, critical observer of this cultural revolution, was the first to sense the ambiguity of the effects of access to this 'reason' – the key to what the Enlightenment had called 'civilization', which had thereby acquired universal prestige. Stendhal was one of the first to grasp the fact that it wrenched the individual from the profounder life of the instincts and the passions. Several times, in his travels through France,[10] Stendhal notes the backwardness of the Midi compared with the North, but especially that of the South-West, Aquitaine. Already, apparently ignorant of Brittany's problems, he guessed that it was here, increasingly, that peasant illiteracy had come to lodge in nineteenth-century

France. Like a worthy son of the Enlightenment (in its Jacobin version), he deplored this illiteracy. But at the same time, he could not help extending to the South of France his sensual affection for Italy and the intellectual blessings which he bestowed upon these lands of sun and passion, reservoirs of natural energy, and hence of superior men. 'A Minister of the Interior,' he wrote in *Henry Brulard*,[11] 'Concerned to do his job rather than intrigue with the King and in the Assemblies, like Mr. Guizot, would do well to request a subsidy of two millions a year to raise, to bring up to the level of education of the rest of the French people, those that live in the fatal triangle stretching between Bordeaux, Bayonne and Valence. They believe in witches, they cannot read and they do not speak French in these parts. They may, by chance, produce a superior being such as Lannes, or Soult, but in general . . . they are unbelievably ignorant.'

Yet the very next sentence, without warning, contradicts that 'by chance': 'I think that because of the climate, and the love and the energy with which it fires the [human] machine, this triangle ought to produce the greatest men in France. Corsica makes me think so. With 180,000 inhabitants, this island has given eight or ten men of merit to the Revolution, whereas the département of the Nord, with its 900,000 inhabitants, scarcely one. And even then, I could not say who that *one* could be.' Finally, without transition, he reverts to his initial pessimism: 'It goes without saying that the priests are all-powerful in this fatal triangle. Civilization runs from Lille to Rennes and stops around Orléans and Tours. To the South-East, Grenoble is a shining outpost.'

Was it so fatal, this triangle? Or was it providential? Was it a sanctuary of clerical obscurantism, or a nursery of future Bonapartes? The interesting thing about this Stendhalian contradiction is not so much its mistaken conception of the Church's part in the acculturation of the Occitanian peasantry (since the said Church was very unevenly represented in this 'triangle' and because where it was strong, as in the Velay or the Rouergue, it acted as a force for basic literacy, either through the school or directly): this erroneous view was consonant with his Jacobin convictions. What is interesting about this incoherent judgement, pronounced by an otherwise acutely perceptive man, was his very modern insight – expressed in his quirky statistical computation of great men – into the ambiguous benefits of written culture: the emergence of a nationality that left no room for witches, but at the same time the impoverishment of powerful spirits through the censorship which it imposes upon individual *furia*. Just as he loved the people yet could not stand contact with them, so he advocated instruction for the people while regretting the passing of all that the old world had allowed in the way of freedom of instinct and passion. For this aristocrat of democracy, the literary vision of a natural, sensual Midi, where rationalization or standardized behaviour are unknown, counterbalances his political conviction of the virtues of 'civilization'. In this, Stendhal speaks less to the reader of 1880, to whom he was ostensibly addressing himself, than to the present-day reader, to whom he still sounds like a brother.

This is because the transition from one culture to another is a slow, partial process, like a long, endless rending asunder. As we can see from the figures, it took three or four centuries: which means that over a very long period (differing from one geographic zone to another, possibly lasting right into the early years of this century in the more backward parts of France), the cultural level of the country was one of restricted literacy. Restricted to certain provinces; restricted to men, to the exclusion of women; restricted to certain social groups, to the exclusion of the poorest peasants; restricted too to the bare minimum, which means that writing was not always taught, and that the age-old loyalty to the subjective ties of solidarity found in oral tradition did not always disappear. Even in Northern France and North-Eastern France, which had achieved high thresholds of literacy by the eighteenth century, it is clear that cultural traditions still lived on in the villages, even where these gradually mingled with book culture. What is more, the upward social mobility coupled with emigration, which schooling offered the more gifted country children, helped to preserve oral traditions through the agency of the mass of those that stayed behind, although these oral traditions had become tinged with regret and, soon, discredit. In the latter half of the nineteenth century, the South of France, fast catching up educationally and culturally, furnished the Third Republic with its officials, although this did not transform village life in the Midi. By offering a chance of escape, and even merely by embodying the image of employment of another kind, the school raised a barrier between the community and its potential 'modernizers'; it helped to entrap the community in its traditions, even though these were now felt to be residual.

So this long history of the literacy process in France was an integral part of a dialectical to-and-fro between institutions and society. Its roots lay in the dominance of written culture, which both society and the state had embraced, encouraged and cultivated from very early on as a harbinger of progress; but for a very long time, and even now, the business of learning and the practice of this culture is intimately bound up with oral communication. For centuries, while slowly being torn from his roots, the French peasant was a cultural half-breed. So much so that this book will some day have to be rewritten, using other sources and facts, looking behind the figures and hypotheses given here to examine the history of this anthropological mutation.

12   LITERACY, JOBS, AND INDUSTRIALIZATION: THE NINETEENTH CENTURY*

Harvey J. Graff

No amount of literary cramming will make a good, loyal, intelligent citizen out of a reluctant child. But a craftsman who loves his work and takes pride in his work, who would rather do his work than joy-ride over the country — such a craftsman cannot be a disloyal, un-intelligent citizen, even though he can neither read nor write. But, of course, he would have mastered these arts without wasting eight years of his life on them, endangering his health to boot.

Frederick Philip Grove
A Search for America (1927)

In 1848, Egerton Ryerson, the Chief Superintendent of Education for Upper Canada, addressed 'The Importance of Education to a Manufacturing, and a Free People'. Commencing from the premise that a system of mass public education was a prerequisite to a system of manufacturing — the symbol of the incoming social order — he proclaimed that 'education is designed to prepare us for the duties of life'. Although, as we have seen, those duties were primarily moral and social, Ryerson did not neglect proper preparation for work. 'How,' he asked, 'is the uneducated and unskilled man to succeed in these times of sharp and skilful competition and sleepless activity?'[1]

One year later Ryerson elaborated his views about the relations between occupational success, formal education, and literacy. Discussing 'Canadian Mechanics and Manufactures', he claimed that the mechanic 'will be a member of society; and, as such, he should know how to read and write the language spoken by such society . . . This supposes instruction in the grammar or structure of his native tongue.' Although one might advance in the working world without education, Ryerson admitted, he would remain fundamentally at a loss:

> I have known many persons rise to wealth and respectability by their industry, virtues and self-taught skill; but from their utter want of training in the proper mode of writing, or speaking, or reading their native tongue, they are unable to fill the situations to which their circumstances and talents and characteristics entitle them, and in which they might confer great benefits upon society.

*Reprinted from *The Literacy Myth: Literacy and Social Structure in the Nineteenth-Century City* by Harvey J. Graff, 195–233, by permission of the publisher, Academic Press, Inc., © Academic Press, Inc. 1979.

232

Social order and progress were the supreme beneficiaries of all education, and, with other Anglo-American educators, Ryerson believed that 'educated labour is more productive than uneducated labour'. By 'productive' he meant a variety of related qualities: less disruptive, more skilled, orderly and disciplined, punctual, and moral. Thus, the 'proper education of the mechanic is important to the interests of society as well as to his own welfare and enjoyment'.

As the preceding chapters have argued, the key issues are much more complex than Ryerson's, or many others', statements allow. How important have literacy and schooling been to occupational and economic success? Traditional wisdom, modern sociology, the rhetoric of modernization, and nineteenth-century school promotion all celebrated the role of education in determining success. Yet not all the evidence, past or present, lends credence to this view. Consider these examples – the first a help-wanted advertisement, the second an educational study:

> Wanted immediately FORTY ABLE BODIED MEN, to serve as JUSTICES OF THE PEACE, for the COUNTY OF HURON. A plain English Education is desirable but not indispensable – each candidate must be able to make his mark, unless he has learned to write his name, and will be expected to produce a character signed by the Deputy Commissioner of the Board of Works and the Collector of Customs Goderich.

and

> For all children, except the 10 percent who will earn a living by the use of their verbal ability there is a case for substituting practical for academic education.

The relationship of education in general and literacy in particular to work, occupation, and their rewards remains an imprecise one, complex and often contradictory. This chapter explores that relationship, examining both the real and the perceived connections surrounding the economic value of literacy. The literacy levels and differentials of the urban Ontario working class are first reviewed in this intellectual context of the economic importance of education. The views of middle-class reformers and working-class spokesmen are examined. Finally, a case study based on the employment-contract ledgers of an Ontario lumbering firm is presented in order to isolate the importance of literacy to workingmen in a specific social situation. In sum, this chapter illuminates the contradictions in the perceived connections between education, employment levels, and economic development, to argue that literacy was not always central to jobs, earnings, and industrialization in the nineteenth century in the manner typically assumed.

I

Ontario in the 1860s and 1870s was an overwhelmingly literate society. Adult

(20 years and older) literacy was over 90% as measured by the censuses of those years. In respect of wealth and occupation, there was superficially a significant degree of stratification by illiteracy; the majority of illiterates labored as semi- and unskilled workers. Large numbers, lacking education, also assumed positions of skill – positions which were maintained over the decade 1861–71.

One hundred and thirty-five illiterates in Hamilton, Kingston, and London held skilled laboring and artisanal occupations in 1861; 44 held higher-ranking jobs. Open to at least some uneducated persons were the occupations of bailiff, engineer, grocer, inn-keeper, mason, merchant, manufacturer, molder, printer, tailor, tavernkeeper, tinsmith, wheelwright, shoemaker, and watch-maker (as is shown in Table 12.1). No single occupation in Hamilton, in fact, comprised a majority of illiterates. Only 25% of adult common laborers, 15% of seamstresses, and 5% of female servants could not read or write. The remainder – and the greatest numbers – of those occupying these low-status positions were literate. Seventy-five percent of the unskilled and 93% of the semiskilled possessed the skills of literacy, but nevertheless were unable to climb higher in occupational level. The acquisition of some education, as signified by their literacy, did not enable them to overcome the dominance of ethnic and class ascription in attaining rank and status in an unequal social structure.

The distribution of wealth in these cities strikingly parallels that of occu-pation. The majority of illiterates whose wealth could be determined (as measured by total annual value in the 1861 city assessment rolls) were poor; that is, below a poverty line struck at the 40th percentile of the assessed population. Nevertheless, sizeable numbers of illiterate workers achieved at least moderate economic standing, and the majority of all poor were literate. Illiteracy did not consign all men to poverty, and, conversely, many literate workers remained poor. Illiteracy could be depressing occupationally or econ-omically, but literacy proved of remarkably limited value in the pursuit of higher status or greater rewards.

More revealing than these occupational and economic profiles is the relationship of literacy to the economic rewards of occupation. Among the unskilled and the semiskilled, very little economic advantage accrued to the literates. Literacy, though, had a greater role in the attainment of skilled or artisanal work and their commensurate rewards. Some illiterates, nevertheless, fared well, especially those few in nonmanual or small proprietary positions.

The possession of literacy did have rewards, though its benefits were hardly clear or unambiguous; overall, they were rather limited ones. The relationship of education to work and earnings was quite complex, as we have seen, complicated by other determinants, usually ascriptive social-structural ones: ethnicity, social class, race, age, and sex. Illiterates' standing, as a result, was far from uniform or homogeneous; they were differentiated and stratified

Table 12.1. *Illiterates: selected occupations, 1861*

	Hamilton	Percentage of Hamilton adult workforce	Kingston	London
Barber	2	10.5	3	1
Blacksmith	8	10.3	–	2
Builder	2	7.2	–	1
Cabinet maker	1	1.9	–	–
Carpenter	14	4.7	4	4
Clergymen	1	3.2	–	–
Clothier	2	13.3	–	–
Constable	1	11.1	–	–
Customs collector	1	33.3	1	–
Dealer	1	9.1	1	–
Dressmaker	1	1.4	2	–
Engineer	1	2.1	1	1
Farmer	3	10.0	3	2
Grocer	1	1.1	1	1
High bailiff	1	50.0	–	–
Innkeeper	1	6.7	3	–
Joiner	1	5.9	–	–
Laborer	205	25.2	105	83
Mail conductor	2	50.0	–	–
Mariner	1	2.0	10	–
Merchant	1	0.9	–	–
Mason	2	3.9	3	1
Molder	2	3.6	–	–
Painter	2	3.2	–	–
Pedlar	2	6.1	1	1
Printer	1	2.5	1	–
Seamstress	8	15.1	2	–
Servant (f)	33	6.1	34	–
Tailor	8	6.2	8	–
Tavernkeeper	7	9.3	1	–
Tinsmith	2	5.1	–	–
Wagonmaker	2	18.2	–	–
Wheelwright	1	50.0	–	–
Gentleman	1	1.5	1	–
Watchmaker	1	7.2	1	–
Porter	3	4.8	1	2
Teamster	4	13.3	–	–
Plasterer	3	6.9	–	2
Clerk	–	–	1	–
Shoemaker	8	5.6	4	4

in the same ways as others in the cities. Consequently, Irish Catholics (illiterate or not), women, blacks, and the aged are generally found in the lowest occupational or economic classes. More than literacy operated in the establishment and maintenance of the rigid stratification of nineteenth-century cities. Education alone seldom altered class or social position dramatically; its influence was overwhelmingly a reinforcing one.

Education and literacy did not reduce the role of class or status as the urban society was gradually transformed by modernization and industrialization. At the same time, social mobility was possible for persisting illiterates, 1861 to 1871, the usual expectations to the contrary. Occupationally, stability was the most common experience, as skilled workers maintained their positions, not falling to lower class ranks. Economically, improvement in wealth and property dominated, regardless of occupation or ethnicity.

An absence of literacy and a lack of education did not remove all opportunities for higher-ranking occupations or the acquisition of wealth. Ethnicity favored some illiterates and hindered others; factors such as chance, personality, and motivation figured too, undoubtedly mitigating some of the disadvantages that illiteracy and ascription could carry. An illiterate could achieve some success in the working world of the nineteenth century. These conclusions form one baseline against which to assess the rhetorical claims of middle-class school promoters and by which to understand the criticisms and aspirations of the working class. Much more than the skills of literacy were at stake to them; other issues were thought to be at least as central to the curriculum of the future workers.

II

Industry, skills, and wealth could be obtained by the individual with no schooling; education, nevertheless, was viewed as fundamental to the development and the maintenance of the economic system, as it was to the social order. The claims of the schoolmen stressed educated, literate labor for productivity and benefit to both society and individuals. As Ryerson stated it, 'Every man, unless he wishes to starve outright, must read and write, and cast accounts, and speak his native tongue well enough to attend to his own particular business.'

Egerton Ryerson long affirmed that education underlay any of the main branches of career pursuits. In his first report, of 1846, he laid the foundation for future statements: 'The establishment of a thorough system of primary and industrial education, commensurate with the population of the country, as contemplated by the Government, and is here proposed, is justified by considerations of *economy* as well as of patriotism and humanity.' With evidence from Switzerland, he argued that uneducated workers have neither the logic for nor capacity of making sound deductions or collecting observations to aid their work. 'This want of capacity of mental arrangements is shown in their manual operations.' Quite simply, it was the well-informed, well-educated workers who were thought to produce the most and the best, to possess superior moral habits, and to save money. Uneducated, illiterate workers, presumably, did not.

Little doubt or hesitation accompanied the proclamations of the benefits of education to the economy or the individual workers. Yet it is important to note, with Alison Prentice, that 'statements relating specific occupational groups to social status tended to be vague and contradictory'. To Ryerson, there were but two kinds of workers: they were either 'rude, simple or un-educated' or they were educated. These were also the classes of society, as status increasingly included demeanor and gentility as well as skills attained. 'And by skills, few school promoters meant manual dexterity.' Literacy was just one skill, important but not the only one; education's benefits involved the transmission of the proper code of behavior, including morality and correct attitudes. Literacy revealed that the training had begun.[2]

More than upward mobility through education, Ryerson emphasized the loss of status and downward mobility, which he claimed would accompany the lack of schooling. Educated men might advance; the uneducated would surely fall. The burden he placed on the shoulders of fathers: 'Does a man wish his sons to swell the dregs of the society – to proscribe them from all situations of trust and duty in the locality of their abode – to make them mere slaves in the land of freedom? Then let him leave them without edu-cation, and their underfoot position in society will be decided upon.' Ryerson further taught that workers were not to be educated to despise their occupations. Not all men should aspire to the highest statuses of work; 'prac-tical' men were needed too, and the supply of farmers and mechanics must not diminish. Education therefore must not alienate labor; and it should not, for labor, he added, did not deaden the mind. The ideal mechanic would combine 'in his own person, the qualifications and skills', of both the manu-facturing superintendent and the operative. All members of the working class thus required that which 'is essential to the successful pursuit of any one of the several departments of human activity and enterprise'. This consisted of 'what is rudimental, or elementary in education'; in addition to reading, writing, arithmetic, and grammar, 'each must learn that which will give him skill in his own particular employments'. Not at all inclusive of specific job skills, this training made for more productive and more easily managed labor; advancing the nation's development took precedence over the individual among education's benefits.

Ryerson was hardly an isolated spokesman for the economic contributions of education; he was joined by many others throughout Anglo-America.[3] Charles Clarke was one such reformer. His 1877 address to the South Welling-ton, Ontario, Teachers Association shows the persistence of the ideas Ryerson had enunciated. 'No unprejudiced man,' Clarke asserted, 'can conceal from himself the fact that education has lightened the toil of the laborer, increased his productive ability, surrounded him with comparative luxuries, and materially increased the purchasing power of his daily wage.' Recent economic and labor history describe the period very differently, of course. Regardless, he argued that uneducated men were heavily handicapped in 'the race of and for life', and that they were 'sinking, more rapidly and certainly than ever, into the position of mere "hewers of wood and drawers of water."'

More so than Ryerson, Clarke, or most others, Horace Mann, the first Secretary of the Massachusetts State Board of Education, fully elaborated these ideas. Mann was Ryerson's contemporary and associate, and the Ontario reformer quoted from his reports and exchanged information with him. For this reason as well as because of Mann's overall contribution to the development of educational thought and institutions in the nineteenth century, his opinion merits discussion.[4]

Horace Mann devoted much of his *Fifth Annual Report* (1842) to the economic benefits of education; in so doing, he entered into much greater detail than Ryerson or most other promoters. Both men favored arguments for education rooted in moral principles and civic virtues, though both made appeals to the economic self-interest of their audiences. As Mann expressed it, such self-interest, of all the 'beneficient influences of education, may, perhaps, be justly regarded as the lowest' yet 'it represents an aspect of the subject susceptible of being made intelligible to all'. Mann's primary objective in the *Fifth Report* was to argue that education was the most productive enterprise that could be undertaken by an individual or a community. To make this claim was certainly not novel; Mann, however, by surveying manufacturers, collected 'hard' evidence to prove his assertions. His questionnaire, sent to selected men, inquired, principally, as follows:

> Have you observed differences among the persons you have employed, growing out of differences in their education, *and independent of their natural abilities* . . . that is, [do] those who . . . have been accustomed to exercise their minds by reading and studying, have greater docility and quickness in applying themselves to work [and] greater appetite, dexterity or ingenuity in comprehending ordinary processes, or in originating new ones?

His major concern was, of course, 'How do those who have enjoyed and improved the privilege of good Common Schools, compare with the neglected and the illiterate?' The answers to the queries were hardly surprising: the manufacturers responded that 'the rudiments of a Common School education are essential to the attainment of skill and expertness as laborers'; 'very few, who have not enjoyed the advantages of a Common School education, ever rise above the lowest class of operatives'. Uneducated labor was unproductive, and the best educated were both the most profitable and the best paid. They were also more moral, loyal, cheerful, and contented as well as more punctual and reliable – or so the replies indicated.

Pleased, Mann proclaimed that these answers 'seem to prove incontestibly that education is not only a moral renovator, and a multiplier of intellectual power, but that it is also the most prolific parent of material riches'. Knowledge, he concluded, must precede industry: intelligence was the 'great money-maker'.[5] Ryerson and Mann joined in recognizing the mid-century spirit of progress and materialism, asserting in their educational promotion the productive contribution of common-school training. Proof was another issue, however, as Mann went further in providing evidence, thinking it insufficient merely to repeat the rhetoric of his witnesses.

Two of Mann's respondents attempted to estimate the wage differentials accruing to literate workmen. One manufacturer noted that literate employees (name-signers as opposed to markers) earned, on the average, about 27% more than illiterate ones; another claimed an 18½% difference. They then calculated the wage differentials between the highest paid literate workers and the lowest paid illiterate ones at 66 and 49%, respectively. Mann throughout his *Report* referred to these estimates as *conclusive* evidence to support his viewpoint, although these data were more impressionistic than statistical. Although his argument was presented in the guise of arithmetical exactness, the analysis of the rate of return to investments in primary education remained vague and overly rhetorical. The only explicit calculation he offered was a new wage difference of 50%.

There are grave problems both with Mann's method of obtaining that figure and with his use of it. He apparently simply averaged the two extreme examples of wages – not the group averages – looking solely at atypical cases. Had he used the average wages reported to him, the result would have been less than half of his 50% differential: 23%, far from such a huge variation, and still unreliable when based on a sample of only two firms. Mann also failed to show that additional education for each child was economically profitable, exaggerating differences between markers and signers, and ignoring the factors of age and ethnicity. He further confused the value of education to parents with its worth to the community, firms, or individuals – these could be very different. Finally, his use of wage rates ignored the imperfections of the labor market, social inequality, and discrimination. In sum, we must agree with Maris Vinovskis, that 'it is likely that Mann's figure of 50% for primary education greatly exaggerates the actual productivity of education during that period. A much more likely estimate would be in the range of 10–20%.'[6] If this is the case, the contributions of education to productivity must be evaluated in very different terms.

Another perspective emerges from the pages of the *Fifth Report*. Each of Mann's respondents concentrated (as did Ryerson) on the fact that educated workers were clean, moral, better able to follow directions, more punctual and reliable, and less likely to be unreasonable or violent during periods of labor unrest. In many ways, these were the most valued, and 'productive', teachings of the common school — more so than cognitive skills. Alexander Field, in examining the 'coincidence' of educational reform and the development of manufacturing in Massachusetts in this period, stresses industry's need for properly socialized labor. Importantly, he discovered that manufacturing expanded in the context of (and with the effect of) declining skill requirements — *not* of increasing skill demands. Manufacturers needed a disciplined, deferential, orderly, and honest labor force, and themselves worked with and through professional school reformers for the expansion of education at state and local levels (as other manufacturers did in Canada and England).

Recent research emphasizes the same point, stressing the importance of the molding of noncognitive personality characteristics as a major aspect of schooling. Gintis, for example, found that the contribution of education to earnings or occupational status can not be explained by the relationship between schooling and cognitive achievement. He demonstrates, rather, that the noncognitive personality traits stressed in schools, such as subordination and discipline, have a more direct influence on worker earnings and productivity. 'The structure of social relations in schools reproduces rather faithfully the capitalist work-environment', he concluded.[7] This was the result of the moral economy and of educational hegemony, expected from the carefully structured provision of literacy.

The contradictions between promoters' emphasis on skills and individual wages (undoubtedly central to popular acceptance of public schooling) and society and industry's behavioral requirements are extremely important in understanding the relationships between literacy, jobs, and development. Dr Edward Jarvis' discussion of the specific ways in which education enhanced the skills of common laborers illustrates the dimensions of the connections, with his amusing and novel presentation of the manifold benefits. Jarvis analyzed the 'processes of labor' of woodcutters, woodsplitters, turners, coalheavers, shovellers, and others in order to compare educated and uneducated workers. He perceived, pseudoscientifically, that

> The discreet shoveller [to take one case] carries his shovel to a point in the circle when the tangential movement, modified by gravitation, shall describe a curve which at its highest part is above the cart-wheel . . . As the blade of the shovel is held at right angles with the plane of the curve of motion, all the contents are carried in a curve of the same radius . . . and all fall together in to the vehicle in a compact mass; none are lost on the way.

In contrast, the uneducated laborer or

> thoughtless workman, unaccustomed to noticing the exact relation to things, and having no comprehensive plan of his operation, places

his cart by accident . . . Or, as chance, not intelligent observation, governs this matter, the receptacle may be so far off as to require the workman to walk a step or two . . . Nor is this dull laborer always mindful of the position of his shovel when he throws its contents.

Experience, knowledge acquired from others, and common sense are ignored, relegated behind the promoted benefits of schooling. Still, it remains unclear how common schooling would aid the worker in the ways Jarvis stressed. What neither Jarvis nor Mann or Ryerson revealed was how education specifically benefited the future workers in opening their eyes, comprehending their work, or applying their powers for best effect. How many sawyers, splitters, coalheavers, or shovellers needed or acquired much education for their jobs, and how much schooling was required to develop these vaunted mental skills? Were the skills of the common schools those necessary for productive labor? These questions went unasked and unanswered, for the primary assumption went unchallenged: 'Education . . . is the economy of force, and gives it a greater power to create value. It enables the intelligent and skilled to add more to the worth of matter than the ignorant.' In addition, they confused knowledge and intelligence with schooling and literacy; skills from experience and what might be termed 'technical literacy' were simply not considered. In this manner, promotion stressed increased skills, productivity, and returns (individual and other) from educational reform and expansion. The results of education added significantly to productivity, economic development, and social order; the process through which they were accomplished was a rather different one from that typically emphasized.

Contemporary sociological debate continues to focus on the relationship between education and occupational attainment, illustrating persisting interest in the importance of this issue. Recent data, significantly, enter into our conclusions about the role of literacy and schooling in the past, contradicting assumptions of a direct link between school achievement and job attainment. The methodological classic of the 1960s, Peter Blau and Otis Dudley Duncan's *The American Occupational Structure*, marked a watershed in the current controversy. Analyzing a special 1962 Current Population Survey, these sociologists found that 'the chances of upward mobility are directly related to education', that mobility for individuals 'is simply a function of their education and their social origins', and that 'occupational status in 1962 apparently is influenced more strongly by education than by first jobs'. Blau and Duncan, though, qualified these sweeping generalizations in three important aspects.

They argued that education, historically viewed, had been less important to occupational status than it has become in recent decades. The evidence presented here could suggest that, in some ways, this might be true. Second, they stressed the importance of social-class origins (ascription), which they found played a major role in accounting for both education and occupation, notwithstanding the amount of mobility they discovered. Finally, they concluded that 'the direct effects of education and father's status are attenuated drastically with the passage of time'. A compensatory effect derived from the increasing importance of the accumulation of occupational experience. Blau and Duncan, nevertheless, maintained the importance of education in their conclusions, aside from these basic qualifications.[8] Other researchers, however, have quickly supplemented their findings, revising them to conclude that education is less directly related to occupational attainment.

Ivar Berg, in particular, demonstrated that these commonly perceived relationships between education and jobs are an endemic part of modern democratic mythology.[9] Berg discovered that it is simply impossible to construct an occupational scale according to the intellectual abilities required by diverse occupations. Recent census data (1950, 1960) also contradict the Blau–Duncan findings. Instead of showing education becoming more important, they reveal 'a distinct drift of "better" educated people into "middle" level jobs and a reduction in the number of "less" educated people who move up into middle-level jobs'. Education has expanded more rapidly than the net change in skill requirements (there may not be much more of a fit in terms of skills than in the nineteenth century). The problem then becomes whether education – at all levels – might offer less in rewards than it engenders in expectations, making underemployment a serious concern, as it is today.

Berg's, and also Squires', examination of job requirements in a number of firms found self-fulfilling prophesies of the value of educated workers to be rampant among managers. Not only is there overeducation for requirements, there has been little, if any, relationship between changes in educational level and changes in output per worker. (Ryerson and Mann would have shuddered!) And in some plants 'educational achievement was *inversely* related to performance'; 'the less productive workers were slightly better educated'. Education, then, may be predictive of initial salary and job title, but not promotion. Finally, in professional and managerial positions, educational achievement, Berg found, was rewarded, rather than performance! 'To argue that well-educated people will automatically boost efficiency, improve organizations, and so on may be to misunderstand in a fundamental way the nature of American education, which functions to an important, indeed depressing extent as a licensing agency.'[10] Schooling of course serves more of the former role among the less-well educated, but this is hardly what is usually meant by productive skills. These arguments, regardless, are a direct legacy from the nineteenth century; their veracity then and now we have good reason to doubt.

To a significant extent the spokesmen of the labor movement in Canada (and the United States and Great Britain) in the last third of the nineteenth century agreed with the voices of middle-class school promoters in their discussions of the benefits of education; they accepted much of the schools' hegemony. To an important degree, however, labor's views were scored by a tension between a hunger for public schooling and very real doubts about the value of the formal education being offered. To them, education represented something more than just the making of better workmen, in spite of their assent to schooling's value.

That workers desired educational provision can not be doubted. Their case was put forth in the first issue of the *Ontario Workman*, in 1872: 'A thorough and general system of education we consider to be one of the first duties of the state; to see that in all its branches it is placed as near as possible within the reach of every son and daughter of the land.' The whole body of workmen should be raised by education and mental training to a higher intellectual level, not merely to permit isolated cases of social advancement. As the Hamilton *Palladium of Labor* claimed, 'An education is the practical side of American industrial success. In the industries where your working people have the best common school education, there you will find them earning the best wages.' This situation, we need to note, was also related to the absence of child labor and therefore to the absence of cheap competition, in labor's didactic participation in educational promotion. For education cut two ways in its benefits for workingmen: First, education was valuable in raising and maintaining wages and standards of labor, while it restricted the supply of workers. Second, 'Educated workmen, skilled workmen, and moral workmen . . . [made] labor respected as well as profitable.'

To make better workers was not the sole emphasis of the labor press, and their educational program was not quite that which Ryerson *et al*. had urged. Education ought to be mechanical, scientific, and technical: for the hand and body as well as the mind. They recommended a combination of work and study, four hours of each per day. Having an idea of common-school education different from that of Ryerson, Clarke, Mann, and Jarvis, the spokesmen of the working class sought a preparation in job skills of a different kind, and articulated a different perspective on the place of literacy. What they wanted was in part a schooling that was practical and related to future occupations. 'It is generally felt,' the *Palladium* echoed, 'that our educational methods are too one-sided. They do not develop the constructive faculties as they might. The adoption of industrial education would do much to enable those of the pupils who, on leaving the school follow mechanical operations to take higher positions than they otherwise occupy by reason of the training secured.' Traditional forms of practical training were found wanting (vocational and industrial education, which never precisely met these desires, were not introduced into the school curriculum until the 1890s and 1900s). *Fincher's Trades Review*, a Philadelphia workingmen's weekly read by and concerned with Canadian labor, reported that apprenticeship was fast declining and that regulation was required; the period of indenture had become too short and incomplete. One problem was that masters neglected the education of their charges.

This neglect was not solely a U.S. concern, as an examination of Upper Canadian indentures reveals. Of the fourteen-odd documents that could be located, representing a handful of nonmanual, skilled, and semiskilled occupations, only half (servant, tailor, carpenter) made any provision for education in the contract. The issue of schooling was not mentioned for a turner, patternmaker, shoemaker, machinist, miller, draper, or a stonecutter. If the sample is tiny and spans without visible trend a lengthy period, the 50% neglect of schooling remains indicative.[11]

The crux of the issue, in labor's interpretation, was that masters wanted the most work for the least costs. 'The desire to make his boys finished workmen, to fit them by night or day schooling for the better comprehension of the business, or to qualify them for advancing in the higher branches, of art and science, scarcely ever enters the master's mind.' The sad results left youngsters conscious of their inferiority, not aspiring to any position higher than the one they had been taught, and often slipping to day labor. 'Botches' were created among the industrious classes each year.

Education nevertheless was not viewed primarily as job preparation; it represented a higher ideal and a different goal. A boy 'should be regarded, rather as the man that will be, than as the future doctor, lawyer, tradesman, farmer or mechanic'. Would such education intersect with economic productivity? The *Workman* suggests that workers were not to be educated to increase the value of capital through their labors. They were not simply *to be* educated: 'They must educate themselves to think; they must also learn to think for themselves.' To a large degree, education was to instill a direction, a goal, and the correct set of personal qualities — all more important than skills or a mere hunger for gold. Education was, in one sense, character-building; it enabled workers to see their calling as useful and dignified. Morals, wisdom, and honorable careers ranked above the skills of the job. Were such men the loyal, punctual, nondisruptive workers the mill-owners desired and Egerton Ryerson promised if allowed to fashion a system of common schools? Education could lead in a rather different direction as the *Palladium* saw it:

> Educate first, agitate afterwards. Ignorance, superstition and timerity [timorousness] are the weapons which our oppressors have used most effectively against us in the past. Secure an education at any cost, put the ballot to its proper use, and then the fall of the venerable structure of legal robbery, alias monopoly, will shake to its centre.

Furthermore, the working class was more than a little ambivalent about education and its value; this tension brought contradiction to their apparent endorsement of mass public education:

> 'A self-made man' awakens in most all a glow of appreciation and regard which we do not feel for the man, equally distinguished for ability and learning he has got, who has been regularly taught in the

schools. The latter has had the counter-sign, and has been invited into the fort, the other has scaled the ramparts and conquered his place.

Success without the assistance of education was admired above that 'aided' by the schools, in sharp contrast to Ryerson's view. A curious tale related in the *Workman* indicates a further lack of esteem for education-related skills. A man in England, the story went, had been jailed. To obtain bail, he was advised that he must sign his name; overnight he taught himself to do so. The implications drawn are important; there was no a priori reason for illiterates or poor workers to be barred from the ballot. Inability to read or write need not disqualify a man from exercising his rights, nor did it signify an inability to carry them out. A final point is implied: When needed, one could quickly and easily gain some skills of literacy.

Ambivalence went even deeper. For example, *Fincher's Trades Review* reprinted 'Proverbs of the Billings Family', which included 'If you kan't git clothes and education too, git the clothes.' A more interesting notice came from the Lawrence, Massachusetts, Mutual Benefit Society. The society began its operations with a system of bookkeeping for accounts, but 'We are now doing it with checks. Our checks are printed on card board, of the following denominations . . . fifty cents, white; one dollar, blue; two dollar, yellow; five dollar, orange; ten dollar, salmon color. We find that this system is much easier than bookkeeping.' Store personnel and society members need not even know the decimal system or how to read numbers; the colors differentiated for them. Literacy need not figure in workers' everyday transactions.

More important in understanding the working class' awareness of the contradictions of educational promotion and programs is their analysis of the 'evils' of the system. The *Palladium* urged its readers to learn a trade, not to be seduced by 'class' education, with its examples in school of millionaires, for 'schools love to dwell too much on the achievements of professional men'. The school curriculum itself was found to be class-biased, and the ideas of classical literature anti-workingmen. Or, as Phillips Thompson expressed it, education 'if perverted by the inculcation of the untruths and half-truths of bourgeois political economy, is a hindrance rather than a help'. This he called 'wrong education', tempting the worker with self-aggrandizement and wealth. The system of state education, compulsory by the 1870s, taught reading but 'then [gave] them dime novels for perusal, having previously given them a taste for such reading'. Such an education – and use of literacy – was hardly desirable; it would not benefit the working class.

The greatest evil of all stood at the pinnacle of the educational system – the university, which all workingmen supported through taxation, but whose expense was prohibitive to most.

It is an injustice that all the farmers, mechanics, and laborers should be taxed to teach the sons of the wealthy merchants and professional men Latin and Greek, and to support a lot of imported professors at high salaries to inculcate false and undemocratic notions of social caste, and to teach an obsolete system of political economy. As a training for practical life and usefulness, the ordinary university education is well-nigh valueless.

The educational system, from the top down, was biased against the working-man and his children. Lest the working class be falsely accused of anti-intellectualism we note that the *Palladium* urged that as good an education could be secured by well-directed reading.

Reading, moreover, was often discussed in terms of amusement, enchantment, comfort, consolation, and leisure — in brief, noninstrumentally. 'Let the torch of intelligence be lit in every household.' The family hearth was the place for the taste for reading ('one of the true blessings of life') to commence, and where parents were to guard against the taint of bad books, magazines, or newspapers. Relief from toil came through literature, making 'study the more refreshing', and the delights of reading and contemplation brought wisdom 'in common with all mankind'. Here lay one real value of literacy to workmen, for knowledge is always power, but not only in an economic or political sense.

Similarly, there were reasons more important than book-learning in the establishment of mechanics' institutes, workingmen's reading rooms, and ancillary public institutions. Workers needed a place to become better acquainted with one another, where their various interests could harmonize, where committees could meet. Two hours of leisure each day (related to demands for reduced hours) spent in mental and physical culture 'would result in the shame and discomfiture of our opponents'. Knowledge, then, could be power in the purely political sense, much as Phillips Thompson would have it. Yet mass literacy need not be a requirement for the development of a shared consciousness, a common political culture, or the exchange of ideas or information. Only a few readers were needed to enlighten a large number if given the chance of congregation and the customary modes of communication. As E.P. Thompson argues, 'Illiteracy by no means excluded men from political discourse.' They could listen and participate in discussion — at work, in reading circles, in pubs, or at ports of call. Activities such as those of the Luddites and 'Captain Swing' support the argument, and contrary to the typical views of historians such as Robert Webb, upheavals can take place without printers. It was the areas lowest in literacy, for example, that experienced the greatest number of 'Swing' actions.

Reading and writing, *Fincher's* found, were less important than the hammer, the sign of workingmen: 'Only the hammer is all powerful and peaceful . . . Without the hammer — a symbol of toil, as the pen is of thought, and the sword is of violence — the world could not exist in comfort and refinement.' 'The ability to read,' moreover, E.P. Thompson reminds us, 'was only the elementary technique. The ability to handle abstract and consecutive argument was by no means inborn; it had to be discovered amid almost overwhelming difficulties.' Much more than literacy or education alone is required for cohesion, consciousness, and activity; social structural and economic factors, leadership and organization, psychology and motivation, numbers and opportunity are equally if not more important. Easier communication, which literacy can advance, may aid the process, but literacy is hardly the key variable.[12]

Labor, in spite of its acceptance of hegemony and an apparent clamor for equal educational opportunity, deviated from the major premises of leading schoolmen who sought more education of the working class for greater productivity. Ambivalent about the proper role, form, and content of education, recognizing some contradictions, and often placing its benefits and application quite aside from their jobs, they sought to be free and independent, powerful in ways that would not have pleased the men who desired to have the masses educated. More fundamentally, they did not always equate education solely with the skills (in either an academic or a practical sense) required to gain and perform a good job.

Estimates, such as Horace Mann's, of a 50% greater return to educated laborers and corresponding increases in productivity from specific skills provided in public schooling, can not be accepted. A 10–20% differential puts the issue into a radically different perspective. Such a difference need not seem so significant to the average workingman, and major questions surround the reasons why he chose – and the majority did – to acquire some education and to send his children to school. An answer must lie in the relationships among the hegemonic functions of the school, the contradictions and ambivalence inherent in working-class attitudes toward education, the noneconomic importance of literacy, and the connection between literacy, skilled work, and its rewards. Equally important questions pertain to how much schooling made a significant difference in wages.

We must ask, moreover, why discussions of the productive contribution of education so rarely addressed specific job skills, beyond abstract thought processes, such as those so disarmingly recounted by Edward Jarvis. Certainly a major answer derives from the recognition of the moral bases of literacy – the moral virtues, attitudes, and behavioral traits – which Egerton Ryerson, Horace Mann, and manufacturers all held central to the making of a productive and malleable labor force. In this, they were undoubtedly correct. As Field and Gintis have found and Dreeben has argued, it is precisely the noncognitive functions of schooling, the concomitants of literacy transmission, which most directly relate to the creation of a workforce acceptable to modern capitalism. Schooling's contribution came from these other kinds of skills. Toward this end, the schools were designed to socialize, prepare, and assimilate the masses – and the schools were attended. Nevertheless, this does not sufficiently answer the basic query of how schooling related to the skills of specific occupations. Neither schoolmen nor labor spokesmen addressed this question to any meaningful degree, although it was a much more serious concern of the latter. So we do not yet know, beyond educated guesses or extrapolations from modern analogues, how much education a carpenter, shoemaker, mechanic, painter, storekeeper, or hotelkeeper would need to do his work. They might need arithmetic, but this could be gained without schooling.[13] Examples of the self-taught readers or writers are almost legendary, and they are central to working-class cultural traditions. But to what extent these skills, the tools based in literacy, were required remains questionable for those not employed in professional or clerical endeavors. Practical job skills were not part of the literacy-centered common school curriculum.

It is very possible that reading was not often required in the search for employment. Advertisements for jobs are rarely found amidst the plethora of announcements and solicitations in nineteenth-century newspapers. Work was most often gained informally, as Gareth Stedman Jones reports for the labor market of London, England, in the second half of the century. Workers circulated among the trades, from one to another in a seasonal pattern:

> Skilled workers could gain information about the availability of work either from press announcements or from local trade union branches. But neither of these channels was really open to the casual worker. The only way he could find out about work was either by chance conversations in pubs or else by tramping around the yards and workshops in his districts . . . being known at local centres of casual work was more important than degree of skills and where character references were not required.[14]

Reading and writing were to such men — a sizeable proportion of the workforce in nineteenth-century cities — relatively inconsequential to their searches for work, perhaps relatively unimportant in doing a good job. Stedman Jones' conclusions probably hold for many skilled workers, journeymen, and artisans as well. The economic — and other — benefits of literacy lay elsewhere.

III

The contradictions of literacy's relationship to work may be further explored in a specific work setting. In this section, we focus on one large lumbering concern, the Hawkesbury Lumber Company, located in the rich timberland of the Ottawa River Valley. Hawkesbury was in important ways a typical large-scale nineteenth-century firm. Lumbering was firstly a primary extractive industry, but it also had a large component of secondary processing (or, more properly, industrial) functions. Lumbering, certainly capitalist-based, may be viewed as a transitional operation between traditional, seasonal rhythms and the discipline and internal control of the factory that milling would represent.

It was a mixture of two historical developments of economic organization. It represents the large work setting, as 795 men were employed, or rehired, during the years 1887 to 1903. The number hired varied from year to year, from a maximum of 208 in 1888 to a low of 6 in 1906. Rather than indicating the introduction of new technology or mechanization, or a drastic response to business conditions, this fluctuation illustrates the stability of the workforce, as most hands retained their positions.[15]

The Hawkesbury Lumber Company is of special interest, for its detailed records of employment contracts have survived. Ledgers of annual contracts were maintained, for 1887–88 (Hamilton Brothers) and 1889–1903 (Hawkesbury). Exceptional records, they provide for each employee, contract date, occupation, name, wage rates, and a signature or mark – a measure of literacy.[16] From these records, the occupational and wage structure and the distribution of literate and illiterate workers may be reconstructed.

The horizontal, or functional, structure of occupations is readily established from these records. As Table 12.2 shows, the largest group of workers were the semiskilled, although the group 'millmen' may well have included some skilled workers. Skilled workers constituted the second largest group, twice the number of the nonmanual, three times the unskilled. The diverse processes of work are easily seen from the list, including the extractive and the processing. The largest number of factory jobs (millman, ironworker, mechanic, millwright, etc.) – perhaps one-third of the total – shows the industrial side of operations. Large variations existed in monthly rates of earnings, from $1.00 (a day's work) to $87.00. The mean wage was $24.00, the median $22.50, certainly not atypical for the area or the period (Table 12.3).[17]

How did literacy intersect with the structure of earnings and occupations? Fifty-two percent of employees were literate and 48% were not, though this measure underestimates the level of reading ability (Table 12.4). This was a high rate of illiteracy for Ontario, Canada, and North America in the last quarter of the century, but it reflects the traditionally high rates of Eastern Ontario and the Province of Quebec, and the French Canadian origins of the greatest number of workers.

As elsewhere, literacy did not always result in higher earnings, a fact supportive of the conclusions of this chapter. Among the lowest paid, at $10 or less per month, illiterates dominated (Table 12.3). The succeeding wage levels show near parity, however. These ranges, $21–$30 (which encompassed a plurality of the workforce) and $11–$20, together comprised over 80% of employees; herein illiterates were hardly disadvantaged. With the exception of the lowest paid (probably casual or part-time), literate workmen fared little better than their illiterate colleagues. Yet there was a limitation on the level of earnings to which the majority of illiterates could aspire, much as tabulations of urban assessed wealth revealed earlier: 92% earned $30 or less, com-

Table 12.2. *Occupational classification and literacy: Hawkesbury Lumber Company*

	N^a	Percentage literate		N^a	Percentage literate
Nonmanual labor (8.5%)			Semiskilled labor (68.8%)		
Foreman	17	88.2	Handyman	21	47.6
Clerk	27	100.0	Teamster	149	36.9
Timekeeper	6	83.3	Courier	1	100.0
Jobber	5	40.0	Lumberman	2	0.0
Lumber inspector	1	100.0	Cook	1	0.0
Contractor	1	100.0	Blockmaker	1	100.0
	—	——	Fuller	1	100.0
Total	57	89.5	Housekeeper	1	100.0
			Stableman	3	66.7
Skilled labor			Chainer/raker	9	66.7
(17.7%)			Picket	8	50.0
Blacksmith	11	81.8	Spareman	3	0.0
Carpenter	19	52.6	Barkman	5	40.0
Cutter	28	64.3	Pileman/piler	69	40.6
Millwright	14	57.1	Stabber	7	71.4
Watchman	5	100.0	Slideman	16	31.3
Mechanic	11	90.9	Chopper	21	28.6
Gardener	2	100.0	Loader/striker	6	0.0
Painter	1	0.0	Boorman	8	50.0
Saddler	6	100.0	Butter	3	0.0
Sawyer	4	50.0	Millman	99	32.3
Trimmer	1	100.0	Road cutter	13	23.1
Wheelwright	1	100.0	Logmaker	14	21.4
Miller	1	0.0		—	——
Plasterer	1	0.0	Total	462	36.8
Filer	1	100.0			
Edger	6	50.0	Unskilled labor		
Ironworker	7	0.0	(5.1%)		
	—	——	Laborer	28	35.7
Total	119	63.9	Choreman/boy	6	16.7
				—	——
			Total	34	32.4

$^a N = 672.$

pared with 70% of literates. Here, however, it was only the top 12% from which illiterates were largely excluded, as they constituted just 20% of those earning $31 or more each month. Nevertheless, some illiterates did make it to these higher levels (8%). What such men lacked in education or booklearning, they no doubt compensated for with skill, experience, or common sense. Pre-

Table 12.3. *Rates of wage and literacy*

Rate/month	N^a	%	Percentage literate
$ 1–10	12	1.6	25.0
11–20	298	39.6	43.3
21–30	341	45.4	49.0
31–40	48	6.4	89.6
41–50	40	5.3	72.5
51–60	2	0.3	50.0
61–70	7	0.9	100.0
70+	4	0.5	50.0
Mean	$24.12		
Median	$22.53		

$^a N = 752.$

Table 12.4. *Literacy of workforce*

	N^a	%
Literate	413	51.9
Illiterate	382	48.1

$^a N = 795.$

sumably their employers did not find that their illiteracy made them less productive; so their work was rewarded.[18]

The rewards possible for illiterate workers are also illustrated by their shares in rising wage rates. The contracts in some cases (24% of all) include two rates of remuneration for a workman: the initial wage, used above, and a subsequent higher wage. These men were employed to hold more than one job, their jobs often varying seasonally, showing a versatility of skill if not necessarily a high initial wage or occupational status. Illiterates predominated among men exhibiting this flexibility. One and one-half times as many of them increased earnings in this way as did literate employees, constituting 70% of all increases from $1–$10 and 50% of larger ones (Table 12.5). These wage differentials strikingly demonstrate the abilities of the uneducated to perform several jobs and to benefit directly in their rewards.

Skills of course relate to occupations, a subject of less significance than economic rewards in attempting to evaluate literacy's role. Occupation is also an inadequate measure of class, status, or skill, but still an important issue. As in the larger society, literacy related directly to occupational status in the Hawkesbury operation. The proportions of the literate increased regularly

Table 12.5. *Differentials and literacy*

Change in wages	N^a	%	Percentage literate
− $ 1	2	0.3	50.0
0	605	76.1	57.6
+ 1–5	125	15.7	31.5
6–10	42	5.3	30.9
11–30	20	2.6	50.0

$^a N = 794.$

with occupational class, with large differences separating the nonmanual from the skilled and the skilled from the remainder. These sharp divisions did not, however, carry over into wages, contradicting analyses of social or class structure based solely on occupations, a quite common sociological procedure. In fact, skilled workers were more highly paid than nonmanual ones despite literacy differences, and several semiskilled men attained high salaries. In addition, the obvious factory occupations were not all marked by high levels of literacy. Some illiterates, moreover, were able to achieve higher-ranking occupations; 11% of nonmanual and 36% of skilled workers were unable to sign their names. Blacksmiths, carpenters, cutters, jobbers, millwrights, mechanics, millers, and ironworkers could be illiterate. Though largely disadvantaged in occupation, illiterates held a great variety of jobs and were only slightly disadvantaged in earnings. Their lack of schooling did not significantly restrict them in the pay envelope or pocket.

Ninety-six men, longer-term employees, signed more than one contract. The influence of literacy both on this form of persistence within the firm and on their changes in wage rates advances the argument. Illiterates outnumbered literate workers in this group, and they dominated among those who increased earnings (Table 12.6A). Literacy apparently was not the salient factor; more probably the key was skills and performance about which the ledgers are silent. Illiterates' greater persistence is significant; their wage changes are intriguing. Literacy's importance is seen more in the magnitudes of the changes, as literate workers gained a greater proportion of the larger increases ($11–$18), but also in the larger decreases (Table 12.6B). Illiteracy may have placed restraints once more on mobility, but these limits operated in the directions both of rising and of falling, regulating the frequency of changes.

An analysis of literacy's role in a specific work situation, the Hawkesbury Lumber Company, reveals the limits of illiteracy. These operated largely in the occupational dimension, but much less in wages, flexibility, or salary increments. Literacy related to occupation strongly, but not completely, and very little to remuneration. This case study supports and extends the con-

Table 12.6. *Changing wage rates: employees with two or more contracts*

	Literate	%	Illiterate	%
A. Same rate	9	20.9	7	13.2
Increasing rate	27	62.8	34	64.2
Decreasing rate	7	16.8	12	22.6
Total[a]	43		53	
B. Increase $ 1–5	15	55.6	23	66.7
6–10	7	25.9	10	29.4
11–18	5	18.5	1	2.9
Decrease $ 1–5	4	57.2	9	75.0
6–8	3	42.8	3	25.0

[a]$N = 96$.

clusions from the urban inquiry. The Hawkesbury experience, on the one hand, contradicts the expectations and perceptions of Ryerson and other middle-class school reformers along with one aspect of working class opinion. On the other hand, it provides further support for working class claims that education figures not always or necessarily in work, but could relate more directly to other aspects of life.

IV

In the partly industrial setting of Hawkesbury, literacy did not significantly relate to individual rewards or to job performance; presumably it did not relate to productivity. This section treats the more general question of the connection between education, literacy, and industrialization. Recent research in economic history and development, if far from complete, has begun to contradict the received wisdom and dominant assumption that education is at once central to the process of industrialization and that it must logically precede 'take-off into sustained growth'. This opinion forms yet another part of the literacy myth. Education and economic development, however, need not be seen as collateral or sequential processes. Productivity and wealth do not necessarily follow from mass literacy, as the histories of Sweden and Scotland, for example, firmly demonstrate. Both achieved mass literacy before the nineteenth century, yet remained desperately poor.

The primary issue is confronted by Roger Schofield, who remarks, 'Today literacy is considered to be a necessary precondition for economic development (and this one may question); but the historian might well ask himself whether this was so in England at the end of the eighteenth century' – or, we might add, North America in the nineteenth. Schofield continues:

The necessity of literacy as a precondition for economic growth is a persistent theme running through many UNESCO publications [and a great many others]. Correlations between measures of industrialization and literacy both in the past and in the present are established in UNESCO *World Illiteracy at Mid-Century* (Paris, 1957), pp. 177—89. These measures are very general and throw no light on the question of why literacy should be considered essential to economic growth.[19]

In various studies, C. Arnold Anderson and Mary Jean Bowman, in particular, have attempted to demonstrate the ways in which literacy should be considered essential to economic development. Proceeding from the premise that education is one of the few sure roads to economic growth, they find an increasingly common tendency among economists and governments to 'justify' education in economic terms (as 'human capital'). In 1965, Anderson claimed that 'about 40 percent of adult literacy or of primary enrollment [which should be conceptually distinguished] is a threshold for economic development'. He added, of course, that the level of education alone is an insufficient condition in a society lacking other prerequisites. Throughout the past decade and a half, their position has been qualified and refined, as they continue to stress the necessity, if not the sufficiency, of a 'literacy threshold' for sustained growth or development, a stage to be maintained until a new literacy level, of 70—80% is attained. They have not shown with any precision or direct historical evidence, however, that these thresholds have the significance that is ascribed to them.[20]

Another social scientist has discovered a different explanatory approach to the literacy-and-education—development connection. From his data, David McClelland finds that investment in education at the elementary or literacy level is inadequate and does not correlate positively with growth rates. He argues that:

> Primary school attendance has a doubtful relationship to significant improvements, in the labor force or even to literacy itself. That is, the marginal product of a primary school education would seem likely to be low, because skilled artisans may function as well without being literate. Furthermore, primary school attendance is not enough by itself to lift a person to the level of being able to perform jobs characteristic of the middle class.

A strong relationship, however, derives from postprimary education, if the lag-time between training and its effect on the economy is considered. 'Education is a long-term investment from the economic point of view', McClelland concludes. This approach seems more sound, for an historical context, though problems do remain, especially when it is applied to the industrial revolution. Nevertheless, distinguishing between levels of training, and critically differentiating literacy from higher and more technical education makes more sense when seeking to explicate and understand education's contribution to economic change; literacy alone should not be seen as representing the level of skills that is required for major development.[21]

What about the past, and the transition to the factory itself, in the transformation of modes of production and the work-setting for industrial capitalism? In the most general sense, as John Talbott has remarked, 'in the first decades of industrialization, the factory system put no premium on even low-level intellectual skills. Whatever relationships existed between widespread literacy and early industrial development must have been quite roundabout'.[22] 'Roundabout' is hardly a precise description, but it is an improvement on theories of linear, deterministic causal connections. We can improve upon that description, I believe.

Firstly, contradicting those who argue for the productive value of educated and literate labor's skills, the relationship in the first, English Industrial Revolution was less than roundabout. Early industrialization was disruptive of education, and literacy rates fell or stagnated as a result. There was little demand for new or increased labor skills, and more importantly, the demand for child labor, in England and elsewhere, greatly reduced the chances for a lower-class child to attend school. Factory schools were, on the whole, rare, ineffectual, and very irregularly attended. Secondary education was unheard of for the children of the working class.[23]

The consequence, Roger Schofield and Michael Sanderson have shown, was reflected directly in the literacy rates of late eighteenth- and early nineteenth-century England. Sanderson found that 'the English Industrial Revolution cannot be seen as one nourished by rising educational standards at least at the elementary level', and from more recent research comes broader, comparative support for his conclusions.[24] The stagnation or decline in literacy, which varied regionally, did not impede the upsurge of economic growth, because the nature of this industrialization made very low literacy demands on the educational system. Or, as Schofield explains:

> Thus, insofar as economic growth in this period entailed the acquisition of a large number of practical skills by a growing proportion of the population, developments in literacy and education were probably largely irrelevant to it. And, insofar as economic growth resulted from the increased productivity of labor brought about the shift from domestic to factory production, literacy and education were also probably largely irrelevant for many of the new industrial occupations recruited a mainly illiterate work force.

'Knack', as Sanderson terms it, and new modes of organizing labor in industrial production were of greater importance than book-learning or literacy skills in the process of industrialization.

In the historical case of English industrialization, there are firm grounds on which to part company with those who must relate mass education directly to economic development. England had reached the 40% 'threshold' of literacy by 1750 (at least for males), and it remains for researchers to isolate an exception to that rule of thumb for economic development. Stephens, for one, finds that literacy levels were 'manifestly related to some extent to the economic function' of urban as well as industrial places. Throughout England, towns that experienced industrial development suffered declining literacy levels, as did other, large and growing centers. In France, with later and slower industrial development, the relationship with literacy and schooling, in the Département du Nord, paralleled the English case. Furet and Ozouf conclude that 'not only does modern industrialization not create a demand for skilled labour, it also tends to depress urban literacy rates'. Peter Flora, finally, in a large-scale macroanalysis of literacy and modernization in 94 countries from 1850–1965, discovers that contrary to the typical assumptions, no direct connection existed between literacy and industrialization (or urbanization). Both the linear causal theories and threshold-level notions seem so vague and overly simplistic, as well as so empirically contradictory, as to be meaningless. The relationship of higher levels of education to development requires further detailed study, although postprimary education played no large role at this early stage (unless, however, it contributed to the development of inventors, technological innovators, and entrepreneurs − a very different matter from these traditionally assumed connections with the main labor force). As Schofield aptly expressed it, 'For England, at least [and we may now add 'elsewhere'], the usual causal relationships between literacy and economic growth might probably be reversed. In this alternative perspective the reduction in illiteracy in nineteenth-century England would appear more as a cultural change brought about by economic growth than as the cause of growth.'[25] Reversing traditional explanations is critically important in disentangling these presumed relationships, and in understanding the historical processes of change and development. Attention to the chronological sequence of developments − in industrialization, economic growth, literacy, and education − (as is suggested presently) introduces a conceptualization that fits the historical contexts.

If not education as preparation for productive skilled labor, then what? We must return to the alternative perspective on skills and literacy elaborated above. Sidney Pollard and Edward Thompson, in path-breaking analyses, have shown that the laboring population had to be trained for factory work and taught industrial habits, rules, and rhythms. Traditional social habits and customs did not fit the new patterns and requirements of industrial life; they had to be discredited and replaced with new, 'modern' forms of behavior, intended to transform, in part, the culture of the working class. Literacy could be far from central in the creation of an industrial (or also commercial, urban) workforce, depending on time and circumstance, although its potential for assimilation was soon recognized. As Pollard illustrates, it was not necessarily

the better worker but rather the stable one who was worth more to manufacturers; 'often, indeed, the skilled apprenticed man was at a discount, because
of the working habits acquired before entering a factory'.[26] The problem of
course was one of discipline, as factory-owners experienced great difficulties
in training men to 'renounce their desultory habits of work, and identify
themselves with the unvarying regularity of the complex automation'. Discipline – and new standards of behavior – were required to produce goods on
time. To orient the factory hands to these routines, rules became the norm:
'Work rules, formalized, impersonal and *occasionally printed*, were symbolic
of the new industrial relationships [emphasis added].' No primacy was to be
accorded literacy (here and at first) in solving the most difficult of industrial
capitalism's conundrums.

   To 'educate' the workers was necessary. But it was not an education in
reading and writing; rather it was 'the need to educate the first generation of
factory workers to a new factory discipline, [part of] the widespread belief in
human perfectibility. . . but one of their consequences was the preoccupation
with the character and morals of the working class which are so marked a
feature of the early stages of industrialization'.[27] Toward this end – the
reshaping of character, behavior, morality, and culture – factory owners and
other capitalists joined with social reformers and school promoters (as in
North America) seeking alternative, more effective and efficient approaches
to socialization. Increasingly, we have seen, they turned to public schooling,
literacy transmission, and mass institutions; the timing of the process made
for crucial differences in economic development on the two sides of the
Atlantic.

   Thompson highlights the transition, focusing more closely on the importance of precise and mechanically maintained clock-time in the shift to the
factory. Regardless of the need for literacy to tell time, 'the bell would also
remind men of [time's] passing . . . Sound served better than sight, especially
in the growing manufacturing districts', as the first generation was taught the
new routine by its masters. The schools could also contribute to this training;
they could be useful in inculcating 'time-thrift', among other industrial habits,
notwithstanding that they might give virtually no attention to specific job
skills. Charity schools, for example, were praised for teaching industry,
frugality, order, regularity, and punctuality. By the time children reached six
or seven years of age, they should have been 'habituated, not to say natural-
ized to Labour and Fatigue'; the training of children of the poor was to begin
at age four. In the attempt to establish the hegemony of the school, instruction intervened in working-class culture, to limit its reproduction in the
interests of social order, properly trained labor, and normatively socialized
citizens. From charity and monitorial schools to 'reformed', less coercive
methods in the 1830s, children were taught the moral bases. Kept constantly
occupied, their ceaseless activity in the school was structured by rules and

discipline in the effort to replace 'that unproductive activity called play', as new forms of behavior and conduct represented the approved and rewarded standard. The parallels between the rules of the school and the rules of the factory were not overlooked by manufacturers or educators either: 'Once within the gate, the child entered the new universe of disciplined time . . . Once in attendance, they were under military rule.'[28] Discipline was modified with time, especially with the further articulation of the moral bases of literacy; both the school and the factory became important agents for productivity and social change, in reciprocal yet subtle balance.

In England, the value of formal education was increasingly recognized. Literacy, it was grasped, could ease the transition and assimilation of the working class and the poor to industrial and 'modern' social habits, if provided in carefully structured institutions. To destroy traditional attitudes, culture, and habits of work was far from an easy or simple task, as many researchers have discovered. Nor was it accomplished in one generation or without great conflict. 'Coercion,' John Harrison summarizes, 'had to be applied in various forms, from strict factory rules to the inculcation [in schools] of precepts of self-discipline.' The latter of course were more effective and efficient in dealing with an increasing population at a time of great change; it also permitted an attempt at the reformation of adults through the inculcation of morality and self-restraints in the children. As a result, the process of assimilation was closely tied to the spread of literacy.[29] Literacy's importance can not be understood in isolation, or in terms of self-advancement or skills; rather, its significance lies in its relation to the transmission of morals, discipline, and social values. As R.P. Dore concluded for a different culture, Tokugawa, Japan:

> But what does widespread literacy do for a developing country? At the very least it constitutes a training in being trained. The man who has in childhood submitted to some processes of disciplined and conscious learning is more likely to respond to further training, be it in a conscript army, in a factory, or at lectures arranged by his village agricultural association.[30]

Training in being trained, as Dore aptly puts it, is the crucial job-preparation and a problem for industrialism. The English example is instructive in this respect, yet the North American experience differed greatly in timing and in the sequence of change. England industrialized well before literacy reached universal proportions (not very much beyond a 40% 'threshold'); formal education was not an integral part of the origins of her transition, and there is little role for a lag-time for educational investments in *early* industrialization. The transition to the factory and industrial capitalism was far from easy — marked by intense conflict, violence, riots, strikes, Luddism, Chartism. Mass schooling tended to follow this first set of changes; its impact was felt later.

On the contrary, North American development, particularly Canadian industrialization, but also that in the United States, came comparatively much later. Importantly, it followed the attainment of near-universal levels of literacy (among the white population) and the establishment and expansion of public systems for mass elementary education (though not much secondary schooling). As the result of the timing – and the linkages on several levels – between changes that were not merely chronologically coincidental, literacy and schooling were intimately related to social and economic development. Alexander Field's Massachusetts case study provides the best analysis available thus far, although it is not flawless. In this, the earliest North American industrial revolution, Field shows that manufacturers actively supported and participated in educational reform and expansion in efforts to resolve the social tensions arising from change and to secure a properly socialized work force, and not a more highly skilled one. Their reasons for promoting education were social as well as economic (the two were inextricably linked) in their response to the perceived need to confront the difficulties of the transformation. To protect society and property, as well as to organize, control, and increase production, they sought – with the school promoters themselves – more moral, orderly, disciplined, deferential, and contented workers: the expected result of the hegemony of the moral economy of literacy. Schooling of course also contributed more broadly to the socialization and formation of the urban, but nonindustrial workforce. In much of North America, moreover, education *preceded* industrialism. While other detailed case studies are urgently required, widely scattered evidence, from educational, working-class, and economic history illustrates the importance of the earlier reform of education in North America and its impact on socioeconomic development.[31]

Therefore, I advance the hypothesis that the transition to both commercial and industrial capitalism in North America was a smoother one than in England, and perhaps elsewhere.[32] Without ignoring or diminishing the significance of conflict and resistance, which certainly were present, their potential may well have been reduced as one direct consequence of the comparatively earlier and more extensive educational development and its intimate reciprocal relationship to economic change and industrialization. Schooling, in this formulation, paved the way for economic transformation, pointing to the function of lag-time at the elementary level. Industrial development apparently did not have the same destructive impact on education either. We also know that North American educational reformers and manufacturers were aware of the problems taking place abroad, and without assigning the conspiratorial or omniscient roles such as would belie their very real confusion and fears, we can allow that they benefited from the English experience and from their not having to face the 'first' Industrial Revolution.[33] This was one key purpose of the education that Ryerson and other middle-class reformers promoted, as they sought to school the masses in the cause of social and national development and greater productivity.

To do so, it was essential to break preindustrial work habits, to 'Canadianize' or 'Americanize' immigrants and workers, removing them from traditional origins and habits. The transmission of literacy in the interests of cognitive skills was of secondary importance. Literacy, though, in its contribution to proper education and its relationship to noncognitive training was central to schooling. Print literacy had important socializing functions, both direct and indirect ones; literacy training, for example, served to regularize and discipline behavior. So, in North America, education could replace some of the coercion of English labor to strict factory rules and internalized self-discipline. In the long run, education was more effective and efficient than overt coercion; certainly, it was less disruptive. The provision of mass schooling; the working class' acceptance of it, though a questioning one; and universal, public education all served in this direction: promoting discipline, morality, and the 'training in being trained' that mattered most in the creation and preparation of a modern industrial and urban work force. These were the purposes of the school – and one use of literacy.[34]

13   THE IMPACT OF THE SCHOOLS,
PROVENCE 1871–1914*

Tony Judt

No discussion of the coming of compulsory education in France would be complete without an initial consideration of the accompanying religious issue, but for the student of political change both imply the eventual question, how important *was* education in determining political choice? This question is all the more worth asking in that it was, as I have suggested, the consideration which lay behind the obsession of nineteenth-century radicals and their opponents with controlling the organisation and content of the school system.

Considerable attention has been paid in recent years to this question, and more specifically to the rôle played by a growing literacy in populations formerly unable to read and write. The apparently obvious assumption, that economic backwardness and illiteracy go hand in glove, and that together they provide an unfavourable context for radical politics, turns out to be false, on at least two counts. In the first place, areas of economic and social backwardness or isolation were often, as we have seen, regions where the influence of the Church was strong. But before the last third of the nineteenth century, the Church was the major source of whatever education was available to the poor. As a result, remote rural areas of strong religious practice were not necessarily regions of highest illiteracy.

Secondly, literacy and radicalisation or even politicisation seem not to have had a very marked historical relationship. This is partly for the reason just suggested – that literacy could often be a function of an active local Church; partly too, through the means by which politics and new ideas came to rural areas, means which did not necessarily exclude the illiterate.

The data in support of such arguments are extensive. Michel Vovelle, discussing the spread of *sociétés populaires* in Provence in the Year II, observes the 'paradoxale divergence du pourcentage des sociétés et du taux d'alphabétisation'. Paul Bois, in his study of the Sarthe, takes care to emphasise the high degree of *scolarisation* in the western fringe of the department – that area where religious practice and conservative politics were most pronounced. In modern Spain, Edward Malefakis has observed that illiteracy was at its highest in those areas where the Church's influence was least pronounced – and where a weak and unconcerned state did not provide compensating facilities. He also points out that these areas are the very ones where revol-

*Reprinted from *Socialism in Provence, 1871–1914: A Study in the Origins of the Modern French Left* by Tony Judt, 187–99, by permission of the publisher, Cambridge University Press, © Cambridge University Press, 1979.

utionary sentiment would have been at its most strong in the Spanish Second Republic of the 1930s. In the Mâconnais, a high level of dechristianisation (by the standard measure of church attendance) was accompanied by a high incidence of illiteracy among nineteenth-century conscripts. Finally, there is the well-documented case of mountain communities; isolated, poor, usually firmly religious and politically conservative or uninterested, they demonstrate a remarkably consistent and high level of literacy, ever since records have been kept. There are special reasons for this, of course – the very isolation tends to an emphasis on education during the winter months, the children not being required for any more productive employment. But as in other instances cited above, we are seeing an example of the impossibility of establishing any sort of simple correlation between religious practice, educational standards and political options.[1]

Bearing this caveat in mind, what was the impact of education on the populations of the Var at this period? Taken on a departmental scale, it appears to have been rather successful. Whereas 6% of the conscript class of 1901 in France were *illettrés*, I calculate that only 3.6% of the 1899 conscripts from the Var (1901 figures not available) were unable to sign their name, although some of these could read, or so it was claimed. Of course the intra-departmental variations were considerable. Table 13.1 shows the official survey of the 1899 conscripts, arranged by canton. From this list it emerges that, by the end of the nineteenth century, most young men in the region could read and write, though few had achieved the distinction of passing the certificate of primary education. It is also clear that, although some isolated and poor regions such as Comps had a high degree of illiteracy, and some Radical or socialist areas such as Barjols had a higher than average percentage of literate conscripts, there is absolutely no correlation between literacy and political behaviour. The canton of Grimaud had a particularly high number of illiterate conscripts – yet three of the five communes in the canton (La Garde Freinet, Plan de la Tour and Grimaud itself) appear on my list of Socialist strongholds. The canton of Cuers, first bastion of Provençal socialism, had a degree of illiteracy well above both the local and national average – but so did Lorgues, a traditionally conservative canton and with a well-established religious community.

Conscript data, while reliable, tell us only about the male youth of a community, the beneficiaries of the Ferry legislation. What of the older generation? We do have some evidence regarding the degree of literacy of the adult population, but it is based on returns completed by local officials, often mayors, and is thus of questionable value. But for what it is worth, we learn that, for example, 54% of the men and 38% of the women in Comps (the commune, not the canton) could read and write in 1872. In Le Luc the figures were 37% and 31% respectively. In Les Salles they were lower still – in 1872 only 21% of the men and 10% of the women were deemed to be

Table 13.1. *Literacy of Var conscripts in 1899*

Canton	Totally illiterate	Able to read but not write
Draguignan	3.1%	0
Aups	0	0
Callas	3.4%	3.4%
Comps	7.1%	7.0%
Fayence	0	1.9%
Fréjus	2.8%	0
Grimaud	9.3%	0
Lorgues	7.7%	0
Le Luc	3.8%	1.9%
St Tropez	0	2.8%
Salernes	2.9%	0
Brignoles	4.9%	0
Barjols	2.0%	0
Besse	0	0
Cotignac	4.8%	0
Rians	6.7%	0
Le Roquebrussanne	3.7%	0
St Maximin	1.7%	0
Tavernes	0	0
Toulon (1e)	3.6%	0.7%
Toulon (2e)	0.8%	0
Le Beausset	4.4%	0
Collobrières	0	0
Cuers	7.8%	0
Hyères	2.5%	2.5%
Ollioules	1.6%	0
La Seyne	3.1%	0
Solliès Pont	5.7%	0

Average percentage of children completing primary education in the Var

Arrondissement	1889	1899
Draguignan	61.0%	81.9%
Brignoles	72.5%	78.2%
Toulon (rural)	63.0%	68.5%
Toulon (city)	73.5%	82.2%

Sources: 'Degré d'instruction des conscrits 1899', *Archives Nationales*, F[17] 14270; *Le Petit Var* 30 December 1889.

literate. Comps of course was a very conservative area, Les Salles and Le Luc bastions of socialism in later years. But in case we were tempted to posit a link between literacy and conservatism, we are reminded that in Tanneron, high on its hill in the east and never noted for its left-wing sympathies, only 26% of the men could read and write in 1872. As for the women, a mere

2.9% (12/404) were classed as literate. We thus learn that the agglomerated communes of the valley such as Le Luc show a much lower differential between male and female literacy than do the villages of the hills (the figures quoted are representative of many other examples), but that otherwise literacy is a poor guide to anything, certainly a hopeless guide to political leanings, likely or actual.

We can be fairly certain, however, that certain kinds of habitat and certain sorts of economy were more or less favourable to educational progress. Dispersed habitats posed a difficulty of transport. Of the 24 schools whose construction was deemed a matter of urgency in 1900, nearly all were in regions of dispersed habitat. Thus there was no school in the hamlet of Les Anges in the commune of Aiguines, a region of very scattered population. Yet 217 of the 549 inhabitants of Aiguines lived in or around Les Anges, and their school-age children had to travel 14 kilometres each way to attend the nearest primary school – which few of them did, understandably enough. Other areas affected in this way were La Martre in the north, the interior hamlets of the Maures, and many of the villages in the Seillans–Callian district in the east-central region of the department.

Economic considerations also counted. Unlike the Alpine villages with their winter period of inactivity, the communes of the lower Var especially had need of labour for much of the year. In Cuers it was rare for the children of the peasantry to attend school in late February on account of the exigencies of the olive harvest. The semi-skilled labour of a young adolescent in the *vinicole* areas was much too precious to waste on an education which in any case bore little relation either to his environment or his future concerns. Thus observers in Le Cannet, for example, a region which combined dispersed habitat with intense cultivation of the vine, affected to be quite astonished at the success of compulsory school attendance in their commune. Notwithstanding the distances involved and the interests of the domestic economy, children were attending school with 'remarkable' regularity.

A further local barrier to the effective implementation of a modern system of education was that of language. As in many parts of France, a national system of *French* education was being imposed on a population whose natural form of communication was a local dialect or language. Thus Provençal came to be the language of the uneducated, French that of the young. This has a distorting effect on statistics of literacy, of course – many older men and women especially could read Provençal but not French; indeed not a few of them must have experienced great difficulty in simply handling questionnaires and official enquiries phrased in bureaucratic French. It is tempting to suppose that, after the initial difficulties experienced by the first generation of children who passed through the primary schools, a distinction developed between the young who spoke French and had access to new ideas, and the old, held back by their inability to communicate in the national language. In fact this appears not to have been the case: partly no doubt because some impact had been made by the primary schools which dated from the Guizot legislation of the 1830s, but more because, in the Var at least, the long-standing links to the outside world, through trade and communications, had reduced the importance of Provençal relative to that of French, at least in the urban villages of the lower Var. The language question was clearly much more important in every way in the Languedoc or the Pyrenees, not to mention Alsace or Brittany. In Provence the conflict over language was linked with an atavistic and in any case largely literary movement associated with the poet Mistral, and it is significant that as an issue it never surfaced in the propaganda of the socialists – though there is some evidence that a number of local socialist groups conversed in Provençal at their meetings. This confirms my sense that socialists' supporters were often older men, and casts further doubt on the hypothesis of a division between Provençal traditionalists and politically advanced francophones.[2]

Despite the dust which it aroused, then, the conflict over the control of education, once reduced to a question of measuring the results of the chief benefit of education at this level – literacy – seems not to have been in the least bit crucial. The Var, like the Limousin, offers no evidence of a relationship between literacy and political tendencies, nor does the degree of education available appear to have varied in any way as a function of political considerations. Just as the clerically-dominated, *notable*-run communes of Comps in the north or Fréjus on the coast varied sharply in the degree of literacy of the youth emerging from their schools, so the politically-advanced town of Le Luc boasted a Cercle founded in 1887 which would be active in socialist politics, and half of whose 26 members signed their adhesion with a mark. I cannot, then, accept Roger Price's conclusion (admittedly in reference to an earlier period) that commerce, Protestantism, good communications and a relatively high degree of literacy tend 'to a high level of political awareness'. Or, more accurately, I can only find evidence of the first and third elements in such tendencies in Provence at least. The fact that the Var was traditionally an area of relatively high illiteracy seems in no way to have reduced its various forms of political awareness; the northern Var certainly conforms to a limited type – neither Provençal nor genuinely Alpine, but a 'société Alpine dégradée', lacking the communal solidarity and the traditions of education of the true Alpine community, but also bereft of the compensating sociability of the bourgs down below. But we have seen that there are exceptions even here – and in any case a linear relationship (isolation – clerical hegemony – low literacy – conservative politics) has little heuristic value without evidence of its inverse in the valleys. And such evidence is not forthcoming.[3]

Of course, there is more to education than mere literacy. Also at issue was the content of what was being offered to children by way of instruction, irrespective of whether or not they could read it for themselves. Hence such incidents as the outburst by the *curé* of Vins in 1880 against the textbook in use at the local primary school, the *Eléments d'éducation civique et morale*, and his warning to parents to burn it and withdraw their children from any school where it was in use. The debate over the content of the educational syllabus raged throughout this period, and it was a real conflict, concerning as it did the means by which competing ruling élites strove to impose their ideological domination upon a newly-educated and socialised mass electorate.

But such issues are not strictly my concern. They are, after all, perennial sources of conflict, and in a rather changed guise they informed much of the educational dispute in France during the 1960s. I am more concerned with a narrower question, concerning the ways by which a political doctrine takes root in the consciousness and political habits of a given region and social class. Since, clearly, there was no question of socialism being presented as a dominant ideology, in the schools or from the pulpit, what mattered were less formal, more voluntaristic forms of 'indoctrination'. Thus my interest in the growth of compulsory primary education in France lies in the extent to which it gave to peasants the tools required for access to modern political communications. But the attainment of literacy appears in itself not to have been a significant prerequisite for radical politicisation. How, then, did the rural populations of the Var gain access to modern ideas? By what means did they absorb the doctrines which would move them in a particular political direction?

Artisans, peasants and politics

For most of human history, myths, popular tales and the like have been transmitted orally. The advent of the printing press changed little, since access to the printed word, both in terms of availability and comprehension, remained the privilege of a tiny minority of even the most advanced societies. It was through the long fireside sessions of the winter, therefore, that peasant women passed on old stories and popular wisdom to their children and grandchildren, and by means of informal social intercourse in fields and village squares that men acquainted themselves and one another with occupational skills and such news as filtered through to their remote communities.

The coming of a modern system of education did not bring about any substantial or immediate changes. Literacy, measured by the minimum standards which were applied in the early years of the primary school, did little to ensure a person's ability to read a newspaper, much less a book. By the middle of the nineteenth century, it is true, the availability of popular literature was much expanded, and in France especially there was quite an active trade in popular almanacs, simple novels and (where permitted) political pamphlets. Nevertheless, these, particularly the last, were never read or even seen by the vast majority of the population. Their sales were understandably greater in artisanal towns and (to a lesser degree) industrial cities; not so much because of any higher level of literacy, particularly in the cities, but rather through a greater degree of opportunity. Modern forms of lighting took a long time to reach the private dwellings of the remote countryside – gas lighting was comparatively unknown in many mountain areas of France even at the very end of the nineteenth century, and as for electricity, it would not reach even some quite accessible parts of the country until the last years of the Third Republic.[4]

And yet, there is little doubt but that much modern thinking, suitably popularised, was entering the consciousness of the peasantry in some parts of France; Provence is a notable example. The first explanation for this relates to earlier observations concerning sociability. It was the very proximity to one another and to the outside world which established for the populations of the Var, from quite an early date, their links with political propaganda and the like.

The link between a peasantry 'vivant urbain' and modern ideas and movements of protest was the café, or in earlier years the *chambrée*, where many, often a majority, of the local working population would meet, sometimes in lunch-breaks, usually in the evenings and on Sundays, to drink and talk. But not just to drink and talk. A centrepiece of many such gatherings was the reading aloud by one of their number of the newspaper to which the *patron*, or perhaps a prominent (and slightly wealthier) member of the society subscribed. Such readings were often lengthy affairs, whole articles being read out with care, often accompanied by a commentary from the reader, his audience or both. Few of the assembled number could have afforded to subscribe to the journal in question, nor would they have thought of so doing. The chances were high that they would have had difficulty in making sense of much of the French (the commentary not infrequently took the form of a translation), but in any case such things were traditionally and best done in a group. Private reading was (and of course remains) an essentially unsocial activity and thus ran counter to the dominant habits of the Provençal community.

The newspaper, and the arguments which accompanied and followed its public perusal, was thus in some sense the 'collective organiser' of populations which it helped to politicise. The rôle is well documented for such periods of rapid and acute political development in the provinces – such as the Second Republic. But the increased prominence of the café, and the liberty of expression and of the press enjoyed after 1880, meant that the rôle of public readings, far from diminishing, probably increased, at least until the early twentieth century.[5]

At this point we encounter a fascinating and tricky problem. *Who* were these readers? *Their* literacy and knowledge, the respect which their opinions earned for them, surely made them vital intermediaries between national politics, strange and new doctrines and theories, and the community of which they were a part but which they also stood just a little outside. One theory is that this vital rôle in the politicisation of the peasantry was performed by rural artisans. In much of France the period 1840–80 had seen the decline in status and means of the traditional artisan. In many trades and skills, the artisan had retained the form of his work – cottage or workshop rather than modern factory – but had seen it deprived of much of its content. He was now not very different from the cottage worker, taking on out-work from merchants or manufacturers, specialising in part of a given product rather than in the manufacture of the whole item, paid by the piece and often short of work for periods of the year. Alternatively his skills might have been pre-served, but his income diminished by direct competition from large-scale urban manufacture, in France or abroad. In either case, his reaction might plausibly have been to turn to various forms of social protest – of which cooperation was a favourite – and, in rural areas, to try and carry with him the surrounding peasantry.

Thus Maurice Agulhon suggests that whereas in the early nineteenth cen-tury artisan leadership of radical movements was confined to the small com-munes of hills and forests, while the liberal bourgeoisie dominated political protest in lower Provence, by the later years the village bourgeoisie having dis-appeared, the artisanat played the central rôle in the political conflicts of the early Third Republic. But this view of the matter has its own problems. We know that in many of the most radicalised villages the artisanat itself was a disappearing class; what is more, many rural artisans (shoemakers, carpenters, cork-workers, even tanners and millers) might equally be described as part-time peasants. Their leadership, if such it was, thus came in some sense as much from within the peasant community as from an educated and distinct class of skilled craftsmen. In rural areas, particularly in Provence where rural occupation and urban habitat overlap so much, the occupational distinctions are often without much meaning.[6]

Agulhon would seem to be inferring for the later period a pattern of social relations which really only fits a slightly earlier era. In 1851 there is absolutely no doubt but that artisans both took the lead and formed a substantial part of the following in the Montagnard movement of that year. In the arrests which followed the insurrection in the Var, artisans (52.6%) were dispropor-tionately over-represented, just as the local bourgeoisie were notable for their absence (4.9%). Even allowing for selective arresting by the authorities, these are relevant data. Similarly, Bezucha's observation of a high level of literacy among the *canuts* of Lyon in the 1830s is obviously important – in artisanal circles within cities such as Lyon there was a high degree of participation and educated political awareness, for example among the protesting silk-workers, and in these early modern revolts the skilled artisanat played a central rôle.[7]

But in later years the pattern is rather different. It was only the most economically backward or isolated communities which appear to have been dependent upon leadership coming 'down' to them from above – either in the form of advice and direction from the local wise-men in Andalusia, or from the distinctly better educated and more socially independent black-smiths or masons of the Alps and the Limousin. By the 1880s the artisan was the vital political link only in the most archaic and closed economies, where the peasantry by themselves lacked means and will to mobilise collectively. In the open communities of lower Provence, the peasantry seem not to have needed such leadership by the end of the nineteenth century – doubtless in part because it was no longer readily available. Thus the complex artisanal base of the population of Lorgues seems to have had no discernible radicalising effect on the surrounding peasantry, while the Cercle des Travailleurs in Cuers in 1876 was already 83% (33/40) peasant.[8]

This is not to deny that the man reading the newspaper in a village café may very well have been at one time a skilled artisan of some kind – perhaps still was. In the same way, the peasantry of the Beaujolais often met and held their discussions in the local forge – with the surprising result that black-smiths emerged frequently at the head of political movements in the region, bonapartist and republican alike. But herein lies the crucial point. Because of their natural advantages and status, artisans not infrequently served as the focus for political life in many rural communities – *but* the precise direction in which they led their peasant following was not thereby determined. The political prominence of the artisan, that is to say, was not a function of what he had to say, but of who he was and what he did. It was circumstances and political developments in a wider sphere which brought the peasantry to pro-test movements, to radical clubs and socialist groups. That we often then find prominent within these organisations the informal dominance of one or more local tradesmen or master craftsmen is a result of the advantage they enjoyed in being able to convey news to the illiterate and spread ideas rapidly among their colleagues in the shop. But the presence of a peasant audience for what they had to say was only very indirectly a result of their own achievements. In the Limousin, rural artisans played an important politicising rôle – but they were also the major source of recruits into the Church.[9]

Thus, in sum, the informal leaders of village discussions and political meet-ings were frequently men whose primary occupation set them apart from their audience in respect of their work and their education. But what they actually said and advocated in these meetings was almost always a reflection of the interests and concerns of their (peasant) audience. I shall not consider this point in more detail here[10] but it is worth noting here that in Flayosc, for example, where there was a heavy concentration of *cordonniers*, masters and employees, the socialist Cercle in 1891 was understandably dominated by their presence (the president was a young man – aged 26 – and skilled: a cutter). But the peasant members of the society seem not to have been at any kind of disadvantage thereby, and the emphasis on cooperation, attacks on high food prices, and sympathy for collective solutions to problems were areas of wide mutual agreement. In so far as artisans led and peasants followed, this must only be construed in the purely formal and organisational sense – and even there it was of limited applicability. So far as the content of such gatherings was concerned, the socialism of the Var was no less a reflection of the peasantry's interests and preoccupations for being occasionally refracted through an artisanal prism.

In this way, then, education and its by-products were important sources of friction within the village community during these years. But the direct link between peasant interest and political literature and ideas was very little affected by the fact that educational reforms were slow to have much impact upon the rural community. To suggest otherwise is to diminish the independence and autonomy of rural society. Just as in the early nineteenth century the peasantry had reacted in atavistic ways for reasons and from fears of their own, acknowledging and needing the leadership of artisans and bourgeois to strengthen the cohesion of inherently disparate rural protests, so in the economic crisis of the last years of the century the Provençal farmers developed their own awareness of a necessity for radical change, their own resentment at their reduced income and prospects. They, too, required an artisanat which could serve as a source of information and education and sometimes of organisation. But they imposed their own needs upon the shoemakers, masons, carpenters and blacksmiths in their villages, making demands upon them, insisting that they subscribe to a particular journal or explain a particular issue, rather than responding passively to the views of the artisans. Nor is this very surprising – by the 1880s many rural artisans had departed, and those who remained were much impoverished, reduced in professional status and totally dependent upon the local community, whose problems they thus shared to the full. They spoke much of the Church, of education, of cooperation and of the need for legislation in various fields. But their audience filtered out the traditional, Radical dogma, taking heed instead of the increasing social element which was entering such political debate. In this way one might almost suggest that, the traditional leadership and access to ideas of the small-town artisan notwithstanding, it was the peasantry which brought the latter to socialism, and not the other way round.

14   LITERACY, EDUCATION AND SCHOOLING – FOR WHAT?*

Johan Galtung

1. Introduction

What would happen if the whole world became literate? Answer: not so very much, for the world is by and large structured in such a way that it is capable of absorbing the impact. But if the whole world consisted of literate, autonomous, critical, constructive people, capable of translating ideas into action, individually or collectively – the world would change. And this is, by and large, the topic to be explored in the present paper.

To do so it may be useful to start out with the distinction between schooling and education that is now rapidly becoming commonplace. This is no sharp dichotomy, schooling obviously serves some educational purpose, but there is, and should be, a concept of education much broader than that which is served by schooling, at present. More particularly, there are important dimensions along which schooling may be said to dilute, even pervert the richer concept of education. And literacy, the major focus of this paper, stands in an interesting in-between position: it can serve as a launching pad for schooling, but it can also be one among several points of departure for education more broadly conceived of.

Let us then proceed with these dimensions along which the schooling-education dilemma can be said to be located. They can conveniently be divided into two parts: form and content, the structure of schooling, vs. the content of that which is transmitted.

2. The schooling paradigm

Structurally speaking, there is little doubt that the entire institution of schooling, as we know it, is *vertical* and *individualistic*. The unit to be schooled is the individual: he or she is the receptacle of knowledge, the unit that moves from one class or school to the other, that performs and ultimately achieves and receives diploma and graduates. And the system is permeated from micro to macro levels with all kinds of verticality: pupils are ranked within classes; classes are ranked by numbers (grades) and often also by letters (the A class and B class of the same grade may be as different in level as the A classes of second and third grades, for instance); schools are ranked

*Reprinted from Johan Galtung, 'Literacy, education and schooling – for what?', in *A Turning Point for Literacy: Adult Education for Development*, ed. Léon Bataille, 93–105, by permission of the publisher, Pergamon Press Ltd., © Pergamon Press Ltd., 1976.

very clearly as conveying primary, secondary and tertiary (also called 'higher') education; but schools are also ranked qualitatively within countries with the best in the center and the poorest in the periphery; and between countries with the best in the Center countries and the poorest in the Periphery countries. There is a corresponding verticality among teachers: the social distance between the professor at a university in the center of a Center country and the village teacher at the lowest grades of a primary school in the periphery of a Periphery country is about the same – we should imagine – as the corresponding difference between their pupils.

Hence, if somebody wanted the schooling system to serve as a tool for placing people in niches in a society that is predominantly vertical and individualistic – the liberal society fostered by the European post-Renaissance tradition, and particularly by the post-Enlightenment, tempered with industrial capitalism – then the system is well constructed. In fact, it is probably too good, for it is much more rational than the society at large. It can be seen as one enormous sorting device absorbing each year new millions of small children, processing hundreds of millions one more step till they either graduate at some level, with some note hung around their necks, or drop out. The system proceeds on the basis of the theory of innate ability combined with the built-in social injustice: the higher one comes up this ladder the better one's life chances, and society is not going to ask too many questions about whether this was because one was favored from the very beginning, e.g. by being born in the center of the Center, or because of innate superior qualities; if such exist at all.

However that may be, the system grinds out a humanity sorted into categories consistent with the way the world economic system divides the same humanity, through all the mechanisms known as 'division of labor', into those who extract something relatively directly from nature, those who process it and those who distribute it and administer this whole process. And by and large these three sectors of economic activity, the primary, secondary and tertiary sectors, receive their 'human resources' from the primary, secondary and tertiary levels of schooling, respectively; when by 'secondary schooling' we also mean vocational, post-elementary schools; and by 'tertiary schooling' we also mean any type of schooling beyond the secondary level. Hence, *schooling is power* because high position in division of labor is power, not only in the trivial sense of by and large being better paid, but also in the sense of having terribly important spin-off effects: often more challenging work, the right to define and prescribe the work of others, easier on-the-job access to other people and other types of activity, easier access to other spheres of society, among them politics. Just think of how a village peasant is tied to a very limited range of activity, compared to a free-floating expert – without glorifying the latter, the difference in impact on their surroundings is considerable, and schooling is the legitimizer of the power of the latter as much as lack of schooling justifies the misery and powerlessness of the former.

In all this there is, of course, the pervasive myth of schooling as the road to mobility, to be trodden by the ambitious, talented and industrious individual. What is not so clearly seen is how this mobility is limited by the constraints set by national and international division of labor. It does not help much to have a certificate from secondary and tertiary schooling if the country only offers job opportunities in the primary and secondary sectors of the economy; unless, that is, the country is in a position of power to adjust its economy so as to fit the schooling delivery system. The countries on top of the international division of labor (by and large those with a high GNP *per capita* since GNP measures essentially degree of processing and marketing) are gradually abolishing the primary sector of the economy, mechanizing and industrializing it and having it carried out in other countries (which deliver raw materials and foodstuffs for processing) thus making secondary and tertiary school graduates more functional, even indispensable. And the countries at the bottom will, precisely for this reason, have difficulties finding jobs for these graduates who, consequently, will engage in brain drain to the countries where their skills can be used because of the division of labor structure. But only few can engage in geographical mobility in order to convert schooling into social mobility − for the majority this is not possible.

Consequently, major contradiction will develop: sooner or later the hungry and angry masses of the Periphery countries will join hands with the educated élite without meaningful jobs and get out of the division of labor and into some pattern of local, national and collective self-reliance. In that case, the Periphery countries will have much to gain, and so with the Center countries which will have to rediscover the primary sectors inside their own countries and overcome the contradiction between that type of work and a pattern of schooling that has emerged whereby several of these countries have between one-third and one-half of the age cohort in tertiary education. In all probability this formula, self-reliance, will also contain some of the basis for a cure to the overdevelopment of the Center countries, just as self-reliance seems to be the new word for the development of the underdeveloped countries.

We mention all this because it belongs to the context in which problems of literacy will have to be understood: it is a clearly economic and political context, domestically as well as globally. And this context also explains some of the *content* of schooling: it is basically knowledge-oriented and basically theoretical − except for the vocational schools. In other words, there is a schooling concept dominating the educational horizon which is predominantly *verbal*, and predominantly geared towards a type of knowledge held to be *uncontroversial*. That type of knowledge, by definition, has to be on the conservative side. To the extent that it is empirical knowledge (e.g. history, geography, natural science of various kinds), it deals with that which *is* rather than that which *might* be to the extent that it contains normative knowledge (religious studies, national myths) it is not likely to instill doubts and to the extent that it deals with instrumental subjects (languages, mathematics and literacy for that matter) they are also seen as unalterable – as it may be argued that to some extent they are (at the very least, one should not change somebody else's language!). The task of schooling seems to be to fill as much as possible of these things into the heads of the pupils, thereby creating people who are as similar as possible. The school is used to reinforce the nation where there is one, to create one where there was none in advance, like in the United States or the Soviet Union.

This immediately spills over into the structure. The type of content mentioned here is entirely compatible with the verticality and the individualism mentioned. As long as the content is so verbal and so knowledge-oriented the superiority of the teacher is almost guaranteed and protected; for it takes some years to accumulate factual knowledge and verbal skills to communicate them. Some children may be almost born with practical skills that emerge and develop very quickly when given the opportunity – and the same may be the case with mathematics and the languages – but hardly with the most fact-oriented subjects. Of course, experience always makes for some verticality, but more in some fields than in others.

Moreover, to memorize things is or can be a totally lonely thing; there is no need for any communication among the pupils at all, nor for any discussion; the receptacles are just being filled, occasionally tapped to check the quality of the knowledge liquid. More particularly, one would not expect any chain effect to arise from schooling, with children running home from the school house, eager to communicate the important findings of that day, to others in the family, to friends, to neighbors – so filled with it that it has to be discussed and tested in some kind of practice. Just to the contrary, one would expect children to separate schooling and the rest of their life into rather watertight compartments, schooling being a very special form of life, relatively unrelated to the rest. This, in turn, has one rather disastrous consequence: since people tend to identify education with schooling, and society tends to support this, they also feel that education ends when schooling is over. They study no more because they have no teachers to check them, and real dialogue they never learnt anyhow.

3. The education paradigm

Let us now contrast this with an image of what education could be. Of course, it is easy to negate everything said above and paint a rosy image of something abstract called 'education' – the problem is to make this image clear, vivid and compelling, partly by means of examples, partly by concrete ideas, and strategies. And that is not easy because it is by no means clear what 'education' stands for. Who is educated, for instance? You? I? Try to think of a person you would call educated — what are the characteristics of that person?

In asking such a question a difficulty of linguistic nature shows up: 'educated' in English is relatively close in meaning to 'schooled', as is *ausgebildet* in German — English does not have the equivalent of the German *gebildet* (Norwegian *dannet*, as opposed to *utdannet*). This concept, on the other hand, has a very bourgeois connotation of somehow belonging to the good class, with nice manners. But it has also some other content which is what we shall draw upon here.

First of all, there is something *autonomous* in the concept of education, something creative and very different from passive receptivity. On the other hand, how does one reconcile the need to receive, at some stage, with the need for autonomy? The answer is obvious: through *dialogue*, and through *self-study*, the two obvious methods of education. The dialogue can be with teachers, with equals, with pupils — as long as it is dialogue and discussion it does not matter so much for that form will in and by itself wash out much of the verticality. Third, and closely related to this: the educated person goes in for *sharing* — an insight is not a private property, but something to be communicated to enrich others, and — through dialogue — to be enriched by them in turn. Fourth, and this is where it would differ from the bourgeois concept: the educated person might go in for the most esoteric subjects but would also be *relevant*, which means that there would be an element of praxis built into the concept of education. *Through schooling the individual is on trial; in education society is on trial* — that may be one way of formulating the difference, and also the simple reason why the societal establishment — right, left or middle — will prefer the former and the anti-establishment the latter, and also why schooling and education will always be dialectically related, in the same way, and paralleling the dialectics between establishment and anti-establishment.

What does this mean concretely in terms of structure and content of education, as opposed to schooling? Less verticality, less individualism, less emphasis on knowledge, less emphasis on verbalism; more dialogue of all kinds, more shared growth, more discussion of values and strategies, more praxis. It is hard not to think of the image we have of education in classical Greece, of citizens combining education and politics using dialogue as the major instrument of either, or another example would be schooling in a People's Commune in China, much closer, it seems, to the Greek ideal than schooling in, for instance, Greece today.

Out of all this let us now pick one element: the notion of 'knowledge'. This is absolutely fundamental, and it is probably relatively safe to say that knowledge presented in at least lower schools is presented as something relatively terminal. The students may be given the idea that further on there is knowledge of a less certain kind, but there are certain fundaments on which to build – and here are some of them for you to *learn*, not to learn how to question. Thus, schools are not known for telling their students how even the most innocent looking arithmetic already has built into so much of Western time concepts (students learn that 5 + 9 = 14, but for a farmer concerned with his work 5 + 9 = 2, if 5 stands for the fifth month, 9 for nine months, and 2 for February – and so it does for a girl who gets pregnant in the month of May: the annual cycle reflects social life better than Western uni-linear time); and capitalist money concepts (students learn that $a+b = b+a$ and are not told that when translated into financial deals this means that the order is unimportant, only the amount, which is another way of cutting down on all kinds of social decorum in favor of a purely quantitative approach to life). Nor do they usually lead up to any discussion of how the language they are taught will structure their thinking – it is taken as an undisputable fact, like the rise of the Sun and the position of the stars.

Instead of the schooling paradigm of knowledge as something about which there is consensus, more or less artificial, education would have another conception of knowledge. The facts would be there, but so would the values, and there would be no effort to stay away from them because of lack of consensus. Values tend to equalize people much more than facts do: of facts one can know more or less, in values one can believe and belief is as good as yours, hence in a dialogue you are no more teacher than I am. *De gestibus non disputandem* – values are not to be discussed – is a deeply reactionary norm, partly because by implication facts are to be discussed, presumably because the last word will be spoken by the older, the more experienced, the more schooled, and partly because values *have to* be discussed, since they are our guiding lights into the future, whether consensus is obtained or not.

But this means that *education should and could be centered around values*, after knowing what *is* mapping out what *might be*, then leading on to discussions of *strategies*, and finally going into *praxis*. Modern countries usually protect themselves against the latter not only by defining such approaches as unscientific and inappropriate for school curricula, but also by constructing nation-states in such a solidified, centralized way that any change has to be from the top, making people into clients of politicians and experts with top schooling, at most capable of exercising some praxis in their own private sphere, their apartment, and their own family life. This idea is also protected by such macro-level oriented ideologies as liberalism and marxism, that both assume that basic changes have to be in the society as a whole, not at the, say, school, farm, factory, firm, village level.

Nonetheless, the moments when this type of education breaks out like a fire, in a school are probably the moments best remembered by students – and by teachers because 'it got out of hand'. These are the moments when a real passionate discussion starts and the teacher does not try to quell it through his authority, nor to act the wise third party but becomes so involved himself that all masks fall and he simply becomes a party, on an equal footing, to the discussion. These are the moments that create chain effects, the moments that will be reported – although often not for its true value as much as for the triumph in having broken the structure – and even small children have a very keen sense of this. And not only does this pattern lead to chain effects – it also leads to a pattern of education by far outlasting schooling as a phase in life: education becomes an existential necessity. Socrates was *old*, meaning not only wise but also one who continued his education beyond schooling.

Thus, there is an intimate relation between form and content; schooling and education are two ways of combining different forms and different contents. Is, then, the answer to all this to abolish schooling and switch to education, creating societies with all kinds of academics where everybody walks peripatetically and dialogues his and her way through life, alternating with People's Communes as a way of coming closer to the ground? No, there is probably also some pedagogical value in the tension between schooling and education, and schools can only be basically transformed if society is transformed anyhow; meaning not necessarily at the macro-level of total society, but at least at the local level. But schools can be, and should be, brought much closer to education – and one way of doing that would be through a critical redefinition of the concept of literacy. To that we now turn.

4. The role of literacy

It is easily seen what role literacy plays in the context of schooling presented above, a context which in turn has to be extended to the economic and political spheres to be fully understood.

First of all, literacy serves as the first rung in the ladder (or succession of ladders) of schooling. If the content of schooling is primarily verbal, as we have argued, then knowing how to read and write is a *conditio sine qua non* for participation. It becomes like an entrance card, and possession of that card becomes like the diploma handed out when the final rungs of the ladders are reached: something ascriptive, 'I can read and write' becomes like 'I am a boy', non-dynamic, undisputable, no longer a question of what for?, why?

Second, literacy, when universally obtained, serves to give a sense of equality. Where everybody is above a certain minimum the discrepancies above that minimum may recede into the background. A national community of 'all us literate' emerges for some time, rapidly yielding to a keen awareness of the tremendous discrepancies between maximum and minimum schooling above that threshold as time passes on and literacy is taken for granted.

Third, literacy is entirely compatible with the typical Western combination of verticality and individualism. In a push-button society a minimum of literacy is needed to know which buttons to push although it is, strictly speaking, not indispensable: like traffic signs they may be ideographic rather than based on letters. However, as the population grows more literate, society will have to make more use of letters and words to make it look functional, to justify the expenses involved, although it only serves as a mask to cover up the alienating nature of work in modern society. By 'alienation', then, we refer essentially to a work structure whereby the work operations become so standardized and routinized — but not necessarily easy to perform — that once they have been acquired these work routines require no more input unless they are changed by somebody higher up.

But does one not have to be able to read to learn how to do it? Yes, that is one way of doing it, both producers and consumers are in need of recipes (there is the magnificent German word *Gebrauchsanweisungen* for this) — but it can probably just as well be acquired through imitation. It is only for more abstract creative work, into the unknown, anticipating through verbal symbols that which is not yet there, in thoughts, on the drawing board, in texts, in discussions that mastery of verbal symbols is strictly speaking necessary. *For that is the fabulous thing about words: they allow us to create images of the potential.* Words do not protest against being put to non-empirical uses, to reflect the non-existing, values rather than facts for instance. The only constraint is that the sentence is correctly formed, and these constraints are internal to the verbal system; they do not reflect the borderline between empirical and potential reality. Like mathematics we would go far to argue that language is empirically neutral, although there probably is some bias in an empiricist direction: after all, languages (and mathematics) are so often used to reflect that which is that there must be some carry-over effect somewhere.

So, the argument is that literacy is not really needed for work in a modern society, for most of the population. It may be needed for consumption though — although producers seem to rely more on commercials and advertising based on the spoken word and symbols than on people's ability to read. And it is, obviously, needed for kinds of creative work, for the reason mentioned, but that is for the few.

Conclusion

Literacy is there to a large extent to create an illusion of equality. It is not really being used, so like a leg never used it will tend to wither away. First goes writing since this is a way of sending a message, and that is incompatible with being located in the lower strata of vertical society — most people, hence, probably have their writing peak at school, particularly during the final exams. After that it may reduce to the legal minimum, the ability to sign a document. But reading, the receiver aspect of literacy, is also threatened if it is not strictly speaking necessary; people soon find out that they can get at more valid knowledge in other ways. People complain of fatigue when they read, and this is protected by the incredible growth in radio and TV, also vertical but no longer with the faintest hope of entering into any dialogue. A teacher can at least be teased into it — it is hard to tease a gadget into a mutually rewarding exchange. In short, the literacy is not functional, it is only a statistical artefact for large groups of the populations — in underdeveloped and overdeveloped countries alike, and probably even more in the latter because they are more routinized in their work structure.

What about individualism? Something of the same applies here. One learns how to read alone and write alone, not how to read for others or tell stories for others, nor how to compose things together. Literacy is privatized, which is natural since capability is used as an arm in the competition with others rather than for co-operative purposes. This is very well reflected in the structure of examinations in ways too obvious to describe in any detail, and the net result is a deepening of the individualization of learning.

Nevertheless, in spite of such critical remarks the conclusion is certainly not to detract from the importance of literacy campaigns, but to enrich them by enriching the concept of literacy in ways to be discussed below. It is very easy for the well educated, not to mention the overeducated, to be scornful about literacy — it smacks of the rich man who says 'believe me, money is not everything' to the pauper. To be literate is like being a citizen or a voter, it means being *in*, being a member. One may certainly criticize what one has become member of, but it is easier for the citizen not to participate, for the voter not to vote and for the literate to let his literacy wither away than for the reverse process to take place.

The problem is certainly not how to reduce literacy campaigns but it is not merely how to reduce literacy either — it is to make them more meaningful. For illiteracy campaigns are conducted very much in the same manner as anti-smallpox or anti-malaria campaigns; illiteracy has to be eradicated so that the country can claim that the territory is free from that plague. However, whereas the alternative to smallpox is no smallpox at all it is not so clear what is the alternative to illiteracy. Is it merely to read or write, or is it to read and write + — and what, in case, does that plus stand for?

5. The broader meaning of literacy

Imagine now that we simply see literacy as the beginning of education rather than as the first rung on a schooling ladder, what would then be the meaning of literacy? Most of it has been spelt out implicitly above, here we shall try to go more into detail.

Evidently, it means training in another type of structure both for the production and consumption of knowledge, in a broad sense, a structure that is at the same time less vertical and less individualist. More concretely, this would mean that the ability to enter into a dialogue would be seen as equal in importance to the ability to read and write. However, there is an important distinction here that could be made between dialogue and discussion or debate: the former is a method, dialectical, for mutual enrichment and mutual growth; the latter is some kind of regulated verbal warfare where the basic point is to win over somebody else. To dialogue (it should also be used as a verb) may involve *pro et contra dicere*, also in the sense that one takes this view and another the opposite view — but this is understood as a method to arrive at some kind of synthesis rather than as a competitive game. It is like the two rowers in a double-sculler: it could turn into a competition in turning the boat around; but it is a co-operative endeavour making use of some of the dynamism of the competitive enterprise.

A more relaxed form of dialogue is the *conversation* which often may be a dialogue, or a debate for that matter, in disguise. It is a profoundly collective undertaking; it respects the other party fully, there is an assumption that time should be about equally shared (it is not a lecture or a teaching session), it is conducted in an atmosphere of respect with a view to mutual enrichment. Of course, it has an air of the bourgeois *salon* and is too polite to be a tool for social transformation — and yet, should it not somehow enter our concept of literacy? Should not literacy be defined more broadly as *how to deal with words in a social setting*, not merely how to read and write them?

We would also argue in favor of knowing how to read and write *together*. The storyteller was an ancient role of tremendous importance — inconceivable with a public, partly destroyed through literacy because the stories are now stored and available to all who care to read them. But in this process the story as a social transaction between human beings disappeared — the book is and remains a rather indirect link between author and reader, between sender and receiver. At least some of this can be re-created through a pattern of joint enjoyment, but today very few people even know anything about how to read so as not to bore others — and few know how, together, to build on a story and create out of it something new.

So much about the form, what about the content?

If education is to be of any use in social transformation it obviously has to include both facts and values, both knowledge of the empirical and the potential, with ample use of the values to criticize the empirical, and of all kinds of knowledge to construct, using the precious tools of words that we humans have at our disposal, a better reality. Education should foster not only the empirical, but also the critical and the constructive mind — and there is no contradiction between the three. On the contrary, to build on only one of them, usually choosing the empirical since it is least threatening and most consensus-oriented, should be seen as promoting some kind of truncated, even castrated type of knowledge.

Concretely this means that education should lead to consciousness, to Paulo Freire's and others' famous conscientization — for what is that if not exactly the keen awareness of the contradiction between the factual and the potential, with ideas about why the factual falls short of the potential and what could make the potential one day become empirical reality. Consciousness is more than mere awareness of the forces working upon one — it is also awareness of how to transcend. To this we would only add one point already alluded to above: a theory that only sees transcendence in terms of macro changes is of little use. Revolutions are rare occurrences in human life; one cannot base education on such macro phenomena that happen once in a generation — at most — that would be like basing astronomy on the appearance of Haley's comet. Hence, the praxis concept to be encouraged should be relevant at the micro levels too — which means that *for literacy to contribute to education society will have to be more decentralized, more capable of diversity at the local level, of permitting people to handle their own affairs locally.* There is a clear connection between education and diversity brought about through more decentralization, and increasing self-reliance, locally and individually, just as there is a connection between schooling and centralization, in fact with nation-state building. Since both may be needed, and at the same time, there should be a scope for both.

6. Literacy, relative to other fundamental needs

Literacy, whether defined narrowly or more broadly, is a fundamental need in a literate society. But what are the other needs, and how does literacy relate to them? The answer to the latter obviously depends on the answer to the former.

Thus, take the usual list of fundamental needs, or *bienes fundamentales* as they would be referred to in Cuba: food, habitat, clothes, health — and then education, at its minimum conceived of as literacy. It is easily seen how literacy narrowly conceived of is instrumental to the satisfaction of these needs when the list is that short and these needs also are narrowly conceived of. Thus, if food becomes a question of reading recipes for increasingly industrialized food-making, habitat a question of signing a contract and being sufficiently knowledgeable of numbers and letters to locate one's own dwelling among similar looking ones, clothes a question of shopping and understanding advertising and health a question of reading instructions of hygiene — well, then, it all combines relatively well. But underneath this smooth surface, there are very substantial problems, and all of them they relate more or less precisely to the problem of what is meant by literacy and education.

First, there is the idea of giving a deeper meaning to the fundamental needs already mentioned. There is a basic structural similarity ('isomorphism' to use the technical term) between being made literate on the one hand, and being fed, sheltered, clad and protected on the other. In all cases one is a receiver, a client, being taken care of by nutritionists and food-makers, by town planners and architects, by manufacturers of clothing, by sanitation engineers and physicians. There is a whole army with tertiary education to take care of you — once you are willing and able to read their instructions! But the significant thing about this is that for all these fields there is something corresponding to the schooling vs. education dilemma, with the former standing for a more quantitative and the latter for a more qualitative approach with autonomy and sharing as basic ingredients.

Take food as an example: food in a qualitative sense is more than calories and proteins, just as education is more than the number of years passed in schools and the number of diplomas received. Food is an act of social communication, of sharing, of doing something together — and just as for habitat, clothing and health: the moment one can master some of it alone or together with the nearest ones (family, friends, neighbors) the whole meaning of these basic aspects of life changes. But that brings them closer to the education end of the spectrum — which means that the type of literacy we have argued above, the broad concept, would be more compatible and probably also lead to deeper quality in the need-satisfaction. This is perhaps most clearly seen in the case of health: to be a patient is not only to admit that you are ill but also to submit to the professional skills of health personnel, denying other roads to cure. In some cases it would be foolhardy not to submit but by no means always — again we are arguing what the Chinese refer to as 'walking on two legs'. A person who has converted his literacy in the education direction, who has become autonomous, capable of dialogue, critical and constructive, will also be far more capable of self-cure and of curing others. The point, one might emphasize, is not so much the precise content of the texts one reads after one has become literate as the structure literacy leads one into, whether it is of the schooling or education varieties — *for the structure is the major message*. Since schooling/education fills increasingly large parts of people's lives that structural message will dominate people in their social behavior — and among other things will have spill-over effect that could lead to a much higher quality of life if the education paradigm is made more dominant.

Second, there are all the other needs — life is not limited to those five alone. How do the two types of literacy relate to these near-fundamental needs? Depends on which they are, and here there is much less consensus. But why is there less consensus? Partly precisely because the needs already mentioned *can* be handled in a way totally consonant with a centralized, standardized, vertical nation-state of fragmented individuals whereas this is clearly not the case for other needs. Take *work*, for instance, not merely interpreted as an employment, as a job with a guaranteed minimum income so as to ensure the satisfaction of basic needs, but as an opportunity to express, to create, to engage in praxis. Today this privilege is probably reserved for a small élite of intellectuals, artists and some others — in a society less bent on standardized production and consumption it could be the birthright of everybody and in that case literacy could become functional for everybody. Or take *freedom*, that holy word which is being usurped precisely by those societies that talk most about it: it should mean more than freedom to choose between different TV channels or newspapers, all the time remaining a passive consumer. It must also imply the freedom to create, but that means that from the very beginning creativity rather than receptivity has to be emphasized, which immediately would favor education rather than schooling.

At this point a very important aspect of literacy should be mentioned: freedom of expression, even in a relatively non-creative way, is meaningless unless the media are available. In modern society one is only permitted to communicate to selected, specific receivers — letters and stamps, telephone calls can be afforded by many, if not by all or even by most — for the letters have to carry an address and the telephone call has to be preceded by dialling a number. Only the establishment, or selected individuals, are permitted to communicate with unspecified audiences, even the nation as a whole, and even beyond that. The ordinary person may not even put up a poster on the town square without permission, even not in countries that boast a very high level of freedom of expression. Our point here is not that everybody should be given prime time on television but that literacy should find more non-privatized outlets that can be afforded by people in general. One possibility is exactly the wall poster — a major Chinese contribution to freedom of expression — another would be to make mimeographing and photocopying services available free of charge to everybody, in addition to cable TV and FM radio-senders. Do this, and literacy would become much more meaningful, immediately.

This also has some implications for the next need in line: the need for *politics*. We are then not merely thinking of politics as a social institution, as an instrument to shape society and hence as a social need. We are thinking of it precisely as a human need, as the need for participating in shaping the conditions of one's own living. One can see it in the facial expressions of people who live in societies where this need is somehow satisfied, at least in some periods: there is an acute sense of being alive — whereas people denied this possibility tend to become dull and to resort to consumerism, passive religiousness or nationalism instead. But to engage actively in politics is to do exactly all those things that we have mentioned under education, and particularly under the broad concept of literacy — whereas schooling would make for citizens who know how to read party programs, and literacy would create people below that, but at least able to behave adequately on election day. Hence, parliamentarism is to real politics what schooling is to real education, which is what the narrow concept of literacy is to the broad concept — which, in turn, is what stones are to bread.

We could continue this list of needs, but it all leads to the same type of conclusion. Thus, is there not a *need for togetherness*, also having such expressions as friendship and love? It is a telling indictment of our schools that many people do not know how to reconcile friendship, love marriage with real dialogue but tend to see dialogue as something one engages in only with half-friends and half-enemies — real enemies are even beyond that. Further, is there not a *need for joy and for giving joy to others* — and is talking together not one, by no means the only one, such source of joy? And what about the *need for having a meaning with one's life* — can that really be reconciled with the kind of structure and content associated with schooling — if the picture drawn above is not too overdrawn, for it is obvious that it applies to some countries and to some periods in history more than to others?

In fact, among all of these dimensions the broad concept of literacy is not only a necessary component; it is so central in the whole social nexus that it comes close to being a major causal factor. But to the extent this is true it becomes rather important, and the question is how that concept is better promoted, in theory and practice. To that we now turn.

7. Conclusion: some strategies

It is not for anybody to translate this into any kind of blueprint — that would be against the whole spirit of the exercise. But a couple of very broad guidelines might be suggested.

First, literacy training must no longer be seen as a question of how to train the largest number as quickly as possible and as inexpensively per head as possible. Rather, much attention must be given to the social structure in which it takes place, and the content of the first verbal messages to be mastered. The structure should be decentralized, close to real life situations — carried out at work if possible, and by equals as much as possible. The content should have maximum relevance, verbal examples should not be contrived, literacy should be experienced as a magnificent instrument to express and understand important things, not as a goal in itself — in that case it becomes a fetish. There is much to learn from the Cuban campaign where this particular point is concerned.

Second, literacy training must include a large variety of training programs in what to do with words, such as composing posters, having dialogues, composing letters-to-the-editor, commenting and criticizing radio programs, behaving in meetings — even when reading and writing are not directly involved. It may well be that a new term should be invented to make a distinction between the narrow and the broad concept, retaining 'literacy' only for the former.

Third, this type of exercise should have carry-over effects into schools, and one vehicle of transformation here might be to give recently alphabetized adults more access to ordinary schools so that their higher level of experience can mix with the more formal training possessed by the children.

Fourth, even given all this a basic condition for literacy to become functional, not only a question of learning and forgetting equally or even more quickly, would be for society to undergo some transformation, particularly in the direction of more administrative decentralization and more economic self-reliance at the local level. For this to happen considerably more than literacy campaigns is needed, but they may be important instruments in that direction. *For just as the structure is the basic message, the content is defined through the use*, and the use will have to be meaningful, which means, ultimately, bordering on or getting into some kind of politics. But this presupposes a sense of local self-respect, which in turn presupposes some kind of *knowledge reform*, not too different from a land reform, whereby the monopolizers of knowledge-production, such as universities, experts, etc., are willing to distribute the tools of knowledge better, and people in general dare respect their own insights more.

So, what would happen if the whole world became literate? Quite a lot, in fact — if we dare define it broadly enough and take the consequence of trusting the people who are given, and themselves develop further, the tools of reading and writing.

15 LITERACY AND INDUSTRIALIZATION – THE DISPOSSESSION OF SPEECH*

E. Verne

Illiteracy: a pedagogic obstacle to industrialization

Since 1965 literacy teaching has functionally served the cause of industrialization while simultaneously serving to justify the existence of two sectors in the Third World: one in which poverty has been modernized, the other in which poverty has been impoverished. The modernization of poverty and the impoverishment of poverty have occurred more or less in step with concentration and expansion of industrial production. Whether modernized or impoverished, poverty can be measured in terms of lack of capital and shortage of information. For it is industrial growth that has led the educational system to assume the social control indispensable to the efficient utilization of conditioned products.†[1]

The patent failure of teachers, instructors and cultural agents in their attempts to eliminate illiteracy; the passive resistance of the illiterate masses; the massive medium term ineffectiveness of mass literacy programmes; all these constitute a *pedagogic limit* to the linear extension of the industrial mode of production. The relative success of intensive and selective literacy programmes, imposed from above by the policy makers' authorities, cannot hide the negative social costs of the type of literacy training that functions as a compulsory gateway to the internalization of the domination of industrial monopolies and of man's industrialization. The ineffectiveness of teachers in extensive literacy programmes is matched by the counter-productiveness of the literacy bureaucracies that have replaced them. The failure of mass literacy campaigns, coupled with the negative impact of voluntarist, narrowly selective literacy campaigns, means that the major political fact in the years to come is going to be the recognition of the significance of and the hopes placed in illiteracy seen as a cultural expression and a manifestation of a balanced interaction with the environment. Taken together with other still more significant indicators, the persistence of masses rendered illiterate does not alter the fact that the political initiative and imagination is gradually shifting in the direction of the Third World.

*Reprinted from E. Verne, 'Literacy and industrialization – the dispossession of speech', in *A Turning Point for Literacy: Adult Education for Development*, ed. Léon Bataille, 211–28, by permission of the publisher, Pergamon Press, Ltd. © Pergamon Press, Ltd. 1976.
†Quotations from English texts are retranslated freely from the French original of this 'paper'.

The foregoing remarks will appear paradoxical only because we have grown used to identifying literacy with development, functional literacy with industrial development and, more fundamentally, underdevelopment and economic lag with illiteracy and dearth. They are surprising only because we have got into the habit of only accepting as literacy the product of the tools of literacy training, much in the same way as we only treat the product of schooling as education. By refusing to examine the positive mentality and the dynamism of the illiterate person who learns how to master his environment and to decide for himself how he wants to live in an open and balanced environment, we betray, just how thoroughly we have internalized, after 15 or 20 years' schooling — for those of us who have managed to break out — the characteristics of dependence and alienation that constitute the essential features of the latent programme of the school system. Utterly dazzled as we are by a handful of individual success stories, as well as by the fact that schooling does free men from traditional hierarchies, we fail to realize that it equally surely binds them to the capitalist hierarchy of certified knowledge and accumulated possessions. Nor do we perceive that scholastic education does not create the conditions in which the child, like the illiterate, can begin to liberate himself. To put it more precisely, we do not perceive that the degree of liberation permitted by the school remains under the control of those who wield the greatest influence in the definition of the aims of our society and who are best able to impose those aims. Literacy campaigns that form part of (or prepare for) programmes of industrialization merely serve to strengthen this kind of control over a fraction of the working masses.

Schooling may help men to break out of a society in which they are born servants and not masters of their own fate, yet in which they are at the same time farmers or craftsmen, disposing of a fair amount of freedom of choice and control over their own daily lives. The sons of farmers or craftsmen, who go to school in order to acquire the right to work in factories or in government offices, will have the opportunity of consuming goods unknown to their parents on the farm or in the village. Yet in so doing they will be surrendering their control over their time and over the social dimensions of their environment.

The counter-productiveness of teaching organizations, and especially with respect to their inability to satisfy the demand for education they themselves have stimulated, ought to lead us to call for radical alternatives to the growing institutionalization of new teaching bodies. The options adopted in Teheran in 1965 at least expressed doubts concerning the school education system; while the World Congress of Education Ministers recommended abandoning the aim of massive literacy campaigns in quantitative terms, having no other purpose than the spread of literacy, in favour of functional literacy campaigns centred around industrial work. Since that time, general agreement has been reached concerning the growing ineffectiveness of constantly rising educational expenditure that entails ever greater social costs. This consensus over the crisis in education grew up before the appearance of the most important signs of a structural crisis that is utterly new in terms of its characteristics and its significance. While the Teheran Congress acted as a trail-blazer in diagnosing the crisis in the school system, it nonetheless failed to diagnose the crisis that was about to hit the system of production itself. And this accounts for the way in which literacy work has been separated from the school system, only to be tacked directly onto the process of industrialization. The crisis in growth today forces us to appraise the impact of this decision and to single it out for critical examination.

At the time when Ministers of Education were establishing a new type of literacy teaching 'tied to vocational training programmes, thereby permitting a rapid rise in individual productivity',[2] people still adhered to an ideology based on unlimited growth; to the extension of industrial monopolies over the entire productive field and to the green revolution; to the productivity of industrial work and to the superiority of scientifically organized work; to the mystification of knowledge and skills as certified by diplomas; to the globalization of technologies and information. Above all, people still believed it was possible to obtain happiness and well-being through the consumption of increasingly insignificant goods.

Today, industrial societies are in a state of crisis. Political, cultural and technological imperialisms have suffered a series of major setbacks and have shown they are incapable of shaping the entire world in their own image. For the rich nations, the end of 25 years of fairly steady growth, the crisis of growth, general environmental degradation; the concentration of power systems; the spread and the growing complexity of mechanisms of dependence; the acceleration of highly unequal industrialization in certain countries, the crisis in institutions responsible for the production of intangible goods; all these lead us to take a rather different view of literacy policies and to put forward alternatives to them whose validity and justification do not reside in needs, aspirations, images, criteria and rationalizations which are themselves created by the domination the industrial world exercises over the whole field of human exchange.

These radical alternatives imply a twofold critique:
1. that of the institutionalization of adult education: this serves to enclose literacy programmes within the school system by subjecting adults to pedagogic action;
2. that of the domination of the industrial monopolies over the content and criteria of literacy: this serves to domesticate men by adapting them to the industrial production machine and by subjecting them to industrially processed information.

This twofold critique has as its object the recognition of the cultural nature of illiteracy in those cases where it implies the recovery, by human groups, of their right to decide for themselves and the rediscovery of their language. The outcome of this critique will be to make the unlearning of literacy a worthwhile project for all those incompetent specialists turned out by the world's knowledge-slicing factories, who have been incapable of limiting the use and the social power of their knowledge. If 'language reflects the monopoly that the industrial mode of production holds over workers' perception and motivations'; if 'language reflects the materialization of consciousness',[3] then literacy training should provide a means of retrieving the convivial function of language. But for language to render the transparency of man's relationships with his tools, we must first begin by reversing the process whereby man is industrialized by his tools.

Literacy and the spread of schooling

In the years 1965–70, no one suspected that by analysing the various aspects of the world crisis in education, by condemning the growing cost of schooling and by unmasking the hidden programme in all scholastic institutions, the main outcome of this destructive critique of 10 or 15 years of compulsory schooling and of continuous full-time education would be to accredit the idea of lifelong education, and to subject people of all ages to the educational process by rendering access to the class-room not merely open, but compulsory. It is as if, in answer to the problems of a declining school system, an alternative solution was being sought that would enable this system to continue to dispense its latent programme. It was evidently essential to begin by imposing upon the public the image of a school system that was no longer capable of carrying out its functions and that was becoming too costly. Once this had been accomplished, it was far easier to argue convincingly that discontinuous and recurrent education in specialized institutions, under the supervision of professional educators dispensing programmes defined by the bureaucracies serving industrial mega-machines was a vital, lifelong necessity. Yet this has been the price paid for the extension of education to all age groups.

Functional literacy training is one of the avatars of school education and of the rising power over life as a whole exercised by those school-orientated norms that are vital to the assimilation of the industrial ethic and to the process of adapting people to its standards. For reasons connected with the current economic situation and with the state of development of the industrial monopolies, it has become necessary to transfer those functions the school is no longer capable of satisfying adequately onto adult education. The deterioration of the school has been recuperated by industrial ideology and made to serve this transfer, much as conscientization has been bent to the service of fascism. Technocrats now hope that by nibbling away at the school's educational functions they will be able to prevent a general educational leakage away from society as a whole. It was via the search for alternatives that would have made it possible to cope with the negative consequences of schooling in the industrial countries while at the same time compensating for the impossibility of providing schooling for all the children in the poor countries, that people gradually abandoned the notion of an educational system solely concerned with the early stages of life in favour of lifelong educational assistance. Because they are concerned merely to tackle the most visible effects, rather than the latent programme and the social *ethos* that go to make up compulsory education, politicians are incapable of thinking in terms other than those of compensation, rectification or limitation of surface dysfunctions. However, the only certain consequence of these innovations will be to dissimulate the latent programme still more effectively through exclusive manipulation of the most visible data; this approach in turn serves to reinforce and to legitimate the school system's latent programme. By seeking replacement strategies, and by imposing fresh legislative and regulatory policies, the experts seem to be implying that individuals and communities have neither the resources necessary to work out their own educational requirements for themselves, nor the ability to decide for themselves how best to satisfy these requirements. On each occasion, these people find themselves just a little more expropriated, just a little more industrialized; this is the only programme, when all is said and done, the school system has successfully managed to inculcate in us all.

The conversion of school system technocrats to belief in lifelong or recurrent education is the best illustration of this transfer of a conception of education that is confined to limitless and endless education; it is also the best evidence we have of the way their power has spread. Because these technocrats have managed to appropriate the entire process, lifelong education will never be able to realize its initial project of dissolving formal schooling into a social fabric that has once more regained significance.

This was a project that would have been bearable to the literacy training of unschooled masses. But functional literacy, on the other hand, does have a place within this paraphernalia; alongside education without schools, schools without walls, open classrooms, educational TV by satellite, teaching machines and multi-media systems. The sleight-of-hand involved in distinguishing formal from informal education by stating that formal education covers everything that happens inside the school-room, while informal education means everything outside the school-building, still cannot hide the fact that, whether formal or not, all institutionalized education cannot convey the same latent programme. We would all like to be able to define education as a process enabling people to become critical and conscious of their own reality with a view to more effective action to transform that reality. But we cannot make this process a compulsory part of institutions that annex this awareness and inexorably programme both consciousness and the action that flows from it.

All these projects, though they reject and generally deny this, are simply modern avatars of all those past illusions — educational, humanist and modernist — which thought that it was by changing man's education that one could change the order of things and the characteristics of institutions. The moment a society is stratified, and the moment the distribution of wealth becomes the yardstick of this stratification, it becomes constantly necessary to lead people to believe in the possibility of a redistribution of opportunities and thereby to ratify the view that these inequalities form part of the natural order of things, while they will be justified secondarily by those whose power they legitimate. The moment social and technical labour are divided, there will be a constant need for a progressive system of qualifications and of apprenticeship; and these qualifications will need to be not merely differentiated, but separate.

The social utility of the avatars of schooling in general and of functional literacy in particular — in order to inculcate their latent programme into the greatest number of people possible — is becoming increasingly evident and necessary: to the survival of the industrial mode of production and for the reproduction of the labour force and of the relations of production. Now that schools and universities are inculcating this programme with diminishing success, these functions which were formally discharged onto the school system, are currently being transferred to adult education. Were it not for this process of transfer, which ensures the continued diffusion of the latent programme of all schooling, it would be hard to understand the lack of energy behind the public authorities' reaction to the deterioration of public education systems and to the rising number of cases where laws regarding compulsory school attendance and child labour are contravened. Life-long adult education therefore appears to be an alternative to the earlier project aiming at providing schooling for all children; it appears to be a riposte to the economic functions the school no longer fulfils; a new opportunity of compensating for the social functions the school never provided; a new rationale behind the teaching act and its supporting administration. In reality it functions like an ideology, the better to cover up the economic bases upon which it resides. Lifelong or recurrent education is undoubtedly the most dangerous, though at the same time the least obvious, trap into which the process of abolishing the school can fall. The elimination of schools from society cannot be compared with the totalitarian, alienating project which lifelong schooling is now becoming at the close of the industrial era.

Lifelong education and its by-products, such as functional education, are nothing more than a present-day avatar of old-fashioned schooling. There are a good many arguments for this view. These run from the description of the way in which adult education is inevitably organized along school lines (the specific age groups of the individuals selected, gathered around a professional specialist, made to learn programmes they themselves have not chosen at predetermined rates, in order to acquire a marketable qualification and so-called greater productivity); from the reproduction of the material basis of the school institution; to the persistence and preservation – through the above reproduction – of the pedagogic notion of education as the only possible medium of transaction between the individual's desire to learn and what he wishes to learn; not forgetting the repetition of the same effects as those produced by the school and the reinforcement of its social functions. In addition to which, lifelong education serves to amplify the industrialization of education and the mercantilization of knowledge; at bottom it is nothing but the continuation of the patent programme of the school system and the confirmation of its most visible effects.

As against this programme, teachers ought now to be concerned with the definition of parameters marking the pedagogic dimensions of the limits to industrial growth. At the very least, they would arrive at conclusions of the following kind: for example, that all educational policies that do not take the trouble to define certain minimal or lower thresholds are condemned to failure and their aim to create a more equitable society, in which fairness and justice will be assessed in terms of evenly distributed amounts of energy and education. But we all know that it only makes sense to guarantee minimal thresholds if maximal ceilings are themselves subject to limitation. As with average *per capita* income, so gross national education (GNE) only takes on meaning within a system that sets both floors and ceilings. We might at least recognize that the chief political problem facing us today is less that of illiteracy than that of the political forces and arrangements capable of calling a halt to overconsumption of education and the excessive remuneration of those who attend educational establishments longest.

What we do know is that, since the beginning of the industrial era, workers throughout the world have wasted their revolutionary energies in the struggle to obtain a guaranteed minimum wage, a minimum of justice, a minimum of work. And that, by their successive struggles, they have managed to raise these minimal guarantees. Yet, they have not been able to change a social structure characterized by maximum domination and by a total dependence on industrialized labour, yet which is incapable of offering them a greater guarantee of an optimal existence. Each time, they are robbed of the fruit of their struggles by an upward shift in the various layers of the social pyramid. How else are we to account for the poor impact of massive schooling upon social inequalities, upon the intensification of social inheritance, intergenerational mobility, social status and income distribution, even where significant reductions in inequalities in the distribution of scholastic capital have been achieved?[4] And who would care to argue that by shifting the educational effort from childhood to adulthood would alter these characteristics of the social system?

The most serious political problem in the next 20 years is no longer going to be that of providing a minimum of education for all, nor of providing a substitute for schooling, nor even of providing limited education-credits to be used as the individual pleases throughout his lifetime. The problem is going to be that of bringing together the political conditions capable of putting a stop to the overconsumption of schooling by the few, the overpayment of those possessing diplomas, and of breaking their monopoly. By attempting to create the political conditions necessary to make these choices – while at the same time ensuring these choices do not result from an excessive concentration of power – one highlights the limitations of political machines and, most likely, just what can and what cannot be asked of them. In view of the fact that political power itself is a kind of specialized instrument and a monopoly, it is more likely that the political conditions required for the creation of a convivial society are going to emerge in the midst of a generalized crisis of all those instruments responsible for the production of intangible goods in which all of these instruments become counter-productive together. Research into ever more sophisticated teaching methods capable of enabling a few individuals to leap across barriers that are in any case going to crop up further along their path, increasingly insurmountable, is not going to have the slightest effect upon this pedagogic limit to industrialization.

Despite every effort and investment, adult literacy is still seen as a kind of remedy against schooling deficiencies to be administered to the 'underprivileged' or the 'deprived' classes. However, the mere fact of being able to read a written message merely leads human communities to subject themselves to instruction *by* and *for* the assembly line. In the best eventualities, it enables them to read comic strip balloons or to puzzle out the sub-titles in foreign films. Its best consequence is that one is sure to learn the standards of a school-based society.

If we have not managed to demonstrate the impact of training on productivity,[5] even though this is a vital effect of functional literacy, then there must be some other explanation for growing expenditure and substantial investment in relation to a frequently very small amount of fixed capital; this expenditure must serve some other function. It may serve the purposes of ideological inculcation, for example and, naturally, for the inculcation of industrial ideology, along with sharpening the appetite for individual advancement and, finally, domesticating the working class to the industrial *ethos*. Control over rising budgets, along with the power and the prestige formerly attaching to the teaching profession, are in the process of passing from teachers and their school to adult educators, with their multi-media systems in order to exercise still more subtle and more pervasive control over individuals. The institutionalization of adult education is going to transform the entire planet into one immense classroom, whether lifelong, intermittent or recurrent. Industrial teaching methods for the purposes of industrialization are about to be replaced by an even more destructive system of post-industrial conditioning. It is becoming increasingly urgent that we open public proceedings to expose the political, cultural and ethical costs of so-called school-free education. Poor countries are still freer than the rich ones to opt for a diversification of learning opportunities within the framework of a convivial way of life through the multiplication of significant personal experiences. All that remains to the rich nations now is the choice imposed upon them by the mega-industrial machines, implying constantly expanding education designed to ensure steadily improving bureaucratic control over men.

Literacy and the industrialization of education

The recognition in Teheran, in 1965, of the virtual uselessness of literacy campaigns undertaken so far, notably due to subsequent illiteracy backlashes; and the appraisal which was made on the occasion of the Teheran Conference regarding the wastage that this expenditure represented for education as a whole; both served as point of departure for the establishment of a consensus on the critique of school-based education systems. Today, one is inclined to wonder whether the consequences drawn from the above consensus − and in particular the recommendation in favour of functional literacy − were not, at bottom, an attempt to mask the real underlying policy, namely one of ignoring the problem and of shirking responsibilities. The abandonment of mass literacy campaigns in favour of campaigns aimed at adults already involved, or about to become involved, in industrial production, and only in those sectors of production where literacy can be considered a factor making for increased productivity, was 'a lucid political and economic decision forced on political leaders by reality; literacy, as with any other kind of education, involves a great deal of expenditure; as a result, it should only be put into effect in those areas where it is liable to be most profitable'.[6] As a result, new forms of financing have been devised and fresh resources have been made available; in the meantime, we are already in a position to say that the resulting wastage is even greater than the one it was supposed to remedy. There is practically no alternative when one can no longer dissociate − not even semantically − the process of teaching people to read and write from what is produced by a specific institution.

Literacy has been hitched up to the waggon of industrialization just as, in the rich countries, the institutionalization of adult education has been linked to the status of salaried employee. Literacy has been transformed into the only way-in to industrial production. We should bear in mind this connivance between literacy and industrialization. This would help to explain why educational expenditure producing only slight yields in terms of investment becomes profitable when one takes into account side effects that rarely come within the purview of assessors. Indeed, assessors never take into account internalization of the curriculum implicit in all education programmes and contained within the concept − as in that of schooling − that 'teaches' an illiterate Mexican peasant-woman whose son is attending school that the reason she herself cannot read is not because she is poor, but because she has never received any education. Schooling has transformed education into a quantifiable commodity, into a knowledge stock capable of being accumulated. Members of society are thus classified in terms of their ability to acquire shares, levels or quantities of this knowledge stock. This ability to acquire shares in this stock is usually measured in terms of knowledge stock certificates. The essential features of this implicit programme are already to be found in the institutionalization of literacy teaching.

In addition to this hidden programme, everyone now knows that the best way for an illiterate worker to achieve integration into the production process and to form an idea of his place in the production chain is to internalize the linear nature of the printed text, to acquire the ability to see things laterally and to equip himself with the spatial scheme necessary in order to learn to read and write. Industrialists have fully understood that the medium constitutes the most important part of the message. The ideological content of the text is of little importance so long as the worker internalizes this linearity and its extensions within industrialized space. He will thereby all the more effectively occupy his place in the production process, constituting a letter that is void of meaning in a line that is alone capable of having any meaning. He will thereby all the more thoroughly internalize the scheme of the division of labour, which is essential to the industrial concept of production.

After all, the book was the first industrial article to be manufactured industrially. And there is a certain structural analogy between the linear logic of the printed sentence and the linearity of the industrial production process. Any process of learning to read and write may thus be seen as functional to the industrial mode of production. European industrialists well know that technological training for immigrant workers means, first and foremost, training in the technology of reading. And that once this has been acquired, or even merely frequented, it makes for improved integration into the organization of industrial space — through internalization of linear schema — and, consequently, makes for greater acceptance of its norms. Managers must at least assume as much, but trade unions defending native workers in the firm[7] must also assume as much when they organize vast literacy campaigns for these workers after production has been halted by wildcat strikes. In view of the fact that the level of combativity of workers attending courses within the framework of lifelong adult education in France tends to decline, it is quite likely that teaching immigrant workers to read and write produces a similar educational effect. The adult educators are on hand to strike the same blow at their autonomy as professional politicians have struck at their capacity for struggle. They will be extending to these workers the task of demobilization that the bourgeois school has already undertaken upon their children. In particular, they will be doing so by holding out the possibility of individual advancement only, and by reducing their combativity by pointing out the competition for jobs in industry and the possibilities of advancement invariably attached to any type of training. 'The rules of recruitment in the infant industries in poor countries are such that only those who have attended school manage to obtain scarce jobs, for they alone have learnt to keep their mouths shut at school.'[8] The school, like literacy courses, serves the purposes of industrialization at least in so far as those who have learnt to read messages that are not their own will realize that what they themselves have to say is of no value. They learn to read so as to learn how to keep quiet.

The Teheran Programme went a little further in the process of linking literacy campaigns to economic development and industrial growth. In so doing, it was merely obeying one of the structural laws inherent in all programmes aiming for the development of schooling, and in all their substitutes. Martin Carnoy has shown that it is impossible to speak of the development of schooling in colonial and non-industrial countries unless one accepts that, once a given country's needs in terms of officials for the colonial administration have been satisfied, the colonial school system serves a further function, namely that of preparing consumers for the products manufactured in the metropolis, as well as a pool of labour ready and waiting for future industrial expansion. The choice made by Education Ministers in Teheran in 1965, calling for an educational programme designed to facilitate a rapid rise in labour productivity, was no different from the call made by President Pardo of Peru in 1873 for an industrial school 'in order to increase the workers' productive capacity and to guarantee order, which is the basis of progress'.[9]

In so doing, moreover, the Teheran Conference laid the basis for what was to become a major argument in favour of institutionalizing adult education within the framework of lifelong or recurrent education. The argument in favour of greater labour productivity was to help direct back into the centre of the industrial production machine those adult education systems which, as with the school system itself, had initially developed on the periphery of industrial activity. Henceforth, they will increasingly be developing under the direct control of business enterprises, with the latter themselves formulating their orders for adult education programmes which, increasingly, they are coming to sanction by means of the hierarchy of recognized qualifications and job evaluation. It is as if the industrial monopolies were making increasingly urgent, ever more feverish demands upon the instruments of education in an attempt to shore up the industrial era.

Thus, the process of industrial transfers makes intense demands for programmed personnel upon the Third World, demands which the schools are incapable of supplying either as rapidly or as narrowly specialized as the process requires. Functional and selective literacy training is intended to remedy this. Multi-national companies, obliged to seek short-term profits and 'who are bereft of horizons over and beyond a dozen or fifteen miserable years',[10] are reluctant to burden themselves with educational investments that could only be expected to bear fruit in the long term. The invention of new, low-cost educational methods, which therefore require a lower level of investment in proportion to fixed capital, thus enables the new bourgeoisies on the periphery and inside the multi-nationals to model a strictly selected work force whose productivity will be greater than the cost of its production. This is especially so where these bourgeoisies are able to make use of the skills acquired by learning on the job by metropolitan workers in order to supervise local work forces they would rather not spend money on training when transferring factories to the periphery. The need for industrial redeployment on a world scale, the new interest of multi-nationals, the rapid and uneven industrialization of a handful of developing countries, at the present time, these are surest guarantees of success of functional and selective adult literacy and education programmes. But this will not be able to prevent there being more unemployed workers in the cities of the Third World, in absolute figures, than workers in the West.

In a society where unemployment and underemployment are endemic, it is hard to see the significance of linking education to jobs and to labour policies. Only the dismantling of the present monopoly of industry overproduction can possibly bring about a redistribution of work and open the way to a more convivial mode of production, where individuals and groups will be encouraged to set up community workshops, collective farms, convivial centres open to all and subject solely to the control of their users. The best chances of an integral literacy programme[11] are at the very least, and for the moment, those emerging within the framework of a project of integrated development that is not exclusively concerned with industrialization, but rather with the creation of community production co-operatives, as in China or in the United Republic of Tanzania. But the hopes for initiatives of this type will be compromised irremediably unless the existing school system is well and truly broken up, so as to ensure a non-formal education for the greatest number. For by safeguarding a private or a public school system for the benefit of a tiny proportion of the population, one would unavoidably impoverish every other form of learning. The law reforming Peru's educational system explicitly allows for this, in view of the degree to which the traditional school system tended to preserve all the social images, the prestige and prospects and attitudes resulting from this. Up to the present time, all the most significant educational reforms have broken down against this highly serious socio-economic option. The experience of several poor countries shows that, even where the school system is only weakly established, it nonetheless represents an image whose power of attraction is far too strong. Rather than allow it to continue to exist, there is no alternative but to dissolve it in a system of informal education in order to avoid the emergence of two parallel educational systems. Barefoot doctors, for example, would be unable to coexist for long with a western Medical Association. It is for reasons of this type that it is essential to put an end to the existing school system.[12]

The rich countries now know that one cannot settle the problem of integrating youth into active life merely by adapting education or training schemes, nor by rendering the teaching system more professional. The poor countries still in a position to exercise their imagination run the risk of taking this course nevertheless, even though it turns out to be a dead end. They too are in the process of adapting their educational systems to the criteria of industrial labour, when they ought to begin by adapting the production process to man. The education problem as it will arise tomorrow will no longer be one of developing fresh educational or training strategies or of institutionalizing educational reforms. The problem is going to be one of changing the characteristics of industrial work so that men can rediscover a relationship with their environment that is not mediatized by tools they neither control nor make themselves.

In the face of the industrial threat and the counter-productivity of machinery, there is still a tendency to deny the importance of an equilibrium between man and the biosphere by means of such palliatives as planning, which aims to equalize the side-effects of both the rate of growth of industrial output and the rate of frustration. Human equilibrium is an open equilibrium, capable of shifting within flexible, though finite, parameters. The model for the dynamics of industrialization, on the other hand, is founded on unlimited growth. And within this industrial dynamic, it is the structure of production that shapes social relations. Only by placing limits upon productive forces can we hope to restore man to a state of open-ended equilibrium.[13]

All those generous outbursts on the part of humanist educators calling for an education 'concretely rooted in the everyday reality of the worker's life, from which it draws both its content and its richness so as to provide him, in turn, with fresh perspectives and dimensions'; all our hopes for a form of teaching 'profoundly rooted in experience so as to set in motion an endogenous process of conscientization and critical elucidation'; all our aspirations towards that 'intellectual adventure wherein man, as the object of his underdevelopment, will gain full consciousness of his place in history';[14] all of these take on their full meaning if accompanied by a critique of the tools of industry, of the radical monopoly exercised by professionals, and of the industrialization of values. But this litany of intentions is a mystification when, as in the Report of the International Commission on the Development of Education, it is accompanied by subjection to a technology whose limits remain undefined. One cannot want, at one and the same time, a form of education that will be a global process, an integral literacy addressed to the whole man, and to adapt the educational system to the acceleration of progress defined in industrial terms. For the result will be a 'literacy action, motivated by and directed towards employment possibilities, that must be integrated into the development objectives of the country or local environment' and whose 'range must be proportionate to that of the overall socio-economic development effort, the strategy behind this effort determining the strategy for literacy programmes'.[15]

I would like to reverse this proposition. We can only hope to set the question of literacy on a new basis by changing the parameters of our tools, by modifying our calculations of the limits of their tolerability, by establishing political control over the dimensions these tools may be allowed to assume. Our aim is not to adapt men to tools they neither make nor control; not to produce a system of objects the better to reify man; but to forbid technologies and the manufacture of tools whose nature is such that they unavoidably render 95% of humanity illiterate.

For there lies the paradox of our society: the fact that it manages to manufacture two types of illiterate. There is the illiteracy of those who are crushed by their physical and human environment, and the illiteracy of those who are crushed by the tools that manipulate them. The Sahel peasant is struggling desperately for survival in a naturally hostile world. His fatalism has grown even stronger now he is increasingly dependent upon outside assistance. He knows he is even poorer today, and he knows he is even more powerless now that green miracle-makers are turning out high-yield seed that can only be used by a minority possessing a twofold fertilizer — chemical, of course, but also the educator. In this way, the right countries are creating a form of illiteracy founded on misery with their uncontrolled technologies.

The most precise definition of functional literacy is to be found in the amendment to the Iranian Literacy Project of 1970. It is there defined as a 'technical and cultural advancement activity integrating, in a synchronized process, vocational training, scientific acculturation, mathematical instruction, civic and socio-economic education, and learning to read and write. This process is designed to improve the productivity of workers, to facilitate their integration into a rapidly modernizing society, and to accelerate development.'[16] As it stands, this definition is of no interest to the highly industrialized countries — which does not matter very much — but neither is it of much interest for the poorest nations. For, in both highly industrialized countries and in non-industrialized countries the problem has ceased to be, or never was, one of adapting the labour force to a tight labour market where jobs are scarce or where jobs never existed in the first place. Education neither creates jobs, nor does it possess the power of conjuring them out of thin air. The main cause of unemployment and of underemployment lies in the existence of more workers than jobs for them. Conversely, adult education tends to disqualify people by devaluing experienced and acquired knowledge. It stands as a threat to the security of those who do have jobs, while disqualifying the experience of those who do not. And unless the production process is modified considerably, it is hard to see how it could offer anything than individual advance, to the detriment of collective advancement.[17] In the rich nations, the problem of underemployment is tackled by readjusting the training of workers to the needs of industry, though no one has bothered to explain in what way lifelong or recurrent education is going to increase the number of jobs available; indeed, the French national statistics institute (INSTE) has observed a net fall in the number of jobs on offer. In the poor countries, schooling offers youngsters three possibilities: they can either be qualified but unemployed; unemployed and unqualified; or else they can work for a qualification in order to forget they are unemployed.

Finally, only a few countries are currently undergoing a process of rapid industrialization and are in a position to push through their industrial revolution within the space of a few years; it is these countries alone that require a literacy process centred upon the rapid reconversion of a strictly selected work force that has been selected strictly with a view to greater productivity. We need have no illusions as to the end result of this decision to encourage literacy for the purposes of the technical, social and international division of labour: namely development for the sake of industrialization alone, and selective training for the purposes of professionalizing each job and trade. The euphoria of rapid industrialization currently being enjoyed by a handful of countries should not blind others to the fact that the various features of the present crisis, whether it be the crisis of dearth in the poor countries or the crisis of overabundance in the rich countries, all lead to the conclusion that we should no longer link individual or communal human development to the ideology of the industrial organization of production and of the capitalist organization of the economy. Educators frequently tend to forget that problems of education are not primordial; that what is primordial is the problem of survival in equity; of autonomy in creativity; and of work in conviviality.

A new understanding of the nature of work

Political realism will eventually lead to the break of the close relationship between institutionalized learning and industrialized employment, between lifelong education and specialized labour as laid down at Teheran. As at the dawn of the Neolithic era, a large part of the human race is able to dispose of its time as it wishes: this represents a huge potential capital, capable of being used to multiply our range of opportunities of significant experiences and to acquire information. The height of political courage in the coming years is going to lie in the determination to link education to the state of not-working. But this presupposes that formal education ceases to devalue − by its very existence − everyday experience and acquired wisdom. By systematically associating education with industrial work, by refusing to recognize as education anything that does not require specialized equipment designed to dispense pre-programmed knowledge by means of pedagogic manipulation at the hands of specialists, we gradually force the unschooled masses out of the habit of making use of their availability on their own initiative. We drive them to associate activity with work, and learning with stored knowledge. 'Men have the innate ability to care for and to comfort each other, to move around, to acquire knowledge, to build homes and to bury their dead. Each of these abilities is matched by certain needs. The means to satisfy these needs are not lacking, provided men remain dependent upon what they can do by and for themselves.'[18]

Industrial tools have become intolerable to us because they have outgrown certain limits. They have become intolerable because they can no longer be controlled by all; and an uncontrollable tool constitutes an unbearable threat to human harmony. Once tooling and equipment grows beyond a certain critical point, it inevitably produces greater and greater quantities of programmed education, functionalized literacy, regulated information, dependence, exploitation and impotence. Man's ability to learn, to achieve fulfilment autonomously and to create is not in doubt here. What is at stake is the super-efficiency of industrial tools, which poses a threat to man's capacities.

We must seek a new meaning in human labour, and some purposes other than industrial work. Over the past 100 years, educational planning has been increasingly concerned with educating man to serve machines, while industrial planning has been seeking to make machines work for mankind. Today, however, we know that the 'machine' will not work and that man will never bend to its demands. Man is a constant factor. He needs tools to work with, not tools that do his work for him. Plans intended to satisfy what is known as 'a positive policy for active life',[19] the enrichment of parcellized jobs, the development of greater flexibility within linear job organization or in career trajectories, greater freedom in the organization of the working day or week, greater participation in an impersonal and technical decision-making process – none of these can be expected to reverse man's relationship to his environment for as long as producers remain enslaved to tools over which they have no control. The structural characteristics of illiteracy will be modified proportionately to the degree of control that workers are able to exercise over the characteristics and dimensions of tools. If we had to attempt an assessment of the social costs entailed by uncontrolled technologies, we would certainly have to take functional literacy into account. And we would also have to include lifelong education, of which it is part, and which, it is claimed, helps fight unemployment by providing workers with qualifications or by reconverting them; enables adults to adapt to technological changes that render their professional skills obsolete; that it helps deprived groups to achieve satisfactory social integration; that it provides workers with the feeling that they have every opportunity of social promotion. On the contrary, it has been our view, in this paper, that adult education, even if it succeeds in bringing about formal changes in institutions, in the way time is used, in the media and in forms of financing, will serve to perpetuate existing social, political and economic conditions just as surely as other school systems.

Resisting the invasion of information

'Science today is capable of helping us simplify tools, of enabling each of us to shape our immediate environment; in other words, it can enable us to take on meaning by filling the world with signs.'[20] The invention of printing started the process by petrifying the letter; radio followed on by appropriating discourse; now television monopolizes the image. It is these three tools that render the greater part of humanity illiterate, depriving it of the right to inscribe its own signs, of making its own voice heard and of producing images of its own. In this respect, if illiteracy is to be measured in terms of the degree to which man controls the tools of his environment, then the Parisian is more illiterate than the African peasant, chatting beneath the palaver tree. The industrially produced book has become, for the literate, the compulsory form of mediation through which they must pass to gain access to deperson-alized discourse. By giving the illiterate the impression that books are the only possible vector of culture one immediately devalues the importance of his own discourse in his own eyes. When rural newspapers start coming out in support of local literacy campaigns organized by people from the towns, the tom-toms are very soon reduced to silence. The book, seen as a form of pro-duction of knowledge, has become a tool running wild, no longer under the control of the human community. The manipulation of signs has become the vital productive ability of the industrial countries,[21] and one has to have done a lot of writing to earn one's right to 'speak up like a man'. The production of knowledge and the scarcity of brainpower are going to become the main productive activity of the rich countries in the years to come. Today, the various sectors of the information industry employ over 50% of the popu-lation of the U.S., as against 20% in 1950, while Parker forecasts the figure will be closer to 60% in 1980. Confronted with this informational invasion, three-quarters of humanity is *ipso facto* robbed of speech. We must reject the notion that the only legitimate question raised by the problem of literacy is that of how to make books and information freely available to all; and we must insistently ask in the name of what are the masses to be robbed of their own discourse, which remains their principal tool.

We should bear in mind that workers are being taught to read and write and are generally being subjected to increasingly long training periods in order to condition them to receive an ever greater flow of uncontrollable infor-mation; so that they will grow used to exchanging conditioned objects rather than devoting their time to speech – their own and others. Whereas today, only industrialized objects and signs are regarded as legitimate means of com-munication. In place of speech as the measure of all things, industrial society substitutes the myth of knowledge seen as the criterion for language, and legitimates the power of those whose authority is founded upon the exclusive possession of uncommunicable knowledge. Industrial society itself is responsible for illiteracy; and it forces us to take as our ideal in the field of literacy the specialized incompetence of the factory worker, chained to his tool, or that of the specialist, bogged down in his area of knowledge, no bigger than a pinhead. The obligation to be literate in order to be eligible for participation in the work of society reflects just one of the least tolerable education side-effects of the non-convivial tool. In a society where the computer programmer has to be reprogrammed himself each time a new generation of computers arrives on the market; where each skilled worker has to be retechnologized each time there is a change in the manufacturing process; then education has become a scarce commodity, of concern only to a minority. 'The recapture of everyday language is the prime pivot of any future political reversal.'

Towards a convivial literary process

A literary process tied to industrial productivity deprives men of their natural tendency to invest their own time in the creation of current values. Everyone, whatever his age, has the right to decide what he would like to learn, how, where and when. And he has the right to decide what he wants to do with it. Knowledge should be constantly available to all. Though it is probably more urgent to make existing knowledge available to all than to carry on developing fresh knowledge for the exclusive use of a handful of specialists; and the latter should be compelled to share their knowledge and give up their professional monopoly of knowledge. No institution can claim a monopoly over knowledge, nor has it the right to control its spread. Learning, living and working are all one, for we learn by living. Learning is a function of life, and man is constantly learning new things, throughout his lifetime. No form of knowledge is superior to another, it is merely different. And all human groups are capable of creating convivial centres; under the control of their users, and for the benefit of their users. In these centres, learning will become synonymous with doing and living.

NOTES

Notes to introduction

1 Robert Disch, ed., *The Future of Literacy* (Englewood Cliffs, N.J., 1973), 4–5. See also, Harvey J. Graff, *The Literacy Myth: Literacy and Social Structure in the Nineteenth-Century City* (New York and London, 1979) and *The Legacies of Literacy*, a history of Western literacy, in progress; M.J. Maynes, 'Schooling of the Masses: A Comparative Social History of Education in France and Germany, 1750–1850', unpub. Ph.D. diss., University of Michigan, 1977.

2 David Olson, 'Towards a Literate Society: Essay Review', *Proceedings*, National Academy of Education (1975–6), 111, 112, 149, 170.

3 See for example, Alex Inkeles and David H. Smith, *Becoming Modern* (Cambridge, Mass., 1974), among the literature linking literacy with modernization and progress. Further citations and a critical review are found in Graff, *The Literacy Myth*, Introduction. See also Charles Tilly's important review of *Becoming Modern*: 'Talking Modern', *Peasant Studies*, 6 (1977), 66–8.

4 Among a large and growing critical literature, see, as examples, Ian Weinberg, 'The Problem of the Convergence of Industrial Societies', *Comparative Studies in Society and History*, 11 (1969), 1–15; Dean C. Tipps, 'Modernization and the Comparative Study of Societies', *ibid.*, 15 (1973), 199–226; Ali A. Mazrui, 'From Social Darwinism to Current Theories of Modernization', *World Politics*, 21 (1968), 69–83; Robert Nisbet, *Social Change and History* (New York, 1969); Charles Tilly, 'Did the Cake of Custom Break?' in *Consciousness and Class Experience in Nineteenth Century Europe*, ed. John M. Merriman (New York, 1979), 17–44.

5 For an outline of this history and a review of sources, see Graff, *The Literacy Myth*, Introduction; Roger Schofield, 'The Measurement of Literacy in Pre-Industrial England', in *Literacy in Traditional Societies*, ed. Jack Goody (Cambridge, 1968), 311–25; Lawrence Stone, 'Literacy and Education in England, 1640–1900', *Past and Present*, 42 (1969), Section I; Graff, *Literacy in History: An Interdisciplinary Research Bibliography* (New York, 1981), Introduction.

6 For further reading and guides to the literature, see the 'Note on Further Reading' (page 11), as well as the notes included with the selections themselves.

7 On these issues, see for example, Graff, 'Literacy, Education, and Fertility, Past and Present: A Critical Review', *Population and Development Review*, 5 (1979), 105–40; Michael Haines, *Fertility and Occupation: Population Patterns in Industrialization* (New York, 1979); David Levine, 'Education and Family Life in Early Industrial England', *Journal of Family History*, 4 (1979), 368–80, and 'Illiteracy and Family Life in the First Industrial Revolution', *Journal of Social History*, 14 (1980), 25–44; John C. Caldwell, 'Mass Education as a Determinant of the Timing of the Fertility Decline', *Population and Development Review*, 6 (1980), 225–55; Charles Tilly, 'Population and Pedagogy in France', *History of Education Quarterly*, 13 (1973), 113–28.

8   Laslett, *The World We Have Lost*, 2nd edn (London, 1971), 207.
9   See for example, in addition to the readings below, Kenneth A. Lockridge, *Literacy in Colonial New England* (New York, 1974).
10   See for example, in addition to the readings, Thomas Laqueur, 'The Cultural Origins of Popular Literacy in England, 1500–1850', *Oxford Review of Education*, 2 (1976), 255–75; R.B. Webb, *The British Working Class Reader* (London, 1955); Margaret Aston, 'Lollardy and Literacy', *History*, 62 (1977), 347–71; Lawrence A. Cremin, *American Education: The Colonial Experience*, and *American Education: The National Experience* (New York, 1970, 1980); Goody, ed., *Literacy in Traditional Societies*; Henry F. Dobyns, 'Enlightenment and Skill Foundations of Power', in *Peasants, Power, and Applied Social Change: Vicos as a Model*, ed. Dobyns, Paul L. Doughty, and Harold D. Lasswell (Beverly Hills, Calif., 1971), 137–66; Inkeles and Smith, *Becoming Modern*.

Notes to chapter 1

1   S.S. Walker, 'Proof of Age of Feudal Heirs in Medieval England', *Medieval Studies* (Toronto) XXXV (1973), pp. 316–20.
2   H. Grundmann, *'Litteratus-Illiteratus', Archiv für Kulturgeschichte* XL (1958), p. 17.
3   In general see the contributions by L. Prosdocimi and Y. Congar to *I Laici nella societas christiana dei secoli XI e XII* ed. G. Lazzati and C.D. Fonesca, Università Cattolica del Sacro Cuore (Milan, 1968), pp. 56–117.
4   P. Riché, 'Recherches sur l'instruction des laics du IX au XII siècle', *Cahiers de Civilisation Médiévale* V (1962), p. 181.
5   J.W. Thompson, *The Literacy of the Laity in the Middle Ages*, University of California Publications in Education IX (1939), p. 170, n. 40. For a contrary view see V.H. Galbraith, 'The Literacy of the Medieval English Kings', *Proceedings of the British Academy*, XXI (1935), pp. 201–2, 211–12.
6   R.W. Southern, 'Master Vacarius and the Beginning of an English Academic Tradition' in *Medieval Learning and Literature: Essays Presented to R.W. Hunt* (1976), p. 268, n. 1, citing *Studia Anselmia* XLI (1957) p. 65. Cf. H.G. Richardson and G.O. Sayles, *The Governance of Medieval England from The Conquest to Magna Carta* (1963) (hereafter R & S), p. 270, n. 4.
7   J.W. Baldwin, *Masters, Princes and Merchants* (1970) II, p. 51, n. 57.
8   Cf. Grundmann, *'Litteratus–Illiteratus'*, p. 52 and Riché, 'Recherches sur l'Instruction des Laics', pp. 180–1.
9   M.M. Sheehan, *The Will in Medieval England*, Pontifical Institute of Medieval Studies: Studies and Texts VI (1963), pp. 260–1, nn. 128, 131.
10   P. Dupuy, *Histoire du differand d'entre le Pape Boniface VIII et Philippe le Bel* (1655), p. 14. G. de Lagarde, *La Naissance de l'esprit laique au déclin du Moyen Age* (1948) I, ch. 12.
11   L.C. Gabel, *Benefit of Clergy in England in the Later Middle Ages*, Smith College Studies in History XIV (1928–9), pp. 68–78.
12   *Ibid.* pp. 82–4.
13   Galbraith's lecture to the British Academy (Galbraith, 'Literacy', pp. 201–38) was published in 1936. Thompson's *The Literacy of the Laity in the Middle Ages* (Thompson, *Literacy*, ch. 7) was completed in the same year, but was not published until 1939.

14   Galbraith, 'Literacy', p. 222, n. 46.
15   *Ibid.*, 'Literacy', p. 215.
16   R & S, p. 278 and (more generally) pp. 269–83.
17   *Ibid.* p. 273.
18   *Ibid.* p. 275.
19   R & S, p. 274.
20   M.B. Parkes, 'The Literacy of The Laity', in *The Medieval World* ed. D. Daiches and A. Thorlby (1973), p. 558, n. 20.
21   Parkes, 'Literacy', p. 560.
22   N. Orme, *English Schools in the Middle Ages* (1973), ch. 1.
23   M.M. Sheehan, *The Will in Medieval England*, Pontifical Institute of Medieval Studies: Studies & Texts VI (1963), pp. 186–7.
24   *Ibid.* pp. 192; 188, n. 90.
25   F. Pollock and F.W. Maitland, *The History of England Law before the time of Edward I*, 2nd edition (1898) II, p. 87, n. 4.
26   Subsequently Anselm and the king came to terms, R.W. Southern, *St Anselm and his Biographer* (1963), pp. 176–9.
27   R.I. Moore, *The Birth of Popular Heresy* (1975), pp. 10–15.
28   II *Corinthians* iii, 3, 6. Cf. B. Smalley, *The Study of the Bible in the Middle Ages*, 2nd edition (1952), ch. i ('The Letter and the Spirit').
29   R.B. Brooke, *The Coming of the Friars* (1975), p. 126.
30   H.E. Butler, *The Autobiography of Giraldus Cambrensis* (1937), pp. 168, 175–6, M. Richter, *Giraldus Cambrensis* (2nd edn, 1976), p. 109.
31   P. Bec, *Nouvelle anthologie de la lyrique occitane* (1970), p. 179.
32   C. Roth, *A History of the Jews in England* (1941), p. 53.
33   C.R. Cheney, 'The Eve of Magna Carta', *Bulletin of The John Rylands Library* XXXVIII (1955–6), p. 340. F. Thompson, *The First Century of Magna Carta* (1925), p. 94.
34   D.L. Douie, *Archbishop Pecham* (1925), p. 113, n. 2.
35   For the meaning of *materna lingua* see C. Clark, 'Women's Names in Post-Conquest England', *Speculum* LIII (1978), pp. 224–5.
36   The story is discussed from a different point of view by A.K. Bate in *Latomus* XXXI (1972), p. 862.
37   *From Script to Print* (1945), p. 145.
38   M.D. Legge, *Anglo-Norman Literature and its Background* (1963), p. 65. Other examples in H.J. Chaytor, *From Script to Print*, pp. 11–12, 144–7. In general see R. Crosby, 'Oral Delivery in the Middle Ages', *Speculum* XI (1936), pp. 90–102.
39   Legge, *Anglo-Norman*, p. 143.
40   C.J. Holdsworth, 'John of Ford and English Cistercian Writing', *Transactions, Royal Historical Society* 5th series XI (1961), p. 124.
41   A description repeated by various scribes but originating in the eighth century, W. Wattenbach, *Das Schriftwesen im Mittelalter*, 3rd edition (1896), p. 495.
42   Thompson, *Literacy*, p. 171, n. 46.
43   F.M. Powicke, *The Christian Life in the Middle Ages* (1935), p. 88. C.H. Haskins, *Studies in Medieval Culture* (1929), p. 83.
44   Their holographs are illustrated by A. Gransden, *Historical Writing in England c. 550–1307* (1974), plates iv, v, x.
45   C.R. Cheney, *Medieval Texts & Studies* (1973), pp. 246–7, gives excellent examples from a letter of the Englishman, Gervase abbot of Prémontré, who died in 1228.
46   R.W. Southern, *Medieval Humanism and other Studies* (1970), p. 119.

47   Galbraith, 'Literacy', pp. 212–13.

Notes to chapter 2

1   The peasants, although illiterate, regarded scripture (in every sense of the word) as an essential reference. See the anxious question of Raymond de Laburat, a Catholic farmer excommunicated for non-payment of tithes: 'Is excommunication to be found in any scripture?' he asked a priest. Similarly a miller: 'The Resurrection is a proven fact, because the priests say it is written in the records and the books.'

2   They were Pierre Clergue the priest; his pupil (*scolaris*); Bernard Clergue; and Prades Tavernier, who stayed for long periods in the village though he did not really belong to it and came from the neighbouring parish. Clergue the priest, his pupil, and perhaps also Bernard Clergue, reputed to be learned, probably also knew some Latin. In all, the literacy rate was about 1.6 per cent, including perhaps two or three with a smattering of Latin.

3   The Inquisition made witnesses and accused persons swear on the Gospel. The friends of the homosexual Arnaud de Verniolles swore on some sacred book. Less sophisticated people swore on their own head, or on bread and wine or on flour.

Notes to chapter 3

1   Since this enabled scattered readers to consult the same book, it may be regarded as an aspect of standardization which is discussed in the next section.

2   Early crises of overproduction of humanist works are noted by Denys Hay, 'Literature, the Printed Book', in G.R. Elton (ed.), *The New Cambridge Modern History* (Cambridge, 1958), II, 365. The failure of printers to assess their markets shrewdly, which accounts for some of these crises, is noted by Curt F. Bühler, *The Fifteenth Century Book: The Scribes, The Printers, the Decorators* (Philadelphia, 1960), pp. 59–61. Inadequate distribution networks at first were largely responsible. Zainer's firm, e.g., turned out 36,000 books when the population of Augsburg was half that number (Bühler, p. 56).

3   Hay, p. 366. By the mid sixteenth century, 'even obscure scholars could possess a relatively large collection of books on a single topic', according to A.R. Hall, 'Science', in Elton (ed.), II, 389.

4   George Sarton, 'The Quest for Truth: Scientific Progress during the Renaissance', in W.K. Ferguson *et al.*, *The Renaissance: Six Essays* (Metropolitan Museum of Art Symposium, 1953 [New York, 1962]), p. 57.

5   These maps are compared and the superiority of manuscript charts to early printed maps is noted by Boies Penrose, *Travel and Discovery in the Renaissance 1420–1620* (New York, 1962), chap. xvi. The logical conclusion – that intelligent, literate sixteenth-century printers did not know what cartographers and mariners in coastal regions did – is, however, not drawn.

6   See R.J. Forbes and E.J. Dijksterhuis, *A History of Science and Technology* (London, 1963), Vol. II, chap. xvi, on how 'technology went to press' in the sixteenth century. A.R. Hall, *The Scientific Revolution 1500–1800: The Formation of the Modern Scientific Attitude* (Boston, 1957), p. 43, states: 'Vesalius' cuts are sometimes less traditional and more accurate than his text.' The cuts were made, however, by a wood-carver, Stephan of Calcar. (See n. 7 below.)

7   Erwin Panofsky, 'Artist, Scientist, Genius: Notes on Renaissance-Dämmerung', in Ferguson *et al.*, p. 160. This whole essay (which passes over the role of printing) is relevant to the above discussion. Stephan of Calcar's role in Vesalius' work is noted on p. 162, n. 36.

8   E. Harris Harbison, *The Christian Scholar in the Age of the Reformation* (New York, 1956), p. 54.

9   G. de Santillana, review of F. Yates's *Giordano Bruno and the Hermetic Tradition, American Historical Review*, LXX (Jan. 1965), 455.

10   See Frances Yates, *Giordano Bruno and the Hermetic Tradition* (London, 1964), *passim*. That ancient Egyptian ingredients *were* present in the third-century compilation is suggested on pp. 2–3, n. 4, and p. 431.

11   On the 'Hieroglyphics of Horapollo' (first printed by Aldus in Greek, 1505, in Latin, 1515) and later developments, see Erik Iversen, *The Myth of Egypt and Its Hieroglyphs in European Tradition* (Copenhagen, 1961), *passim*. Additional data is given by E.P. Goldschmidt, *The Printed Book of the Renaissance: Three Lectures on Type, Illustration, Ornament* (Cambridge, 1950), pp. 84–5, and Mario Praz, *Studies in Seventeenth Century Imagery* (Rome, 1964), chap. i. Yates implies that baroque argumentation about *hermetica* ended with Isaac Casaubon's early seventeenth-century proof that Ficino had translated works dating from the third century A.D. But Greek scholarship alone could not unlock the secrets of the pyramids. Interest in arcana associated with Thoth and 'Horapollo' continued until Champollion. By then the cluster of mysteries that had thickened with each successive 'unveiling of Isis' was so opaque that even the decipherment of the Rosetta stone could not dispel them.

12   Myron Gilmore, *The World of Humanism 1453–1517* (*Rise of Modern Europe* [New York, 1952]), p. 189.

13   Sarton, p. 66.

14   On what follows, see remarks by M.H. Black, 'The Printed Bible', in S.J. Greenslade (ed.), *The Cambridge History of the Bible* (Cambridge, 1963), pp. 408–14.

15   The word 'not' had been omitted from the seventh commandment (*ibid.*, p. 412).

16   How important this was is stressed both by Gilmore, p. 189, and Sarton, p. 66.

17   The historical importance of new standardized images is spelled out most clearly by Ivins. K. Boulding, *The Image* (Ann Arbor, Mich., 1961), pp. 64–8, who incorrectly assigns to the invention of writing the capacity to produce uniform spatiotemporal images. His remarks about the 'dissociated transcript' do not seem applicable to scribal culture.

18   Ernst Curtius, *European Literature and the Latin Middle Ages*, trans. W. Trask (New York, 1963; 1st ed., 1948), exemplifies erudite humanistic scholarship at its best. Yet his remarks on scribal book production are remarkably fanciful, on changes wrought by printing entirely vacuous (p. 238). His failure to consider how all the issues he deals with were affected by the new technology is shared by most literary scholars and historians of ideas.

19   See S.H. Steinberg, *Five Hundred Years of Printing* (rev. ed., Bristol, 1961), p. 25.

20   The probable effect of title-page ornamentation on sixteenth-century fine arts and the necessity of taking printing into account when dealing with new aesthetic styles is noted by André Chastel, 'What is Mannerism?' *Art News*, LXIV (Dec. 1965), 53.

21   This applies particularly to the publisher–printer (or printer–bookseller) as

described, e.g., by Elizabeth Armstrong, *Robert Estienne Royal Printer: An Historical Study of the Elder Stephanus* (Cambridge, 1954), pp. 18, 68. It is also applicable to many independent master printers, to some merchant–publishers (who, literally defined, were not printers at all and yet closely supervised the processing of texts – even editing and compiling some themselves), and finally to some skilled journeymen (who served as correctors or were charged with throwing together, from antiquated stock, cheap reprints for mass markets). The divergent social and economic positions occupied by these groups are discussed by Natalie Z. Davis in 'Strikes and Salvation at Lyons', *Archiv für Reformationsgeschichte*, LXV (1965), 48, and in 'Publisher Guillaume Rouillé, Businessman and Humanist', in R.J. Schoeck (ed.), *Editing Sixteenth Century Texts* (Toronto, 1966), pp. 73–6. Within workshops down through the eighteenth century, divisions of labor varied so widely and were blurred so frequently that they must be left out of account for the purpose of developing my conjectures. Accordingly I use the term 'printer' very loosely to cover all these groups throughout this paper.

22 Cited by Davis, 'Guillaume Rouillé', p. 100.

23 Steinberg, p. 28. A detailed account of the effects of printing on punctuation is given by Rudolph Hirsch, *Printing, Selling, Reading 1450–1550* (Wiesbaden, 1967), pp. 136–7.

24 The 'diagrammatic tidiness' imparted by print to 'the world of ideas' *is* discussed by Walter J. Ong, S.J., *Ramus: Method and the Decay of Dialogue from the Art of Discourse to the Art of Reason* (Cambridge, Mass., 1958), p. 311. See also his 'System, Space and Intellect in Renaissance Symbolism', *Bibliothéque d'humanisme et Renaissance – travaux et documents*, XVIII, No. 2 (1956), 222–40; and his 'From Allegory to Diagram in the Renaissance Mind', *Journal of Aesthetics and Art Criticism*, XVII (June 1959), 4. Father Ong's somewhat abstruse discussion has recently been substantiated and supplemented by a straightforward study of changes registered on repeated editions of a popular sixteenth-century reference work, which provides detailed confirmation of the above discussion. See Gerald Straus, 'A Sixteenth Century Encyclopedia: Sebastian Münster's *Cosmography* and Its Editions', in C.H. Carter (ed.), *From the Renaissance to the Counter Reformation: Essays in Honor of Garret Mattingly* (New York, 1965), pp. 145–63. See also the discussion of Robert Estienne's pioneering work in lexicography (in Armstrong, chap. iv), and Davis, 'Guillaume Rouillé', pp. 100–1.

25 The interplay between the printing of existing laws and laws pertaining to (or necessitated by) printing is an instance of complex interaction that deserves special study.

26 H.J. Graham, '"Our Tongue Maternall Marvellously Amendyd and Augmentyd": The First Englishing and Printing of the Medieval Statutes at Large, 1530–1533', *U.C.L.A. Law Bulletin*, XIII (Nov. 1965), 58–98.

27 *Ibid.*, p. 66.

28 G. Sarton, 'Incunabula Wrongly Dated', in D. Stimson (ed.), *Sarton on the History of Science* (Cambridge, Mass., 1962), pp. 322–3. Arabic numerals appear for the first time on each page of the Scriptures in Froben's first edition of Erasmus' New Testament of 1516, which also 'set the style' for the well-differentiated book and chapter headings employed by other Bible-printers (Black, p. 419). See also Francis J. Witty, 'Early Indexing Techniques: A Study of Several Book Indexes of the Fourteenth, Fifteenth, and Early Sixteenth Centuries', *Library Quarterly*, XXV (July 1965), 141–8.

29   Steinberg, pp. 145–53.

30   Thomas Kuhn, *The Copernican Revolution* (Cambridge, Mass., 1957), p. 131.

31   Ortelius' 'epoch-making' *Theatrum orbis terrarum* was published in Antwerp in 1570. (Although Mercator's 'milestone' was published in 1569, his new projection remained little known until 1599, when Edward Wright published a set of rules for its construction.) See Penrose, pp. 324–7. Febvre and Martin, p. 418, point to the fact that Copernicus' *De revolutionibus orbium cælistium* (1543) was not republished in a second edition until 1566 to support the view that printing did not speed up the acceptance of new ideas. In 1551, however, Erasmus Reinhold issued a 'complete new set of astronomical tables', based on the *De revolutionibus*. These so-called Prutenic Tables were widely used. See Kuhn, pp. 125, 187–8. The duplication of Napier's logarithms and their use by Kepler in constructing his Rudolphine Tables also seem to me to argue against Febvre and Martin's thesis. See Arthur Koestler, *The Sleepwalkers* (London, 1959), pp. 410–11. J.J. Scaliger's *De emendatione temporum*, which 'revolutionized all received ideas of chronology', was published in 1583; R.C. Christie and J.E. Sandys, 'Joseph Justus Scaliger (1540–1609)', *Encyclopædia Britannica* (11th ed.; New York, 1911), XXIV, 284. Theodore Besterman, *The Beginnings of Systematic Bibliography* (Oxford, 1936), pp. 7–8, 15–21, 33, argues that Conrad Gesner's *Bibliotheca universalis* (1545), a 1,300-page tome listing 12,000 Latin, Greek and Hebrew works, does not warrant calling Gesner the 'father of bibliography', since Johannes Tritheim's much smaller and restricted *Liber de scriptoribus ecclesiasticus* (1494) preceded it. The 'foundations of systematic bibliography were well and truly laid' at any rate before 1600.

32   The issues dealt with by studies such as F. Smith Fussner's *The Historical Revolution: English Historical Writing and Thought 1580–1640* (London, 1962) and Wylie Sypher's 'Similarities between the Scientific and Historical Revolutions at the End of the Renaissance', *Journal of the History of Ideas*, XXV (July–Sept. 1965), 353–68, need particularly to be reviewed in the light of the above discussion.

33   For the most part I have omitted from this section issues relating to historical consciousness and historiography, since I have discussed them elsewhere; Elizabeth L. Eisenstein, 'Clio and Chronos: An Essay on the Making and Breaking of History-Book Time', *History and the Concept of Time* (*History and Theory*, Suppl. 6 [1966]), pp. 42–64. Certain portions of this essay seemed too pertinent to be excluded, however. They have, therefore, been repeated in a slightly altered form and reworked along with fresh material into a different context here.

34   Kuhn, p. 73, remarks on this 'incredibly long time'.

35   The strategic position occupied by this unique ancient message center (which apparently swallowed up the contents of its only rival in Pergamum in the first century B.C. to make up for losses suffered in the famous fire) has only recently become apparent to me. Possibly it is well known to specialists in ancient history, but it still needs to be spelled out in more general accounts. According to Edward A. Parsons, *The Alexandrian Library* (Amsterdam, 1952), p. xi, the actual use of the museum by scholars over the course of seven (maybe nine) centuries 'is still a virgin field of inquiry'.

36   Like almost all other Renaissance scholars, Kristeller (P.O. Kristeller, *Renaissance Thought*, Vol. 1: *The Classic, Scholastic and Humanist Strains* (New York, 1961), p. 17), while noting that a selection of the 'classics' circulated in medieval times, singles out as the special contribution of Renaissance humanism

that 'it extended its knowledge almost to the entire range of . . . extant remains'. This boils down to the fact that most of what was recovered in the trecento and early quattrocento was not again lost. But it came very close to being lost. The manuscript of *De rerum natura* found by Poggio Bracciolini in 1417 *has* disappeared. The future of the copy that was made remained uncertain until 1473, when a printed edition was issued. Thirty more followed before 1600. A school of pagan philosophy intermittently revived and repeatedly snuffed out was thus permanently secured. See Danton B. Sailor, 'Moses and Atomism', *Journal of the History of Ideas*, XXV (Jan.–Mar. 1964), 3–16. Other findings from palimpsests and papyri would come later, as Kristeller notes. They came too late to be inserted into a curriculum of classical studies that was 'fixed' (by typography) in the sixteenth century. Hence they are regarded as being somewhat peripheral to the central corpus of classical works.

37 These same criteria, employed implicitly by Kristeller, are more explicitly and forcefully set forth by Erwin Panofsky, *Renaissance and Renascences in Western Art* (Stockholm, 1960), pp. 108, 113. The capacity to view antiquity from a 'fixed distance' is, in my view, placed much too early in this study.

38 Burckhardt notes as a 'singular piece of good fortune' that 'Northerners like Agricola, Reuchlin, Erasmus, the Stephani and Budaeus' had mastered Greek when it was dying out – with the 'last colony' of Byzantine exiles – in the 1520s in Italy; Jacob Burckhardt, *The Civilization of the Renaissance in Italy*, trans. S.G.C. Middlemore (New York, 1958), I, 205. The Aldine Press (among others) had already insured its perpetuation, however. All these 'northerners', one notes, were close allies of scholar–printers or (as with the 'Stephani', i.e., Estiennes) famous printers themselves.

39 Compare abundance of relevant data in Febvre and Martin, chap. viii, with what is missing in H. Stuart Hughes, *History as Art and as Science* (New York, 1964), pp. 38–40, where the relation between linguistic fixity and nationalism, individualism, capitalism, and the nation-state is discussed. Hughes urges historians to make use of linguistic studies, but linguists, while careful to discriminate between 'spoken' and 'written' languages, say little about scribal versus printed ones. Judging by my own experience, books on linguistics are most difficult to master and seem to lead far afield. I found the reverse to be true when consulting literature on printing.

40 Steinberg, pp. 120–6. Cases pertaining to Cornish, Cymric, Gaelic, Latvian, Estonian, Lithuanian, Finnish, Pomeranian, Courlander, Czech, Basque, etc., are cited. Of course, other factors may have been at work in other instances than those cited, but the number of instances where sixteenth-century type-casting seems to have been critical is noteworthy.

41 R.M. Kingdon, 'Patronage, Piety, and Printing in Sixteenth-Century Europe', in D.H. Pinkney and T. Ropp (eds.), *A Festschrift for Frederick B. Artz* (Durham, N.C., 1964), pp. 32–3, offers a detailed view of how Plantin's Antwerp firm implemented the Erastian policy of Philip II in order to evade payments to a rival firm (none other than Manutius) that had been granted the concession to print Catholic breviaries by Rome. Graham, pp. 71–2, also shows how closely allied Thomas Cromwell was with a circle of law-printers led by Thomas More's brother-in-law, John Rastell – an independent crusader for 'Englishing' all law, French or Latin, canon or civil.

42 By pursuing this line of inquiry, one could usefully supplement the theoretical views developed by Karl Deutsch (*Nationalism and Social Communication: An Inquiry into the Foundations of Nationality* [Cambridge, Mass., 1953]) with a more empirical, historically grounded approach.

43   J.C. Holt, *Magna Carta* (Cambridge, 1965), pp. 288–90.

44   Graham, p. 93.

45   Franklin Ford, *Robe and Sword (Harvard Historical Studies*, Vol. LXIV), (Cambridge, Mass., 1953), p. 80, describes this mechanism – not, however, how it was altered. See also his remarks about the 'great advance in publicity techniques' and how major parlement remonstrances were being 'published' by 1732 in printed form (p. 101).

46   A landmark in the history of literary property rights came in 1469, when a Venetian printer obtained a privilege to print and sell a given book for a given interval of time. See C. Blagden, *The Stationers Company, A History 1403– 1959* (London, 1960), p. 32. According to Forbes and Dijksterhuis, I, 147, although occasional privileges had been granted previously, the state of Venice was also the first to provide legal protection for inventors in 1474.

47   Raymond Birn, 'Journal des savants sous l'Ancien Régime', *Journal des savants* (1965), pp. 29, 33, shows how diverse fields of learning (and a division between 'serious' and 'frivolous' literature) were clearly defined by the terms of the official privilege granted this journal to cover a wide variety of different topics of serious concern. Both this article and Fredrick S. Siebert's *Freedom of the Press in England 1476–1776, The Rise and Decline of Government Control* (Urbana, Ill., 1952), *passim*, suggest how laws regulating printing raised new issues pertaining to privilege and monopoly, which became an acute source of conflict down through the eighteenth century.

48   P.O. Kristeller, *Renaissance Thought*, Vol. II: *Papers on Humanism and the Arts* (New York, 1965), p. 11.

49   Burckhardt, I, 149–50.

50   See a witty discussion of these terms by Robert K. Merton, *On The Shoulders of Giants: A Shandean Postscript* (New York, 1965), pp. 83–5.

51   The issue of authorship versus authority is discussed by McLuhan, pp. 130–7. The nature of medieval scribal authorship is brilliantly illuminated by Goldschmidt, *Medieval Texts*, Part III.

52   See the citation from Glanvill's *Essays* of 1676 cited by Merton, p. 68 n. Ramus, in the 1530s, had already stated: 'All that Aristotle has said is forged', according to H. Baker, *The Wars of Truth* (Cambridge, Mass., 1952), p. 93.

53   Lucien Febvre and H.J. Martin, *L'Apparition du Livre (L'Evolution de l'Humanité*, vol. XLIX [Paris, 1958]), p. 410. Additional data on the production of vernacular as opposed to Latin works during the first century of printing is supplied by Hirsch, pp. 132–4.

54   Hans Baron's 'The Querelle of the Ancients and Moderns as a Problem for Renaissance Scholarship', *Journal of the History of Ideas*, XX (Jan. 1959), 3–22, like many other treatments of this battle of books, passes over the possible role played by printers. Curtius, pp. 251–6, covers the scribal use of terms such as 'ancients' and 'moderns' but fails to note how they were altered after printing. All of Merton's (tongue in cheek) treatment of the giant and dwarf aphorism is also relevant and points to a vast literature on the topic.

55   Harbison, p. 5.

56   E. Rosen, 'The Invention of Eyeglasses', *Journal of the History of Medicine and Allied Sciences*, XI (1956), 34, n. 99, regards an early fourteenth-century preacher as inconsistent when he is recorded as saying in one sermon, 'Nothing remains to be said . . . today a new book could not be made nor a new art' and in a preceding one as referring to 'all the arts that have been

found by man and new ones yet to be found'. *Finding* a new art was not, however, necessarily equivalent to *making* one.

57 The Italian word for 'invention' has been located only once in fourteenth-century literature – a reference by Petrarch to Zoroaster as the *inventore* of the magic arts (*ibid.*, p. 192). Thoth (or 'Hermes Trismegistus') was responsible for inventing writing and numbering or measurement. Adam had, of course, named all things and (in a prelapsarian state) may have also known all things. A full inventory would include countless other (often overlapping) ancient claimants to the role of originators.

58 Sarton, 'The Quest for Truth', p. 66.

59 The most recent study is Frances Yates' *The Art of Memory* (London, 1966), which centers on use made of 'memory theaters'. According to J. Finegan, *Handbook of Biblical Chronology* (Princeton, N.J., 1964), p. 57, the term 'Amen' encapsulated in the three Hebrew letters aleph, mem, and nun (to which different numbers were assigned) a scheme for remembering four ninety-one day seasons of the solar year. When consulting works on this topic, I find it difficult to decide whether the ingenuity of modern scholars or that of ancient ones is being displayed.

60 Bennett, p. 158, notes a 'striking difference' between the large number of pagan classics translated into French in the sixteenth century and the greater number of 'edifying' devotional works translated into English.

61 How this was done in sixteenth-century England is traced with remarkable clarity by William Haller, *The Elect Nation: The Meaning and Relevance of Foxe's Book of Martyrs* (New York, 1963), *passim* – an exceptional work that integrates printing with other historical developments. Children's books about Elizabeth I are still being written from bits and pieces drawn from Foxe's massive *apologia*.

62 The most important exceptions are France and Geneva, where by the mid seventeenth century two differently oriented native literary cultures coincided with a single cosmopolitan one. A sounding board was thus provided for Rousseau, Mme de Staël, Sismondi, and other Genevans who might otherwise have been as obscure as their German, Swiss, or Dutch counterparts. The reasons for the conquest of the Gallic tongue (which paradoxically linked the most populous and powerful consolidated dynastic Catholic state with the tiny canton that had served as the protestant Rome and with the cosmopolitan culture of civilized Europe) deserve further study. Louis Réau, *L'Europe française au Siècle des Lumières* (*L'Evolution de l'humanité*, Vol. LXX [Paris, 1938]), although devoted to this important topic, slides over issues that need more rigorous analysis. David Pottinger, *The French Book Trade in the Ancien Regime 1500–1791* (Cambridge, Mass., 1958), offers some useful statistics, pp. 19–23, as does Steinberg, p. 118. Some further consequences of the spread of French are touched on in Eisenstein, 'Some Conjectures', pp. 51, 52.

One might note that the reaction to French armies and the rejection of French influence, among Germans and eastern Europeans in the early nineteenth century, necessarily involved disowning the cosmopolitan culture of the Enlightenment as well.

63 R.A. Sayce, 'French Continental Versions to c. 1600', in Greenslade (ed.), p. 114, contrasts the deep penetration of vernacular scriptural versions into the literary culture of German and English-speaking peoples with the shallow effect of French Bible translations. From Pascal to Gide, he notes, Latin

citations from the Vulgate appear most frequently when biblical references are evoked. The immense repercussions of the decision taken by the Council of Trent to proscribe vernacular translations and uphold the 'authenticity' of the Vulgate are difficult to locate throughout this massive collaborative volume. A clear view of how, when, and where the decision itself was taken is not offered. F.J. Crehan, S.J., 'The Bible in the Roman Catholic Church from Trent to the Present Day', pp. 199–237, ostensibly covers this issue but actually obfuscates it.

Notes to chapter 4

1 Robert Mandrou, *De la culture populaire aux 17e et 18e siècles. La bibliothèque bleue de Troyes* (Paris, 1964), pp. 9–10, 18, 22. Geneviève Bollème, 'Littérature populaire et littérature de colportage au 18e siècle', in *Livre et société dans la France du XVIIe siècle* (Paris, 1965), p. 65; *idem, Les almanachs populaires aux XVIIe et XVIIIe siècles. Essai d'histoire sociale* (Paris, 1969), 'Avant-propos'. See also Marc Soriano, *Les Contes de Perrault. Culture savante et traditions populaires* (Paris, 1968), pp. 480–1.

2 Louis B. Wright, *Middle-Class Culture in Elizabethan England* (Ithaca, New York, 1958 [1st ed. 1935]), p. 18. Mandrou, *Culture populaire*, pp. 19–20, 162. Bollème, however, has expressed some doubts about *whose* world view is revealed in almanacs and other popular literature.

3 A.H. Schutz, *Vernacular Books in Parisian Private Libraries of the Sixteenth Century, according to the Notarial Inventories* (University of North Carolina Studies in the Romance Languages and Literatures 25; Chapel Hill, 1955), pp. 39, 78, n. 85. Albert Labarre, *Le livre dans la vie amiénoise du seizième siècle. L'enseignement des inventaires après décès* (Paris, 1971), p. 274.
   Bollème admits to the wide range in the social background of readers of almanacs in the seventeenth and eighteenth centuries (*Almanachs*, p. 15).

4 Schutz, *Vernacular Books*, p. 34 (Arnaud de Villeneuve, to whom the *Tresor des povres* was attributed), p. 81, n. 137. E. Coyecque, *Recueil d'actes notariés relatifs à l'histoire de Paris et de ses environs au 16e siècle* ('Histoire generale de Paris', Paris, 1924), no. 106.

5 Mandrou, *Culture populaire*, pp. 162–3. Noel Taillepied, *Psichologie ou traité de l'apparition des esprits* (Paris, 1588), chap. 6.

6 Jean-Paul Sartre, *Qu'est-ce que la littérature?* (1948), cited by Robert Escarpit in his valuable essay 'Le littéraire et le social' (R. Escarpit, ed., *Le littéraire et le social. Eléments pour une sociologie de la littérature* [Paris, 1970], p. 18).

7 J.R. Goody, ed., *Literacy in Traditional Societies* (Cambridge, 1968). Elizabeth L. Eisenstein, 'Some Conjectures About the Impact of Printing on Western Society and Thought: A Preliminary Report', *Journal of Modern History* 40 (1968), 1–56; *idem*, 'The Advent of Printing and the Problem of the Renaissance', *Past and Present* 45 (Nov. 1969), 19–89; *idem* (with T.K. Rabb), 'Debate. The Advent of Printing and the Problem of the Renaissance', *Past and Present* 52 (Aug. 1971), 134–44; *idem*, 'L'avènement de l'imprimerie et la Réforme', Annales ESC 26 (1971), 1355–82. For a study of popular culture that uses a 'relational' approach, see M. Agulhon, 'Le problème de la culture populaire en France autour de 1848', Davis Center Seminar, Princeton University (May 1974).
   For a critique of some of the techniques used by social historians in the study of books and literary culture in the eighteenth century, see R. Darnton,

'Reading, Writing and Publishing in Eighteenth-Century France: A Case Study in the Sociology of Literature', in Felix Gilbert and S.R. Graubard, eds., *Historical Studies Today* (New York, 1972), pp. 238–50.

8 Lucien Febvre and Henri-Jean Martin, *L'apparition du livre* (Paris, 1958), pp. 285–6, 173–237; Henri-Jean Martin, *Livre, pouvoirs et société à Paris au XVIIe siècle (1598–1701)* (Geneva, 1969), pp. 319–26. N.Z. Davis, 'Publisher Guillaume Rouillé, Businessman and Humanist', in R.J. Schoeck, ed., *Editing Sixteenth Century Texts* (Toronto, 1966), pp. 72–7.

Schutz, *Vernacular Books*, pp. 31–73 (first appearance of craftsmen and small merchants among book-owners in the 1520s); Coyecque, *Recueil*, nos. 270, 588. Roger Doucet, *Les bibliothèques parisiennes au XVIe siècle* (Paris, 1956), 171–5 (lists names and occupations of book-owners in 194 Parisian inventories after death from 1493–1560). Out of 94 inventories from the years 1540–60, ten percent relate to persons below the level of the commercial and legal elite. Calculating from Martin's analysis of Parisian inventories after death in the seventeenth century (*Livre, pouvoirs et société*, p. 492), we get roughly ten percent of the book collections in the hands of lesser merchants, barber-surgeons, painters, and craftsmen.

9 Roger Vaultier, *Le folklore pendant la guerre de Cent Ans d'après les lettres de rémission du trésor des chartes* (Paris, 1965), p. 106. Bernard Guenée, *Tribunaux et gens de justice dans le bailliage de Senlis à la fin du moyen age (vers 1380–vers 1550)* (Paris, 1963), pp. 277–8, 317. Michel Devèze, *La vie de la fôret française au XVIe siècle* (Paris, 1961), 2: 112–13.

10 Emmanuel Le Roy Ladurie, *Les Paysans de Languedoc* (Paris, 1966), pp. 345–7. Yvonne Bézard, *La vie rurale dans le sud de la région parisienne de 1450 à 1560* (Paris, 1929), pp. 249–52, 185–6. Guenée, *Tribunaux*, pp. 187–93. Jacques Toussaert, *Le sentiment religieux en Flandre à la fin du moyen age* (Paris, 1963), pp. 60–6. M. Gonon, *La vie quotidienne en Lyonnais d'après les testaments, XIVe–XVIe siècles* (Paris, 1968), p. 54 and p. 54, n. 2 (none of the testaments that prescribe the placing of children in school are from peasant parents). Bernard Bonnin, 'L'éducation dans les classes populaires rurales en Dauphiné au XVIIe siècle', in *Le XVIIe siècle et l'éducation*, supplement to *Marseille* 88 (1972), 63–8 (I am grateful to Daniel Hickey for calling this article to my attention). A major new study of literacy in France from 1650 to the twentieth century is now under way by François Furet.

Isabelle Guérin, *La vie rurale en Sologne aux XIVe et XVe siècles* (Paris, 1960), p. 231, n. 5. Coyecque, *Recueil*, nos. 4078, 4806, 5380.

The seventeenth and eighteenth centuries were periods when rural schools spread significantly.

E. Campardon and A. Tuetey, eds., *Inventaire des registres des insinuations du Châtelet de Paris pendant les règnes de François 1er et de Henri II* (Paris, 1906), no. 735. ADR, B, Insinuations, Testaments, 1560–61, ff. 9r–10v; Henri and Julien Baudrier, *Bibliographie lyonnaise* (Lyon, 1895–1912), 9, 306.

11 No books are mentioned in the reviews of household possessions and wills made by Bézard, *Vie rurale*; Guérin, *Vie rurale*; Gonon, *Vie quotidienne*; and Raveau, *Agriculture*. Note the remarkably infrequent mention of books in notarial acts in the rural Mâconnais even in the seventeenth through nineteenth centuries (Suzanne Tardieu, *La vie domestique dans le mâconnais rural préindustriel* [Paris, 1964], p. 358 and p. 358, n. 2).

12   Prices taken from inventories after death in Labarre, *Livre*, p. 274, n. 20. Coyecque, *Recueil*, nos. 196, 96. The evaluation of Books of Hours varies considerably, depending on illustrations and bindings. The prices attributed to the same books when found in quantity in printers' stock are lower, the *Trésor des povres* at about eight deniers the volume (115s. 6d. for 165 copies) and the *Calendrier des bergers* at about six deniers the volume (69s. for 150 copies) in an inventory of 1522 (Doucet, *Bibliothèques*, p. 102, nos. 134, 150). Presumably these are wholesale prices for books that might not yet have been bound.

13   Martin, *Livre, pouvoirs et société*, pp. 319—20. When the Sire de Gouberville acquired books for his little library at the manor of Mesnil-au-Val in Normandy, they were purchased in Paris and Bayeux (A. Tollemer, *Un Sire de Gouberville, gentilhomme campagnard au contentin de 1553 à 1562* [Paris, 1972], pp. 204—9). In the 1570s and early 1580s, the bibliophile François de la Croix du Maine found it much harder to acquire books in Le Mans and vicinity than in Paris. It seems unlikely that books were sold at the Beaucaire fairs a century earlier.

14   On the variety of speech and dialect in sixteenth-century France and the growing separation between written and spoken language, see F. Brunot et al., *Histoire de la langue française des origines à 1900* (Paris, 1905—53), 1: xiii—xiv, 304ff; 2: 174—5.

15   Bollème points out that the *Shepherd's Calendar* did not become part of the peddlers' literature, in a cheap edition, until the mid-seventeenth century (*Almanachs*, p. 40). Yet she sees the intended public for the work as always the peasants ('L'auteur qui, symboliquement, ne sait pas écrire donne au lecteur qui ne sait pas lire le moyen de sa conduire mieux selon la sagesse naturelle . . . Le Berger parle au berger, au laboureur, au paysan' – p. 16). I am suggesting, however, that the initial public for the work was not the peasants ('Who wants to have knowledge of the heavens . . . like the shepherds without letters [can have it]. It is extracted and composed from their calendar and put into letters so that everyone can understand and know it like them'. *Cy est le compost et kalendrier des bergiers nouvellement reffait* [Paris; Guy Marchant, 1493], f. h. vii^v).

16   L. Petit de Julleville, *Histoire du théâtre en France. Les mystères* (Paris, 1880), 1: 373—4. Arnold Van Gennep, *Manuel de folklore français contemporain* (Paris, 1943), 1, 1: 209.

17   Petit de Julleville, *Théâtre*, 1: 384. Coyecque, *Recueil*, no. 4470. Perhaps the Saint Victor referred to here is Victorinus, the rhetorician and teacher of Jerome, who, while still a pagan, had a statue made to him in the Forum. The tale of the three-year-old martyr and his faithful martyred mother Julithe (d. 230) was well known in France, where numerous villages were named after him. He is included in the *Golden Legend*. See also G. Hérelle, *Les théâtres ruraux en France . . . depuis le XIVe siècle jusqu'à nos jours* (Paris, 1930).

18   F. Lesure, 'Eléments populaires dans la chanson français au début du 16e siècle', in *Musique et poésie au XVIe siècle* (Colloques internationaux du CNRS, Sciences Humaines, 5; Paris, 1954), pp. 169—75. Patrice Coirault, *Recherches sur notre ancienne chanson populaire traditionnelle* (Paris, 1927—33), pp. 82—3. *Notre chanson folklorique* (Paris, 1942), pp. 158—64.

19   Vaultier, *Folklore*, pp. 111—12; Mandrou, *Culture populaire*, p. 18; André Varangnac, *Civilization traditionelle et genres de vie* (Paris, 1970), pp. 96—7,

209; Tardieu, *Vie domestique*, pp. 154–62. Maurice Agulhon, 'Les Chambrées en Basse Provence: histoire et ethnologie', *Revue historique* 498 (1971), 359–60.

20   The *veillée* at which these tales are told is supposed to have occurred not in 1547, but in the youth of one of the peasants. E. LeRoy Ladurie, 'Mélusine ruralisée', Annales ESC 26 (1971): 604–6. On women as storytellers, see, for instance, Soriano, *Contes de Perrault*, p. 79.

21   French editions of Aesop: Lyon, 1490 and 1499, prepared by the Augustinian Julien de Macho; new rhymed edition by Guillaume Corrozet, Paris 1542 and after. Greek and Latin editions: Elizabeth Armstrong, *Robert Estienne, Royal Printer* (Cambridge, 1954), p. 97. Germaine Warkentin, 'Some Renaissance Schoolbooks in the Osborne Collection', *Renaissance and Reformation* 5, 3 (May 1969): 37. Urban ownership of Aesop: Labarre, *Livre*, p. 208; Schutz, *Vernacular Books*, pp. 72–3.

      Editions of the *Roman de la Rose* in its 'ancient language': fourteen between 1481 and 1528 in Paris and Lyon; three prose versions 'moralised' by Jean de Molinet, 1500–21, four editions between 1526 and 1538 in the translation attributed to Marot. No further editions until 1735! (Clearly the *Roman* did not become part of the peddlers' literature.) On these editions, on interest in the *Roman* among poets, and on Marot as probable translator, see Antonio Viscardi, 'Introduction', in *Le Roman de la Rose, dans la version attribuée à Clément Marot*, ed. S.F. Baridon (Milan, 1954), pp. 11–90. Urban ownership of the *Roman*, Labarre, *Livre*, p. 210; Schutz, *Vernacular Books*, p. 67; Doucet, *Bibliothèques*, p. 87, n. 39.

      I am grateful to F. Howard Bloch, Joseph Duggan, and John Benton for suggestions on this subject. Though many medieval manuscripts remain of the *Roman de la Rose* – some 300 – they are unlikely to have circulated among the peasants in this form. There is a short version of the *Roman* in manuscript, with much of the philosophical material omitted (E. Langlois, *Les manuscrits du roman de la Rose. Description et classement* [Lille, 1910], pp. 385–6). Here again there is no evidence that these excisions were made to prepare it for reading to peasants.

22   O. Douen, 'La Réforme en Picardie', BSHPF 8 (1859), 393. Crespin, *Martyrs*, 2: 468–9; P. Chaix, *Recherches sur l'imprimerie à Genève de 1550 à 1564* (Geneva, 1954), p. 194. Bernard Palissy, *Recepte véritable par laquelle tous les hommes de la France pourront apprendre à multiplier et augmenter leurs thrésors, in Oeuvres complètes* (Paris, 1961), pp. 104–5.

23   On the carter Barthélemy Hector: *Livre des habitants de Genève*, ed. P.-F. Geisendorf (Geneva, 1957), p. 55; H.-L. Schlaepfer, 'Laurent de Normandie', in *Aspects de la propagande religieuse* (Geneva, 1957), p. 198; Crespin, *Martyrs*, 2: 437–8. On the peddlers in the Lyonnais, ADR, B. Sénéchaussée, Sentences, 1556–9, Sentence of July 1559. Two of them, the dressmaker Girard Bernard, native of Champagne, and the shoemaker Antoine Tallencon or Tallenton, native of Gascony, purchased books from Laurent de Normandie a few months before their arrest (Schlaepfer, 'Laurent de Normandie', p. 200).

24   See, for instance, Marcel Cauvin, 'Le protestantisme dans le Contentin', BSHPF 112 (1966): 367–8; 115 (1960): 80–1. Le Roy Ladurie, *Paysans*, 348–51. For a picture of Protestant congregations in the seventeenth century in which individual *laboureurs* play their part, see P.H. Chaix, 'Les protestants en Bresse en 1621', *Cahiers d'histoire* 14 (1969): 252–4.

25   Chaix, *Recherches sur l'imprimerie*, pp. 120–2; Eugénie Droz, 'Le calendrier

genevois, agent de la propagande' and 'Le calendrier lyonnais', in *Chemins de l'hérésie* (Geneva, 1970–74), 2: 443–56; 3: 1–29. See also Jean Delumeau, 'Les réformateurs et la superstition', *Actes du colloque l'Amiral de Coligny et son temps* (1972) (Paris, 1974), pp. 451–87.

The Protestant *Calendriers* were not the first to use historical material. A 1550 *Heures de Nostre Dame a l'usage de Romme*, published by Magdaleine Boursette, includes dates in its calendar: the death of the scholar Vatable, the Concordat of Leo X and François 1er, the birth of Henri II, etc. (Paris, 1550).

26   Vinson, *Essai*, nos. 3–4; L. Desgraves, *L'imprimerie à la Rochelle 2. Les Haultin* (Geneva, 1960): 1–3. The only other example I know of French Protestant publications in regional dialect is the catechism in 'bernois', published by Pierre du Bois at Pau in 1564 at the request of Pastor Merlin for the 'catechistes de ce pays de Bearn' (Schlaepfer, 'Laurent de Normandie', p. 205, n. 1).

27   Crespin, *Martyrs*, 2: 438. The publisher of Protestant propaganda sometimes shared part of the risk with the peddler, contracting, for instance, that if the books were seized within a two-month period by the 'enemies of the Gospel', the *libraire* would bear all the loss (Schlaepfer, 'Laurent de Normandie', p. 199, n. 10; Chaix, *Recherches*, p. 59).

28   N. Weiss, 'Vidimus des lettres patentes de François 1er, 1529', BSHPF 59 (1910), 501–4; LeRoy Ladurie, *Paysans*, 380–404; Bézard, *Vie rurale*, 289–90; V. Carrière, *Introduction aux études d'histoire ecclésiastique locale* (Paris, 1936), 3: 319–52. S. Gigon, *La révolte de la gabelle en Guyenne* (Paris, 1906); G. Procacci, *Classi sociali e monarchia assoluta nella Francia della prima metà del secolo XVI* (Turin, 1965), pp. 161–73, 213–30; Choppin, *Oeuvres* (1662–63), 3: 22 (*'la multitude des Rustiques de la Guyenne, qui alloient tumultueusement armée de villages en villages en l'an 1594'*). Jean Moreau, *Mémoires . . . sur les Guerres de la Ligue en Bretagne*, ed. H. Waquet (Archives historiques de Bretagne, 1; Quimper, 1960), pp. 11–14, 75–6. A. Le M. de La Borderie and B. Pocquet, *Histoire de Bretagne* (Rennes, 1906), 5: 173–81; Henri Drouot, *Mayenne et la Bourgogne. Etude sur la Ligue (1587–1596)* (Paris, 1937), 1: 39–55; 2: 291–2. Claude de Rubys, *Histoire veritable de la ville de Lyon* (Lyon, 1604), pp. 430–1; Daniel Hickey, 'The Socio-Economic Context of the French Wars of Religion. A Case Study: Valentinois-Diois' (unpublished Ph.D. dissertation, Dept. of History, McGill University, 1973), chap 4; L.S. Van Doren, 'Revolt and Reaction in the City of Romans, Dauphiné, 1579–80', *Sixteenth Century Journal* 5 (1974): 72–7. See also Madeleine Foisil, *La révolte des Nu-Pieds et les révoltes normandes de 1639* (Paris, 1970), 178–83, on nicknames and organization of the Nu-Pieds.

29   Jean-Pierre Seguin, *L'information en France de Louis XII à Henri II* (Geneva, 1961), p. 52.

30   The Lyon analysis is based on a study of hundreds of contracts in ADR, 3E, for the decades of the 1560s and 1570s. LeRoy Ladurie, *Paysans*, pp. 333, 347, 882.

31   LeRoy Ladurie, *Paysans*, p. 333. According to André Bourde, in a lecture given at the University of California at Berkeley in December 1972, it was only in the course of the seventeenth century that French made important gains among the patriciate of Marseille, while the people continued to speak Provençal.

32   The Amiens figures are calculated by me from the data given in Labarre, *Livre*, pp. 118–26 and 62–104. I have defined the 'artisanal' group slightly differ-

ently from M. Labarre for purposes of this paper; that is, I have *excluded* from my count the unskilled workers included on pp. 124—6 and *added* some of the goldsmiths, butchers, etc. that Labarre has categorized with the *'classe marchande'*.

33 Labarre, *Livre*, pp. 260—3. Coyecque, *Recueil*, nos. 3768, 3791. A one-book library in Lyon in 1563 in a room rented by a mason's helper from a miller's daughter: *'une bible en francois'*. A five-book library in Lyon belonging to a merchant with a lot of paintings and furniture: *'Le livre des croniques, Les ordonnances des privileges des foyres de Lyon, Les troys miroirs du monde, La premiere partie de nouveau testament, Une Bible en francoys'* (ADR, 3E7179, ff. 467^r—468^r, 576^r—577^v).

34 The relation of prices to wages and purchases is, of course, rough:

Book	*Price, place, date*
Jean de Vauzelles, *Police subsidaire . . . des povres*	5 deniers, Montpellier, 1535
Livre d'arismetique	1½ deniers wholesale, Paris, 1522
Jacques de Bourbon, *Prinse . . . de Rodes*	3 sous, Paris, 1547/48
La bible des Noelz	2 sous, Paris, 1547/48
Philippe de Commines, *Les croniques du roy Loys unze*	5 sous, Paris, 1547/48

Sources: L. Galle, 'Les livres lyonnais', *Revue du Lyonnais* 23 (5th ser., 1897): 341; Doucet, *Bibliothèques*, pp. 92, 119, 118, 126.

In the 1520s in 'normal' years at Lyon, a loaf of *pain farain* cost 5 deniers. In the 1530s and 1540s, a pair of children's shoes might cost 4s. 6d.; a pound of candlewax, 2s. Painters' journeymen and printers' journeymen had wages roughly equivalent to 8s. per day in the 1540s; journeymen and workers in the building trades, about 5—6s. per day.

35 Schlaepfer, 'Laurent de Normandie', p. 207: 4s. per copy of the New Testament, 16°. Presumably this is a wholesale price. Bibles and New Testaments varied enormously in price depending on format, illustration, etc. An illustrated New Testament in an Amiens Library in 1564 was estimated at 5 livres (Labarre, *Livre*, p. 311).

36 Coyecque, *Recueil*, no. 588. Medieval university students often used manuscripts as security for loans. Crespin, *Martyrs*, 2: 430.

37 Henri Hauser, *Ouvriers du temps passé* (5th ed.; Paris, 1927), pp. 82—5. Hauser points out how often regulations against night work were violated. Even when they existed, they prohibited work after 8, 9, or 10 p.m. In 1539, the Lyon printing ateliers ran till 10 p.m.; in 1572, they closed at 8 or 9 p.m.

38 For further information on de Norry and the commercial arithmetic, see N.Z. Davis, 'Mathematics in the Sixteenth-Century French Academies: Some Further Evidence', *Renaissance News* 11 (1958), pp. 3—10; and 'Sixteenth-Century Arithmetics on the Business Life', *Journal of the History of Ideas* 21 (1960): 18—48.

39 Eisenstein, 'Advent of Printing', p. 68.

40 Crespin, *Martyrs*, 1: 527.

41 Eugénie Droz, 'Bibles françaises après le Concile de Trents', *Journal of the Warburg and Courtauld Institutes* 18 (1965): 213.

42 E. Delaruelle et al., *L'Eglise au temps du grand schisme et de la crise conciliaire (1378—1440)* ('Histoire de l'Eglise depuis les origins jusqu'à nos jours',

14; Paris, 1964), 2: 712–21. Droz, 'Bibles françaises', p. 222. See also, Martin, *Livre, pouvoirs et société*, pp. 102–4.

43   On this process, see Brunot, *Histoire de la langue française*, 2: 36–55; Howard Stone, 'The French Language in Renaissance Medicine', BHR 15 (1953): 315–43; V.-L. Saulnier, 'Lyon et la médecine aux temps de la Renaissance', *Revue lyonnaise de médecine* (1958): 73–83; C.A. Wickersheimer, *La médecine et les médecins en France à l'époque de la Renaissance* (Paris, 1906), pp. 128–78. Alison Klairmont of the University of California at Berkeley is considering these subjects anew in her doctoral dissertation on the medical profession in sixteenth-century France.

Notes to chapter 5

1   Elizabeth Eisenstein, 'Some Conjectures about the Impact of Printing on Western Society and Thought: A Preliminary Report', *Journal of Modern History* 40, no. 1 (1968): 1–56.

2   The same point is made in a different context by Natalie Z. Davis, *Society and Culture in Early Modern France* (Stanford, Calif., 1975), p. 221.

3   Lawrence Stone has considered both religion and the political drive for social control as factors determining educational policy, institutions, and procedures: 'Literacy and Education in England, 1640–1900', *Past and Present* 42 (1969): 76–86. I do not find that Protestantism – at least in its sixteenth-century German version – gave as great a stimulus to mass education as he suggests (pp. 76–83). There was a wide gap between programmatic announcements by governments and consistories, on the one hand, and the public response to these on the other. The incentive to become literate arose mainly from pragmatic considerations.

4   Andrzey Wyczanski, 'Alphabétisation et structure sociale en Pologne au 16e siècle', *Annales, E.S.C.* 29, no. 3 (May–June 1974): 705–13. Wyczanski takes a sample of about a thousand tax self-assessments containing signatures from the years 1564–65 in the Cracow region, enabling him to relate literacy (= ability to take pen in hand and sign) to social standing. For a discussion of the relationship of signatures to literacy, see F. Furet and W. Sachs, 'La croissance de l'alphabétisation en France, XVIIIe–XIXe siècle', *Annales, E.S.C.* 29, no. 3 (May–June 1974): 714–37. The authors conclude (after much hedging) that signatures are a valid measure of literacy. See also Pierre Goubert, *L'ancien régime*, Vol. 1. *La société* (Paris, 1969), pp. 244 ff. Goubert utilizes the unpublished work of Louis Maggiolo with signatures and marks on marriage contracts and concludes that four-fifths of all Frenchmen, and an even greater part of Frenchwomen, were totally illiterate in 1685 (78.7% and 86%, respectively, based on 219,047 cases). Literacy was greater in the north of France than in the west, center, and south. It seems to have been tied to the existence of village schools, and Protestantism 'ne s'accommode jamais de l'ignorance totale' (p. 244). Goubert's data were used before him by M. Fleury and A. Valmary, 'Les progrès de l'instruction élémentaire de Louis XIV à Napoléon III . . . ', *Population* (January–March 1957), pp. 71–92, who conclude, however, that no correlation exists between the prevalence of schools and the ability to sign. Emmanuel LeRoy Ladurie, measuring the frequency of signatures of artisans in Montpellier and Narbonne in 1575, finds only 25% of them illiterate in the former place, 33% in the latter. In the countryside he finds 72% illiteracy among peasants in Montpellier, 90% among rural workers

in the Narbonne region: *The Peasants of Languedoc*, trans. John Day (Urbana, Ill., 1974), pp. 150, 161–4. Natalie Davis, 'City Women and Religious Change', in her *Society and Culture in Early Modern France* (Stanford, Calif., 1975), pp. 72–3, studies 1,200 contracts from Lyon in the 1560s and 1570s, concluding that 28% of women, all of them from merchant and publisher families, and a much higher proportion of men, including artisans, could sign their names. For some English evidence in the late sixteenth and the seventeenth and eighteenth centuries, see Peter Clark, 'The Ownership of Books in England, 1560–1640: The Example of Some Kentish Townfolk', in *Schooling and Society: Studies in the History of Education*, ed. Lawrence Stone (Baltimore, 1976), pp. 102–3, 106, 109. Clark finds a notable extension of literacy to 'lower ranks of respectable society', i.e., artisans. Also R.S. Schofield, 'The Measurement of Literacy in Pre-Industrial England', in *Literacy in Traditional Societies*, ed. Jack Goody (Cambridge, 1968), pp. 311–25, especially p. 319, for discussion of signatures as indicators of literacy. Also Victor E. Neuburg, *Popular Education in Eighteenth-Century England* (London, 1971); Lawrence Stone, 'Literacy and Education in England, 1460–1900', *Past and Present* 42 (1969): 69–139. Cf. also Carlo M. Cipolla, *Literacy and Development in the West* (Baltimore, 1969), and H.J. Martin, *Livre, pouvoirs et société à Paris au 17e siècle* (Geneva, 1969), and Harvey J. Graff, 'Notes on Methods for Studying Literacy from the Manuscript Census [in nineteenth-century Canada]', *Historical Methods Newsletter* 5, no. 1 (December 1971).

5   Rudolf Engelsing, *Analphabetentum und Lektüre: Zur Sozialgeschichte des Lesens zwischen feudaler und industrieller Gesellschaft* (Stuttgart, 1973), especially chaps. 5–7, is a disappointingly general and superficial book that in no way justifies its promising title.

6   On the vernacular literature of the time in relation to its society, see Inge Leipold, 'Untersuchungen zum Funktionstyp "Frühe deutschsprachige Druckprose . . . " ', *Deutsche Vierteljahrsschr. Literaturwiss. Geistesgesch.* 48, no. 2 (May 1974): 264–90. On the entertainment literature generally, see Hans Rupprich, *Die deutsch Literatur vom späten Mittelalter bis zum Barock*, vol. 2, in H. DeBoor and Richard Newald, *Geschichte der deutschen Literatur*, 4² (Munich, 1973): 165–84.

7   Jörg Wickram *Derr irr reintende Pilger* (1556), in Roloff, ed., *Jörg Wickram*, 6: 84–5:

> Holding the Bible, he drew near
> To the good pilgrim, saying, 'hear
> How I find my greatest pleasure
> And spend my evening hours of leisure.
> My labor done in field and stable,
> I place the Bible on my table
> And study it two hours or three.
> On holidays, when I am free
> Of work, I spend the day
> Reading the Scriptures, for my way
> To church is far, two hours to reach
> My parish to hear the pastor preach.'

How, the pilgrim wanted to know, could such a simple man be sure that he understood the Bible correctly?

> The peasant answered, 'here by my side
> I have some other books, to wit

Explanations of Holy Writ,
And these I use to teach myself.'
He showed the pilgrim a tall shelf
Filled with bound volumes: history,
Chronicles and theology,
All German titles, well selected,
Which this simple person had collected.

There are many references to reading peasants in the pamphlet literature of the time.

8   Pierre Goubert, *l'ancien régime* (1969), pp. 244—5, ties literacy to the presence of village schools. The most literate regions had two or three times as many schools easily accessible to its population as less literate regions.

Notes to chapter 6

1   Sources are discussed and some figures given in R.S. Schofield, 'The measurement of literacy in pre-industrial England', in Jack Goody (ed.), *Literacy in traditional societies* (Cambridge, 1968), pp. 311—25; R.S. Schofield, 'Illiteracy in pre-industrial England: the work of the Cambridge Group', *Educational Reports Umea*, II (1973), 1—21; Lawrence Stone, 'Literacy and education in England, 1640—1900', *Past and Present*, XLII (1969), 98—112; Margaret Spufford, *Contrasting communities, English villagers in the sixteenth and seventeenth centuries* (Cambridge, 1974), pp. 192—205; David Cressy, 'Literacy in pre-industrial England', *Societas*, IV (1974), 229—40. Another source is introduced in Richard T. Vann, 'Literacy in seventeenth-century England: some Hearth Tax evidence', *Journal of Interdisciplinary History*, V (1974), 287—93. Wills and depositions are compared in David Cressy, 'Literacy in seventeenth-century England: more evidence', *Journal of Interdisciplinary History* (forthcoming).

2   Cf. R.D. Altick, *The English common reader* (Chicago, 1963), pp. 18—19.

3   Schofield, 'Measurement of literacy', p. 319.

4   Ibid. p. 317.

5   Lawrence Stone, 'The educational revolution in England, 1560—1640', *Past and Present*, XXVIII (1964), 43. Almost half of a sample of early seventeenth century criminals sentenced to death pleaded Benefit of Clergy and saved their lives by reciting the 'neck verse'.

6   The procedure follows R.S. Schofield, 'Sampling in historical research', in E.A. Wrigley (ed.), *Nineteenth century society* (Cambridge, 1972), pp. 146—84.

7   Alan Everitt, 'Farm labourers', in Joan Thirsk (ed.), *The agrarian history of England and Wales, 1500—1640* (Cambridge, 1967), p. 398, estimates more than a third of the population were labourers in a fertile corn growing area.

8   Protestation Returns, House of Lords Record Office, summarized in Schofield, 'Illiteracy in pre-industrial England', p. 11; Essex figures are derived from returns to the Protestation of 1642, the Vow and Covenant of 1643 and the Solemn League and Covenant of 1644, David Cressy, 'Education and literacy in London and East Anglia, 1580—1700', Cambridge University Ph.D. thesis, 1972, pp. 283—94. Declarations from three Suffolk and one Norfolk parishes preserved in local collections show 46 per cent illiteracy in Suffolk and 72 per cent in Norfolk, Cressy, thesis, p. 294, and Breckles, Norfolk, parish register with incumbent. None of the Protestation Returns in the H.L.R.O. can be used to calculate more acceptable figures for Norfolk or Suffolk.

9   The social order is most conveniently outlined in Peter Laslett, *The world we have lost* (2nd edn, London, 1971), p. 38.

10 Much of this material is discussed in Mildred Campbell, *The English Yeoman under Elizabeth and the early Stuarts* (London, 1967), pp. 407–22.

11 Some examples are printed in Charles Sisson, 'Marks as signatures', *The Library*, 4th ser., IX (1928–9), pp. 1–37.

12 Spufford, *Contrasting communities*, pp. 206–18, discusses the importance of reading in the village community.

13 Women in London, however, made substantial progress in the second half of the seventeenth century, reducing their measured illiteracy from 90 per cent to a mere 52 per cent by the 1690s. Cressy, 'Literacy in pre-industrial England', p. 233. Perhaps the complexity of London life required better literacy. Men in London were also far more literate than their rural counterparts.

14 See Spufford, *Contrasting communities*, pp. 182, 196, for the unsatisfactory nature of wills. My comparison of wills and depositions in the diocese of Norwich in the 1630s finds yeomen 61 per cent illiterate instead of 32 per cent, husbandmen 91 per cent illiterate instead of 86 per cent, and tradesmen 60 per cent illiterate instead of 49 per cent, calculations from Norwich Record Office, Wills.

15 To test whether an age effect was at work a check was made by grouping the tradesmen and craftsmen into their appropriate birth decades and comparing their ability to sign as they grew older. No significant difference was observed until they were aged over sixty.

16 London, 1969, esp. pp. 279–97, and table p. 373.

17 Cressy, thesis, pp. 218–37; Lawrence Stone, 'The size and composition of the Oxford student body 1580–1910', in Lawrence Stone (ed.), *The university in society* (Princeton, N.J., 1974), I, 91.

18 G.R. Elton, *Reform and renewal, Thomas Cromwell and the common weal* Cambridge, 1973), pp. 29–32.

19 A.F. Leach, *English schools at the Reformation* (2 vols., London, 1896); Joan Simon, *Education and society in Tudor England* (Cambridge, 1967), pp. 179–96, 215–44.

20 The characterization originates with Stone, 'Educational revolution', loc. cit.

21 Figures are derived from the Vicar General's books, Greater London Record Office DL/C 333–4, and a licensing record, Norwich Record Office, SUN/2, discussed in Cressy, thesis, pp. 149–54.

22 Stone, 'Oxford student body', pp. 17, 28–9.

23 The total of matriculations in the 1590s is extrapolated from the number of graduations in that decade and the numerical relationship between matriculations and graduations in the previous and following decades. The Cambridge matriculation register was poorly maintained in the 1590s, another symptom of decline.

24 The figures are derived from episcopal visitation records in the Norwich Record Office, VIS/1–6, VSC/1–2, REG/16.

25 Idem.

26 For good intentions and slight achievements during the Revolution see Charles Webster, *Samuel Hartlib and the advancement of learning* (Cambridge, 1970) and W.A.L. Vincent, *The state and school education 1640–1666* (London, 1950), passim.

27 Cf. Lawrence Stone, 'The alienated intellectuals of early Stuart England', *Past and Present*, XXIV (1963), 101–2.

28   M.G. Jones, *The charity school movement* (London, 1964), p. 73. See also Joan Simon, 'Was there a charity school movement?', in Brian Simon (ed.), *Education in Leicestershire* (Leicester, 1968), pp. 55–100.

29   R.S. Schofield, 'Dimensions of illiteracy, 1750–1850', *Explorations in Economic History*, X (1973), p. 450.

Notes to chapter 7

1   I should like to thank Dr Roger Schofield for reading and commenting on this piece. I am also very grateful to Miss Sandy Harrison for collecting details from those autobiographies I could not myself see. The autobiographies have been extensively discussed in Owen C. Watkins, *The Puritan Experience* (1972) and Paul Delaney, *British Autobiography in the Seventeenth Century* (1969). Neither man is particularly interested in literacy, or the social origins of the humble autobiographer; indeed, the latter work includes the quite mistaken statement: 'Before 1700, no autobiographies by agricultural labourers or yeomen are known' (142, n. 25). Thirty-one of the 141 autobiographers whose works I have been able to examine describe the social status of the autobiographer's parents, and give some fragmentary details of the autobiographer's education. (Watkins, *op. cit.*, 241–59, lists autobiographies, and I have used this list as my base.) In addition, five more of the autobiographers give some information on their education alone, and another dozen on their background alone. I have used this information to help build up a picture of the age at which reading and writing were taught. I have also used the diaries of men born in the seventeenth century of non-gentle rural origin, and, for good measure, the educational experience of the early eighteenth-century day-labourer poet, Stephen Duck. Much of this material is re-used in Chapter 2 of *Small Books and Pleasant Histories: Popular fiction and its readership in seventeenth-century England* (Methuen, 1981).

2   It is possible that the Quaker autobiographers were less exceptional, for the Quakers seem to have had an entirely deliberate policy of using print for evangelism and polemic. Quaker autobiographies are therefore much the most common. For the whole subject of humble autobiographers, see David Vincent's forthcoming study of the autobiographies of working men in the first half of the nineteenth century, *Bread, Knowledge, and Freedom* (Europa, 1981). I am very much indebted to Dr Vincent for drawing my attention to the relevance of the seventeenth-century autobiographer to my work. His second chapter discusses both the seventeenth-century autobiographers and the eighteenth-century 'uneducated poets' as forerunners of the nineteenth-century working-class autobiographers, and was my point of departure.

3   R.T. Vann, *The Social Development of English Quakerism, 1655–1755* (1969), ch. 2.

4   The whole question of the use of signatures to provide a measure of the diffusion of literary skills over time, and of the crucial relationship of writing ability to reading ability, is discussed in R.S. Schofield, 'The measurement of literacy in pre-industrial England', in J.R. Goody (ed.), *Literacy in Traditional Societies* (1968), 318–25 and 'Some discussion of illiteracy in England, 1600–1800' (unpublished). A part of the latter has appeared as 'Dimensions of illiteracy, 1750–1850', *Explorations in Economic History*, X, 4 (1973), 437–54. I am very grateful for Dr Schofield's permission to use the unpublished, definitive discussion of the relationship between signing and reading ability.

5   David Cressy, 'Educational opportunity in Tudor and Stuart England', *History of Education Quarterly* (Fall 1976), 314, and 'Literacy in seventeenth-century England: more evidence', *Journal of Interdisciplinary History*, VIII, 1 (Summer 1977), 146–8. Also *Historical Journal*, XX (1977), 4–8.

6   Cressy, 'Educational opportunity', 309–13.

7   Ironically, in view of his recent care to stress restricted access to education in 'Educational opportunity', the best survey of elementary educational facilities and their effects is in David Cressy, 'Education and literacy in London and East Anglia 1580–1700' (Cambridge Ph.D. thesis, 1972) which lists all schoolmasters appearing in the Dioceses of London and Norwich and shows them relatively well provided with masters in rural areas in the 1590 and early seventeenth century. Alan Smith 'A study of educational development in the dioceses of Lichfield and Coventry in the seventeenth century' (Leicester Ph.D. thesis, 1972) and 'Private schools and schoolmasters in the Dioceses of Lichfield and Coventry', *History of Education*, V, 2 (1976) shows that in these dioceses there were more unendowed schoolmasters teaching in more places between 1660 and 1700 than in 1600–40. This might, of course, indicate merely an improvement in the records. On the other hand, it may indicate that the periods when most elementary education was available differed in different parts of the country. In this case, Cressy's periodization of improvement and stagnation in literacy rates does not necessarily apply to the whole country.

8   Schofield, 'The measurement of literacy in pre-Industrial England', 313–14, and 'Some discussion of Illiteracy in England, 1600–1800'.

9   See Cressy, *Education in Tudor and Stuart England*, 70–2.

10 This coincides well with the expectations of the early nineteenth-century monitorial schools, in which a child was expected to learn to read in eleven months. Schofield, 'Measurement of literacy in pre-Industrial England', 316.

11 *Pace* Peter Clark, who suggests that my argument that 'the husbandman who depended entirely on familial labour was probably . . . unable to afford the loss of labour which his child's school attendance entailed . . . is stronger in the context of higher education than in the case of primary instruction. It does not take into account those many *longeurs* in the agricultural year . . . when parents were probably quite happy to send a noisy son out to school for a month or so.' Peter Clark, *English Provincial Society from the Reformation to the Revolution: Religion, Politics and Society in Kent, 1500–1640* (1977), 191. The acquisition of the ability to sign was certainly normally acquired young, probably between seven and eight, and Cressy's evidence shows quite conclusively that economic status determined education to this level.

12 Extract from *Board of Trade Papers*, printed in H.R. Fox Bourne, *The Life of John Locke* (London, 1876, reprinted Aalen, 1969), p. 366.

13 Alice Clark, *Working Life of Women in the Seventeenth Century* (1919), 131. In the 1640s unskilled agricultural labourers were earning 12*d*. a day (Joan Thirsk (ed.), *Agrarian History of England and Wales*, IV, *1560–1640*, 864). This rate was the same as that for building labourers, which remained constant at 12*d*. a day until just after 1690. (E.H. Phelps Brown and Sheila V. Hopkins, 'Seven centuries of building wages', in E.M. Carus-Wilson (ed.), *Essays in Economic History*, II (1962), 172–3 and 177.) These children were earning a sixth of a man's wage. Exceptionally skilled children, like Thomas Tryon, could earn a third of a man's wage at eight.

14 I. Pinchbeck and M. Hewitt, *Children in English Society* (1969), i, 161.

15 *Ibid.*, 154–6.

16   *Ibid.*, 10.

17   J. Thirsk (ed.), *Agrarian History of England and Wales*, IV, *1500–1640*, 865. In 1586 in London their day-wages without food had been fixed at 13*d*. a day, along with masons, coopers and glaziers under the Statute of Artificers. This compared with 9*d*. a day for 'common labourers'. R.H. Tawney and Eileen Power (eds.), *Tudor Econ. Documents*, I (1924), 369–70.

18   The autobiographers whose parents were prosperous enough to enable them to go to university quite frequently went as early as fourteen. This conflicts with Cressy's findings that the mean age for entry to university was sixteen (*thesis cit.*) and bears out the suggestion that the autobiographers were probably an exceptionally gifted group.

19   The term 'husbandman' can be misleadingly used in a literary sense. Otherwise, it normally describes the group of farmers with medium-sized farms between fifteen and fifty acres who were becoming increasingly rare in arable areas in the seventeenth century. The plotting of values of the goods of men described as 'husbandmen' by their neighbours who drew up their inventories shows this quite clearly, although the range of values of husbandmen's goods is wide, and will overlap considerably with the bottom of the range of values of the more prosperous 'yeomen's' goods. Margaret Spufford, 'The significance of the Cambridgeshire Hearth Tax', *Cambridge Antiquarian Society*, LV (1962), 54, n. 3.

20   When Mrs Leavis wrote of the literary inadequacy and emotional poverty of twentieth-century mass fiction in 1939, she was unaware of the existence of the voluminous chap-literature of the seventeenth and eighteenth centuries, the content of which would have provided her with an apt comparison with modern bestsellers. She wrote of Bunyan's prose, as if only the *Authorised Version* was available to form his style, and of the cultural contacts of working-class men up to the 1850s as if only the *Bible*, the *Pilgrim's Progress*, *Paradise Lost* and *Robinson Crusoe*, with works by Addison, Swift and Goldsmith and so on, were on the market. 'No energy was wasted, the edge of their taste was not blunted on bad writing and cheap thinking', Q.D. Leavis, *Fiction and the Reading Public* (1939), 97–102, 106–15.

21   In eighteenth-century France, about one eighth of children had lost their fathers by this age, and by fourteen, the age at which apprenticeship normally seems to have started, a quarter of children had lost their fathers. Calculated from Harvé Le Bras, 'Parents, grands-parents, bisaieux', *Population* (1973), 34. I am told by the Cambridge Group for the History of Population and Social Structure that these figures should apply to seventeenth-century England.

22   Vincent, *op. cit.*, Ch. 5.

23   Although it seems that there was no hard and fast distinctive line drawn between a schoolmaster licensed to teach 'reading, writing and arithmetic' and one licensed to teach 'grammar'. At one visitation a man might well be licensed to teach grammar, who had previously been licensed to teach reading and writing, and vice versa. It does not seem as if there was a clear distinction, in the small 'private' schools which were both so numerous and so impermanent in the seventeenth century, between 'English', or 'petty' schools, and grammar schools. The masters probably taught according to the aptitudes of the different children, the desires of their parents, and the length of time the children could be spared for education from the labour force, as well as their own ability and training. The flexibility frequently found in seventeenth-century education is indicated by the licenses to Thomas Orpe, *literatus* 'to

teach boys in English as well as in Latin as long as they were able' at Norton, Salop, in 1695. Alan Smith, 'Private schools and schoolmasters in the Dioceses of Lichfield and Coventry in the seventeenth century', *History of Education*, vol. 5, no. 2, (1976) 125; Margaret Spufford, *Contrasting Communities* (1974), 187.

24 Cressy, 'Educational opportunity in Tudor and Stuart England', 314.

25 Schofield, 'The measurement of literacy in pre-Industrial England', 313.

26 David Cressy, 'Illiteracy in England, 1530–1730', *Historical Journal*, XX, 1 (March 1977), 8–9.

27 Eleven of the thirty-one, including six of the nine orphans.

28 A similar situation of course already existed a century earlier amongst at least a group of the yeomanry. C.J. Harrison, 'The Social and Economic History of Cannock and Rugeley, 1546–1597' (unpublished Ph.D. thesis, University of Keele, 1974), 118–23, demonstrates the social importance of the court Leet meeting and also the legal capacities and attitudes, and network of correspondents, of a sixteenth-century yeoman farmer. He himself, although technically untrained, acted as both under-steward and steward of the manor, advising his lord on legal affairs in Staffordshire. A small group of such men regularly acted as legal advisors and representatives of the other peasantry in the manor court.

29 Cressy, 'Educational opportunity in Tudor and Stuart England', *passim*. To him, of course, yeomen's sons at university appear a minority, sober and straitened group. This, as an overall view, is undoubtedly correct.

Notes to chapter 8

1 *Aperçu de la Démographie des divers Pays du Monde 1929–1936* (The Hague, 1939), p. 28.

2 UNESCO, *Progress of Literacy in Various Countries* (Paris, 1953), p. 88.

3 UNESCO, *World Illiteracy at Mid-Century* (Paris, 1957), p. 29.

4 Carlo Cipolla, *Literacy and Development in the West* (London, 1969), p. 61.

5 For Swedish progress see *Svenska folkskoland historia* (The history of the Swedish elementary school), I–III (Stockholm, 1940–42), W. Sjöstrand, *Pedagogikens* II–III: 2 (History of education) (Lund, 1958–63); C.I. Sandström, *Utbildningens idéhistoria* (The history of the ideology of education) (Stockholm, 1975); and for older literature, see references in Egil Johansson, *En studie med kvantitativa metoder av folkundervisningen i Bygdeå socken 1845–1873* (Study with quantitative methods of popular education in the parish of Bygdeå 1845–1873) (Umeå, 1972).

6 Johansson, *En studie*, pp. 76–80.

7 H. Pleijel, *Husandakt, husaga, husförhor* (Family prayers, caning, and church examinations) (Stockholm, 1965), and references in this work.

8 For the conflict regarding Consistorium generale in the seventeenth century, see e.g. Y. Brilioth, *Svensk kyrkokunskap* (Knowledge of the Swedish Church) (Uppsala, 1946), p. 96.

9 For family prayers, home instruction, and caning, see Pleijel, *Husandakt*.

10 O. Isaksson, *Bystämma och bystadga* (Village council and village laws) (Uppsala, 1967), pp. 252ff.

11 R. Gullstrand, *Socknarnas självstyrelse i historick belysning* (The autonomy of the parishes in a historical perspective) (Stockholm, 1933).

12   E. Alexanderson, *Bondeståndet i riksdagen 1760–1772* (The farmers in the Swedish Riksdag 1760–72) (Lund, 1975), pp. 41–6.

13   Pleijel, B. Olsson, and S. Svensson, *Våra äldsta följkbocker* (Our oldest population registers) (Lund, 1967).

14   B. Widén, 'Literacy in the Ecclesiastical Context', in Johansson, E., (ed.), *Literacy and Society in a Historical Perspective – A Conference Report*, Educational report no. 2, Pedagogiska Institutionen, Umeå Universitet (Department of education, University of Umeå), 1973, p. 38.

15   Johansson, *En studie*, pp. 80–1, Royal Decree of 1723.

16   Each of the five articles in the Small Catechism is introduced with the words 'huru man må det ungt folk enfaldeligen förehålla' (how easily to explain it to young people).

17   J. Naeslund, *Metoden vid den första läsundervisningen* (The learning to reading instruction) (Umeå, 1956), pp. 20 ff.; I. Wilke, *ABC-bücher in Schweden* (Stockholm, 1965).

18   R. Wagnsson, *ABC. Var folkundervisning från medeltid till enhetsskola* (ABC. Our popular education from the middle ages to the comprehensive school) (Malmö, 1955), 33, 49, 66.

19   E. Nygren, 'Våra kyrkoarkiv' (Our church archives), *Tidskrift för det svenska folkbildningsarbetet* (The journal of Swedish popular education) 1922, pp. 15–36, A. Sandberg, *Linköpings stifts kyrkoarkivalier* (The Church archives for the diocese of Linköping) (Lund, 1948), and R. Swedlund, *Kyrkarkiven i länsarkivet i Österund* (The Church archives in the County archives of Österund) (Lund, 1939).

20   E. Johansson and S. Åkerman, *Demografisk Databas* (Demographic database) (1973): The material for Fleninge (1975), The material for Svinnegarn (1976).

21   S. Rönnegård and U. Lundberg, *Folkundervisningen i Leksand och Forshem* (Popular education in Leksand and Forshem). *ÅSU* (Annual reports of the history of Swedish education), vol. 115 (Falun, 1966), p. 11.

22   The complete report can be ordered from the author, Umeå University, S-901 87 Umeå, Sweden. New publications in English on the reading tradition in Sweden are forthcoming.

Notes to chapter 9

1   Kenneth A. Lockridge, *Literacy in Colonial New England: An Enquiry into the Social Context of Literacy in the Early Modern West* (N.Y., 1974); all other information is from early versions of essays on literacy in England, France, Sweden by Roger Schofield, François Furet and Jacques Ozouf, and Egil Johansson, save for the data on signatures in Sweden, which is from research by the author.

2   This does not of course exclude the possibility that at all times a significant but essentially constant portion of young men were educated outside the schools and at older ages.

3   This is based on an analysis of 2000 inventories in New England, sampled on the same basis as the wills, save that every fourth inventory was sampled beginning with a random number *n*.

4   University of Illinois at Chicago Circle, unpublished memo, 1974. Published version appeared in the *William and Mary Quarterly*, January 1975.

5   Unpublished paper, 1974–75, David Cressy. Possibly the New England estimate of age bias should have been higher still, because, compared with the slightly younger Englishmen who made depositions, these men leaving wills

were more likely to be *physically* unable to sign their names. But other studies limited this component of age-bias to a maximum of 5%, a proportion of which is already captured in the English estimates, leaving only an extra 3–4% to add to the New England estimates of age-bias. This in turn is probably offset by the fact that some younger men, quite unlikely to forget, are involved in the New England sample. (Whether or not the various effects of age declined in England, the evidence was that they probably did so in eighteenth-century New England.)

6   Women's literacy probably did move upward, albeit late and for reasons not directly connected to the Church. Roger Schofield suggests that the emergence of various private small-schools in England in the middle of the eighteenth century meant that a very large proportion of women eventually learned to read. As many as 85% of women who could not sign could read, in one early nineteenth-century English village. The same may have been true in New England. This essentially passive literacy skill supplied women rather late and through informal schooling would not alter the fact that the basic literacy achievement in colonial New England was Protestant and masculine.

7   It is only fair to point out that F. Furet and Jacques Ozouf have found no reliable correlation between the availability of schooling (or population density) and male signatures across a wide range of communes in mid-nineteenth-century France. One reason may be that their sample includes some areas of heavy industry where density was high but the schools had degenerated and, whether because of this or of in-migration, literacy was low. Another may be the substantial role of the Army in teaching youths from low-density rural areas to read and write. The net result would be a low correlation of schools with literacy because, at the extremes, schools were not related to literacy. Moreover, the correlation is further weakened by the tendency in north-eastern France of economic 'pulls' to excite literacy even where schools did not exist. Otherwise, in south-west France, where the secular 'push' for literacy *via* schools most closely resembles circumstances in New England and in nineteenth-century Sweden, there is a closer correlation of the availability of schools to literacy. Here, to make schools available was, again, to make reading and writing universal almost regardless of other conditions.

8   Some allowance for the net upward bias of the data originally used for English farmers and artisans might bring them down closer to their American cousins, but the recent data of David Cressy and Roger Schofield still give the edge in literacy to English artisans over American, and to English yeomen over Virginia planters and farmers of the early and middle eighteenth century. Also, the data showing higher literacy among Americans in the higher ranks of wealth is from Virginian and English wills, and the biases here are parallel, leaving the point intact.

9   Fine generational distinctions might, of course, reveal in America a literacy increasing slowly from generation to generation beginning with those educated around 1750 and dying circa 1790, under the impact of increasing economic necessity and, eventually, of other social changes of uncertain import.

10   This view was first presented in an outline of the second half of a paper on modernization presented at Edinburgh in July 1973. Daniel Scott Smith seems to agree; see his review of *Literacy* in the *Journal of American History*, 1975. The chief theoretical background for this broader and still rather sceptical or conservative portrayal of modernization may be found in articles by E.A. Wrigley, *Journal of Interdisciplinary History*, 1971, and Charles Tilly, *History*

of Education Quarterly, 1973. Subsequent data analysed by J. Hanson and the author indicate that, in New England, England, and Virginia, the general withdrawal from voluntary social charity in wills was accompanied by a trend toward making the will even farther in advance of death, a further evidence of an emerging mentality of rational family- and self-oriented planning.

Notes to chapter 10

1   For example, see M. Blaug, *An Introduction to Economics of Education* (London: Allen Lane, 1970).

2   C.A. Anderson and M.J. Bowman, eds., *Education and Economic Development* (London: F. Cass, 1966), chs. 17, 18, 20.

3   Anderson and Bowman, *Education and Economic Development*, p. 350.

4   L.S. Stone, 'Literacy and Education in England 1640–1900', *Past and Present*, 42 (1969), 109.

5   M.J. Bowman and C.A. Anderson, 'Concerning the Role of Education in Development', in *Old societies and New States*, ed. C. Geertz (New York: Free Press of Glencoe, 1963), pp. 247–9, reprinted in *Readings in the Economics of Education*, ed. M.J. Bowman *et al.* (Paris: UNESCO, 1968).

6   For example, the survey of education in Westminster in 1837–1838 reported that school attendance in winter was down to between a quarter and a half of the number of children enrolled. Second Report of a Committee of the Statistical Society of London, appointed to enquire into the State of Education in Westminster, *Journal of the Statistical Society of London*, 1 (1838): 193–215.

7   These surveys have been well summarized and discussed in R.K. Webb, 'Working Class Readers in Early Victorian England', *English Historical Review*, 65 (1950), 333–51; and R.K. Webb, *The British Working Class Reader, 1790–1848* (London: Allen & Unwin, 1955), ch. 1.

8   For example, a survey of education in Newcastle-upon-Tyne in the late 1830s reported, 'In making such enquiries our agent was universally regarded as interfering with what they thought he had no concern and they gave answers which he knew in the majority of cases to be false'. William Cargill, Esq., and a Committee of the Educational Society of Newcastle, 'Educational, Criminal, and Social Statistics of Newcastle-Upon-Tyne', *Journal of the Statistical Society of London*, 1 (1838): 355–61.

9   H.S. Schuman, A. Inkeles and D.H. Smith, 'Some Social Psychological Effects and Noneffects of Literacy in a New Nation', *Economic Development and Cultural Change*, 16 (1967), 1–14.

10 Compare the figures cited by Webb, 'Working Class Readers', and the figures given in the Registrar General's *Annual Reports*. See also the opinions of an educational inspector of the time: J.F. Fletcher, 'Moral and Educational Statistics of England and Wales', *Journal of the Statistical Society of London*, 10 (1847): 212. Signatures as measures of literacy are discussed more fully in R.S. Schofield, 'The Measurement of Literacy in Pre-Industrial England', in *Literacy in Traditional Societies*, ed. J. Goody (Cambridge: Cambridge U.P., 1968).

11 Only Jews, Quakers, and members of the royal family were exempt; 26 George II c. 33, usually known as Lord Hardwicke's Marriage Act.

12 A rough idea of the proportion of the population never marrying and thus escaping observation in the marriage registers is given by the proportion of the

age group 50–54 that was still unmarried. In 1851 11% of men and 12% of women were unmarried in this age group. These figures do not represent exactly the proportions of men and women never marrying, because although over 99% of all first marriages took place before either partner had reached fifty years of age, it was probably not the case at this period that the mortality of single people below the age of fifty was equal to that of married people. See Great Britain, *Parliamentary Papers*, vol. LXXXVIII (1852–1853), '1851 Census of England and Wales', pt. 1, p. cci; and Registrar General of England and Wales, *Annual Report of Births, Deaths and Marriages* (1851–1852), p. viii. Information of sufficient quality on the distribution of ages at marriage is first available in 1851. In this year 73% of all bridegrooms and 70% of all brides were between 20 and 29 years old. A further problem lies in the double-counting of further marriages of widows and widowers, especially if the risk of widowhood and the propensity to remarriage prove to have been social class specific. In 1851, 14% of the bridegrooms and 9% of the brides were widowers and widows respectively (Registrar General, *Annual Report* (1851–52), p. viii).

13   Registrar General, *Annual Report* (1839–1840).

14   W.L. Sargant, 'On the Progress of Elementary Education', *Journal of the Statistical Society of London*, 30 (1867), 80–137.

15   For local studies see, for example, W.P. Baker, 'Parish Registers and Illiteracy in East Yorkshire', *East Yorkshire Local History Society*, 13 (1961), and R.C. Russell, *A History of School and Education in Lindsey* (Lindsey County Council Education Committee, 1965). For the use of marriage licenses, see L. Stone, 'Literacy and Education'.

16   The parishes are Cheshire: Chester St. Mary; Cornwall: Budock; Derbyshire: Littleover; Devonshire: Eggesford, St. Paul's Exeter, Kentisbeare, Ottery St. Mary, Plymstock, Wembury; Hampshire (I.O.W.): Brightsone; Lancashire: Caton, Overton, Pennington, Walton-on-the-Hill; Lincolnshire: Thurlby near Bourne, Cherry Willingham; Northumberland: Earsdon; Nottinghamshire: East Drayton; Oxfordshire: Horley; Rutland: Bisbrooke; Somersetshire: Dunster, Staple Fitzpaine; Suffolk: Woodbridge.

17   For example, see the survey of education in Westminster cited above, *Journal of the Statistical Society of London*, 1: 193–215.

18   'The struggle between the disciplines of labour and literature for the control of the Charity School curriculum ended in the defeat of labour. If success had crowned the efforts of the working Charity Schools the history of elementary education in the British Isles would have followed a different course.' M.G. Jones, *The Charity School Movement* (Cambridge, University Press, 1938), p. 95.

19   For example, see the survey of education in Westminster cited above, *Journal of the Statistical Society of London*, 1: 193–215.

20   This is visible both in the sample parishes and also in the data printed by the Registrar General in his *Annual Reports*. Since this paper was written, an investigation of the ability to sign in Lancashire has confirmed for a key industrializing area some of the national results presented here. In particular, literacy was found to be *declining* in Lancashire in the later half of the eighteenth century 'down to about the 1820s or 1830', and the author concluded that 'the English industrial revolution cannot be seen as one nourished by rising educational standards at least at the elementary level'. Michael Sanderson, 'Literacy and Social Mobility in the Industrial Revolution in England', *Past and Present*, no. 56 (August 1972), pp. 75–104.

21   Bowman and Anderson, 'Concerning the Role of Education in Development'.
22   Registrar General, *Annual Report* (1846).

Notes to chapter 11

1   Nothing has changed in this respect: A Darbel's remarkable article ('Inégalitiés régionales ou inégalités sociales? Essai d'explication des taux de scolarisation', *Revue Française de Sociologie*, 8 [1967]) on regional and social inequalities in school enrolment rates concludes that 'geographical inequalities are fundamentally of the same nature as social inequalities'.

2   J. Goody, ed., *Literacy in Traditional Societies* (Cambridge, 1968).

3   G. Duverdier, 'La pénétration du livre dans une société de culture orale: le cas de Tahiti', *Revue française d'histoire du livre* (1971).

4   R. Cagnac, a peasant at Lugagnac (Lot), interviewed by F. Furet (Jan. 1976). The strictest interpreter of this notion that for women to remain submissive and innocent was to exclude them from written culture was Restif de la Bretonne, who 'even' looked askance at reading: 'All women should be prohibited from learning to write and even read. This would preserve them from loose thoughts, confining them to useful tasks about the house, instilling in them respect for the first sex, which would be all the more carefully instructed in these things for the second sex having been neglected' (Cf. N. Restif de la Bretonne, *Les Gynographes ou Idées de deux honnêtes femmes sur un projet de règlement proposé à toute l'Europe pour mettre les femmes à leur place et opérer le bonheur des deux sexes*. [Paris, 1977]).

5   This example, and the passage that follows, is taken from a doctoral thesis prepared by M.-H. Froeschlé, 'Les dévotions populaires dans les diocèses de Vence et de Grasse, 1680–1750' (unpublished thesis, presented in June 1976 at the University of Paris-Sorbonne).

6   L. Stone, 'Literacy and Education in England, 1640–1900', *Past and Present*, 42 (1969).

7   M. de Certeau, D. Julia, J. Revel, *Une politique de la langue: La Révolution française et le patois: enquête de Gregoire* (Paris, 1975).

8   This analysis of the secularization of rites through writing is based on an unpublished study by Véronique Nahoum.

9   To borrow David Riesman's expression.

10   Stendhal, *Mémoires d'un touriste* (1838), Paris, Le Divan, 1928.

11   Stendhal, *La vie d'Henry Brulard* (1890), Paris, Le Divan, 1929.

Notes to chapter 12

1   For English parallels, see Central Society of Education, *Papers* (London, 1837–1839). On the centrality of morality in nineteenth-century education see esp. Alison Prentice, 'The School Promoters: Education and Social Class in Nineteenth Century Upper Canada', unpub. Ph.D. Diss., University of Toronto, 1974. (Published as *The School Promoters* [1977]; Graff, *The Literacy Myth: Literacy and Social Structure in the Nineteenth-Century City* (New York: Academic Press, 1979), ch. 1.

2   Prentice, 'School Promoters', 150, 174.

3   For English examples, see Richard Johnson, 'Educational Policy and Social Control in Early Victorian England', *Past and Present*, 49 (1970), 96–119, 'Notes on the schooling of the English working class, 1780–1850', in *Schooling and Capitalism*, ed. R. Dale, G. Esland, and M. MacDonald (London:

Routledge, Kegan Paul, 1976), 44–54; E.G. West, *Education and the Industrial Revolution* (London: Batsford, 1975), 'The Role of Education in 19th Century Doctrines of Political Economy', *British Journal of Educational Studies*, 12 (1964), 161–74. For the U.S., see Alexander J. Field, 'Educational Reform and Manufacturing Development in Mid-Nineteenth Century Massachusetts', unpub. Ph.D. Diss., University of California, Berkeley, 1974, summarized in 'Educational Expansion in Mid-Nineteenth-Century Massachusetts', *Harvard Educational Review*, 46 (1976), 521–52; Michael B. Katz, *The Irony of Early School Reform* (Cambridge, Mass.: Harvard University Press, 1968), 'The Origins of Public Education', *History of Education Quarterly*, 14 (1976), 381–407; Samuel Bowles and Herbert Gintis, *Schooling in Capitalist America* (New York: Basic Books, 1976).

4   See David Onn, 'Egerton Ryerson's Philosophy of Education: Something Borrowed or Something New?' *Ontario History*, 61 (1969), 77–86; Ryerson, 'Report upon a System'. On Mann, see Jonathan Messerli, *Horace Mann* (New York: Knopf, 1971); Katz, *The Irony*; Field, 'Reform'.

5   On the biases inherent in Mann's survey, see the *Annual Report, passim.*; Maris A. Vinovskis, 'Horace Mann on the Economic Productivity of Education', *New England Quarterly*, 43 (1970), 550–71. Soltow and Stevens ('Economic Aspects of School Promotion', *Journal of Interdisciplinary History*, 8 [1977], 236) provide an Ohio example.

6   Vinovskis, 'Mann', 568. This discussion is indebted to the work of Vinovskis, Part II. See also, Frank Tracey Carleton, *Economic Influences upon Educational Progress in the United States, 1820–1850* (Reprinted: New York: Teachers College Press, 1965), Ch. 4; Field, 'Educational Reform'. On the relationship between literacy and inventiveness, so prized by Mann, see the fascinating article by Eugene Ferguson, 'The Mind's Eye: Nonverbal Thought in Technology', *Science*, 197 (1977), 827–36. See also, A.F.C. Wallace, *Rockdale* (New York: Knopf, 1978), 237 ff.

7   Field, 'Reform', esp. Chs. 8–9; Herbert Gintis, 'Education, Technology, and the Characteristics of Worker Productivity', *American Economic Review*, 61 (1971), 266–79; Bowles and Gintis, *Schooling*, Part Two; Robert Dreeben, *On What is Learned in School* (Reading, Mass.: Addison-Wesley, 1968). See also E. Verne, 'Literacy and Industrialization', in *A Turning Point for Literacy*, ed. Léon Bataille (New York: Pergamon Press, 1976), 211–228; Ivar Berg, *Education and Jobs* (Boston: Beacon Press, 1971); G.D. Squires, 'Education, Jobs, and Inequality', *Social Problems*, 24 (1977), 436–50; Alex Inkeles and David H. Smith, *Becoming Modern* (Cambridge, Mass.: Harvard University Press, 1974); James Bright, 'Does Automation Raise Skill Requirements?', *Harvard Business Review*, 36 (1958), 85–98, 'The Relationship of Increasing Automation and Skill Requirements', in *Report* of The U.S. National Commission on Technology, Automation, and Economic Progress, Appendix Vol. II (Washington, D.C.: G.P.O., 1966), 203–21. See also note 34.

8   (New York: John Wiley, 1967), 156, 159, 170, 180, 195, 187; among a large literature. See also, John Porter, *The Vertical Mosaic* (Toronto: University of Toronto Press, 1965), 189–95. Revision of traditional relationships has just begun in Canadian sociology, and while there is no critical study yet published, many sociologists support the critiques elaborated below as highly relevant to the Canadian scene. The issues, needless to add, are highly controversial and value-laden, especially in their implications for the nature of modern society and social policy.

9   *Education and Jobs: The Great Training Robbery*, Ch. 1. See also, Squires,

'Education', for additional evidence; Jencks *et al.*, *Inequality* (New York: Basic Books, 1972), as examples. See too, David Noble, *America by Design* (New York: Knopf, 1977), esp. Chs. 8—9; Harry Braverman, *Labor and Monopoly Capital* (New York: Monthly Review Press, 1974); Bright, 'Automation'.

10   Berg,*Education*,40—1,59,80—3,Ch. 5,87,104;Squires, 'Education', 439—40.

11   The indentures examined are all those located in the Archives of the Province of Ontario (Toronto). See also D.T. Ruddell, 'Apprenticeship in Early Nineteenth Century Quebec', unpub. M.A. Thesis, Laval University, 1969.

12   Ironically, Mechanics' Institutes in Canada, as in Britain, tended to be middle class in inspiration and in membership: see J. Donald Wilson, 'Adult Education in Upper Canada before 1850', *Journal of Education* (U.B.C.), 19 (1973), 43—51; Foster Vernon, 'The Development of Adult Education in Ontario, 1790—1900', unpub. Ed.D. Thesis, University of Toronto, 1969; J.A. Eadie, 'The Napanee Mechanics' Institutes', *Ontario History*, 68 (1976), 209—21; E. Royle, 'Mechanics' Institutes and the Working Classes, 1840—1860', *The Historical Journal*, 14 (1971), 305—21. See also John Foster, 'Nineteenth Century Towns — A Class Dimension', in *The Study of Urban History*, ed. H.J. Dyos (London: Edward Arnold, 1968), 281—300, *Class Struggle in the Industrial Revolution* (London: Weidenfeld and Nicolson, 1974); Patrick Joyce, 'The Factory Politics of Lancaster in the Later Nineteenth Century', *Historical Journal*, 18 (1975), 525—53; E.P. Thompson, *The Making of the English Working Class* (New York: Pantheon, 1967), 712—13; R.K. Webb, *The British Working Class Reader, 1790—1848*, (London: Unwin, 1955); Hobsbawm and George Rudé, *Captain Swing* (New York: Pantheon, 1969), Charles Tilly, *From Mobilization to Revolution* (Reading, Mass.: Addison-Wesley, 1978).

13   *Massachusetts Teacher*, 15 (1862), 10, May, *Essays*, 23, reinforces the point: 'Men who could neither read nor write have lived, some of them not unsuccessfully; but without Arithmetic nobody has ever lived, or can live.' Not only did children come to school knowing how to count, as the *Massachusetts Teacher* reported, May implies that arithmetic literacy neither implies or correlates with alphabetic literacy. See also, Bright, 'Automation'.

14   Jones, *Outcast London* (Oxford: Oxford University Press, 1971), 82—3; see also E.J. Hobsbawm, 'The Tramping Artisans', in his *Labouring Men* (Garden City, N.Y.: Doubleday Anchor, 1967), 41—74. Skilled literate, and organized, workingmen could of course read about economic conditions, and therefore employment opportunities, in the working class press. The development, circulation (including oral transmission of news, group and shop reading aloud), and impact of the Canadian labor press in this period is obviously critical and merits separate and detailed study. See also, E.P. Thompson, *Making*; Webb, *Reader*; J.F.C. Harrison, *The Early Victorians* (New York: Schocken, 1971).

15   The company was begun by George and William Hamilton of Quebec in 1797, and transformed into a joint-stock venture upon its sale to Blackburn, Egan, Robinson, and Thistle in 1889, taking on the new name of Hawkesbury. A few summary statistics suggest the scope: by 1885, 30 million feet of timber were cut annually and milled by 350 hands, by 1909, the annual yield was 50 million feet. Hawkesbury continued to operate until 1936. The records are found in the Archives of the Province of Ontario (Toronto). On lumber industry, see in general, Michael S. Cross, 'The Dark Druidical Groves: The Lumber Community and the Commercial Frontier in British North America to 1854', unpub. Ph.D. Diss., University of Toronto, 1968; Edward McKenna. 'Unorgan-

ized Labour versus Management: The Strike at the Chaudière Lumber Mills, 1891', *Histoire Sociale*, 5 (1972), 186–211; and A.R.M. Lower, *The North American Assault on the Canadian Frontier* (Toronto: Ryerson Press, 1938).

On work rhythms, see E.P. Thompson, 'Time, Work-Discipline, and Industrial Capitalism', *Past and Present*, 38 (1967), 56–97; Sidney Pollard, 'Factory Discipline in the Industrial Revolution', *Economic History Review*, 16 (1963), 254–71.

16   On signatures and literacy, see Roger Schofield, 'The Measurement of Literacy in Pre-Industrial England', in *Literacy in Traditional Societies*, ed. Jack Goody (Cambridge: Cambridge University Press, 1968), 311–25; Kenneth A. Lockridge, *Literacy in Colonial New England* (New York: Norton, 1974). Signatures, it should be noted, slightly underestimate the level of reading literacy, as some men would be able to read and not write.

17   For comparative wage data see McKenna, 'Labour', 190; *Royal Commission on the Relationships of Labor and Capital* (Ottawa, 1889), Ontario Evidence. A useful compendium of its four volumes has been edited by Gregory Kealey (University of Toronto Press, 1973).

18   Information on workers' ages not included in these records, could be very revealing in this regard. This analysis may be confirmed and supplemented by an examination of the receipt book of the Madawaska Improvement Company (1888–1903) (Provincial Archives of Ontario). These data also show little disadvantage in wages for illiterates, although the records are less complete than the Hawkesbury material. Obviously, more studies of this kind are needed.

19   Schofield, 'Measurement', 312. See also E. Verne, 'Literacy'.

20   Anderson, 'Literacy and Schooling on the Development Threshold: Some Historical Cases', in *Education and Economic Development*, ed. Anderson and Bowman (Chicago: Aldine, 1965), 347–62; Bowman and Anderson, 'Concerning the Role of Education in Development', in *Old Societies and New States*, ed. Clifford C. Geertz (New York: Free Press, 1963), 247–79; Bowman and Anderson, 'Education and Economic Modernization in Historical Perspective', presented to the Fourth International Congress of Economic History, 1968, now published in *Schooling and Society*, ed. Lawrence Stone (Baltimore: Johns Hopkins, 1976), 3–19. The latter contains the best summary of their work. The roots of the human capital school of economists, largely dominated by Gary Becker and Theodore Schultz are found in these approaches. For a useful critical analysis of approaches to the economics of education, see W.G. Bowen, 'Assessing the Economic Contribution of Education', in *The Economics of Education*, 1, ed. Mark Blaug (Harmondsworth: Penguin, 1968), 67–100.

21   'Does Education Accelerate Economic Growth?', *Economic Development and Cultural Change*, 14 (1966), 262, 266. See also, M.W. Flinn, 'Social Theory and the Industrial Revolution', in *Social Theory and Economic Change*, ed. Burns and Saul (London: Tavistock, 1967), 9–34; David Landes, *The Unbound Prometheus* (Cambridge: Cambridge University Press, 1969).

22   'The History of Education', *Daedalus*, 100 (1971), 141. For contrary views, see Webb, *Reader*, 15, *passim*.; Bowman and Anderson, 'Education'. See also D.J. Treiman, 'Industrialization and Social Stratification', in *Social Stratification*, ed. E.C. Laumann (Indianapolis: Bobbs Merrill, 1970), 207–34. The most recent restatement of the normative view may be found in E.G. West, 'Literacy and the Industrial Revolution', *Economic History Review*, 31 (1978), 369–83. I find it no more persuasive than other versions.

23   Michael Sanderson, 'Education and the Factory in Industrial Lancashire,

1780–1840', *Economic History Review*, 20 (1967), 266, 'Social Change and Elementary Education in Industrial Lancashire, 1780–1840', *Northern History*, 3 (1968), 131–54. David Levine, in *Family Formation in An Age of Nascent Capitalism* (New York: Academic Press, 1977), 28ff and in unpublished work, presents important additional evidence of this effect of early industrialization. The labor press cited above made many of the same points, as did both the commissioners and the witnesses in *The Royal Commission on the Relations of Labour and Capital*.

24   'Literacy and Social Mobility in the Industrial Revolution', *Past and Present*, 56 (1972), 75, 102. See the critique of this paper by Thomas Laqueur, *ibid.*, 64 (1974), 96–107 and Sanderson's reply, 108–12; Laqueur's *Religion and Respectability* (New Haven: Yale University Press, 1976), 'Working-Class Demand and the Growth of English Elementary Education', in *Schooling and Society*, ed. Stone, 192–205. In support of Sanderson's interpretation, see Levine, *Family Formation*; Richard Johnson, 'Notes'; W.B. Stephens, 'Illiteracy and Schooling in the Provincial Towns, 1640–1870', in *Urban Education in the 19th Century*, ed. David Reeder (London: Taylor and Francis, 1977), 27–48, among Stephens' studies.

25   'Dimensions of Illiteracy, 1750–1850', *Explorations in Economic History*, 10 (1973), 452–3, 454; Stephens, 'Illiteracy', 32. See François Furet and Jacques Ozouf, 'Literacy and Industrialization', *Journal of European Economic History*, 5 (1976), 26, 5–44, for France, and their *Lire et écrire* (Paris: Éditions de Minuit, 1977); Peter Flora, 'Historical Processes of Social Mobilization', in *Building States and Nations*, ed. S.N. Eisenstadt and S. Rokkan (Beverly Hills: Sage, 1973), I, 213–58, for additional cross-cultural, aggregative evidence in support of the argument; Verne, 'Literacy'.

26   Pollard, 'Factory Discipline', 225. See also, his *Genesis of Modern Management* (Harmondsworth: Penguin, 1968), esp. Ch. 5; Thompson, 'Time, Work-Discipline'; Keith Thomas, 'Work and Leisure in Pre-Industrial Societies', *Past and Present*, 29 (1964); Robert Malcolmson, *Popular Recreations in English Society, 1700–1850* (Cambridge: Cambridge University Press, 1973); Herbert Gutman, 'Work, Culture, and Society in Industrializing America, 1815–1919', *American Historical Review*, 78 (1973), 531–88; J.F.C. Harrison, *Victorians*; Field, 'Reform'; Johnson, 'Notes'; Stephen Marglin, 'What Do Bosses Do?', *Review of Radical Political Economics*, 6 (1974), 60–112, 7 (1975), 20–38; Inkeles and Smith, *Modern*, Ch. 11.

27   Richard Arkwright, quoted in Pollard, 'Factory Discipline', 258, 258 (emphasis added), 268; Johnson, 'Notes', provides additional examples.

28   Thompson, 'Time, Work-Discipline', 64, 84–5; Johnson, 'Notes', 46–8, *passim*. See, for example, Allan Greer, 'The Sunday Schools of Upper Canada', *Ontario History*, 67 (1975), 169–84. See also, Bowles and Gintis, *Schooling*; Gintis, 'Education'; Field, 'Reform'; Inkeles and Smith, *Modern*.

29   Harrison, *Victorians*, 135–6; Johnson, 'Notes'; Phillip McCann, ed., *Popular Education and Socialization in the Nineteenth Century* (London: Methuen, 1977); A.P. Donajgrodzki, ed., *Social Control in Nineteenth Century Britain* (London: Croom Helm, 1977).

30   *Education in Tokugawa Japan* (London: Routledge, Kegan Paul, 1967), 292.

31   See, in support of this approach, the important recent studies of Field, 'Reform'; Gutman, 'Work'; Marglin, 'Bosses'; Katz, 'Origins of Public Education'; Daniel T. Rodgers, 'Tradition, Modernity, and the American Worker', *Journal of Interdisciplinary History*, 7 (1977), 655–81; Bowles and Gintis, *Schooling*. For one representative, contemporary view, see John Eaton,

Illiteracy and its Social, Political and Industrial Effects: An Address (New York, 1882).

32   At this stage of research, this contention must remain largely hypothetical. We know all too little about the transition in Canada, and comparative studies of Anglo-America are sadly lacking. Recent work by Charles Tilly and Edward Shorter on strikes in France suggests one approach, though an exclusive focus on strike action would obscure many issues.

33   The writings of Ryerson and Mann, with their frequent European references, make this clear. See also the important discussion by Thomas Bender, *An Urban Vision: Ideas and Institutions in Nineteenth-Century America* (Lexington: University of Kentucky Press, 1975).

34   This is, of course, the mere sketch of a theory, for many questions surrounding the actual experience of schooling remain unanswered: the lines of future research should be clear, however. There is, for example, the problem of irregular attendance which was widespread. Did this militate against the schools' 'success'? Quite simply we do not yet know how much exposure to the routine and the message of schools was required for sufficient training. The role of non-English-speaking immigrants must be considered as well. For a fascinating argument on a closely related theme, that of the sanitation movement, see Richard L. Schoenwald, 'Training Urban Man', in *The Victorian City*, ed. H.J. Dyos and Michael Wolff (London: Routledge, Kegan Paul, 1973), 669–92.

    The presumed effects of literacy and 'alphabetization' on personality and the regularization and standardization of behavior may be important in this regard. See below, but see also the speculations of Marshall McLuhan, *The Gutenberg Galaxy* (Toronto: University of Toronto Press, 1962), *Understanding Media* (New York: McGraw-Hill, 1964); G.H. Bantock, *The Implications of Literacy* (Leicester: Leicester University Press, 1966); Jack Goody and Ian Watt, 'The Consequences of Literacy', in *Literacy in Traditional Societies*, ed. Jack Goody, 27–68; Goody, *The Domestication of the Savage Mind* (Cambridge: Cambridge University Press, 1977). There is also a large but very inconclusive psychological literature in this area. Among recent work, the most interesting include the studies of Michael Cole, Sylvia Scribner, and Patricia F. Greenfield.

    The cognitive consequences of illiteracy and literacy are far from clear, although *formal training* in literacy does seem to be closely associated with more abstract thought processes, generalization of solutions, classification and association, changes in concept formation, use of language in description, *in some contexts and some tasks*. As Scribner and Cole put it, 'differences in the social organization of education promote differences in the organization of learning and thinking in the individual . . . the school presents a specialized set of educational experiences which are discontinuous from those encountered in everyday life and that it requires and promotes ways of learning and thinking which often run counter to those nurtured in practical daily activities', 'Cognitive Consequences of Formal and Informal Education', *Science*, 182 (1973), 553, 553–9. Among a large and generally murky literature, see also, Scribner, 'Cognitive Consequences of Literacy', unpub. paper, 1968; Scribner and Cole, 'Research Program on Vai Literacy and its Cognitive Consequences', *Cross-Cultural Social Psychology Newsletter*, 8 (1974), 2–4; Jack Goody, Cole, and Scribner, 'Writing and Formal Operations: A Case Study Among the Vai', *Africa*, 47 (1977), 289–304; Patricia M. Greenfield, 'Oral or Written Language: The Consequences for Cognitive Development in Africa, the United States and

England', *Language and Speech*, 15 (1972), 169–78. See also, H.E. Freeman and G.C. Kassebaum, 'The Illiterate in American Society', *Social Forces*, 34 (1956), 371–5; Don A. Brown, 'Educational Characteristics of Adult Illiterates: A Preliminary Report', *New Frontiers in College-Adult Reading*, 15th Yearbook of the National Reading Conference (Milwaukee, 1966), 58–68. However else illiteracy may have handicapped urban residents in these nineteenth-century cities and however else their experiences may have prepared them, the conclusion that they were not prepared to stand well in the formal context of judicial proceedings seems warranted.

To this we must add the important function of class and cultural differences in speech pattern, which may well have contributed further to a poor showing and disadvantagement. See, among his many writings, Basil Bernstein, 'Some Sociological Determinants of Perception', *British Journal of Sociology*, 9 (1958), 159–74; Doris R. Entwhistle, 'Implications of language socialization for reading models and for learning to read', *Reading Research Quarterly*, 7 (1971–72), 111–67, 'Developmental Sociolinguistics: Inner-City Children', *American Journal of Sociology*, 74 (1968), 37–49. These areas obviously require further attention, perhaps in a situational, phenomenological, or ethnographic actor-oriented framework.

The experience of Quebec in the nineteenth century illustrates vividly the problems of the transition in a society without mass literacy; see *Royal Commission on the Relation of Labor and Capital*, Quebec Evidence. See also Michael Bliss' interesting attempts to explain manufacturers' lack of understanding of these problems: 'Employers, as representative as anyone else of prevailing social mores, were often confused and puzzled when faced with insistence that the familiar rules of the game should not be changed, and not in their favour', 'A Living Profit: Studies in the Social History of Canadian Business, 1883–1911', unpub. Ph.D. Diss., University of Toronto, 1972: 137, 148, 157; published as *A Living Profit* (Toronto: McClelland and Stewart, 1974), Ch. 3.

Notes to chapter 13

1   M. Vovelle in *Atlas historique de Provence* (Paris, 1969), pp. 63–4; P. Bois, *Paysans de l'Ouest* (Paris, 1971), abridged edn, p. 65; E. Malefakis in Bezucha (ed.), *Modern European Social History* (Lexington, Mass., 1972), p. 202; G. Garrier, *Paysans du Beaujolais et du Lyonnais 1800–1970* (Grenoble, 1973, 2 vols.), p. 320, n. 52, quoting P. Goujon on the Mâconnais. See also Vovelle, *Pieté baroque et déchristianisation en Provence au 18e siècle* (Paris, 1973), p. 455, on literacy and schoolteachers in the eighteenth-century Alps.

2   On the language question at this time, see the perceptive comments in E. Weber, *Peasants into Frenchmen: The Modernisation of Rural France 1870–1914* (London, 1977), esp. pp. 67–95, 303–39; also *Le Cri du Var*, 19 November 1911, where the Aups Section of the Socialist Federation requested that minor business be discussed in the local sections, prior to the taking of decisions at Federal Congresses. That way, local militants would have the chance to express their views on the matters in question – in Provençal.

3   See A. Corbin, *Archaïsme et modernité en Limousin au 19e siècle* (Paris, 1974, 2 vols.), p. 991; *AD Var* VIII M 16, for the membership of the Cercle de la Liberté in Le Luc; Price (ed.), *Revolution and Reaction*, p. 51; C. Cippola, *Literacy and Development in the West* (London, 1969), lists the Var 24th in a ranking of French departments for the years 1786–1790 according to the

percentage of newly-weds who signed the register with their mark. Provence, the Midi generally and the western Massif Central all appear as particularly illiterate regions – and would all become strongholds of the left. Karl Deutsch suggests that, while literacy and economic progress do not necessarily correlate, there may be a relationship between growing literacy and political instability. But, as with the geography of dechristianisation, are we not here dealing with parallel effects, rather than a causal link? See K. Deutsch, 'Social mobilisation and political development', in *American Political Science Review* LV, 1961.

4   See J.-J. Darmon, *Le colportage de librairie en France sous le Second Empire* (Paris, 1971), esp. parts I, IV, V.

5   See M. Agulhon, 'La diffusion d'un journal montagnard, le Démocrate du Var, sous la Seconde République', *Provence Historique* X, 1960, pp. 18, 27.

6   Agulhon, *La vie sociale en Provence* (Paris, 1970), p. 305; on artisan tailors, see the interesting contribution by Christopher Johnson in Price (ed.), *Revolution and Reaction: 1848 and the Second French Republic* (London, 1975), pp. 87–115.

7   Y.-M. Bercé, *Croquants et nu-pieds. Les soulèvements paysans en France du 16e au 19e siècle* (Paris, 1974), p. 204; *AD Var* IV M 24 (2–3). See also Bezucha (ed.), *Modern European Social History*, p. 107.

8   On the diffusion of anarchist propaganda among Andalusian *braceros*, see the contribution by Waggoner in Bezucha (ed.), *Modern European Social History*, esp. p. 161. On the Limousin, see Corbin, *Archaïsme et modernité*, p. 794. On the social rôle of the blacksmith's forge in the Lyonnais countryside, see Garrier, *Paysans du Beaujolais*, p. 198. Demographic and occupational data concerning Lorgues in *AD Var* XI M 2 (119) and *AD Var* XIV M 19 (4). Membership of the Cercle des Travailleurs in Cuers in *AD Var* VIII M 16.

9   Corbin, *Archaïsme et modernité*, p. 308.

10   For more details, see Judt, *Socialism in Provence*, ch. 9.

Notes to chapter 15

1   The following paper is essentially founded on the critique of the industrial mode of production as exposed by Ivan Illich, most notably. The critique aims to show that two-thirds of humanity can still hope to avoid passing through the industrial era if they rapidly opt for a mode of production founded in post-industrial equilibrium. The critique of functional literacy seen as an alternative to the school system and as an industrial alternative falls within this framework. Cf. *Celebration of Awareness, Deschooling Society, Tools for Conviviality, Medical Nemesis*. More especially, the themes dealt with here, as with the demonstrations they presuppose, formed the topics of discussion of an international group that met on July/August 1975, at the CIDOC, Cuernavaca. This group was especially concerned with examining the problem of the counter-productivity of the institutionalization of lifelong education. Preliminary results of this examination will be published appearing in several languages at the end of 1976.

2   Unesco, *Final Report* of the World Conference of Ministers of Education on the Eradication of Illiteracy, Teheran, 8–19 September 1975. Paris, Unesco, ED/217, p. 37.

3   I. Illich, *Tools for Conviviality*, Glasgow, Fontana/Collins, 1973, p. 104.

4   R. Boudon, *L'Inégalité des chances. La Mobilité sociale dans les sociétés industrielles*, Paris, Colin, 1973; C. Jenks, *Inequality. A Reassessment of the Effect of Family and Schooling in America*, New York.

5   For a good many reasons, one of which is methodological, indicated by C.E. Beeby: 'if functional literacy is not associated with economic development programmes, it is not functional; whereas if it is so associated, then it is impossible to evaluate functional literacy's role in the change brought about at the end of the project'. Cf. A. Meister, *Alphabétisation et développement. Le rôle de l'alphabétisation fonctionnelle dans le développement économique et la modernisation*, Editions Anthropos, 1973, p. 220. Meister nonetheless makes his own appraisal of the impact of functional literacy on productivity, pp. 215–69.

6   Meister, *op. cit.*, p. 22.

7   Cf. A. Castanhimira, *Niangane Ladji*; Où est l'éducation ses travailleurs migrants? Deux travailleurs migrants parlent . . . , in *Perspectives*, IV 3 Autumn 1971, 401–9 (Unesco).

8   I. Illich, *Tools for Conviviality*.

9   M. Carnoy, *Education as Cultural Imperialism*, New York, 1974.

10   Samir Amin, 'Le tiersmonde doit larguer les amarres', in *Le Nouvel Observateur*, Special No., June 1975.

11   Cf. A. Salazar Bondy, *Hacia une alfabetizacion integral*, Ministerio de la Educación, Lima, Peru; along with the forms taken by the ALFIN programme in Peru.

12   I. Illich, *Deschooling Society*, International Corporation on Education, Unesco, 1971. Series B. Opinions. Text partially reproduced in *l'Education en devenir*, Unesco, 1975.

13   I. Illich, *Tools for Conviviality*.

14   M. Rahnema, *L'institutionalisation de la réforme de l'éducation*, International Commission on the Development of Education, Series B. Opinions, Unesco, 1971, p. 3. Cf. also *l'Education en devenir*, Unesco, 1975.

15   M. Faure *et al.*, *Learning to Be*, Unesco, 1972, p. 235.

16   Cited by P. Furter in *l'Education en devenir*, *op. cit.*, pp. 373–4.

17   Cf. *Cuernavaca Manifesto: The Price of Lifelong Education*, doc. CIDOC, 1974.

18   I. Illich, *Tools for Conviviality*, p. 68.

19   OECD, *Education and Active Life in Modern Society*, Report of the Secretary-General's *ad hoc* working party on the relationship between education and employment, 1975.

20   *Tools for Conviviality*.

21   J. Attali, *La Parole et l'outil*, PUF, 1975.